P9-BYJ-564

ADVANCE PRAISE FOR
KANGAROO SQUADRON

"With his exquisite eye for detail and spellbinding talent as a storyteller, Bruce Gamble takes readers on an unforgettable journey through the perilous early months of World War II in the Southwest Pacific."

—Colonel Walter Boyne, author and former director of the National Air and Space Museum

"Fast-paced and packed with vivid descriptions and valuable information, *Kangaroo Squadron* shines a bright light on the valiant American fliers who took on the Japanese in the first engagements in the Pacific. Bruce Gamble brings these heroes out of the shadows and makes them come alive. A must-read for anyone interested in World War II."

—John Darnton, Pulitzer Prize–winning journalist and author of *Almost a Family*

"Bruce Gamble demonstrates again why he is one of the best aviation historians in the business. In *Kangaroo Squadron* he has crafted a fascinating account of men and machines, painting a compelling picture of what it was like to fight as an American aviator during the very darkest days of the Pacific War. Outstanding!"

—Jonathan Parshall, co-author of *Shattered Sword: The Untold Story of the Battle of Midway*

"Bruce Gamble's excellent history of the U.S. Army's B-17 bombers in the Pacific, officially the Southern Bomber Command but colloquially known as the Kangaroo Squadron, is a triumph. The characters are vivid and the narrative gripping; the story of the downed B-17 later known as the 'Swamp Ghost' is especially riveting. Throughout, Gamble's mastery of aircraft characteristics is impeccable, and his fast-paced storytelling is irresistible."

—Craig L. Symonds, author of *World War II at Sea: A Global History*

"Flying Boeing B-17s, the Kangaroo Squadron's aircrews and maintenance men fought not only Imperial Japan but weather, geography, and a perennial shortage of everything—except courage and dedication. Their example remains an inspiration to Americans three generations later, thanks to Bruce Gamble's in-depth research and deft writing."

—Barrett Tillman, author of *On Wave and Wing: The 100-Year Quest to Perfect the Aircraft Carrier*

KANGAROO SQUADRON

BOOKS BY BRUCE GAMBLE

The Black Sheep: The Definitive Account of Marine Fighting Squadron 214 in World War II

Black Sheep One: The Life of Gregory "Pappy" Boyington

The Rabaul Trilogy:

Invasion Rabaul: The Epic Story of Lark Force, the Forgotten Garrison, January—July 1942

Fortress Rabaul: The Battle for the Southwest Pacific, January 1942—April 1943

Target: Rabaul: The Allied Siege of Japan's Most Notorious Stronghold, March 1943—August 1945

Swashbucklers and Black Sheep: A Pictorial History of Marine Fighting Squadron 214 in World War II

KANGAROO SQUADRON

AMERICAN COURAGE IN THE DARKEST DAYS OF WORLD WAR II

BRUCE GAMBLE

Da Capo Press

Copyright © 2018 by Bruce Gamble

Hachette Book Group supports the right to free expression and the value of copyright. The purpose of copyright is to encourage writers and artists to produce the creative works that enrich our culture.

The scanning, uploading, and distribution of this book without permission is a theft of the author's intellectual property. If you would like permission to use material from the book (other than for review purposes), please contact permissions@hbgusa.com. Thank you for your support of the author's rights.

Da Capo Press
Hachette Book Group
1290 Avenue of the Americas, New York, NY 10104
dacapopress.com
@DaCapoPress, @DaCapoPR

Printed in the United States of America

First edition: November 2018

Published by Da Capo Press, an imprint of Perseus Books, LLC, a subsidiary of Hachette Book Group, Inc. The Da Capo Press name and logo is a trademark of the Hachette Book Group.

The Hachette Speakers Bureau provides a wide range of authors for speaking events. To find out more, go to www.hachettespeakersbureau.com or call (866) 376-6591.

The publisher is not responsible for websites (or their content) that are not owned by the publisher.

Print book interior design by Amy Quinn

All maps by the author using modified Google relief-style images

Library of Congress Cataloging-in-Publication Data

Names: Gamble, Bruce, author.
Title: Kangaroo squadron: American courage in the darkest days of World War
   II / Bruce Gamble.
Description: First Da Capo Press edition. | Boston: Da Capo Press, [2018] |
   Includes bibliographical references and index.
Identifiers: LCCN 2018021086| ISBN 9780306903120 (hardcover) | ISBN
   9780306903106 (ebook)
Subjects: LCSH: United States. Army Air Forces. Bombardment Squadron, 435th.
   | B-17 bomber—History—20th century. | World War, 1939-1945—Pacific
   Area. | World War, 1939-1945—Aerial operations, American. | World War,
   1939-1945—Regimental histories—United States.
Classification: LCC D790.263 435th .G36 2018 | DDC 940.54/4973—dc23
LC record available at https://lccn.loc.gov/2018021086

ISBNs: 978-0-306-90312-0 (hardcover), 978-0-306-90310-6 (ebook)

LSC-C

10 9 8 7 6 5 4 3 2 1

For all the fine young men who served overseas with the Kangaroo Squadron:
You were the tip of the spear during our time of need.

PREFACE

It is neither an exaggeration nor boastful arrogance to say that I was born to write this story. When I came into this world—on the anniversary of the Japanese attack on Pearl Harbor, no less—I became part of a large, extended family living in an old stone farmhouse in Bucks County, Pennsylvania. Three generations resided in that wonderful home, including my uncle, John Steinbinder, a navigator in the squadron whose story is described herein.

My immediate family later moved from Bucks County, so I had little awareness of Uncle Johnny's military service during my youth. Instead I paid more attention to my father's experiences as a B-29 pilot over Japan, which inspired me to serve as a flight officer in the U.S. Navy during the closing years of the Cold War. It wasn't until much later, after I was medically retired and began writing, that my interest in Uncle Johnny's wartime adventures revived. Sadly, by the time I began work on my trilogy about Rabaul, he had been diagnosed with Alzheimer's. But fate took a turn. Not long before his death, I took possession of a footlocker containing his military papers and other memorabilia, including a handwritten diary filled with details of his combat tour with the Kangaroo Squadron in 1942. Many of his entries revealed the intense drama he experienced during combat missions, which made even the day-to-day commentary seem all the more interesting. And the more I learned about his squadron, the more impressed I became with the achievements those young men accomplished during the darkest days of the war.

While I worked on other books, I began gathering as much information on the Kangaroo Squadron as I could find. Considering the early period of the war, when setbacks and retreats were a daily occurrence and official records were frequently lost or neglected, it was a pleasant surprise to find that a wealth of documentation had been preserved by the Air Force Historical Research Agency (AFHRA) at Maxwell AFB in Montgomery, Alabama. Later, thanks to the assistance of numerous colleagues, I managed to track down the diaries, memoirs, and photograph collections of several other squadron members to supplement the official records and my uncle's material. Now, almost sixty years after my arrival on that winter night, it is my honor and privilege to share this narrative account of the Kangaroo Squadron and its brave crews. My only regret is that so few members of Uncle Johnny's generation are still extant. We can't slow the march of time, of course, but it is my sincere hope that this book will enable another generation of readers to appreciate the courageous efforts of a few American aviators during the opening months of World War II. May their actions be remembered for just a little while longer.

KEY INDIVIDUALS

Lieutenant General Henry H. "Hap" Arnold: Aviation pioneer, chief of the U.S. Army Air Forces

Sergeant Mervyn C. Bell: One of six Royal Australian Air Force (RAAF) pilots attached to the Kangaroo Squadron

First Lieutenant Frank P. Bostrom: Native of Bangor, Maine, and the most decorated pilot in the Kangaroo Squadron

Major Richard H. Carmichael: West Point graduate, former pursuit pilot, first commanding officer of the Kangaroo Squadron

Frank Allan Champion: Australian born in New Guinea, former seafarer, resident magistrate of the Northern District

First Lieutenant Frederick C. Eaton Jr.: Reservist raised in suburban New York City, pilot of the Kangaroo Squadron's first bomber lost in combat

Vice Admiral Shigeyoshi Inoue: Commander of operations in New Guinea and the Japanese Southeastern Area

Lieutenant General George C. Kenney: Commander of Allied Air Forces in Australia

Captain William Lewis: Former airline pilot, second commanding officer of the Kangaroo Squadron

General Douglas MacArthur: Supreme commander, Southwest Pacific Area

Manuel Quezon: Exiled president of the Philippines

Brigadier General Ralph Royce: Chief of air staff, U.S. Army Forces in Australia

Lieutenant (Junior Grade) Jun-ichi Sasai: Japanese Naval Academy graduate and division leader, Tainan Air Group

First Lieutenant John J. Steinbinder: First-generation American, Kangaroo Squadron navigator, author's uncle

Sergeant Earl T. Williams: Assistant crew chief, tail gunner, aircraft mechanic. Last known surviving member of the Kangaroo Squadron

THE HEROES WHO DIDN'T COME HOME

The crew of *Chief Seattle*, missing in action over the Solomon Sea on August 14, 1942:

Flight Sergeant George S. Andrews, RAAF, copilot, Brisbane, Australia

Private David B. Beattie, radar specialist, native of Scotland raised in Flint, Michigan

First Lieutenant Wilson L. Cook, pilot, Bradley, Oklahoma

Second Lieutenant Joseph R. Cunningham, bombardier, Travelers Rest, South Carolina

Staff Sergeant John J. Dunbar, assistant flight engineer, Tujunga, California

Corporal Charles M. Hartman, assistant radio operator, Gettysburg, South Dakota

Technical Sergeant Irving W. McMichael, radio operator, Lincoln, Nebraska

Second Lieutenant Hubert S. Mobley, navigator, Tampa, Florida

Corporal Richard K. Pastor, gunner, Lynbrook, New York

Staff Sergeant Elwyn O. Rahier, flight engineer, Itasca County, Minnesota

Killed in action by Japanese fighters in the vicinity of Rabaul, New Britain, on October 9, 1942:

Corporal Ralph C. Fritz, tail gunner, Detroit, Michigan

*7:30 A.M.; February 23, 1942; 26,000 feet
above Rabaul, New Britain*

Major Dick Carmichael must have been amazed, teetering on the edge of disbelief, at the realization that so many aspects of his squadron's first bombing mission could go so completely wrong. Hell, even before it started, the mission was tainted by misfortune and mistakes. The downward spiral seemed to have no end, and he could not shrug it off as a case of Murphy's Law. It was worse than that.

Carmichael's twelve B-17 Flying Fortresses, the first combat-ready U.S. Army squadron to deploy across the Pacific after the Japanese attack on Pearl Harbor, had arrived in Australia only days earlier. Dubbed the Southern Bomber Command, the squadron was under special orders to conduct one of the first heavy bombing campaigns of the Pacific war, beginning with a 1,600-mile raid on the Japanese stronghold at Rabaul. It was both a remarkable opportunity and an enormous responsibility for a twenty-eight-year-old squadron commander, but right from the beginning, the carefully organized plans had begun to unravel.

En route to Australia, a tropical cyclone had forced part of the squadron to divert to an airdrome near Brisbane, where one of the B-17s was damaged by a civilian airliner that slid out of control on the rain-slicked grass field. Then a second B-17 was damaged after its tail wheel became mired in mud at the Royal Australian Air Force (RAAF) base near Townsville, Queensland, and later a third was grounded with mechanical trouble at a dispersal field in the outback. The raid on Rabaul was scheduled to commence on the night of February 22, but three more B-17s were forced out of the mission—one with contaminated fuel, the other two after colliding on the ground—leaving Carmichael with only half of his original squadron. And the troubles continued. Only an hour after the mission began, the six remaining bombers encountered a huge, violent storm that forced one aircraft to turn back. The rest split up into two widely scattered elements.

Now, as he approached the target at daybreak on February 23, Carmichael had only two B-17s remaining on his wing. What could he hope to achieve with three bombers? Moreover, Rabaul was obscured by a solid undercast, preventing the bombardier up forward from picking out enemy ships down in the harbor. Carmichael was also worried about fuel consumption: his new B-17s were not only using far more gas than anticipated, they still faced another five hundred miles to the nearest friendly airdrome at Port Moresby, New Guinea.

But the young major had no time to dwell on the problems. Just when it seemed that the situation couldn't get much worse, the shooting started. First the small formation was rocked by heavy bursts of antiaircraft fire from large-caliber guns. Soon after the barrage abated, the B-17s were intercepted by enemy fighters. Breathtakingly fast and agile, the Japanese planes made pass after pass, concentrating most of their fire on the exposed bomber on the outside of the formation. Their gunfire was accurate, scoring hits on Lieutenant Harry Brandon's right inboard engine, which burst into flames from a ruptured oil tank. Carmichael and his other wingman slowed to keep pace with the smoking cripple, closing ranks to maximize the bombers' defensive firepower as they fought off the slashing attacks for nearly an hour. Bristling with machine guns, the Flying Fortresses held their own against the darting enemy fighters, although two of Carmichael's crewmen were wounded in the legs by ricocheting bullets. Ignoring their pain, they continued to return fire until the Japanese ran low on fuel and gave up the chase.

Their own tanks nearly empty, the three B-17s barely made it to the refueling stop at Port Moresby. There, Carmichael learned that two additional Fortresses had attacked Rabaul, but one was now missing in action. With that, the attempt to mount a damaging strike from Australia ended in disappointment. Twelve heavy bombers might have landed a solid punch on the enemy's nose, but the litany of mishaps, errors, and unforeseen difficulties had whittled the effort down to a meaningless outcome. It was a perfect microcosm of the overall situation in those early days of the Pacific war. The scattered Allied forces, woefully unprepared to fight, could mount little resistance against the Japanese offensive that swept southward toward Australia, crushing defenders at every turn.

Although the first mission could hardly have gone worse for the squadron, there was no lack of commitment or courage among the 111 men under Carmichael's command. More than half had been present when the Japanese attacked Pearl Harbor, witnessing firsthand the destruction, the smashed planes, the capsized ships, the torn bodies. A few had been wounded; all were fighting mad.

Determined to even the score, Carmichael and his men drew strength from an intense desire to strike back at the Japanese, unaware that they would represent the *only* combat-capable American bomber squadron in Australia for the next six weeks. In fact, as the battle to save Australia unfolded, they would shoulder the responsibility for all heavy bomber operations during the next few months.

Despite the disappointing results of the first mission, there would be many more opportunities to avenge Pearl Harbor. The American airmen were not only equal to the demands thrust upon them, they would crisscross Australia and the entire Southwest Pacific numerous times during their nine-month deployment, collectively flying millions of miles while battling the numerically superior Japanese. Operating with an unusual degree of independence, they developed a reputation for pulling off the impossible, which made them the darlings of the press. As some of the first Yanks to begin combat operations Down Under, they adapted almost seamlessly to their host country. Fittingly, they came to be known across the Pacific as the Kangaroo Squadron.

This is the story of their bravery, determination, and sacrifice.

ONE

LONG NIGHT'S
JOURNEY INTO WAR

Of all the breathtaking panoramas that grace this blue-and-white marble of a planet, few can rival the beauty of a sunrise over the Pacific Ocean. As dawn broke on the seventh day of December 1941, the crews of twelve B-17 bombers flying westward toward Hawaii were treated to a spectacular view. Almost imperceptibly at first, the first pinkish rays of sunlight peeked over the horizon behind the bombers, revealing their graceful silhouettes. Soon, blazing higher, the sun's full glory reflected off distant pillars of cumulus clouds, turning them the color of molten gold.[1]

It had been a long night. Twelve hours in the air already, mostly flying above a moonlit layer of clouds. The bombers cruised at altitudes ranging from six thousand to ten thousand feet, where the ambient temperature was reasonably comfortable. But not the noise. Acoustically, the interior of a B-17 was little more than an aluminum barrel that rattled with every bump and accentuated the unmuffled roar of the four Wright "Cyclone" radial engines. Quilted padding filled with cotton insulation alleviated the noise in some compartments, and the crewmembers wore headsets, but the earphones caused their own aggravation after pressing against the skull for hours on end.

Despite the noise and discomforts, most of the crewmen had managed to relax or even fall asleep. All were exhausted, having spent the past several days preparing for a two-year deployment to the Philippines. Their present destination, Hickam Field in the Territory of Hawaii, was merely the first stop on a journey of almost ten thousand miles. After refueling and arming the bombers at Hickam, the crews faced another week of island-hopping flights across the Pacific.

Not everyone could enjoy the luxury of a nap. Aboard each bomber, two crewmembers were compelled to stay alert throughout the flight. Radio operators, sitting in their insulated compartments amidships, passed the long hours trying to tune in any signal they could find. Strict radio silence was in effect, which meant no transmitting except in an emergency, but the operators were keen to pick up a commercial radio station in Honolulu to aid with direction-finding. And then there were the navigators: shuffling between their charts and octant mounts with nervous energy, they periodically "shot the stars" and referred to celestial navigation tables to update their plane's estimated position. Most, fresh out of training, still received cadet pay. Among them, only one or two had ever conducted an ocean crossing. And because the B-17s flew independently rather than in formation, each navigator was responsible for guiding his aircraft to a safe landfall.

The pilot of the lead aircraft, Major Truman H. "Ted" Landon, gave a long leash to his newly winged navigator. Fully qualified in navigation himself, Landon sensed a gradual drift to the right. He held his tongue, however, allowing Second Lieutenant Chester L. Budz to figure out his own calculations. "It is much better to be on a known side of a course than to not know where in the hell you are," Landon would later comment. "So I let him continue."[2]

As the commanding officer of the 38th Reconnaissance Squadron, it wasn't easy for Landon to ignore the temptation to micromanage his young navigator. The challenges of crossing that particular stretch of ocean were demanding, regardless of experience. From the rocky outcroppings of the California coast to the shores of Oahu, the bombers would cross 2,400 miles of uninterrupted ocean. On such a long overwater flight, a drift of only three degrees could potentially cause an aircraft to miss the islands by more than a hundred miles. The risks were great, but the opportunity for a neophyte navigator to gain experience was equally important.

Daybreak therefore offered more than just a lovely view. It brought a sense of relief, banishing the gremlins that teased the greenhorn navigators into constantly second-guessing their calculations. The lifting veil of darkness also gave the crews an opportunity to scan the horizon for their squadron mates. Most found nothing but clouds in an otherwise empty sky. After cruising all night at slightly different speeds and headings, the bombers had become widely separated. Lieutenant David G. Rawls, piloting a brand-new B-17E of the 88th Reconnaissance Squadron, spotted one bomber off to his left at a distance of twenty miles, practically the limit of his vision. He regarded the lone aircraft, though it was little more than a speck, as "a welcome sight after the solitude of the night."[3]

DOWN ON THE ocean's surface some two hundred miles west of the bombers, six aircraft carriers shouldered through heavy swells and intermittent rain showers north of Hawaii. Dawn would not come for another hour, but there was plenty of activity onboard as the flattops steamed behind a protective phalanx of battleships, cruisers, and destroyers. From the halyards of every vessel snapped a large white flag with a unique geometric design: a blood red disk, offset from the center, with sixteen rays extending in a sunburst pattern. Symbolic of the dawn that was about to come, the flags represented the nation proudly referred to by the sailors as Nippon, "Land of the Rising Sun."

The six flattops, stalwarts of the Imperial Japanese Navy's *Kido Butai*, or Mobile Force, had stealthily approached Hawaii for more than a week. Now, upon reaching their assigned coordinates without detection, the crews underwent last-minute preparations for a massive airstrike. On each wooden flight deck, dozens of single-engine aircraft sat idling, their pilots and aircrews anxiously awaiting the signal to take off. After a twenty-minute delay caused by foul weather, the first planes began to roll, cheered enthusiastically by hundreds of cap-waving sailors lining the catwalks and observation galleries. Despite the darkness, the six carriers collectively launched more than 180 aircraft in only fifteen minutes. The warplanes circled above the task force while gathering into assigned formations according to type: level bombers, dive bombers, torpedo planes, and fighters.[4]

As soon as the launch cycle was complete, the carrier crews shuttled more planes up to the flight decks, readying a second wave of attackers with remarkable efficiency. Overhead, just as the sky began to lighten, the first wave turned southward and flew off toward the same island the American B-17s were approaching.

For the Japanese, of course, Oahu was not a destination. It was their target.

ON A KNOLL near the northernmost tip of Oahu, two U.S. Army privates prepared to wrap up their shift in a new, high-tech outpost. The remote site, located in the Opana district more than five hundred feet above Kawela Bay, provided a striking view of the ocean. But the two men were immune to the postcard scenery. For the past few hours they had been seated inside the darkened van of a Signal Corps truck filled with electronic equipment. The vehicle housed the receiver and oscilloscope of an early warning radar, designed to detect aircraft at long range. Manufactured by Westinghouse, the first-generation SCR-270B was classified as a mobile radar unit, although moving it was a major undertaking that required four trucks, including a flatbed tractor-trailer to haul the forty-five-foot-tall antenna. Five virtually identical units had been established at strategic points around Oahu, and a sixth was preparing to come online. When active, their operators searched the oscilloscope displays for "blips" representing unidentified aircraft, which were reported by telephone to the Information Center at Fort Shafter, several miles east of Pearl Harbor. There, personnel maneuvered icons representing the bogies on a room-sized plotting map. Collectively, the radar sites and the Information Center were part of a newly established unit with a convoluted name: Signal Company Aircraft Warning Hawaii (SCAWH). Despite the impressive title, the radar network was underfunded, undermanned, and underutilized.

Like many new technological developments, the first radar establishments in the Army Signal Corps were underappreciated by the old-timers who had forged careers in the infantry, artillery, or cavalry. Among them was the commander of army forces in Hawaii, Lieutenant General Walter C. Short. Although he had seen impressive demonstrations of the radar center's capabilities during recent war games, the sixty-one-year-old Short either failed to fully grasp the new technology or lacked confidence in the information it provided. Perhaps both.[5]

And it wasn't simply a matter of old versus new. Island-wide, the military struggled with complacency. Despite specific warnings from the War Department about the possibility of a Japanese attack, an entrenched peacetime attitude prevailed. Army units in Hawaii worked five days a week, scheduling only essential personnel for duty on weekends and holidays. General Short took this a step further with the radar sites, restricting them to three hours of operation per day, from 4:00 A.M. to 7:00 A.M. The odd schedule was supposedly established to preserve the limited supply of spare parts—especially the delicate glass transmitter tubes—but at least one historian has suggested that Short wanted to prevent the radar branch from "interfering with normal army operations during the day."[6]

On this particular Sunday morning, privates George E. Elliott Jr. and Joseph L. Lockard were the only personnel on duty at the Opana station. Lockard, who possessed the most experience, monitored the oscilloscope. At 6:54 A.M., after nearly three hours with no activity, the Information Center phoned in and advised the two men to shut down their unit. They were about to comply, as Elliott would later explain, when a spontaneous suggestion led to an unexpected discovery:

> Lockard began to power down, but I reminded him that we had received previous permission from our platoon sergeant to keep the system operating so that I could learn how to operate the oscilloscope. I had less than three months' radar experience under my belt and Lockard agreed to keep the unit running.
>
> At 0702 I was sitting at the controls while Lockard peered over my shoulder and instructed me on how to detect planes. Suddenly, there appeared the largest blip either of us had ever seen on an oscilloscope.
>
> "What's this?" I asked him. Lockard thought the unit had either malfunctioned or was giving us a false reading. He quickly tested the equipment and determined everything to be working perfectly.
>
> We calculated the blip to be a large group of aircraft approaching quickly from 3 degrees east approximately 137 miles out to sea. I suggested to Lockard that we should notify our Information Center.
>
> "Don't be crazy!" he laughed. "Our problem ended at seven o'clock."
>
> However, I was insistent and after a long discussion he said, "Well, go ahead and send it in if you like."[7]

Elliott tried the primary phone line, but his call went unanswered. Due to the scheduling limitations, almost everyone in the Information Center had gone off duty at seven o'clock and promptly left the facility. Trying again on an administrative line, Elliott reached the switchboard operator. "I nervously explained what we'd seen," he recalled, "and asked him to get someone in charge to call us back as soon as possible." At 7:20, the only other person on duty in the Information Center phoned the radar site.[8]

This was Lieutenant Kermit A. Tyler, a twenty-eight-year-old fighter pilot from Iowa and second in command of the 78th Pursuit Squadron based at Wheeler Field. He had been in the Information Center exactly twice before: once for an introductory tour, followed a few days later by his inaugural duty as the pursuit officer. Tyler understood the principles of radar—if called upon he would direct airborne fighters to intercept hostile aircraft— but he had received no formal training. To him, it was all theoretical. Lacking practical experience, and knowing his shift was about to end, he listened with probably less than complete attention as Lockard described the large radar return.

By now the unidentified bogies had closed to within seventy-five miles of Oahu. Lockard, who answered the call from Tyler, mentioned that the blip was the largest he had ever seen. Unfortunately, his subjective comment gave the inexperienced Tyler no basis for analysis or comparison, but the information presented by Lockard jogged Tyler's memory. While driving to Fort Shafter early that morning, he had listened to a Honolulu radio station on his car radio. "I had very good reason to believe that there was a flight of B-17s en route to the islands from the mainland," Tyler would later testify. "I had a friend in the bomber command who told me that any time the radio stations were playing this Hawaiian music all night, I could be certain that a flight of our bombers was coming over."[9]

This was indeed true. Commercial radio waves could be used as a homing signal, so the army paid station KGMB in Honolulu to stay on the air throughout the night whenever long-distance flights were scheduled to arrive. (Coincidentally, the leader of the first wave of Japanese planes, Commander Mitsuo Fuchida, was at that very moment tracking KGMB in his Nakajima bomber.[10]) Tyler rationalized that the huge blip represented a formation of B-17s approaching from the mainland. "Well," he said to Lockard, "don't worry about it."[11]

Viewed with the cold eye of hindsight, both Lockard and Tyler had committed errors, mostly of omission. Considering the shortcomings they faced, from a dearth of comprehensive training to the lackadaisical attitude of the peacetime army, their blunders were predictable. If Lockard had been more empirical about the *size* of the radar return, which he later described as "probably more than fifty" aircraft, Tyler would almost certainly have paid more attention. Conversely, on just his second shift as the pursuit officer in the Information Center, Tyler lacked the experience to seek additional clarification regarding Lockard's verbal report.

Speculation aside, the burden of responsibility fell on Tyler, who ultimately made not one but two incorrect assumptions. The first was equating the radar blip with a possible flight of B-17s, an assessment based more on hearsay than official information. His second mistake was to presume the inbound bombers would be flying in formation, thus creating a large radar return. No one had briefed him on the particulars of transpacific bomber flights, such as the fact that the aircraft flew independently. Had he known this, the young lieutenant would not have been so cavalier about the large radar return.

The die had been cast, an opportunity fumbled. Soon enough, Tyler and the two radar operators would realize that the equipment had detected an inbound formation of hostile aircraft, a scenario they never considered. Ultimately, all three men would be linked with the first wartime use of radar in American history—but not heroically. By the time comprehension settled over them with a sickening reality, it was too late to sound the alarm. The newfangled radar had silently done its job. The human element had not.

THE B-17S APPROACHING Hawaii were not only scattered across hundreds of square miles, some were far off course. Major Landon's bomber, a brand-new E model, had drifted approximately a hundred miles north of the intended route. With adequate fuel remaining in the tanks, Landon was not overly concerned when his navigator keyed the interphone and reported their destination was due south, requiring a ninety-degree turn to the left. However, soon after Landon completed the turn, the direction finder locked onto station KGMB and revealed that a southeasterly heading was required to put Oahu on the nose. This meant the bomber had already flown well beyond the islands and was actually doubling back.

The other new E model in Landon's flight, flown by German-born Lieutenant Karl T. Barthelmess, had also drifted off course. As a result, the squadron's four obsolescent B-17Cs had overtaken both of the E models during the night. This was not unusual, considering the weight difference between the two variants. The B-17E, with its electrically powered machine-gun turrets and an enlarged empennage to accommodate a tail gun, was some nine thousand pounds heavier than the older C model. The first bomber to make landfall, therefore, was a B-17C named *Skipper*, flown by Lieutenant Robert H. Richards.[12] His crew had affectionately named the plane after a terrier-mix puppy that had been flying with them since he was only a few weeks old. Even now, the little mutt was a passenger under the watchful eye of the crew chief, Staff Sergeant Joseph S. Angelini, who had gone to great lengths to fashion a doggy-size oxygen mask and flotation device for the four-legged mascot.[13]

In addition to an unorthodox passenger, Richards had two cadet navigators on board his B-17. Neither had made a long overwater flight before, but their combined efforts proved remarkably accurate. As *Skipper* approached the eastern shore of Oahu, a small fighter strip named Bellows Field appeared straight off the nose. From there, a meandering flight around the island's southern coastline would bring the airplane to the approach pattern for Hickam Field. Keeping just offshore, Richards banked gracefully around the contour of Koko Head, then took a westerly heading past the more famous landmarks of Diamond Head, Waikiki Beach, and the still-sleeping city of Honolulu. Dead ahead lay John Rogers Field, a civilian airport serving Honolulu. Just beyond that, Hickam Field was easily identified by its Moorish-inspired water tower. The tapered octagonal structure, its concrete exterior gleaming in the early morning sunlight, soared to a height of more than 170 feet.

Their long flight almost over, Richards and his crew approached Hickam Field with visions of sandy beaches, palm trees, and hula girls in their heads—but a different welcome was in store.

INSIDE THE OPERATIONS building at Hickam, the arrival of the B-17s was highly anticipated. The commander of the airfield, Colonel William E.

Farthing, arrived early and climbed the control tower to enjoy the fabulous view. Several officers from the Hawaiian Air Force, the controlling authority for army aviation in the territory, were also on hand to welcome the big bombers. Among them was the operations officer, Major Roger Ramey, eager to greet his good friend and West Point classmate Ted Landon. While waiting for the B-17s to arrive, he and the base operations officer, Captain Gordon A. Blake, swapped stories in the latter's downstairs office.[14]

Unbeknownst to all of them, the first wave of Japanese aircraft had already received the attack signal from the strike leader, Commander Fuchida. A formation of fifty-one Aichi D3A dive bombers divided over central Oahu, the first element peeling off to attack Wheeler Field, the second continuing straight ahead. After a sweeping turn, the second formation separated once again, one group heading east to bomb the naval air station at Kaneohe, the other circling around to initiate simultaneous bombing runs against Hickam Field and Ford Island.

Known to the Japanese as Type 99 dive bombers, each of the fixed-gear planes carried one 250-kilogram bomb in a centerline rack and two 60-kilo bombs on wing racks. Their objective was to smash the airfields across Oahu and destroy as many planes as possible on the ground, thereby reducing the possibility of counterattacks against the *Kido Butai*.[15] At 7:55, just as a formation of Type 99s rolled into their dives over Ford Island and Hickam Field, the horizontal bombers and torpedo bombers initiated simultaneous attacks against the warships in Pearl Harbor. Except for a few minor glitches, none of which affected the outcome, the strike had been almost perfectly coordinated.

In the control tower at Hickam, the first indication that something was wrong came with the thump of distant explosions followed by the roar of radial engines straining at full power. Several low-flying aircraft were seen racing eastward from the direction of Pearl Harbor, giving the impression that U.S. Navy planes were taking off from Ford Island. Then came the distinctive whine of aircraft diving from altitude. Colonel Farthing figured some Marines from nearby Ewa Field were practicing maneuvers, until the lead aircraft dropped a dark object over Ford Island. A heavy explosion mushroomed skyward and the plane zoomed up, heading straight for the control tower. Momentarily stunned, Farthing could see the red insignia of Japan on the underside of the bomber's wings.

Downstairs, Captain Blake and Major Ramey were startled by a different explosion. Running outside, they saw a dive bomber swoop up after scoring a direct hit on the Hawaiian Air Depot, a large repair facility down the street. Despite the shock of seeing Japanese markings on the airplane, Blake had the presence of mind to remember the incoming B-17s. Dashing inside and up to the control tower, he grabbed a microphone. Radio silence was no longer in effect.

LIEUTENANT RICHARDS AND the crew of *Skipper* were already in trouble. Puzzled by the sight of smoke rising over Pearl Harbor, they were even more astonished when an unfamiliar plane pulled alongside. Moments later came the biggest surprise of all—the impact of machine-gun bullets rattling against the B-17's aluminum skin. The attack seemed so incongruous, so unexpected, that one crewman thought the unidentified planes were firing wax bullets as part of a realistic exercise. Sergeant Angelini knew better, shouting, "We got goddamn holes in our wings!"[16]

Richards yanked the bomber into a nearby cloud. As soon as the B-17 popped out the other side, however, more fighters swarmed in. They were Type 0 carrier fighters (Mitsubishi A6M2s), the undisputed pride of the Imperial Japanese Navy. A nine-plane division of Zeros led by Lieutenant Commander Shigeru Itaya, leader of the first-wave fighter element, had already strafed a Hawaiian Airlines DC-3 idling on the pavement at John Rogers Field. The commercial airliner, filled with passengers, burst into flames but was successfully evacuated without serious injuries.

Now, after regaining altitude, Itaya and his pilots turned their aggression on Richards's unarmed B-17, which they mistook for a large transport. As Angelini had noted so emphatically, one of the initial bursts of gunfire hit the left wing of the Fortress, shredding the aileron and damaging the inboard engine. Bullets from the next attack buzzed through the fuselage, wounding two crewmen. The most seriously injured was the bombardier,

Staff Sergeant Lawrence B. Velarde, who moments earlier had suggested the bullets were made of wax.

The crew had no ability to fight back. The bomber's machine guns were stowed in the rear fuselage, "pickled" in rust-preventative Cosmoline gel, and in any event there were no ammunition belts for them. With two long-range auxiliary fuel tanks in the bomb bay and the fuselage crammed with baggage, tools, and supplies, the B-17 had been at its maximum gross weight when it left California. There was neither space nor legal weight allowance for heavy boxes of ammunition.

Defenseless, almost out of fuel, with two crewmen wounded and Hickam Field under attack, Richards decided to abort the landing attempt. Turning eastward, he raced back toward Bellows Field, where the situation had seemed peaceful a few minutes earlier.

LIEUTENANT BRUCE G. Allen, piloting the second B-17 to reach Oahu, was likewise curious about the pall of smoke rising over Pearl Harbor. At first he thought a large tract of sugarcane was being burned off, then he presumed that a realistic exercise was under way. Suddenly a voice boomed in his earphones, stating that the island was under attack. In the control tower, Gordon Blake keyed his microphone again to warn Allen that an enemy fighter was directly behind him. Startled by "the peculiar feeling of being told by the tower that a Jap was on my tail," Allen landed immediately. The sight of parked aircraft in flames on the flight line seemed surreal as he taxied to the grassy dispersal area near the eastern boundary of the field. The weary crew jumped out, disoriented by the sudden events, but their adrenaline surged again as enemy planes roared down to strafe them. Trying to make himself invisible in grass only three inches high, Allen distinctly heard "the flat reports of machine guns and the thud of bullets impacting the earth."[17]

Miraculously, no one among his crew was hit. During a lull in the strafing, all nine men jumped up and ran for the shelter of some nearby woods. Compelled to remain there for the rest of the morning, they watched the attack unfold while fighting off swarms of mosquitos.

THE THIRD B-17C to approach Hickam Field carried one of the more experienced crews in the 38th Reconnaissance Squadron. Its pilot was twenty-nine-year-old Captain Raymond T. Swenson, a somewhat overweight alumnus of the University of Minnesota, where he had played trumpet in the marching band. The veteran of a ferry flight to Hawaii in May 1941, he had put on shiny new captain's bars in early November. He still enjoyed playing his trumpet, which was carefully packed with his personal belongings amid a pile of B4 garment bags, footlockers, and crates labeled "PLUM," the code name for the Philippines.

The navigator was likewise experienced. Lieutenant Homer R. Taylor had not only made the trip to Hawaii in May, he subsequently spent several months ferrying Lend-Lease bombers across the North Atlantic to Great Britain. The long overwater flights had provided a wealth of experience no classroom syllabus could ever teach.

By far the oldest member of the crew, and one of the oldest men in the squadron, was Master Sergeant Leroy B. Pouncey, the flight engineer. Born in 1900, he had enlisted as a teenager when the United States entered World War I; now, after twenty-four years of continuous service, he was the squadron's wizened sage, a mentor who could solve almost any mechanical problem.

By contrast, the assistant flight engineer was barely half Pouncey's age. Sergeant Earl T. Williams, assigned to the squadron straight out of boot camp, had enlisted in the Air Corps in 1939, a matter of weeks after Hitler invaded Poland. A former Eagle Scout with excellent mechanical skills, the slender Ohioan had earned a First Class Aircraft Mechanic rating and his sergeant's stripes within only two years. For that, the army paid him eighty-four dollars a month. "It was pretty good pay," he acknowledged, "for that economy."[18] Although not technically a member of the combat crew, Williams flew so routinely as an assistant engineer that he was included in the air echelon for the squadron's deployment.

Other members of the crew were still cutting their teeth as aviators. Second Lieutenant Ernest L. "Roy" Reid, the twenty-one-year-old copilot, had been in the squadron for only six months. During that time he had accumulated about one hundred hours of right-seat time, and needed at least four hundred more before he could qualify as a command pilot. One of his routine copilot duties was to check the engine instruments every hour and record the various readouts in a logbook. At precisely eight o'clock that morning, several miles east of Hickam Field, he began entering the final updates.

Sitting in the observer's seat directly behind Roy Reid, the squadron's newly assigned flight surgeon could scarcely contain his enthusiasm. The overseas deployment seemed like a grand adventure to First Lieutenant William R. Schick, who pulled out his new camera, a farewell gift from his wife. "This is spectacular," he said to Earl Williams between snapshots of Diamond Head. "I wouldn't take a million dollars for this view. It's really beautiful."[19]

While the flight surgeon took photographs, Williams decided to move aft. After stepping through the bomb bay on a narrow catwalk, he joined Staff Sergeant Joseph J. Bruce, the radio operator, and his assistant, Private Bert Lee Jr., in the soundproofed radio compartment. All three men gazed out the side window while Sergeant Bruce, another veteran of the ferry flight six months earlier, pointed out famous landmarks. They had just passed the pink stucco extravagance of the Royal Hawaiian Hotel when a vee of single-engine planes flashed by in the opposite direction. "Oh, that's probably the navy," offered Bruce. "They always welcome us when we come from the States."[20]

Up on the flight deck, rising columns of black smoke caught the eye of both pilots. "Swede" Swenson, like Bruce Allen in the preceding B-17, presumed the smoke was coming from controlled burns of sugarcane. Roy Reid noticed the smoke, too, but it wasn't until the B-17 was on final approach, heading directly toward Hickam, that full realization sank in. "What I saw shocked me," he remembered. "At least six planes were burning fiercely on the ground."[21]

Seconds later, the Zero fighters led by Lieutenant Commander Itaya attacked Swenson's B-17 from behind.

In the radio compartment, Sergeant Bruce was startled by "a noise in the ship like a string of firecrackers exploding."[22] He thought a control cable had snapped and was flailing around inside the fuselage somewhere. That idea evaporated when the plastic canopy covering the retractable machine-gun mount, located in the roof of the compartment, suddenly shattered. At the front of the compartment, Earl Williams jumped to his feet and looked aft through the jagged opening, wondering what the hell had happened. To his surprise, a fighter maneuvered directly behind the B-17. Remembering what Joe Bruce had said about the navy, Williams presumed the aircraft was friendly—even after it began spraying bullets. The aggression seemed so incomprehensible, he figured that "somebody must have forgotten to load its guns with dummy ammunition."[23]

The pale gray fighters were anything but friendly. Now leading a three-plane tactical formation called a *shotai*, Itaya poured 7.7mm bullets into the unarmed bomber from close range. The stunned crew, recalled Williams, had nowhere to hide.

Bullets were coming through the radio compartment in massive amounts. The cotton from the insulated padding was swirling inside the radio compartment like snowflakes. Then the fighters hit the flare locker on the right side of the aircraft, and the whole compartment burst into flames. My parachute was sitting on one of the seats. I picked it up, but it was on fire. I thought I'd better go up front and tell the pilot.

I went forward toward the cockpit and closed the door between the radio compartment and the bomb bay, but that heat came through the door and singed my hair. I could feel the heat on my neck and ears and the back of my head. I got to the flight deck and told the pilot what was happening aft, but he was quite aware of it. Black smoke filled the flight deck, and he was having a hard time seeing the instruments.

The flare locker, filled with 37mm signal cartridges resembling huge shotgun shells, burned with an intensity no portable fire extinguisher could cope with. In a matter of seconds, the magnesium-fed flames began to melt through the bomber's aluminum skin and even its structural framework.

The only means of escape for Joe Bruce and Bert Lee was to retreat aft, so they jumped through the compartment's doorway into the rear fuselage.

In the cockpit, both Swenson and Reid were saved by the heavy armor plating installed on their seats just before they left the mainland. As the Zeros raked the bomber, bullets ricocheted from the backs of the seats like angry bees. "If we hadn't had that armor plate," observed Williams, "the pilots would have been hit and that would have been the end of it."[24]

Even as deformed bullets zinged through the confined space, Lieutenant Schick warned that additional gunfire was coming up from the ground. He was right. American antiaircraft gunners had jumped to their weapons and were beginning to fight back, but in the furious chaos of explosions and fire that swirled across the island, they shot at everything in the air. It didn't help their recognition skills that the inbound B-17s had been freshly painted with olive drab upper surfaces and light gray undersides, whereas the B-17s based in Hawaii wore a natural aluminum finish. Nor did it help that the U.S. national insignia featured a bright red circle in the middle of the traditional white star, easily mistakable for the red disk of the Japanese insignia. Some observers on the ground even assumed the big planes belonged to the enemy. "My God," swore one navy pilot, "they have four-engine bombers. Where are they coming from?"[25]

But the real threat to Swede Swenson's B-17 came from Itaya's nimble fighters. Lieutenant Schick had no sooner commented on the antiaircraft fire when he cried out, "God damn it, those are real bullets they're shooting, I'm hit!"[26] Two other crewmen were also wounded during the flurry of gunfire. Earl Williams discovered blood trickling into his mouth from a crease in his scalp, and Homer Taylor, the navigator, was nicked in the ear. Both men had avoided potentially fatal head wounds by inches. Although they bled profusely, the injuries proved superficial.

Swenson and Reid, blinded by smoke so thick they could barely see each other, struggled to maintain control of the B-17. Swenson slid open his side window to evacuate some of the smoke, while Reid's first instinct was to raise the wheels and duck into a cloud to throw off the attackers. Swenson overruled him. "Get that gear back down," he ordered.[27] Reid cycled the switch and the electrically operated landing gear, already partially raised, whirred down slowly. It locked in position only a few feet above the ground. Seconds later the crippled bomber, its midsection burning fiercely, touched down with a jolt and caromed back into the air. "It took both of us on the controls to get the wings level after that first bounce," Reid would later recall. "Then the tail came down. Almost immediately, the plane began to buckle and collapse, breaking in the middle where the fire had burned through."[28]

Still rolling down the runway at high speed, the B-17 physically collapsed, its back broken. The rear fuselage, attached by one or two twisted spars, dragged along the pavement in a shower of sparks. Sergeant Bruce and Private Lee held on for a wild ride, then jumped out as soon as the flaming wreckage slid to a stop. The baggage, supplies, and personal belongings stored in the rear compartment, including Captain Swenson's prized trumpet and Earl Williams's high school yearbook, were consumed in the fire.

The forward section of the B-17 continued to roll down the runway on the trailing edge of the main wing, its four propellers spinning at a crazy angle. As the Fortress swerved to a stop, the pilots shut down the engines and secured the electrical system. Purely out of habit, Roy Reid took the time to set the parking brake, a superfluous action that placed him a few seconds behind Swenson in a mad scramble to evacuate the burning airplane. The two-hundred-pound Swenson took longer than Reid liked in squeezing through the upper escape hatch, so Reid gave the pilot a hefty shove on the bottom before following him out. Just as Reid emerged from the hatch, a gust of flames rolled over his head, singeing off his hair and eyebrows. Spurred by the heat, he jumped onto the main wing, crawled up its awkward slope, and leaped from the leading edge—now some twelve feet off the pavement—without feeling the jolt.[29]

While the pilots climbed through the upper hatch, the remaining crewmembers in the forward section evacuated through the belly door. By no small miracle, all nine men escaped the crash landing without additional injuries, but their ordeal was far from over. Noticing that the hangars and flight line were under attack, a few crewmen ran toward the dispersal area, where Lieutenant Allen's B-17 was parked. The rest, including Williams,

Schick, and both pilots, decided to seek shelter in the hangars. Before any of them could reach safety, however, several Zero fighters dived toward the burning Fortress and commenced a series of strafing attacks.

Roy Reid took a few strides across the flight line, but changed his mind. "Obeying my first impulse to get away from the ship before it blew up," he remembered, "I ran a few feet and came out of the smoke just in time to see a Jap plane making another pass at us down the runway. I decided to chance the ship blowing up rather than the Jap, and ran back to the plane."[30]

The heavy mass of the landing gear offered good protection from bullets, so Reid climbed onto the left tire and took cover beneath the inboard engine. Earl Williams also sought shelter beneath the bomber's wing. Seventy-five years later, his memories of the attack remained vivid: "Schick got out, I got out, and the Japanese were still strafing us. Instead of staying with the airplane, Lieutenant Schick went toward the hangars. I thought, jeez, the thickest part of the airplane is the landing gear, so I'm staying here until the strafing ends."[31]

Schick, evidently slowed by the bullet wound in his leg, got only halfway across the flight line before a Zero caught him in the open. Twin streams of machine-gun bullets stitched across the ramp and the doctor tumbled to the ground, struck in the face by a ricocheting bullet or chunk of pavement. Sprawled on the flight line, he lay motionless, stunned but still alive.

Three other crewmen were also hit by the strafing Zeros. The bombardier, Aviation Cadet GC Beale (his full legal name), started running toward the dispersal area but was knocked to the ground by a bullet that smashed his left femur, causing a compound fracture a few inches above the knee. Almost simultaneously, Leroy Pouncey took a bullet in the shoulder and Bert Lee was shot downward through the groin. The only men from Swenson's crew *not* wounded were the pilot, the radio operator, and the copilot, although Reid's hair was singed off.

TWENTY MILES DUE east of Hickam, Lieutenant Richards lined up to land at Bellows Field. The winds were out of the east, which permitted a straight-in approach, but even under the best of circumstances the attempt was almost foolhardy. The runway, only two-thirds of a mile long, was barely adequate for the single-engine fighters stationed there—but Richards had no choice. Smoke poured from the number two engine, the fuel tanks were nearly empty, and the wounded bombardier needed immediate medical attention. The control tower at Bellows was obviously unaware of the B-17's approach, for just as Richards neared the field, a crew chief taxiing a P-40 fighter started to cross the runway. Forced to pull up, Richards lacked the fuel to go around for another approach into the wind. Quickly reversing direction, he lined up for a downwind landing in a desperate attempt to put the big bomber down before it ran out of gas. He tried to flare the B-17, which seemed enormous to eyewitnesses on the ground, but it was halfway down the runway before the main wheels touched down. Not surprisingly, the Fortress was still rolling at high speed when the pavement ended. Richards either retracted the landing gear or it collapsed as the bomber sailed over a drainage ditch, then flopped onto its belly.

Unaware of the attacks occurring at Pearl Harbor, airfield personnel rushed to the damaged bomber in disbelief and assisted the shaken crew. Velarde, the wounded bombardier, received prompt attention from the medicos. After he was carted off, the responsibility for securing the top-secret bombsight went to the flight engineer, Joe Angelini. He climbed into the nose compartment and began to remove the device, but its various connections proved vexing. While he struggled to detach "that damn Norden bombsight," another flight of Zeros attacked the airfield.[32] They made multiple strafing runs on the B-17, evidently trying to burn it, but the bomber refused to ignite. Up in the nose, a frustrated Angelini decided not to risk life and limb for the sake of the bombsight. Abandoning the fruitless effort, he gathered up his puppy and went off in search of a weapon.

TWO OF THE first three B-17s to reach Oahu had been forced down or crash-landed, and neither would ever fly again. Eight personnel among their crews had been wounded, some severely, one mortally. As for the nine remaining bombers that approached Hickam Field that morning, most would benefit from the assistance of Gordon Blake, whose calm voice from the control tower guided them toward safe landings. But not necessarily at Hickam. Shot at by enemy aircraft and nervous American gunners with equal enthusiasm, the crews of the defenseless B-17s anxiously dodged shell bursts and streams of tracer fire as they tried to find safe places to land before running out of fuel.

The spectacular sunrise had been forgotten. Fourteen hours after lifting off from the peaceful coast of California, the B-17s had flown straight into a brand-new war.

TWO

BOEING'S BIG, BEAUTIFUL BOMBER

For the dozens of B-17 crewmen and one six-week-old puppy who arrived over Oahu in the midst of the Japanese attack, the distinction of being aboard the first U.S. Army bombers to engage in aerial combat in World War II was unwelcome. Caught completely by surprise, unable to fight back, and nearly out of fuel, the B-17s should have been slaughtered. Fortunately, the aircraft themselves provided a singular advantage—one that had been engineered into them from the very beginning. As thousands of aircrews would learn over the next few years, the B-17 could absorb terrific amounts of battle damage and still fly. No plane was invincible, but as the men of the 38th and 88th Reconnaissance Squadrons discovered that fateful morning, their bombers were extremely durable. Despite the many disadvantages they faced, all twelve B-17s managed to land under their own power. Of equal importance, only a few crewmen were wounded in the air.

Destined to become one of the most beloved aircraft of all time, the rugged B-17 is as much a part of the Kangaroo Squadron story as the men who flew it. Therefore, in order to adequately illustrate the squadron's combat history, a brief overview of the B-17's development is well worth narrating here. It also provides an interesting account of how one design saved a struggling company, ultimately helping to transform it from a medium-sized business into a global leader in the aerospace industry. And the story began, curiously enough, in the midst of the worst economic depression in American history.

In the spring of 1934, a circular was sent from the Materials Division of the U.S. Army Air Corps to two reputable airplane manufacturers, the Glenn Martin Company and the Boeing Aircraft Company. At stake was a potential government contract worth millions, possibly the difference between financial success and ruin. It was not a time for half-hearted commitments. The nation was in the throes of the Great Depression, and dozens of aircraft companies had already gone belly-up.

Neither company had ever attempted anything like the concept dreamed up by the Air Corps. The requirements for "Project A," as it was called, bordered on science fiction: design an aircraft capable of carrying a ton of bombs over a range of five thousand miles at an average speed of two hundred miles per hour. Such performance characteristics were unheard of. Based on the desired speed, it would take a bomber more than twenty-four hours to cover the proposed distance. The prototype would therefore have to carry a tremendous amount of fuel and provide amenities for the crew such as bunks, a galley, and even a toilet. No aircraft then in existence came close to meeting the stated goals.

Only thirty years had elapsed since the Wright brothers' first powered flight. If aviation had outgrown its infancy, it was still adolescent. Despite numerous advances, the world of aeronautics in the mid-1930s was dominated by fabric-covered biplanes with fixed landing gear and open cockpits. Such configurations created excessive drag, resulting in overall performance that had not improved significantly since World War I. The Air Corps' frontline bomber, in fact, was the twin-engine Keystone biplane, with an almost laughable cruising speed of 102 miles per hour and a range of barely eight hundred miles.

In the boardrooms of the competing companies, the directors understood that they would have to fund the construction of their respective prototypes. The Air Corps project did not include money up-front, nor was there any guarantee of an eventual payoff. Rising to the challenge, Boeing's engineers produced a preliminary design that was both futuristic and gargantuan. No name was bequeathed, simply a sequential number assigned by the company. But if her generic identity lacked a soul, it soon became obvious that Model 294 would be an extraordinary machine. Her specifications were astonishing. Whereas the Keystone bomber weighed around 14,000 pounds fully loaded, Model 294 would tip the scales at more than 70,000 pounds. Her cylindrical fuselage, eighty-seven feet in length, would be manned by a crew of ten. Designed from the outset for long-range reconnaissance and bombing, the giant plane would boast an eight-thousand-pound payload. Furthermore, at a time when "multi-engine" typically referred to two or perhaps three motors, Model 294 would have *four* powerful engines mounted on her main wing. Other innovations included access tunnels inside the wing to allow crewmen to make minor adjustments to the engines in flight, an autopilot, de-icers, and machine guns in pivoting turrets for defense. Enormous yet elegant, Model 294 promised to stand the aviation world on its ear.[1]

In June 1934, Boeing was awarded a contract to develop a prototype. The army called it the XBLR-1 (Experimental Bomber, Long Range), but the concept proved to be too advanced, too large. No airplane of such complexity had ever been produced, and there were no factories in existence big enough to build it. The design would have to wait while Boeing constructed a huge new plant. Thus more than two years passed before a single prototype, assigned a new designation as the XB-15, emerged from the factory's gaping doors. Although the design never went into production, the prototype served as a test platform, conducting several record-setting flights before its eventual conversion into a one-of-a-kind transport.

In the meantime, a somewhat smaller, more manageable design had been submitted to the Air Corps. With a slender fuselage and tapered main wing, four engines, and pivoting gun turrets, Boeing's Model 299 shared several common features with the Model 294. Boardroom approval to commence the project was given in late September 1934, and construction began three months later with full awareness that the investment represented a major percentage of the company's financial resources. In a truly remarkable feat of engineering and modern fabrication techniques, the prototype of Model 299 was completed in only seven months.

Touted as the largest land plane yet constructed in the United States, the gleaming bomber was an instant sensation when it emerged from Boeing's red brick factory on July 16, 1935.[*] Collectively, Model 299's massive wingspan, supercharged radial engines, retractable landing gear, and streamlined fuselage represented an astonishing combination of aeronautical design and technology; yet for all her jaw-dropping brawn, she was aesthetically pleasing, even elegant. But the feature that caught the eye of many observers, including a local journalist, was the plane's defensive armament. Machine guns protruded from several blisters and turrets, prompting Richard Williams of the *Seattle Post Intelligencer* to describe the aircraft as a "15-ton flying fortress."[2] The Boeing company liked the description so much it copyrighted the Flying Fortress name.

The airplane, like its nickname, had panache. But appearances would mean nothing if the machine did not live up to the hype. After a series of high-speed taxiing tests and adjustments, Boeing's chief test pilot, Leslie R. Tower, took the airplane on its maiden flight on July 28. Any concerns about the handling characteristics of such a big airplane were immediately dispelled. When asked how it handled, Tower answered laconically, "Just like a little ship, only a little bigger."[3]

Less than a month later, Boeing personnel flew the prototype to Wright Field outside Dayton, Ohio, for the army's competitive fly-off. The nonstop flight of two thousand miles, completed in just over nine hours, grabbed the attention of the Air Corps even before the competition began. The experts were astonished to discover that the huge aircraft cruised at speeds approaching the *top* speed of the army's fastest pursuit planes. Over the next few weeks, the evaluation team noted that Model 299's performance was consistently superior to the Martin and Douglas entries, both of which were twin-engine aircraft. The competition seemed all but locked up—but then tragedy struck.

---

[*] The Boeing was dwarfed by the Soviet Union's Tupolev ANT-20 "Maksim Gorky," introduced in 1934. Designed as a propaganda platform, the plane carried an onboard printing press for creating leaflets to be dropped over isolated stretches of the USSR. The forty-five-ton aircraft, powered by eight engines, had a wingspan of two hundred feet, carried an eight-man crew, and could accommodate more than sixty passengers.

Because of her size, Model 299 had been designed with a device called a "gust lock" to prevent the rudder and elevators from slamming against their limits when the plane was parked in high wind conditions. On October 30, 1935, the chief of the Flying Branch at Wright Field, making his first flight in the prototype, took off without releasing the elevator lock. Climbing too steeply, the big plane stalled and pancaked into a nearby field, then burst into flames. Four men escaped from the burning wreckage, but the pilot and Les Tower, who had been riding as an observer, were fatally injured. Before succumbing, Tower managed to explain what had happened and took responsibility for the oversight.[*4]

An accident board determined that the cause of the crash was the direct result of the locked controls, essentially exonerating the airplane from any contributing flaws, but the fatal crash disqualified the Boeing entry since it could not complete the entire series of tests. The Douglas Model DB-1, based on the company's popular DC-2 airliner, won the lucrative contract, in large measure because its production cost per airframe would be roughly half the price of a four-engine Boeing. By 1940 Douglas sold 350 twin-engine bombers, designated as the B-18, to the United States and Canada. Boeing, meanwhile, had more than doubled its initial investment, sinking more than $600,000 into Model 299. Thus, in addition to the tragedy of losing its chief test pilot, the Seattle-based company teetered on the brink of bankruptcy.

Fortunately for Boeing, the Air Corps was too impressed with the initial performance of the prototype to ignore its potential. In early 1937, through a procurement loophole, the army awarded a contract for a small number of aircraft, identified as YB-17s, for evaluation. Thirteen examples were delivered to the Air Corps by August 1937, of which twelve went to the 2nd Bombardment Group at Langley Field, Virginia. (The other airframe went to Wright Field for experimental testing and development.) The new bombers made a splash with both the Air Corps and the public, flying approximately 1.8 million miles over the next two years without a major accident.

---

* One direct outcome of the accident was the Air Corps' development of a cockpit checklist. The safety benefits were immediately apparent. To this day, cockpit checklists are a staple of the routine aviation safety procedures practiced worldwide.

Constant improvements and upgrades resulted in record-setting achievements that garnered worldwide attention. The most widely publicized event, carefully orchestrated to demonstrate the capabilities of the YB-17, occurred in the spring of 1938. On May 12, three Flying Fortresses took off from Mitchel Field, Long Island, for a long-range "interception" of the Italian liner *Rex* as it steamed toward New York City. Among the three crews were some of the rising stars in the strategic bombing community, including Lieutenant Colonel Robert Olds, commander of the 2nd Bombardment Group, and a young lieutenant named Curtis E. LeMay, the mission's lead navigator. Despite bad weather, the B-17s found the sleek ocean liner more than seven hundred statute miles east of Sandy Hook. During a series of low flyovers, an NBC crew aboard one of the bombers presented a live radio broadcast. The following day, stunning aerial photographs showing two B-17s just off the port rail of the *Rex* were published nationwide.

The attention almost backfired. Senior members of the navy, resentful of the Air Corps' intrusion into their area of responsibility, criticized the flight as a publicity stunt. Even the army failed to capitalize on the event, primarily because of long-standing rivalries within the War Department. Some members of the General Staff were dismayed by all the publicity, which reminded them of the aerial demonstrations staged by Colonel William "Billy" Mitchell in 1921. A political circus had ensued after he famously bombed captured German warships to show the world what his airplanes were capable of. Ultimately antagonizing too many of his superiors, the outspoken Mitchell was court-martialed and convicted of insubordination in 1925, though he resigned before the army could officially suspend him from duty.

After the high-profile interception of the *Rex*, pushbacks from rivals and political opponents of strategic bombardment hindered the further acquisition of B-17s. Ironically, this played right into Boeing's hands. As the performance capabilities of military aircraft improved exponentially, the Air Corps realized that the Douglas B-18's mediocre range, service ceiling, and payload had already rendered it obsolete as a bombing platform, opening the door for the B-17. During the interim, Boeing had made numerous improvements to the original design. Boasting bigger engines fitted with turbosuperchargers, the B-17 could now fly higher and significantly faster than any pursuit aircraft in the U.S. inventory. In August 1937, the army agreed to order ten of the company's newest variant, designated as the B-17B. The contract was subsequently increased to a total of thirty-nine bombers, enough to equip three squadrons, which Boeing fulfilled in March 1940. By then, the next model was already coming down the assembly line inside the company's gigantic new factory at Boeing Field. The delivery of thirty-eight B-17Cs commenced in the summer of 1940, followed by forty-two D models beginning in the late winter of 1941.

Visually alike, with a delicately tapered fuselage topped by a spade-shaped vertical stabilizer, the first three production models were becoming obsolescent. Almost six years had passed since the rollout of the prototype, with relatively minor changes aft of the main wing. In the spring of 1941, twenty C models (known to the British as the Fortress I) were delivered to the Royal Air Force, where they performed poorly in combat against the Luftwaffe. The speed and range of the B-17 had no equal among operational Allied bombers, but the defensive armament that had seemed so impressive in 1935 now proved woefully inadequate. Boeing had made few changes to the armament, primarily due to the belief that the B-17 could outrun any pursuer, but in fact the bomber's defenses against attack from the rear quarter were its primary weakness. What the Flying Fortress needed, based on the RAF's experience, was more heavy machine guns, especially a tail gun position.

The engineers at Boeing responded with the first major redesign of the B-17. Although the bullet-shaped nose compartment for the bombardier and navigator remained essentially unchanged, a powered dorsal turret housing twin .50 caliber machine guns was added behind the cockpit, and a remote-controlled turret with another pair of "fifties" was grafted into the belly. The most obvious change involved the expanded rear fuselage. Gone was the slender tail, replaced by a dorsal tailfin and much larger vertical stabilizer. Lengthened by ten feet, the new design also provided space to install a twin machine-gun position in the tail. The extensive alterations added a whopping nine thousand pounds to the new model, which Boeing partially compensated for by upgrading the engines.

After worrisome months of haggling over unit prices and contractual obligations during the summer of 1940, Boeing received orders to build 512 redesigned B-17s. A lengthy and complicated period of retooling and acquisition of raw materials followed, but the contracts eventually propelled the company into an era of growth from which it never looked back. Interestingly, when the first B-17Es appeared in the fall of 1941, some observers thought the much-enlarged tail section spoiled the aesthetics of the original design. Old-timers even referred to the new model as the "big ass bird." The veterans were entitled to their opinion, of course, but for thousands of others, especially the pilots and crewmen who had recently begun training for war, the Flying Fortress in all its forms eventually became one of the most revered bombers that ever flew.

Boeing had created a fabulous machine. Dazzling from the day it emerged from the factory, the B-17 captured the world's attention like no other big airplane before it. But without highly trained people to fly it, guide it, operate its systems and defenses, and properly maintain it, the conglomeration of parts would never have become more than an inert machine. It took a group of uniquely qualified men—volunteers who had joined the Air Corps years before World War II began—to fly the amazing bomber into a glorious new chapter in aviation history.

THREE

OFF WE GO!

The young Americans who came of age during the Great Depression faced a grim future. Theirs was a nation in which half the banks had failed, industrial production was down fifty percent from the boom years before the crisis, and prairie states turned to dust from a prolonged drought. Unaware that they would be called upon to save their country from global tyranny in the next decade, the youth of America became intimately familiar with the stark realities of a severe economic disaster: abandoned factories, vacant farms, homeless families struggling to survive in squalid camps, long lines of unemployed waiting for handouts of bread or soup.

And yet the decade known as the "Dirty Thirties," although often gloomy, was not unbearable. Americans benefited from numerous developments and advancements, especially in technology and the arts. At the beginning of the decade only ten percent of rural homes and farms had electricity. A federal program enacted by the Roosevelt administration gradually brought power to millions of isolated households, leading to a boom in affordable electronic appliances. Furniture-sized radios became the centerpiece of home entertainment, and families gathered in their living rooms to listen to news, sports, music, and a wide variety of comedy skits and dramas. The Golden Age of radio broadcasting provided a welcome diversion from the dismal economic outlook.

During the same period, advances in aeronautics were nothing short of phenomenal. Doctor Robert Goddard launched the first gyroscope-equipped

rocket in 1935; two years later Frank Whittle, an engineering genius and former Royal Air Force pilot, developed the first turbojet engine. Although the
practical applications of those inventions were still years in the future, other
new developments made an immediate impact. All-metal construction, en-
closed cockpits, retractable landing gear, and instrument navigation were
some of the breakthroughs that enabled planes to fly ever faster, higher, and
farther in almost any type of weather. More than a few developments were
outgrowths of the National Air Races and their overseas equivalents. The
annual events drew hundreds of thousands of spectators and made front-
page headlines, fostering intense competition between airplane designers,
engine builders, and a host of aviation industries. Pilots fortunate enough
to win a Bendix Trophy (or a Pulitzer, Schneider, or Thompson Trophy) not
only reaped financial rewards, they basked in worldwide glory.

One hallmark of aviation in the 1930s was the trend in bright, almost
gaudy paint schemes, a spinoff of the art deco movement. Aluminum-clad
planes often wore a highly polished bare finish complemented by bold graph-
ics, and military aircraft were painted in vibrant colors. One eye-popping
example was the U.S. Army's sleek Curtiss P-6E Hawk, a fixed-gear biplane
with brilliant yellow wings and dazzling black and white accents. The 17th
Pursuit Squadron even decorated its Hawk fighters by painting "talons" on
the teardrop-shaped wheel pants.

The public's embrace of aviation was fed by a proliferation of pulp novels and hobby magazines devoted to flying escapades, many featuring the
heroes of the Great War. The youth of the 1930s devoured serialized stories
such as *G-8 and His Battle Aces* and eagerly awaited the newest issues of
Flying Aces and *Popular Aviation*. Filled with adventure stories, technical articles, model-building plans, and advertisements for flying lessons and trade
schools, the publications provided easy access to the latest news about aviation around the world.

But the public was far more enthralled with the pilots, who had a mystique unmatched by any other profession. A leather flight jacket, leather
helmet, and goggles perched on the forehead could transform an average
individual into a dashing idol. Military flying was a particularly dangerous

vocation—the army suffered fifty-nine fatalities in well over four hundred aircraft accidents during 1936 alone—but the public adored fliers of every stripe. The feats of civilian aviators Charles and Anne Lindbergh, Wiley Post, Clyde Pangborn, Amelia Earhart, and many others inspired a lifelong interest in aviation among millions of Americans.

Many a young man dreamed of a career in the Air Corps, but severe cutbacks during the Depression created a major obstacle. Due to double-digit unemployment rates nationwide, jobs in the military were highly coveted. The pay was better than average, such that even a lowly private could make ends meet. Most personnel lived in barracks or base housing, everyone took advantage of the reduced prices available at post commissaries and exchanges, and hardly anyone complained about the status quo. "No one in the military service ever worked very hard in those days," wrote Norman E. Borden, a reserve pilot in the mid-1930s. "A normal day's duty always ended at 3:30 in the afternoon to allow time for recreation. Wednesday was a half-holiday and no one ever dreamed of working at night."[1]

Competition for new openings in the Air Corps was keen, and the army could afford to be highly selective. But eventually, toward the end of the decade, a confluence of world events would provide new opportunities for thousands of recruits.

ALTHOUGH MILLIONS OF Americans endured hardships during the Great Depression, not everyone suffered equally. It was a foregone conclusion, for example, that Frederick C. Eaton Jr. would attend Dartmouth College. His father and uncles were Dartmouth men, and for an eighteen-year-old like Fred, acceptance to an Ivy League school was the pinnacle of prestige. Raised in an affluent suburb of New York City, educated in good public schools, and shaped by a community of faith in his local church, Eaton possessed the attributes to succeed at almost anything. Handsome, athletic (he excelled at squash), and affable, he attracted friends wherever he went.

In the late summer of 1936, Eaton entered his freshman year at Dartmouth. He became fast friends with an Ohio native named Daniel Conway and they joined Sigma Chi fraternity, cramming their college days (as Fred would later reminisce) "with the wonderful times, the grand friendships, and the various unforgettable experiences that one lives through with a roommate."[2] But not everything went the way Fred planned. By the end of his junior year, struggling with a heavy workload in mathematics and economics, he faced the embarrassment of academic dismissal.

The likely cause of the setback was an off-campus distraction. Shortly after his twenty-first birthday, Eaton became a student at Bugbee Flying Service in Vermont, just across the state line from Dartmouth. He soloed on May 13, 1939, after eight hours of instruction, and the timing of his sudden interest in aviation was no coincidence. For the past several months, nationwide attention had been focused on a new defense spending bill that stemmed from a secret meeting at the White House between President Franklin D. Roosevelt and the chief of the U.S. Army Air Corps. Roosevelt had verbally pledged to Major General Henry H. "Hap" Arnold that he would expand the army's aerial branch tenfold, from 2,200 planes to 20,000. In a special message to Congress on January 12, 1939, Roosevelt requested $300 million for the Air Corps. Heeding the president's message about the growing threat of war and the need for a strategically deterrent air force, Congress approved the requested funding within three months.

The emergency defense bill earmarked $170 million to expand the Air Corps to a total of five thousand aircraft, and $130 million for proportionate increases in personnel, training facilities, and airfields. Almost overnight, while the manufacturing sector tooled up to meet the demand for new airplanes, the Air Corps prepared to train thousands of new pilots, crewmembers, and maintenance personnel. As far as Fred Eaton was concerned, the timing was perfect. In the spring of 1939, just when his dismissal from Dartmouth looked certain, the recruiting floodgates opened.

Together with Dan Conway, Eaton said goodbye to Dartmouth. Transcripts in hand showing credit for at least two years of college, the two men enlisted in the Air Corps, passed a series of rigid physical exams, and qualified for the Aviation Cadet Training Program. Anticipating a life of grand adventure, they headed off to Nebraska for primary flight training. Their destination was the Lincoln Airplane and Flying School, a civilian facility under contract with the army, renowned as the same school (under different owner-ship) where Charles Lindbergh had started his incomparable aviation career.

The pace at Lincoln was fast and furious. After a few lectures on basic navigation and the principles of flight, the students began flying with an instructor. Throughout the twelve-week program they flew simple, light-weight, forgiving aircraft—typically a Piper Cub or similar design—as they progressed from dual instruction to solo flight. For the first few hours in the cockpit, instructors demonstrated basic maneuvers along with emer-gency procedures, including forced landings and techniques for recovering from dangerous situations such as spins and stalls. Incrementally the stu-dents performed more of the actual flying as they advanced through the syllabus, learning figure-eights and other maneuvers before they progressed to more challenging aspects, especially landings. Many would-be pilots "washed out," but Eaton and Conway were among those who advanced to the aerobatic stage where they practiced loops, rolls, chandelles, and more. To complete the program successfully, students had to log a minimum of sixty-five flight hours (at least fifty percent solo) along with a total of 175 touch-and-go or full-stop landings.[3]

Attrition among student pilots averaged about forty percent, with the highest failure rate occurring in the primary stage. Despite a fierce desire to fly, many young men were disappointed to learn that they lacked the temperament, coordination, or common sense to handle a complex piece of machinery in the three-dimensional realm of flight. Some students out-smarted themselves by overanalyzing situations; others became rattled when instructors berated them, a telltale indicator that they would not perform adequately during the stress of combat. Sometimes, in the blink of an eye, mistakes turned deadly. As the flight training program mushroomed, so did the cost in lives, quadrupling from 51 aviation deaths in 1939 to 199 in 1941. A great majority of the fatal accidents were attributable to pilot error in the training command—and the statistics would get much worse in the years to come.

After completing the primary stage in January 1940, Eaton and Con-way traveled south to Texas. Their next phase was basic flight training at

Randolph Field, on the northeast perimeter of San Antonio. It was all army now—no more civilian instructors—with a curriculum that was naturally more comprehensive. Cadets marched and learned close-order drill in addition to their classroom studies in aerial navigation, meteorology, and Morse code. In the air they learned to master a more complicated trainer, with emphasis on precise, smooth flying.

Eaton and Conway passed the basic course without delay and proceeded to the advanced syllabus at fabled Kelly Field, on the opposite side of San Antonio. But here their paths diverged. Conway was selected for instruction in single-engine aircraft, the course for pursuit pilots, whereas Eaton entered advanced multi-engine training. For the final twelve-week stage, he flew a series of modern twin-engine monoplanes with features such as retractable landing gear, variable-pitch propellers, and complex electrical and hydraulic systems. By the end of the syllabus he had accumulated more than 215 flying hours, most of them solo.

With a respectable overall grade of "Very Satisfactory," Eaton graduated from pilot training with Class 40-C on June 21, 1940. Despite the ninety-degree heat on the parade ground that summer day, he stood tall in his new Class A uniform. At five feet, eight inches tall he was perfectly average for his generation, but the shiny gold lieutenant's bars and the pair of wings pinned on his uniform made him looked larger than life. In the span of nine months, the army had turned a struggling college student into a confident, professional pilot.

Dan Conway also graduated that day. As a testament to his skill, he was "plowed back" for a year of instructor duty at Randolph Field and later moved to a new training center at Curtis Field outside Brady, Texas. Although he could expect to receive a choice assignment at the end of the obligation, a year of teaching cadets at a tiny airfield in rural Texas would seem like purgatory.

Eaton, by comparison, was all smiles. He had received orders to the 7th Bombardment Group (Heavy), based at Hamilton Field near San Francisco. In addition to living in sunny California, he would get paid to fly the nation's frontline bombers, including the fabulous new B-17. Never mind that most of the country was still crawling out of the Great Depression. Never mind that a war raged in Europe. For a freshly winged pilot, this was a dream come true.

As THE UNITED States drew closer to involvement in the escalating war, the massive military expansion that began in 1939 was constantly revised upward. Speaking again before Congress in May 1940, President Roosevelt stated, "I should like to see this nation geared up to the ability to turn out at least fifty thousand airplanes a year."[4] And again, Congress increased the military budget. Based on the unprecedented executive backing, the Air Corps planned to expand to fifty-four combat groups. The bombardment units alone would need 12,000 pilots, 2,500 bombardiers, and more than a thousand new navigators, but after more than a decade of fiscal restraint, the Air Corps was ill-equipped to handle such an ambitious expansion.[5] Virtually everything required to meet the enormous new goals was lacking, from airplanes to personnel to facilities. Although the training pipeline was beginning to produce a flood of qualified pilots and crewmen, the aircraft factories and associated industries would take years to reach their full manufacturing potential.

Not surprisingly, the rapid expansion led to unexpected changes. One that impacted Lieutenant Eaton was the relocation of the 7th Bombardment Group. Hamilton Field was a jewel of an airbase, with handsome buildings reflecting California's popular mission-style architecture and big white hangars covered with gracefully arched checkerboard roofs, but the airfield also had a flaw. Its runways and taxiways, constructed prior to the introduction of the B-17, were not sturdy enough to withstand the daily stresses exerted by squadrons of heavy bombers. In late August 1940, only a month after Eaton reported for duty, the War Department decided to move the group to Salt Lake City, Utah, opening up Hamilton for the arrival of two pursuit groups.

Although he spent only a brief time in California, Eaton began his bomber career in tall cotton. With a second lieutenant's monthly income of $250 per month (including flight pay), he earned an annual salary of $3,000, equivalent today to more than $51,000.* And because he shared a rented room with a classmate from flight school, his expenses were minimal. Flush with cash, he followed the example of many newly winged pilots and purchased a car. Not just any car, but a 1940 Buick Roadmaster with two-tone paint, whitewall tires, and a powerful eight-cylinder engine. The big sedan was ideal for hauling his substantial collection of household goods—snow skis, golf clubs, rugs, lamps, books, and a closet full of uniforms and civilian clothing—the six hundred miles to Fort Douglas on the outskirts of Salt Lake City. There, assigned to the 22nd Bombardment Squadron, he began the long process of learning to fly the most glamorous bomber in the world.

WHEN THE 7TH Group moved to Salt Lake City in the late summer of 1940, there was no lack of energy or enthusiasm among the local populace. The arrival of twenty-one gleaming aluminum B-17s and B-18s was a huge event, drawing an estimated crowd of 20,000 to the municipal airport. Unfortunately there were no military facilities adjacent to the field, so group personnel were housed at Fort Douglas. Originally built during the Civil War and vacated recently by an infantry regiment, it was located inconveniently on the other side of the city. Furthermore, the fort was too small to accommodate the entire group, which grew by the day with the arrival of newly trained aircrews, maintenance personnel, and staff. As part of the overall shuffling of air groups, the 88th Reconnaissance Squadron moved to Salt Lake City from its former base in Tucson, placing additional strain on housing. Junior enlisted men bedded down in a hastily built encampment of tents, and with the onset of cold weather—winter came early at that elevation—daily life became miserable. Before long, the half-frozen troops began calling their camp "Valley Forge."[6]

Had the group been saddled with an unpopular commanding officer, morale might have plummeted, but the 7th was fortunate to have Lieutenant Colonel Ralph Royce in charge. A graduate of West Point, the fifty-year-old Michigan native had been a pilot in the army since 1915. His career was filled with adventure, from his participation in General John "Black Jack"

---

* 2017 dollars based on the historic standard of living index.

Pershing's expedition to hunt down Pancho Villa in Mexico to his leadership of the 1st Aero Squadron (and later the 1st Observation Group) in France during the Great War, where he earned the Croix de Guerre. After the war he had remained as active as the peacetime budget would allow. In 1930, having risen to the rank of major, he led an expedition to test winter flight conditions in open-cockpit pursuit planes and won the Mackay Trophy. Four years later, as the operations officer of a long-distance expedition led by Hap Arnold (then a lieutenant colonel), Royce piloted one of ten bombers in a mass flight from Washington, DC, to Fairbanks, Alaska, and back.* More recently, he had served for two years as the air officer of the Philippine Department prior to assuming command of the 7th Group in 1939. His familiarity with the overseas territory would later become important.

FOR THE MEN of the 7th Group, everyday life in Salt Lake City bore little resemblance to the country-club atmosphere that had existed before the expansion. But it was still an exciting time for eager young pilots and crewmen on their first operational duty. As one of many new arrivals in the 22nd Squadron, Fred Eaton's primary duty was to study and fly. The squadron operated B-18s as well as B-17s, each requiring a lengthy qualification process. Trainees started over again on the bottom rung, attending weeks of classroom lectures on the complicated systems and equipment used in operational bombers, followed by orientation flights, followed by hour after hour in the air to accumulate time in the copilot's seat. Not only did trainees have to master the airplanes' systems, they had to be certified as aerial navigators (including proficiency at celestial navigation) *and* log a minimum of five hundred hours in the copilot's seat before qualifying as a 1st Pilot. It typically took up to two years to obtain the rating.

Eaton chipped away at the requirements, qualifying as a celestial navigator in late May 1941, ten months after joining the squadron. By that time

---

* Suspended for several years during World War II, the Mackay Trophy has been awarded since 1912 for the most meritorious flight of the year conducted by an individual or unit in the U.S. Air Force (or its predecessors). Hap Arnold was the first recipient in 1912 and won it again in 1934.

the group had acquired about twenty B-17s, which were divided among the four squadrons, resulting in plenty of competition for flight time. Counting only the second lieutenants, there were thirty-eight individuals ahead of Eaton in the pecking order established by date of rank. Some had been winged a class or two ahead of him, others had achieved a higher class standing upon graduation, and all were trying to work their way through the qualification process as quickly as possible. Nobody could predict, in those early stages, who would excel or who would struggle during the transition from comparatively simple training aircraft to operational bombers.

One of the pilots ahead of Eaton was an anomaly among the junior lieutenants. Born in 1907, Frank P. Bostrom had earned his army wings in 1930, a year after graduating from the University of Maine with a degree in mechanical engineering. Trained as a pursuit pilot, he had spent a decade serving intermittent periods of active duty interspersed with longer holds on inactive reserve, and he wanted something permanent. A superb pilot, he was willing to fly bombers—even if he had to start all over at the bottom— in exchange for a regular commission. Now, a second lieutenant at the age of 33, he was older than most of the captains and even a few of the majors in the group.

Another noteworthy pilot, a few years older than Bostrom and recently promoted to captain, had an equally interesting backstory. Thirty-six-year-old William Lewis Jr., a pursuit pilot during the early 1930s, was no stranger to Salt Lake City. Married to the daughter of a local dentist, he had been based there as an airline pilot with Western Air Express after serving his army stint. Tall and slender, he was fortunate to have survived two major aviation accidents, including a recent B-17 crash. During maneuvers on the East Coast in February 1941, a pilot in the 9th Bomb Squadron had ground-looped while taking off from Langley Field, Virginia. The heavily loaded B-17C burst into flames, but all twelve passengers and crew, including Lewis, escaped without serious injury.[7]

It was a far better outcome than Lewis's first crash. On January 12, 1937, while piloting a Boeing 247 airliner carrying ten passengers and three crew, he encountered heavy rain and fog during his descent to Burbank,

California. Trying to find his way in near-zero visibility, he suddenly spotted a craggy mountain slope mere seconds before impact. Cutting the throttles and pulling up sharply, Lewis avoided a head-on impact that would surely have killed them all. But the crash was violent nonetheless, killing one passenger instantly. The copilot and three other passengers, including famed naturalist and explorer Martin Johnson, died later of injuries. Lewis himself was badly hurt, with a compound leg fracture and severe facial injuries. A full investigation by the Bureau of Air Commerce attributed the accident to a combination of adverse weather and pilot error, but Lewis was widely praised for his actions. By pancaking into the mountainside at the last second, he had saved eight lives. Never timid in the cockpit, Lewis returned to active duty in the Air Corps ten months after the crash, joining the 7th Bomb Group at Hamilton Field. Regarded as one of the best pilots in the 22nd Squadron, if not the entire group, he always demanded the utmost of his crew.

In contrast to Lewis's serious demeanor, one of the new pilots in the 22nd Squadron was a consummate prankster. Second Lieutenant Henry M. Harlow, who had graduated from flight school in October 1940, was a renowned athlete at the University of Virginia. Known there by his middle name of Maynard, but nicknamed "The Bull" by his teammates, Harlow was a middleweight pugilist at the peak of collegiate boxing's popularity. In an era when five thousand spectators routinely packed field houses for dual meets, Harlow qualified for the biggest event of the year, the 1938 national championship tournament in Sacramento. Cheered by his Cavalier teammates, he won the junior middleweight title in one of the closest decisions of the event. In the Air Corps, his favorite prank was to sneak up behind unsuspecting squadron mates and light a match under the sole of their shoe. It was a common joke, made easier to accomplish by the fact that the squadron lounges were already hazy with cigarette smoke. A master at getting a victim to leap up from his chair with a yell, Harlow acquired the new nickname of "Hotfoot" from his squadron mates.

Surrounded by such personalities, Fred Eaton not only enjoyed his assignment to the 22nd Squadron, he thrived. Between the proficiency flights, bombing practices, and navigation exercises, no two days were ever the same. Eaton and his fellow fliers developed a confident swagger, wearing their leather jackets with pride. They took the stays out of their service caps, a taboo alteration in the other branches of the army, but the aviators were permitted because they wore the caps in flight: the stiffeners prevented their headphones from fitting properly. In truth the aviators loved the casual look. Their "crush caps" and leather jackets were what set them apart from the rest.

The trainees played as hard as they worked. Weekends were for outdoor recreation, for hunting and fishing excursions in the spectacular Wasatch Mountains or a visit to Lagoon Amusement Park a few miles north of Salt Lake City, for dinner parties and rum-and-Cokes at the officers club, and for jitterbugging at clubs like the Coconut Grove—one of the largest dance halls in America—to the sassy big bands of Jimmy Dorsey, Artie Shaw, Harry James, and Glenn Miller. Many of the enlisted men played just as hard (if not harder) in the NCO clubs and the dozens of drinking establishments in the city, but the off-duty hours weren't exclusively for boozing and frivolity. The patriotic townsfolk frequently invited men of all ranks and rates to visit for a few hours and enjoy a homecooked meal. Compared with the frustrations of the previous decade, the summer of 1941 was a carefree time.

In late July, Fred Eaton took a weekend off to fly down to Texas for the wedding of his friend Dan Conway. He then got right back to the business of qualifying as a 1st Pilot, flying as often as he could, but opportunities began to diminish that summer as the 7th Group turned its B-18s and older B-17s over to other units.

Elsewhere, major changes that would eventually impact the 7th Group were already under way. One was the consolidation of the Air Corps and General Headquarters Air Force, which for the past six years had been separate entities in the War Department, into a single command that would eventually achieve autonomy and equality with the ground forces. Officially activated on June 20, 1941, the United States Army Air Forces (US-AAF) placed all of the aviation elements under the command of General Arnold. But the changes took months to trickle down through the chain of command to the squadron level, and many fliers still called their branch of service the Air Corps well into 1942.

Halfway around the world, meanwhile, the Japanese had established control over the southern half of French Indochina in late July 1941, completing the occupation they had begun the previous year. President Roosevelt's cabinet responded by halting the export of oil to Japan, adding to earlier embargoes on fuel, scrap iron, and steel. Though not immediately crippling, the sanctions threatened Japan's planned military and industrial expansions, central to their intention of creating a "co-prosperity sphere," a euphemism for the domination of Asia. This, in turn, led to an accelerating collapse in diplomatic relations between Tokyo and Washington.

Realizing that America's interests in the Philippines were at risk, President Roosevelt and the service chiefs formulated plans to bolster military strength overseas. Douglas MacArthur was recalled to active duty and placed in charge of a new command, the U.S. Army Forces in the Far East (USAFFE), headquartered in Manila. American ground units were increased by approximately half, with even bigger reinforcements proposed for the aerial component, the Far East Air Force. General Arnold, planning to deploy four heavy bombardment groups (a total of 272 bombers) and two pursuit groups (130 fighters) to the Philippines by February 1942, was counting on the fulfillment of contracts with Boeing for the production of 512 new B-17Es. However, due to delays caused by shortages in aircraft-grade aluminum and other materials, the first E models would not be available until late September 1941.[8]

In the meantime, Fred Eaton enjoyed himself tremendously. Over the Labor Day weekend he flew a long cross-country training flight to Boston, where a favorite aunt and uncle lived, and his parents came up from New York to proudly inspect the parked B-17. Writing to his family a few weeks later, Eaton was pleased to report, "We have been speeding up and getting a lot more flying in since I got back. The old Army efficiency has really been clicking."[9]

But in the coming weeks, Eaton and his squadron mates would be shockingly reminded that the rapid expansion of the AAF—the very thing that had enabled them to join such a dynamic and adventurous fraternity—incurred the possibility of a heavy debt. The army's accident rate soared that year, with mishaps affecting almost every unit. And for Eaton, it was personal. On September 17 he flew back East again, this time to attend a funeral. Two days earlier, his close friend and recently married classmate Dan Conway had been killed when his two-seat trainer, piloted by a student during instrument flight training, crashed near Curtis Field. Then, less than a month after Conway's funeral, Eaton lost another friend and Kelly Field classmate, killed when an overloaded B-17C from the 19th Bomb Group crashed while taking off from Duncan Field near San Antonio. Statistically, Eaton's friends were but two drops in a bucket that was growing deeper by the day. Army aviation was marred by 233 fatal flying accidents during 1941, resulting in 417 deaths and another eighty-six personnel injured.[10]

Although subdued by the loss of his friends, Eaton did not let the accidents affect his determination. Surging ahead, he completed his qualifications on November 1 and was promoted to first lieutenant. His first flight in the pilot's seat, conducted in a new B-17E, made for "a mighty big day."[11] The aircraft was brand-new, one of the first E models to arrive at Fort Douglas, providing a clear measure of the army's trust in Eaton's qualifications. Not just any twenty-four-year-old was handed the keys to a spanking new bomber that cost American taxpayers more than a quarter of a million dollars.[12]

EATON HAD MORE big news for his family, but he was certain they would be worried about it. A few days before he qualified as a 1st Pilot, the group received orders to prepare for overseas duty of up to two years' duration in the Philippines, code-named PLUM. The rapidly deteriorating situation with Japan had convinced General Arnold that he could not afford to wait for Boeing and Consolidated (which built the army's new B-24 Liberator) to complete the hundreds of heavy bombers earmarked for the Far East. Instead he scraped together several existing squadrons, few of which were fully operational, and sent them piecemeal across the Pacific as soon as they were deemed ready. The 19th Bombardment Group (Heavy), based in Albuquerque, had been ordered to PLUM two months earlier, but its squadrons were still not trained. Therefore the 14th Squadron, based in Hawaii, became the first outfit to island-hop across the ocean to Clark Field on Luzon, making the trip in mid-September with nine B-17Ds. A month later, two squadrons of the 19th Group were released for overseas deployment and commenced a similar island-hopping journey across the Pacific. They arrived safely in early November, adding another twenty-six B-17Cs and Ds for the defense of the Philippines. Then came the announcement that the 7th Bomb Group would be next, but instead of deploying with obsolescent B-17Cs and Ds, the individual squadrons scrambled to obtain a full complement of new Es.[13]

The bombardment community was also badly in need of navigators. The shortage was so acute, in fact, that some pilots served as stand-ins after qualifying as celestial navigators. This included Second Lieutenant George B. Munroe, a twenty-three-year-old Missourian assigned to Eaton's crew. Tall and thin, with distinctly arched eyebrows, he was a rated pilot and undoubtedly felt slighted by the temporary assignment. There was no getting around the fact that pilots and copilots, in that order, were at the top of the heap. Navigators were less respected because of the general assumption that they had either washed out of flight school or did not meet the rigid requirements for eyesight. To his credit, Munroe stoically accepted the assignment and performed professionally while awaiting his opportunity to resume his 1st Pilot qualifications.

Throughout the rest of November, the 7th Bomb Group prepared for its overseas deployment. The ground echelon—almost 1,100 officers and men from the maintenance and staff departments of each squadron, plus the headquarters staff—packed their tools, spare parts, office equipment, files, and all the other operational necessities into crates marked "PLUM." Personal belongings were likewise packed in a veritable mountain of footlockers and B4 bags, all of which were trucked to the Salt Lake City railroad terminal. The ground echelon departed on November 13 for a two-day train ride to San Francisco, then sailed for the Philippines on November 21 aboard the USS *Republic*. An aged passenger liner (formerly named the *President Grant*) converted to a transport, she had already spent almost forty years on the high seas.

The flight crews, whose date of departure was uncertain, shipped personal belongings such as radios, books, golf clubs, and other bulky items to the Philippines with the ground echelon. Fred Eaton sold his fancy Buick, and notified his parents to be on the lookout for eighty-six pounds of household goods that he sent back to Scarsdale by train. But his mind was not on possessions. In a letter to his parents on November 14, he proudly mentioned that he would fly his own B-17 overseas. "There are still eight of my class here who have not been checked off as 1st Pilots," he wrote. "Therefore, I feel quite flattered and elated to have a ship and crew of my own with no older pilot going along."[14]

But no one in the 7th Group was feeling elated a few days later, when yet another accident marred preparations for overseas duty. Major Robert E. L. Pirtle, the commanding officer of the 88th Reconnaissance Squadron, decided to bring his wife and three daughters out to Salt Lake City before he deployed. He drove them part of the way from their home in Kansas but apparently fell behind schedule, and therefore arranged for one of the squadron's B-18s to pick him up in Denver on the evening of November 16. During the flight back to Salt Lake City, the twin-engine plane encountered a violent storm and severe icing near Park City, Utah. Shortly after midnight, with control of the aircraft all but lost, Pirtle gave the order to bail out. One crewmember never jumped, while Pirtle and five others took to their parachutes. But in a freakish twist of fate, the pilotless bomber circled around and struck Pirtle's parachute. Torn by a radio antenna, the canopy collapsed, sending the major to his death. Moments later the B-18 smashed into Iron Mountain, instantly killing the crewman who had remained aboard. The other jumpers landed among the rugged slopes with comparatively minor injuries.[15]

With the squadron about to deploy, there was barely time to mourn the loss of two experienced aviators. A new commanding officer, Captain Richard H. "Dick" Carmichael, transferred from the 9th Bomb Squadron to take over the 88th. Oddly, it was the second time in only four months that he had assumed command of a squadron due to a storm-related fatality. On July 23, while serving as the executive officer of the 9th Squadron, he had gone fishing on Yellowstone Lake with the commanding officer, Major Julius T. Flock. Caught in a severe thunderstorm that capsized their boat, the two men were immersed in the bitterly cold lake for hours. Flock was overcome by hypothermia and drowned, but Carmichael, a twenty-eight-year-old Texan and West Point graduate, survived six hours in the frigid water before his eventual rescue.* His feat defied all odds, but Carmichael was charmed that way. One day in 1938, while flying a Boeing P-26 Peashooter with the 6th Pursuit Squadron in Hawaii, he started to pull out of a practice dive-bombing run only to find that his control stick was hopelessly jammed. He bailed out at extremely low altitude—one observer estimated that his parachute opened at two hundred feet—and struck the ground with enough force to break his left knee. After months of excruciating rehab in California, he could flex the knee enough pass a flight physical for bomber duty and was subsequently assigned to the 7th Group.[16]

Throughout the remainder of November, pilots were periodically detailed to pick up new B-17Es in Seattle. The bombers, coming off the Boeing assembly line at a rapidly increasing pace, were parked in neat rows outside the gargantuan factory. To prepare them for acceptance, Boeing personnel had already run the engines for the recommended break-in period, a methodical process known as "slow-timing," prior to completing satisfactory test flights.

Fred Eaton got his opportunity to pick up a brand-new bomber on November 29. One of six B-17s accepted that day by the 7th Group, the aircraft was painted matte olive green with a light gray belly and lower wing surfaces, looking every inch the strategic bomber it was designed to be. But the new plane was not yet ready for combat. With the exception of the dorsal and belly turrets, installed as subassemblies with their guns already in

---

* According to the National Park Service, Yellowstone Lake usually thaws in late May or early June but the water remains very cold throughout the summer with an average temperature of 41°F. Swimming is discouraged, as survival time is "estimated to be only 20 to 30 minutes in water at this temperature."

place, the aircraft had no armament. After the AAF took delivery, the B-17s were eventually ferried to a depot in Sacramento, where additional defensive armament and other military-grade equipment was installed. Finally, after compasses and flight instruments were adjusted, the new bombers underwent shakedown flights.

Although he was heartsick that he would not be home for Christmas for the first time in his life, Eaton enthusiastically told his family about his new B-17. "I just got back here yesterday from Seattle," he wrote to his aunt and uncle on December 2. "I flew a new ship down from the factory. They are putting out a beautiful ship nowadays. I do wish I could take you both for a ride in mine."[17] (Eaton's use of "ship" to describe an airplane was almost ubiquitous in that era, both conversationally and in writing. It stemmed from the earliest days of aviation, when the first powered airplanes as well as lighter-than-air dirigibles shared nautical terminology. Their structural components included spars and keels, and they were steered with rudders. The huge rigid airships operated by the U.S. Navy were even considered ships of the fleet, the USS *Akron*, USS *Macon*, and USS *Shenandoah* among them.)

Eaton telephoned his parents that same evening to share his excitement in person. The topic of a possible war with Japan evidently came up, compelling him to write a follow-up letter to his mother the next day. "I know it looks as if we might get into a shooting war with Japan, but don't worry one second about your son Fred," he assured her. "My B-17E can get out of reach of any Japanese planes. Also, I don't think anything more will come of this situation than a big bluff."[18]

But as events would soon demonstrate, young Eaton was wrong on both counts.

FOUR

HAP'S FAREWELL

The delight of seeing the world from the air never got old. On the afternoon of December 6, 1941, as his twin-engine transport descended over San Francisco Bay, Major General Hap Arnold was treated to an expansive view of the California coast. The cities and farmlands of the Central Valley spread before him, framed by the deep blue of the Pacific, the craggy brown mountains, and a cloudless sky. It was a privilege Arnold had enjoyed many times before, but on this particular Saturday the fifty-five-year-old chief of the U.S. Army Air Forces was not on a sightseeing excursion. Urgent business awaited at Hamilton Field, a few miles north of the Golden Gate Bridge.

Responsible for AAF organizations scattered all over the United States and several territories overseas, Arnold was accustomed to long flights and even longer workdays. During the past two years, as the nation girded for war, he had almost single-handedly pulled the air forces out of the doldrums. Moving adroitly between the War Department, the industrial sector, and miserly politicians, he campaigned tirelessly to obtain funding for more airplanes, more men, better facilities, better pay, better training, and whatever else was necessary to build a world-class air force. He visited factories to urge more production, met with engineers to encourage the design of bigger, faster airplanes, and inspected the units under his command to gauge their readiness and professionalism. Arnold particularly enjoyed chatting with his young pilots and crewmen; they, in turn, almost universally adored him.

Quick with a laugh, his congenial personality was accentuated by the crow's feet etched in his face from years of flying in open-cockpit planes.

Already legendary as an aviation pioneer—he learned to fly in 1911 at the school operated by Orville and Wilbur Wright—Arnold had direct connections to virtually every aspect of aviation's progress over the past thirty years. Some of the credit for his professional success could be attributed to luck, for he had managed to survive the crash-filled days when pilots flew frail, kite-like airplanes made of wood and linen, "quaint flying front porches" as one reporter called them.[1] So many of Arnold's friends and acquaintances were killed in crashes over the years that at one point, after surviving a couple of serious mishaps himself, he stopped flying altogether. But Hap (short for "Happy") eventually got back in the cockpit. Rising steadily through the ranks, he established a reputation as an intuitive leader with a knack for solving complicated problems. He pinned on his first star as a brigadier general in 1935 and was named assistant chief of the Air Corps that December. Less than three years later his boss, Major General Oscar Westover, was killed while piloting an advanced, single-engine attack aircraft, whereupon Arnold became the new chief of the Air Corps. He added a second star, commensurate with his advancement, though it was not the way he wanted to reach the pinnacle of his chosen profession.

Because of Westover's fatal crash and his own advancing years, Arnold was no longer authorized to fly solo on official business. His aide, Major Eugene I. Beebe, doubled as the pilot of the chief's C-41 transport, a brightly polished, specially configured version of the famed Douglas DC-3 airliner. Fiercely loyal, Beebe was accustomed to the general's demanding schedule. "His idea of a good time," he would later say, "was to work all day, then . . . fly all night to Los Angeles, arrive in the morning, visit about five aircraft plants, then go to someone's house for dinner that night."[2]

Arnold's current trip was a perfect example. Departing from Washington, DC, on the morning of December 4, he spent two days in Knoxville, Tennessee, while inspecting the world's largest sheet aluminum plant ("I want to find out what makes Alcoa tick," he told reporters).[3] On the sixth, he and Beebe continued to California, where Arnold intended to address the squadrons preparing to deploy to the Far East. He had initially hoped to send sixty-five new B-17s and thirty LB-30s (the export version of the Consolidated B-24 Liberator) to the Philippines by February 1942, but unforeseen delays had slowed the process to a crawl. Disappointed that fewer than half of the B-17s and none of the LB-30s had been delivered thus far, Arnold was beginning to lose patience and decided to investigate the situation personally.

Two squadrons were scheduled to depart for the Philippines that very night. Arnold wanted to determine their readiness, especially since both had recently suffered fatal accidents. Two pilots in the 38th Reconnaissance Squadron had been killed in the B-17 crash near San Antonio in October, and the following month the 88th Reconnaissance Squadron lost its commanding officer in the storm-related B-18 crash near Park City. Were the squadrons ready for their strenuous deployment, not to mention the likelihood of combat in the coming weeks?

Arnold's initial impression left him wondering. Before addressing the squadrons, he phoned General George C. Marshall, the U.S. Army chief-of-staff, and expressed his concern that the bomber crews were too cavalier. "These damn fellows don't realize how serious this thing is," he said.

"Well," replied Marshall, "you are there, and they are your people. You start them out."[4]

It was superfluous advice for Arnold. Never one to command from behind a desk, he had crossed the continent to send the crews off with a personal farewell. If a visit and a few words of encouragement from the top man in the Army Air Forces didn't get their attention, nothing would.

HAMILTON FIELD WAS a scene of frantic activity. Except for the inspiring lineup of B-17s sitting on the flight line, everyone and everything seemed to be in motion. Fuel trucks trundled from plane to plane; tractor tugs shuttled spare parts and baggage from the big white hangars; flight crews scurried with eleventh-hour urgency to check equipment, top off gas tanks, and make final engine adjustments before the 2,400-mile overwater flight to Hawaii.

The men of the 88th Squadron were already exhausted. Days earlier, having picked up eight new B-17Es from Boeing, they were on a long shake-down trip to Tucson when Dick Carmichael received an urgent message: the jump-off for the Philippines had been moved up. He was to fly his planes immediately to the air depot in Sacramento for final equipment installation, then bring the squadron straight to Hamilton Field. There was no time to return to Salt Lake City, no time for crewmembers to say goodbye to their families or sweethearts.

At the air depot, described as "poorly organized, with more red tape than any place in the Air Corps," the crews were frustrated by the sluggish peacetime work ethic.[5] And they chafed because the forecast called for a few nights of clear weather with favorable tailwinds, but by December 5 most of the B-17s were still being fitted out at Sacramento. "Crews tell tales of waiting, waiting," wrote the squadron adjutant, Second Lieutenant Walter H. Johnson. "Property had to be checked time and again. A plane [wasn't] released for over two days simply because nobody would ok its release. Nobody was sure who it should be released to."[6]

Due to the depot's molasses-in-winter pace, there would not be enough time to install the machine guns in the new E models. Instead, slathered in Cosmoline gel, the guns were stowed in crates for the first leg of the journey. All of Carmichael's bombers were eventually released—one wild rumor had it that President Roosevelt himself had intervened—the last one arriving at Hamilton on the afternoon of the sixth, mere hours before departure.

The floor of the hangar assigned to the 88th Squadron was a madhouse. "Personal equipment, B4 bags, and flying jackets were all mixed up with bomb racks and bomb bay tanks," recalled Carmichael. "It was a hell of a mess."[7] While crewmembers sorted through the gear and stowed it aboard the airplanes, Carmichael conferred with his counterpart in the 38th Squadron, Major Landon. A fellow West Pointer, class of 1928, Landon had commanded the 38th for the past two years. The last squadron of the 19th Group ordered to PLUM, the 38th currently had eight B-17s, though at least half were older C models.

Throughout the afternoon, navigators from both squadrons nervously attended to their preflight planning. Most were still aviation cadets, having recently completed the intense course at Coral Gables, shortened by several weeks due to the shortage in qualified personnel. With a bare minimum of long-distance experience, they now faced the most challenging leg of the deployment: crossing 2,400 miles of water to reach a small, isolated chain of islands. In the days before global positioning systems, aerial navigation was part science, part instinct. A navigator's tools included radio direction-finding equipment, an octant for celestial navigation, a circular slide rule, almanacs, and a bookbag full of aerial charts. But there were numerous factors that could cause such flights to go terribly wrong. A change in wind speed or direction, equipment failure, distractions, mathematical errors, or simple ineptitude could cause a navigator to become hopelessly lost. During an ocean crossing, position estimates could not be confirmed until the crew spotted a landmark or locked onto a radio beacon. Thus, accuracy in plotting was paramount. Well aware that the lives of the entire crew were in their hands, the navigators worked and reworked their calculations and worried about passing their first real-world test.

That evening, in one of the big checkerboard hangars, the crews gathered for a briefing by Brigadier General Jacob E. "Jake" Fickel, commander of the Fourth Air Force in California. A genuine old-timer, legendary in army aviation as the first American to conduct aerial gunnery tests, Fickel discussed the basic profile of the deployment. Destination: Luzon, with refueling stops at Hawaii, Midway, Wake Island, Port Moresby, and Darwin. The 10,000-mile route, pioneered only three months earlier, had been successfully completed by the first thirty-five B-17s that attempted the trip, but as Fickel pointed out, those were C and D models, thousands of pounds lighter than the new B-17Es. Furthermore, because the fuel consumption of the new model had not been thoroughly calculated, the aircraft would make the flight to Hawaii without ammunition for the guns, thereby saving hundreds of pounds of dead weight.

Listening to Fickel's briefing, one navigator grew more uncertain by the minute. Second Lieutenant Charles E. Bergdoll, who had just recovered from injuries sustained in the B-17 crash near San Antonio, already harbored doubts about his first overwater flight. "Then to top it off," he recalled, "we were told that even if we performed a perfect job of navigation, we might end up in the ocean because of the questionable range of the plane."[8]

At the conclusion of his speech, Fickel told the crews to be prepared to do whatever was required of them. "By the way," he added, "I have a surprise for you. It just happens that General Arnold is here and he would like to say a few words to you."[9]

The paternal-looking chief of the AAF decided to be blunt. "War is imminent," Arnold told the assembled men. "You may run into a war during your flight."[10] He followed with a speech similar to Fickel's, then asked if there were any questions. Major Landon piped up, asking why the planes would not be fully armed right from the start. The absence of working guns evidently caught Arnold by surprise, for he had no ready answer except to reiterate Fickel's explanation about minimizing the weight of the B-17Es. Landon therefore announced that he was going to lay over in Hawaii until the guns were mounted. Arnold bristled at this, but rather than voicing approval or disapproval, he simply told Landon to get his bombers to the Philippines as soon as possible.[11]

Before dismissing the crews, Fickel offered some prophetic parting words. "Good luck, and good shooting," he said. "It looks as if you might get to do some of that."[12]

SHORTLY AFTER THEIR royal sendoff, sixteen crews began final preflight checks and boarded their heavily loaded B-17s. Pilots flipped master battery switches to ON, providing internal power for the aircraft, then began the standardized checklist procedures, their flashlights filtered to preserve night vision. Outside, crew chiefs and their assistants followed the routine for cold engine starts, pulling the propellers by hand through three revolutions to drain excess oil from the bottom cylinders. In each cockpit, pilots and copilots verbally read through each item in the detailed, challenge-and-response checklists, setting engine controls and switches before attempting to start the number one engine, outboard on the left wing. Presently the whine of inertia starters could be heard, followed by staccato barks as fat radial engines coughed to life, belched smoke, then settled down to a steady rumble.

By the time all sixteen bombers were involved, the combined roar of more than sixty 1,200-horsepower radials produced a racket that could be heard for miles.

Despite all the careful preparations, two B-17s from the 38th Squadron and one from the 88th encountered mechanical trouble that prevented their departure. There they sat, crews cursing their bad engines or faulty generators, watching in frustration as the remaining thirteen bombers began to taxi toward the departure end of the runway. The first to go was Major Landon. At 9:00 P.M. he pulled onto the runway, revved up his engines for final checks, and released the brakes. Roaring at full power, the B-17E slowly gathered speed. Eventually the tail came up, but instead of lifting gracefully into the night sky, the bomber seemed glued to the runway. Landon's takeoff, his first in a new E model, almost ended in disaster. Accustomed to the B-17Cs he'd been flying, he had set the elevator trim based on their characteristics. "It looked like we were not going to get off," he later recalled. "Well, my copilot was George Newton, who was smarter than I was about that airplane. I was just sweating trying to get that nose up in the air. George reached down and moved the [trim wheel], and immediately we jumped off. He saved our necks right there."[13]

Lieutenant Karl Barthelmess followed in another new E model, after which four B-17Cs thundered aloft at ten-minute intervals. Next in line, beginning at 10:10 P.M., Dick Carmichael led the seven remaining bombers of the 88th Squadron into the air at evenly spaced intervals. Climbing over San Francisco Bay, the bombers turned westward toward the Golden Gate Bridge, their red, white, and green position lights gradually receding in the darkness.

Hap Arnold and Jake Fickel watched them go. Just as surely as they would soon knock back a few drinks and reminisce about the bygone days when they squinted in the sunlight in their open-cockpit biplanes, silk scarves trailing in the slipstream, the two aging generals felt tremendous pride in the happy-go-lucky youngsters flying those fabulous new B-17s across the ocean. Both men knew their protégés faced the very real possibility of a war. They just didn't realize how soon it would come.

FIVE

SURFBOARDS AND SUBMARINES

Over the span of an hour and a half, thirteen heavily loaded B-17s took off from Hamilton Field on the night of Saturday, December 6, to begin their deployment to the Philippines. Gaining altitude slowly, they passed abeam San Francisco, described by one crewman as "a fairyland of lights," then turned southwesterly toward the black abyss of the Pacific Ocean.[1] At approximately midnight, Lieutenant Richard F. Ezzard of the 88th Reconnaissance Squadron broke radio silence to report that he was turning back due to engine trouble. Within a few hours, the twelve remaining bombers reached the fuel-critical demarcation known as "the point of no return" and continued toward Hawaii.*

But that didn't mean they were immune to trouble. As the night wore on, newly commissioned navigator Charlie Bergdoll experienced several anxious moments in the B-17E flown by Lieutenant Barthelmess. All too aware of his limited experience, Bergdoll felt particularly isolated after Barthelmess and the copilot set the switches for the automatic flight control equipment (AFCE) and fell asleep. Shortly before dawn, with memories of the horrific crash in Texas still raw in his mind, Bergdoll was alarmed to

---

* Plotted by the navigators, this was an estimated position beyond which the aircraft would not have enough fuel to return to its departure point in the event of trouble. Several factors, including the prevailing winds, affected this arbitrary point.

discover that the B-17 was in a gradual descent, already passing through three thousand feet. Rushing to the flight deck, he tried without success to rouse Barthelmess but finally managed to waken the copilot, Lieutenant Larry J. Sheehan, who corrected the descent and guided the bomber back up to six thousand feet. After inspecting various switch settings, the flight engineer discovered that the bombardier, asleep in his seat in the nose compartment, had somehow activated the toggle switch that gave him control of the plane during bombing runs. If not for Bergdoll, the aircraft might have continued descending until it smacked into the ocean.

Rather than feeling relieved, Bergdoll realized that the changes in altitude had invalidated most of his celestial navigation calculations, giving him no confidence in the bomber's actual position. With unease turning to dread, he went back up to the flight deck and explained the situation to the pilots, who came fully awake. By this time the sun had risen, preventing Bergdoll from shooting the stars for navigation. Resorting to the inexact science of dead reckoning, he made some quick calculations and updated his estimated time of arrival at Hickam—but the ETA came and went with no land in sight. Their own concerns increasing, the pilots decided to break radio silence and call Hickam tower on the radio. Nobody answered. With the fuel gauges hovering near empty, it was time to make a tough decision: search a little longer, or prepare to ditch.

From nose to tail, word of the bomber's predicament spread rapidly. The radio operator, Staff Sergeant Nicholas H. Kahlefent, overheard Bergdoll explaining that he was essentially lost and needed help locating an island so that he could get a position fix. "We looked and looked," Kahlefent recalled, "but all we could see was water, clouds, and more water."[2] At approximately 7:15 that morning, the flight engineer entered the radio compartment and asked Kahlefent if he or the assistant radio operator knew how to swim. "Hell, no," answered Kahlefent. The engineer told him they might have to learn soon if they didn't spot land, as the plane had only an hour's worth of fuel remaining. Several minutes later Kahlefent spotted an island (which turned out to be Oahu) and reported it to Bergdoll. "He breathed a sigh of relief," Kahlefent wrote, "and said he knew where we were."[3]

The pilots immediately turned south and reduced speed, trying to conserve as much fuel as possible. Moments later, the entire crew was distracted by the sight of numerous aircraft. Bergdoll later related the details.

> Shortly after altering course . . . we were suddenly overtaken by a group of twelve to fifteen light [colored] planes marked with large red circles. They flew above, under, and abreast of us, and our first thought was that this was a group of planes sent out from Hickam to escort us to the field. All of us heaved a sigh of relief, removed our life jackets which we had donned when it looked like we would end up in the ocean, and began waving greetings to our escort.
>
> Someone remarked about the peculiar markings on the planes, but it was decided that they were having maneuvers in Hawaii similar to those which had been held in the States, thus accounting for the strange insignias.[4]

The B-17, far off course to the north, had crossed paths with the first wave of Japanese carrier planes en route to Oahu. For a few moments the opposing fliers scrutinized each other. The notion that the light gray planes might be hostile never occurred to the American crewmen, nor did any of them recognize the distinctive features of the Aichi D3A dive bombers, such as non-retractable landing gear and streamlined wheel pants. Instead, the Americans waved naively at the Japanese.

Staff Sergeant Lee R. Embree, an aerial photographer, grabbed his personal Graflex camera, aimed it from the waist gunner's window on the left side of the bomber, and took the first American aerial photograph of the Pacific war. His fancy "Speed Graphic" captured two Japanese dive bombers as they cruised above the B-17, their fixed landing gear clearly visible. Moments later, more enemy planes overtook the Flying Fortress. "They passed us so close on the left I could see the pilots' faces," Embree recalled decades later. "They were grinning from ear to ear."[5]

Although the dive bombers were armed with machine guns, the disciplined Japanese kept their hands away from the triggers. Having not yet received the attack signal, they knew it was imperative to maintain the element of surprise. Undoubtedly perplexed to see the B-17 crewmen waving at them, the Japanese surged ahead, leaving the Americans mystified but none the wiser.

By the time Barthelmess entered the landing pattern for Hickam Field and overflew the ship channel, the Japanese attack on Pearl Harbor was under way. Even then, the fatigued bomber crewmen mistook the flames and explosions and bursting antiaircraft shells as part of an elaborate military exercise. Upon calling the control tower for landing instructions, Barthelmess was told to go around: another B-17 was in the pattern ahead of him. While Barthelmess made a complete orbit in the midst of the attack, Sergeant Embree snapped a few additional photographs from the side gunner's position. Asked later why he didn't take more, he explained: "I was so flabbergasted at what was happening that I momentarily forgot the camera in my hand."[6]

During his second approach, Barthelmess was again instructed to go around. The awful reality of the enemy attack had still not registered with the entire crew, although Sergeant Kahlefent heard the announcer at station KGMB in Honolulu exclaim, "This is not a mock battle, this is the real McCoy!"[7] Finally, after three aborted landing attempts, the lack of fuel forced Barthelmess to commit to his next approach, regardless of instructions from the tower.

Cool under pressure, he landed without incident. His crew, stunned by the sight of ships overturned in the harbor and wrecked planes burning on the flight line, jumped out as soon as their Fortress rolled to a stop at the eastern perimeter of the dispersal area. Joining the crews of Ted Landon, Bruce Allen, and Lieutenant Earl J. Cooper, they could see the remains of "Swede" Swenson's B-17 in flames alongside the runway. Sergeant Embree, standing near his parked bomber, took several photographs of the devastation, framing the heavy columns of black smoke that rose above Hickam and Pearl Harbor with the Fortress's wing. One of his iconic images appeared a few weeks later in *Life* magazine.

THE SIX B-17S of Dick Carmichael's 88th Reconnaissance Squadron, which had departed from California more than an hour after Major Landon took off, arrived over Oahu just as the first wave of Japanese planes wrapped up devastating strikes all over the island. "I called in and asked for landing instructions," Carmichael remembered. "The answer came back, 'Land from west to east, but use caution, the field is under attack.'"[8] During his approach, Carmichael realized that conditions at Hickam were simply too dangerous. "Things had gone to hell in a handbasket," he remarked later. So he flew north to try landing at Wheeler Field, which he knew well from his days as a pursuit pilot, but the whole hangar line was on fire. Next, turning eastward toward the Marine Corps air station at Kaneohe, he discovered that its runway was blocked by a burning aircraft. Now getting dangerously low on fuel, he doubled back around the Ko'olau Mountains to Haleiwa, the site of a small auxiliary fighter strip near the north shore of the island. Too pumped up with adrenaline to worry about the hazards of landing on a 1,200-foot runway, Carmichael swooped down and planted the big bomber as though flying a fighter. Braking hard, he stopped the B-17 just before it reached the far end of the runway, then taxied back toward a line of trees adjacent to the beach. There he found the B-17 flown by his operations officer, Lieutenant Harold N. "Newt" Chaffin, who had arrived a few minutes earlier.

For about twenty minutes it seemed that the bombers were out of danger at the remote airstrip. After unpacking a few machine guns, the crew chiefs went off to find ammunition. Carmichael and his friend Captain James W. Twaddell Jr., a West Point classmate and the squadron's weather officer, were standing near their B-17 when they suddenly spotted a Japanese fighter coming straight at them in a strafing attack. Sprinting to the beach, the two officers found an overhang in the rocks with enough space to crawl under. They took cover beneath the overhang, then nearly drowned when the surf rolled back in. "So there we were," Carmichael later recalled with a chuckle, "the brave squadron commander and the weather officer, hiding under the rocks, and all the sergeants were out trying to shoot down the enemy."[9]

In the meantime, three of Carmichael's B-17s had landed helter-skelter at Hickam Field. Fired upon by several Japanese planes and American anti-aircraft guns, Lieutenant Harry N. Brandon, a twenty-eight-year-old West Pointer from Arkansas, waved off his first approach when he saw ground crews pulling a burning bomber (undoubtedly Swenson's B-17C) off the runway. The tower then cleared him for a downwind landing, a tricky procedure that Brandon accomplished without incident. He taxied directly to a remote corner of the field, where his bomber was refueled and armed, ready for takeoff again in two hours.

Lieutenant Robert E. Thacker, a classmate of Fred Eaton's in flight school, handled his baptism of fire with cool professionalism despite minimal hours as a 1st Pilot. Rocked by antiaircraft bursts as his B-17 approached Hickam, the twenty-three-year-old Californian saw massive oil fires in the harbor and wrecked planes burning on the flight line, and considered landing elsewhere. He got no response when he first radioed the control tower but finally heard, "You're number three to land. Land [west] to east." He too made a downwind approach, coming in fast as bullets popped all around. The brakes overheated during his high-speed rollout, causing one of the tires to burst into flames, and when he reached the end of the runway Thacker had to reef the big Fortress around in a screeching ground loop to stop. The crew used a fire extinguisher to snuff the minor blaze.[10]

The third B-17 from Carmichael's squadron, flown by Dave Rawls, had a close encounter with enemy fighters over Hickam. He later provided a nothing-to-it statement:

> The air was rough, and when we realized that we were being fired upon by antiaircraft, we made a quick 180-degree turn and began to climb. We leveled off at 8,000 feet and decided to try landing at Wheeler, but found it burning as badly as Hickam. We had to find a place to land for our gas was low, and so we determined to land at Hickam. Boiling smoke from the burning *Oklahoma* furnished a screen for the let-down, but proved not to be effective, for just as we emerged from the smoke a Jap pursuit spotted us and headed for our tail. Flaps down and wheels down we knew we had

no chance of out-flying him, and so we continued to approach. We were 200 feet off the ground when he opened up. One bullet hit the No. 2 propeller and another went through the main spar of the left wing. Numerous other hits were scored but we got in. Sergeant [Robert K.] Palmer shot at the Jap with the only weapon we had available, a .45 caliber pistol.[11]

The trickiest and most innovative landing among 88th Squadron pilots was pulled off by Frank Bostrom. Flying one of the last B-17s to take off from California, he was also among the last to arrive over Oahu—and the only one who didn't land on a prepared runway. During his approach to Hickam an antiaircraft shell exploded off the right wing, and Bostrom could see the obvious mayhem on the ground below. "I grabbed my mic and asked the tower what the hell was going on," he related, "and they finally told us that we were being attacked by enemy aircraft. We were then at 700 feet and ready to sweep onto the field and land, but four or five destroyers shot at us and cut off our approach." Climbing to his left, Bostrom cut across Oahu to the northwest, hoping to return to Hickam during a lull in the fighting. A call to the control tower revealed that the airfield was still under attack, so he sought temporary shelter in a layer of broken cumulus clouds. Within a few minutes, however, his B-17 was attacked from behind by a Zero, and shortly thereafter three more enemy fighters joined in. "We were using full power and our gas was nearly exhausted," continued Bostrom, "so we broke away from the clouds and were warned by the radio operator that another Jap was on our tail."[12]

Bostrom ordered his assistant flight engineer and tail gunner, Private Herbert M. Wheatley Jr., back to the tail position to report on enemy aircraft. "A Jap started after us," Wheatley later recalled, "and I saw my first tracer shots. They looked as if they were coming right for the tail gunner's compartment; actually they hit the fuselage on either side. I grabbed the interphone, and was so scared I couldn't get a sound out. I ran all the way up forward and pointed."[13]

Flying above the coastline of Oahu, Bostrom and his crew failed to spot the auxiliary field at Haleiwa where Carmichael and Chaffin had already landed. But as the B-17 rounded the northernmost tip of the island, Bostrom spied a golf course. This was the oceanfront club at Kahuku, only a few miles from the Opana radar site, and it featured a long, relatively flat par-five fairway parallel to the shore.[14] Knowing he had only minutes to spare, Bostrom dropped down and got a quick peek at the 552-yard fairway of the seventh hole, then reversed course with a maneuver that flabbergasted his crew. "[He] did a vertical around a smokestack as if he were flying a trainer," reported Wheatley, "and made an incredible landing. We cut up the golf course, but we were okay. The owner of a sugar cane plantation and his wife came out, thinking we had been forced down. We told them there was a war on. They took us up to the house, served us big highballs. We were prepared to stay there for the duration."[15]

BOSTROM'S FEAT OF airmanship was a fitting conclusion to the arrival of the B-17s from California. Considering the scores of enemy fighters in the skies above Oahu and the heavy antiaircraft fire directed at the B-17s, it was miraculous that no Fortresses were shot down. The two that crash-landed never flew again, but the other ten had sustained only minor combat damage and were soon back in service. More important, all but one of the crewmembers wounded aboard the two shot-up Fortresses eventually recovered.

The lone exception was Dr. William Schick, the flight surgeon. Initially hit in the left leg aboard Swenson's B-17, then wounded in the face as he ran across the flight line at Hickam during a strafing attack, Schick was transported to the base hospital by ambulance. But even before the first wave of attacks subsided, the small facility was overwhelmed with wounded personnel. Stretcher cases overflowed onto the manicured lawn as trucks and vehicles of every description brought in casualties, many with grievous burns or missing limbs. The hospital's commanding officer, Captain Richard Lane, observed one individual who seemed out of place.

> He was a young medical officer who had arrived with the B-17 bombers
> from the States during the raid. When I first noticed him he was sitting on
> the stairs to the second story of the hospital. I suppose the reason that my

attention was called to him was that he was dressed in a winter uniform which we never wore in the Islands, and had the insignia of a medical officer on his lapels. He had a wound in the face and when I went to take care of him he said he was all right and pointed to the casualties on litters on the floor and said, "Take care of them." I told him I would get him on the next ambulance going to Tripler General Hospital, which I did.[16]

Schick's head wound, caused by a ricocheting bullet or a piece of pavement kicked up by the strafing attack, did not initially appear to be life-threatening. He was lucid, sitting upright, and neither he nor Dr. Lane believed his wounds required immediate treatment. But sometime during the next twenty-four hours, after being transported to the main army hospital at Fort Shafter, the newly qualified flight surgeon died. The fact that he was sitting and talking with Dr. Lane soon after the attack strongly suggests that he had sustained a traumatic brain injury, either from the ricochet or perhaps from striking his head on the pavement when he was knocked down. Brain hemorrhages were poorly understood then, and even more difficult to diagnose. Hence, the sole fatality from the B-17 flight was probably avoidable. Due to the triage conditions that existed that day, with hundreds of wounded personnel pouring into the hospitals, Schick's condition was sadly overlooked. He died not knowing that his wife was one month pregnant and thus never met his son, born the following August on what would have been his father's thirty-second birthday.

Although not directly related to the B-17 flight, two men in Carmichael's squadron had been killed during the Japanese attack—and both occurred on the ground at Hickam Field. On December 4, two days before the B-17s left California, Lieutenant Ted S. Faulkner had departed from Hamilton Field in a brand-new B-24A Liberator. Seconded to the ferry command several weeks earlier, Faulkner had qualified in the new bomber for the purpose of conducting secret photoreconnaissance missions over some of the islands that had been mandated to Japan by the League of Nations after World War I. His aircraft, one of two B-24s slated for the special duty, was undergoing weapons installation at the Hawaiian Air Depot when the attack occurred. Several members of the crew were asleep in the big new "million dollar barracks" at Hickam, but Faulkner and three others happened to be checking on their aircraft when the first bomb landed only thirty feet away. Strafing attacks later set fire to the Liberator, which burned to the ground. Faulkner's navigator and one enlisted crewman were killed—the latter in the barracks—and three crewmembers suffered serious wounds, including a junior officer whose leg was later amputated. With no airplane and half his crew dead or hospitalized, Faulkner eventually joined Carmichael's echelon as a spare pilot.

IN THE CONFUSION and disarray that reigned after the attack, practically everyone on Oahu expected the Japanese to invade. Most of the crews from the incoming B-17s spent the night near their planes, still parked along the perimeter of the field. They were joined by Carmichael and Chaffin, who put just enough gas in their bombers to fly them down from Haleiwa. Despite the crews' collective weariness from long days of preparation and the fourteen-hour flight from California, almost no one slept. The hours passed anxiously, punctuated by frequent bursts of antiaircraft fire from nervous gunners. "That night under the mosquito nets, occasionally dampened by showers, put the crews a long, long way from the mainland and their loved ones," wrote Walt Johnson, the 88th Squadron's adjutant. "A lot of itchy fingers touched the triggers of their guns . . . and made the first night of war very real."[17]

The next morning, five thousand miles to the east, President Roosevelt presented an impassioned, seven-minute speech to a joint session of Congress. Barely half an hour later, Congress voted almost unanimously—only a single representative voted against the resolution—to declare war on Japan. Twenty-three years after the conclusion of the so-called "war to end all wars," the United States was embroiled in another global conflict.

AT HICKAM FIELD that morning, the crews of the 38th and 88th squadrons moved into one of the undamaged barracks, an old wooden facility originally constructed as temporary housing. Captain Twaddell was promptly grabbed for duty with the weather detachment at Hickam, and soon thereafter the 88th Squadron combat crews were attached to the 31st Bombardment Squadron/5th Bombardment Group, which operated under the authority of the Hawaiian Air Force. Frank Bostrom and his crew spent a few days making hasty repairs to their B-17 and stripping it of all unnecessary weight; then, with a skeleton crew aboard, Bostrom successfully took off from the golf course on December 10 and hopped over to Hickam.

Due to the widespread destruction among the airfields, the ten airworthy B-17s were among the few functional defenses still available on Hawaii. Two days after the attack, a handful of crews began flying long-distance patrols out of Hickam at dawn and dusk, searching the seas surrounding the islands for signs of the enemy—and finding nothing. "The Japs," noted Walt Johnson, "had struck and gone."[18]

All across the island, the grim work of cleaning up the wreckage progressed rapidly, as did the process of reinforcement. Ferry crews arrived from California with more B-17s on December 11, by which time the 38th and 88th squadrons knew they were no longer destined for the Philippines. Clark Field had been smashed by Japanese aircraft mere hours after the attack on Pearl Harbor, and two other AAF bases on Luzon were targeted on December 10. Within a span of forty-eight hours, General Douglas MacArthur's vaunted Far East Air Force had been cut to pieces.

And so, beginning in mid-December, the Hawaii squadrons commenced a routine of daily long-range patrols that would define their operations for the next several weeks. Crews were assigned specific sectors, each covering ten degrees of the compass along radials that extended six hundred nautical miles out to sea. The daylong missions, conducted at altitudes low enough to spot a submarine periscope, resulted in nine to ten hours of sheer boredom. Rarely did the crews see anything but boundless sea and sky, and they returned to Hickam tired and hungry. Those not scheduled for a patrol mission typically stood alert duty, ready to take off and attack the enemy invasion fleet that many still believed would materialize.

Back in California, where fears of a Japanese invasion were still rampant, the 22nd Bomb Squadron had been performing similar patrol work.

Led by Major Kenneth B. Hobson, the flight crews had departed from Salt Lake City by train on December 3 and traveled to Sacramento, where they picked up eight new B-17Es and reported to Hamilton Field. They originally planned to leave for Hawaii on the night of December 7, but the shocking news of the attack on Pearl Harbor brought everything to a standstill. That afternoon, out of concern that the B-17s were vulnerable to an enemy attack along the coast, Hobson was ordered to disperse his squadron to a facility known as Muroc Dry Lake (the present site of Edwards Air Force Base) in the California desert. There, Fred Eaton dashed off a letter to his family. "We were all set to leave tonight when the news of the war came," he wrote. "As a result, I imagine we will do patrol duty out over the Pacific for a while instead of leaving immediately for PLUM."[19]

His guess was correct. For the next week and a half, the 22nd Squadron flew patrols two hundred miles out to sea along a line from Los Angeles to San Francisco, terminating the flights inland at either Muroc or Sacramento. Following up with another letter on the morning of December 10, Eaton wrote, "It is 10:30 and I have just gotten up after sleeping 18 hours straight. . . . The last few days I have worked harder than the last two years combined."

The daily patrols found no sign of the Japanese, but as Eaton noted in his next letter, the anxiety on the West Coast persisted. "It has been rumored that there is a fleet of many ships about 700 miles off the coast," he wrote on the night of December 11, "and we will go out and try to take care of them. My ship is all loaded with 600 lb. bombs and gas."[20]

There was no enemy fleet, of course, but the crews continued to fly patrols over the Pacific for several more days before Hobson received orders to take his squadron to Hawaii. After a delay due to bad weather and strong headwinds, the squadron departed from Hamilton on the night of December 17. Riding with them—he bumped Fred Eaton's assistant radio operator for a seat—was Brigadier General Clarence L. Tinker, making his way to Hickam to take command of the Hawaiian Air Force.[21] Born in the Osage Nation in 1887, renowned for a long and stellar military career, Tinker would soon be promoted to major general, becoming the first Native American to achieve that rank.*

For the first hundred miles out of California, Hobson and his pilots flew on instruments before finally breaking out into a clear, starry sky. But a few hours later one of the newly winged navigators discovered a serious discrepancy. Aviation Cadet John J. Steinbinder, raised on a farm near Oberlin, Ohio, realized that his calculations of the bomber's ground speed and fuel consumption didn't add up. After only six hundred miles, well short of the estimated point of no return, it became obvious that the bomber lacked enough fuel to reach Hawaii. The pilot, Lieutenant James R. "Dubby" DuBose Jr., promptly turned around. The cause of the fuel loss was discovered the next day, when a thorough inspection at Sacramento revealed a split in the B-17's right wing tank. With a new tank installed, DuBose and his crew made a solo crossing three days behind the rest of the squadron.[22]

Naturally, the crews who landed at Hickam on the morning of December 18 had a different impression of Hawaii than those who had arrived in the midst of the Japanese attack. Much had changed in the span of eleven days, but the sight of the carnage was sobering. "There was still smoke from burning vessels in Pearl Harbor and an oil slick all over the water," recalled John W. Fields, a pilot and backup navigator aboard Bill Lewis's aircraft. "It was really a mess. Ships, those that weren't burning, had been damaged, and the *Arizona*, of course, was sunk."[23]

At Hickam Field, the scenes of bombed-out buildings and pieces of charred aircraft looked equally grim to Fields, who went by his middle name of Wallace. What he didn't realize, however, was how much worse it had been. Shocked, angry, but always resilient, the American troops on Oahu had recovered quickly from the disaster. Much of the debris had already been cleared away, and the daily routine was mostly back to normal.

Christmas was but a few days off when the 22nd Squadron arrived.

---

* Six months later, Tinker became the first American general killed during World War II. He and his crew died when their B-24 bomber crashed into the ocean on June 7, 1942, during a mop-up mission after the Battle of Midway.

Instead of the winter weather most of the young men were accustomed to on the mainland, they found the climate on Oahu delightful. Fred Eaton, for one, could scarcely contain his enthusiasm when describing the island to his family. "As you can well imagine, we are on the alert most of the time," he wrote two days after his arrival. "However, I love it here. I mean it. I never have seen such a beautiful place. The weather is perfect and they say it is always the same. I have never in my life seen a place I liked better."[24]

Less than a week later, on Christmas Day, his crew was among several that conducted a long patrol mission. Eaton passed the time by writing another letter to his family, and despite a touch of homesickness, he was still infatuated with Hawaii.

> I'm out over the Pacific looking for enemy ships or submarines. We left before dawn this morning, and I won't be back in sight of land until after dark tonight. A fine Christmas!! I really don't mind, though. The weather is perfect, and all I'm doing is sitting here watching and letting "Hotfoot" Harlow do most of the flying. I want to get him ready to check off as 1st Pilot.
>
> Yesterday, and two days before that, I spent on the beach at Waikiki. I am acquiring a good tan already, and after a few months of this life, I will be healthier than I have ever been. Capt. Bill Lewis has a friend here who belongs to the Outrigger Club, which is the ritzy place we went swimming. I have a guest card and can go whenever I want. We patrol one day and have the next day off, so I hope to spend every other day on the beach. They have great steak dinners at the club, which sure taste good after a swim and surfboarding. What a life!!! What a war!!![25]

Eaton's attitude wasn't cavalier or immature, he simply had not lost his youthful innocence. The war, to him, was remote. Some of his peers, on the other hand, had gained a different outlook. Among them was copilot Roy Reid of the 38th Squadron, who had grown up only fifty miles from Eaton in New Haven, Connecticut, and was almost three years younger. But the things Reid had experienced on December 7, both in the cockpit and on the ground, had left silent scars. After first escaping from his burning B-17 with his hair singed off, then dodging the strafing attack that badly wounded three of his fellow crewmen, Reid found his way to the base hospital. When an ambulance pulled up, he instinctively checked to see if Lieutenant Schick was inside. "I went to the rear of the ambulance as they opened the door," he recalled, "and met a horrible sight of this poor man being pulled [out] with his leg blown off right at the hip."[26]

Planning to be a doctor himself, Reid had observed major surgeries and even an autopsy during his college days, but the gore he witnessed in the back of that ambulance nearly caused him to faint. He sat on the hospital steps for a few minutes to clear his head, and in just that short amount of time the medical staff was swamped with incoming wounded. That was how Reid, all of twenty-one years old, spent his first hour in Hawaii. The shock of war, experienced close enough to smell it, left an unwanted imprint.

LIFE ON OAHU wasn't always pleasant, even for Fred Eaton. The day-on, day-off routine of patrol missions became exceedingly dull. During their time off, the crews found it difficult to relax in the cramped, dirty rooms of the temporary barracks. A dusk-to-dawn curfew restricted them to the base beginning at 5:00 P.M., so there was no nightlife in Honolulu, which was blacked out anyway. Just as frustrating, only a trickle of mail arrived from the States. Many of the men, denied the opportunity to say goodbye to their loved ones before their sudden departure from California, relied on cryptic messages via Western Union to let their families know they were safe. Starved for news from home, especially during the holidays, they were frustrated by the absence of mail.

Walt Johnson, in his role as the 88th Squadron's adjutant, decided to research the postal system. He was appalled to discover that all incoming mail worked its way through a veritable maze, with at least five separate handlings after it reached Hawaii. "First our letters go to the Honolulu post office," he noted, "then either to Fort Shafter or the Hickam post office, thence to the Hickam message center, thence to the 5th Group, to the 31st Squadron, and then maybe to us."[27]

A further aggravation affected the B-17 squadrons shortly before Christmas. In one of his first acts as commander of the Hawaiian Air Force, General Tinker commandeered the B-17Es and gave the crews flying patrols the older C and D models. The seemingly endless hours they spent searching for enemy submarines—no one expected to find Japanese surface ships in the area by this time—were as fruitless as they were boring. But the crews could never let their guard down.

A few days before Christmas, on one of his first patrols, Lieutenant Rawls flew six hundred miles outbound on his assigned radial before discovering that he could not use the fuel in the auxiliary tank mounted in the bomb bay. The fuel pump had failed, and someone had removed the emergency hand pump that was supposed to be stored in the airplane. To lighten the bomber, everything that could be removed was tossed overboard, including the auxiliary tank, and Rawls squeaked back to Hickam with only a few minutes' worth of fuel remaining.

Days later, the search sectors were extended out to eight hundred nautical miles. The total round-trip, which included a perpendicular track from the outbound leg to the inbound radial, now covered almost two thousand statute miles, equivalent to flying from Los Angeles to Atlanta. Depending on wind conditions, the missions often lasted eleven to twelve hours and required two auxiliary fuel tanks, leaving no room for bombs. The crews simply reconnoitered their assigned sectors and reported any noteworthy sightings. "Deacon" Rawls, a former country preacher from the Florida panhandle, was far out to sea one day when he received a coded message to bomb a submarine at a specified location. His two-word response: "What with?"[28]

On December 26, the first day of the extended patrols, the B-17C flown by Earl Cooper of the 38th Squadron failed to return. The news hit everyone hard. Cooper's crew had been among the twelve that landed during the Japanese attack, and the men of the 38th and 88th squadrons shared the same floor of the temporary barracks. "Our neighbor squadron has had plenty of bad luck," wrote Walt Johnson, "having lost two ships on December 7, and their doctor."[29] It was obvious to everyone that even if Cooper's crew had ditched successfully, their chances of being found in such a wide expanse of ocean were minuscule. Not surprisingly, four days passed with no word on the missing crew. Then, on the night of December 30, the squadrons learned of a miraculous outcome: Ensign Frank M. "Fuzzy" Fisler, flying a PBY Catalina of Patrol Squadron 51, was searching his assigned sector when his crew spotted life rafts on the stormy sea. Because of the rough conditions, headquarters at Pearl Harbor denied Fisler's request to attempt a water landing, so he put the choice to his crewmembers. They voted to give it a try. In a feat of superb flying, Fisler and his enlisted copilot landed the ungainly flying boat without seriously damaging its hull, then spent a few anxious hours transferring nine cold, wet, and hungry survivors into the bobbing Catalina. Even more amazingly, Fisler got the flying boat airborne again despite the additional weight and delivered the grateful men safely to Pearl Harbor.[30]

Word of the successful rescue electrified the crews at Hickam. "When the news came in during the evening, both the 88th and the 38th were out in the halls, everyone with something to say," Johnson wrote happily. "It was as if a sigh of relief were echoing out of the chatter, for the spirits of every man rose."[31]

Cooper and his crew had almost given up hope after three nights of stormy weather, their only meal an albatross they shot and ate raw, along with the undigested fish in its stomach. Their mishap, blamed on a combination of faulty navigation and erroneous communications, served as a cautionary tale. The heroics of Fisler and his copilot, Aviation Machinist's Mate 1st Class Leonard H. Wagoner, were fittingly recognized by Admiral Chester W. Nimitz, who awarded both men the Navy Cross on New Year's Eve.

As the routine patrol missions continued into 1942, no additional incidents tarnished the effort. But the long flights put a tremendous strain on the crews as well as the B-17s. Squadron commanders campaigned for operational schedules that would allow a full day off between missions, though most of the young crewmen tended to play just as hard, if not harder, than they worked. On their days off they headed straight to Waikiki Beach, where they forgot about the scarcity of mail and the shabby living quarters.

Fortunately, a few letters began to trickle in. Fred Eaton was excited to report home about his first piece of mail. "At last! A letter, the first one that I have received since I have been here," he wrote on January 12. "You have no idea how welcome it is. . . . I'm still fighting a terrific war over here. On the beach at Waikiki every other day. Today I'm out over whitecaps patrolling again. All engines purring like kittens and no submarines in sight. . . . I can picture you having a cold, slushy New York winter. You should be here with me getting a good tan and really having a perfect time. All that is wrong here is that I can't go in town and have a date at night."[32]

The routine remained unchanged throughout the first month of 1942. "The men are used to the stuffy rooms and the blackout," wrote Lieutenant Johnson on January 31, "and used to staying in during the evenings. Naturally there are a number of card games going on, and some read books, some gossip. That's all the recreation there is."[33]

The first real break in the monotony did not occur until the beginning of February, when housing originally assigned to married officers stationed at Hickam was made available to the officers of bomber crews. The enlisted crewmen moved into repaired sections of the modern, nine-wing consolidated barracks known as the "Hickam Hotel."

But the men had barely settled into their new accommodations when everything changed. Dick Carmichael, recently promoted to major along with Jim Twaddell, was selected to form a new squadron and lead it across the South Pacific to Fiji. Much to his liking it would be an independent outfit, cobbled together with crews from three different squadrons for the purpose of supporting a U.S. Navy task force. Those who were selected for the operation reacted with excitement. After two months of patrolling the ocean for submarines and surfing the waves at Waikiki Beach, they were eager to engage the enemy. Thus far the opening blows of the war in the Pacific had heavily favored the Japanese. Perhaps Carmichael's back-channel squadron, with twelve new B-17Es and some of the best-trained heavy bomber crews in the army, could even the score.

SIX

TO FIJI, AND BEYOND

Prior to the attack on Pearl Harbor, most Americans had a poor grasp of Pacific Ocean geography. And little wonder. An attitude of isolationism had prevailed for decades, Hawaii was not yet a state, and few people even knew where to find Pearl Harbor on a map. The more remote atolls dotting the enormous ocean—Canton, Midway, Samoa, Palmyra, and many others—were about as familiar as the dark side of the moon.

The vastness of the Pacific had much to do with America's isolation. Covering a fourth of the earth's surface, it seemed almost infinitely huge in the days before overseas air travel. It took the fastest ocean liners at least four days to reach Hawaii from the West Coast, while a voyage to the Far East required weeks at sea. But in 1936, thanks to an influential American entrepreneur, the world began to get smaller. Juan Trippe, the founder of Pan American Airways, had already established regular aerial service to the Caribbean, Cuba, and Latin America from the airline's home base in Miami. He accomplished this with a fleet of flying boats that could operate from sheltered harbors, eliminating the need to build and maintain big, expensive airports in foreign countries. Subsequently, as seaplanes increased in size, range, and dependability, Trippe set his sights on an aerial route across the Pacific.

Trippe's concept represented a tremendous breakthrough in world travel, but the island-hopping journey would still take six days. Pan American's four-engine Martin M-130 flying boats, with their massive hulls and drag-inducing outriggers, cruised at less than 130 miles per hour. Hence the leg from San Francisco to Honolulu, the longest overwater stretch of the entire route, required an all-night endurance run lasting more than sixteen hours. And there were numerous potential hazards to consider. Unfavorable winds, fuel leaks, or mechanical failures could easily spell doom. In the previous decade, thirteen aviators had perished attempting to cross various stretches of the Pacific, most disappearing somewhere between California and Hawaii.[1]

Deeply committed to maintaining his airline's reputation for safety and reliability, Trippe hired the most experienced pilots, navigators, and communications experts available. He also retained Charles Lindbergh as an advisor, an affiliation that helped Pan Am obtain long-term leases for the construction of refueling facilities and other necessary infrastructure on islands under American jurisdiction. Before the facilities could be built, however, Trippe and his employees had to overcome several obstacles.

At the time, hardly anyone except mariners knew what lay beyond Hawaii. For aviators, the Pacific was the last great frontier. There were no electronic aids to navigation or aerial meteorology stations for thousands of miles. The long stretches of open water between widely scattered atolls were as daunting and unforgiving as a trek across the Sahara Desert. To further complicate matters, several island groups had been mandated to the government of Japan after World War I. Strategically located and closely guarded, they were strictly off limits to Westerners. Consequently, Trippe's aerial route would have to be indirect, giving the mandated islands a wide berth.

Scouting far across the ocean, Pan American survey teams soon determined that the U.S. territories of Guam and Midway, which already supported an undersea telegraph cable and naval communications facilities, would make suitable stopping points. Wake Atoll, only a few feet above sea level and previously uninhabited, could also be developed into a refueling station.

Despite the tremendous distances involved, Pan American constructed the necessary support facilities in only two years. The infrastructure included refueling and maintenance services, accommodations for crew rest, and lodges worthy of the rich and famous. Because of their remoteness, the latter featured cutting-edge innovations such as hydroponic gardens, where the staff raised fresh vegetables for hotel dining rooms. Every clipper passenger traveled first class, and Pan Am's standard for luxury was reflected in the ticket price. In the depths of the Great Depression, when the average household income in the United States was approximately $1,600 per year and unemployment hovered around twenty percent, the price of a one-way ticket from San Francisco to Manila was set at $950—equivalent to more than $16,000 in today's value.[2]

With great fanfare, an M-130 named *China Clipper* made the first aerial crossing of the Pacific in November 1935, carrying airmail but no commercial passengers. One year later, proudly proclaiming, "It's a smaller world than ever now," Pan American inaugurated weekly passenger service from San Francisco to Hong Kong.[3] Magazine ads touted the luxury and speed of the company's "giant flying clipper ships," an ingenious marketing concept created by Trippe, who likened the romanticism of his Martin flying boats to the famous tall ships of the nineteenth century.[4]

But the Pacific would not be tamed easily. Pan American's top navigator, Frederick J. Noonan, left the company in early 1937 to join Amelia Earhart on her attempted flight around the world. Starting out from California, the pair flew easterly across an equatorial route of some 22,000 miles before reaching Lae, New Guinea. They commenced the first leg of their Pacific crossing on July 2, planning to refuel at Howland Island, but in one of the most intriguing mysteries of all time their Lockheed Electra vanished.[*5] Then, just six months later, the *Samoan Clipper* exploded in midair during a survey flight in the South Pacific, killing Pan Am's most experienced pilot, Captain Edwin C. Musick, along with his entire crew.[6] And six months after that tragedy, the *Hawaii Clipper* disappeared with six passengers and nine crew en route to Manila from Guam.[7]

Considering these and other high-profile accidents, particularly the *Hindenburg* disaster in May 1937, the safety of commercial aviation was

---

* Interest in the disappearance of Earhart and Noonan has never entirely waned, mainly because dramatic new theories are floated periodically to keep the mystery alive. To date, no airtight proof of their crash-landing or ditching location has ever been produced.

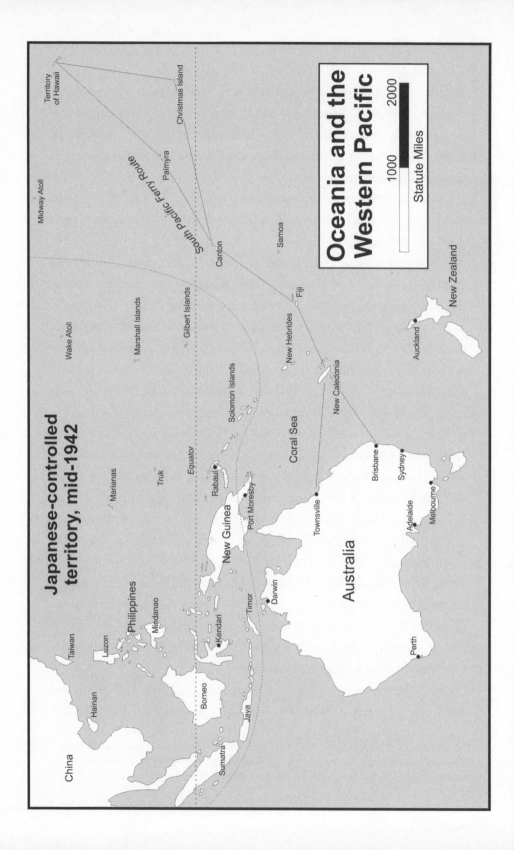

Oceania and the Western Pacific

Japanese-controlled territory, mid-1942

Statute Miles

0   1000   2000

China
Hainan
Taiwan
Luzon
Philippines
Mindanao
Borneo
Sumatra
Java
Timor
Kendari
Marianas
Truk
Marshall Islands
Wake Atoll
Midway Atoll
Territory of Hawaii
Palmyra
Christmas Island
South Pacific Ferry Route
Canton
Samoa
Gilbert Islands
Equator
Rabaul
New Guinea
Port Moresby
Solomon Islands
New Hebrides
Fiji
New Caledonia
Coral Sea
Darwin
Townsville
Brisbane
Sydney
Adelaide
Melbourne
Perth
Australia
Auckland
New Zealand

frequently scrutinized. The public did not lose trust in Pan American, but with only one M-130 remaining in service, the Pacific crossings were curtailed temporarily. Then in early 1939, when the fabulous new Boeing Model 314 was introduced, the transpacific flights resumed on a regular schedule. The massive yet elegant flying boats, which used the same wing and engine nacelles as the XB-15, boasted luxurious cabins seating seventy-four passengers for daytime flights and convertible berthing for thirty-six overnight travelers. Just as on a steamship, the captain dined with the passengers. Inflight meals, prepared by renowned chefs, were served on fine china by white-jacketed stewards. More than any other airplane in history, the Boeing clippers epitomized the glitz and glamour of overseas travel. But their glory days were brief. Less than three years after the Model 314s entered service, the transpacific flights were abruptly suspended. The attack on Pearl Harbor put an end to the grand overseas adventures.

When the Japanese offensive began on December 7, 1941, America's collective naivety about the Pacific vanished. Guam was captured only three days later, and Wake Atoll, valiantly defended by elements of a Marine Corps battalion and the surviving pilots of a decimated fighter squadron, fell silent on December 23. For the families of the men deployed to those far-off islands, the holidays were especially bleak: all American personnel at both locations, including civilian contractors, were believed to have been killed or captured.[*]

Compared with the damage inflicted in Hawaii and the Philippines, the loss of two small islands might have seemed relatively insignificant. But the aerial route pioneered by Pan American had underscored the importance of the islands as stepping stones across the Pacific. As early as February 1941, in fact, the Roosevelt administration had approved the construction of airfields on Wake and Midway to support movements by long-range heavy bombers. (Guam was not considered a viable refueling stop for land-based planes, in

---

[*] The lone exception was Radioman First Class George Tweed, USN, who managed to avoid capture for two years and seven months. Aided by local Chamorros, many of whom were later executed for their suspected collusion, Tweed was rescued when U.S. forces recaptured Guam in June 1944.

part because of its proximity to Saipan, a mandated island in the northern Marianas.[8]) The wisdom of constructing the new airfields was demonstrated that September, when Major Emmett "Rosie" O'Donnell led the first group of B-17s from Hawaii to the Philippines.[9] Two months later, an even larger group was ferried to Clark Field via the same route. However, that route was severed with the fall of Wake.[10] Only one alternate route remained potentially available—and it was not yet ready for use.

FULLY TEN MONTHS before the Pacific war began, the vulnerability of the ferry route across the Central Pacific concerned members of the War Department.[11] One was the assistant chief of the Air Corps, Major General George H. Brett, who lobbied hard for the construction of an alternate route via the South Pacific. This would require the construction of several new airfields on extremely remote atolls, an expensive commitment, and the idea was rejected with the explanation that "neither the War nor the Navy Department has any plan for operations that would require the movement of long-range Army bombardment aviation to the Orient, nor can the need for such a plan now be foreseen."[12]

But only eight months later, as the threat of war with Japan grew far more ominous, the War Department did an about-face. General Marshall, the chief of staff, not only authorized the development of a South Pacific route, he placed Lieutenant General Short, commanding general of the Hawaiian Department, in charge of the project. Marshall originally set a completion date of June 1942, but mere weeks after the project started he was notified by Hap Arnold that the southern route had become "a matter of extreme urgency." In early November, therefore, Marshall shortened the deadline to January 15, 1942.[13]

Given only two months to complete the enormous project, General Short pulled off a minor miracle. Shiploads of heavy equipment, construction personnel, and civilian contractors were unloaded on the chosen islands, where the workmen bulldozed, graded, and paved new five-thousand-foot runways. Three of the tiny atolls were under U.S. jurisdiction, but the 5,700-mile route also required the cooperation of three Allied nations. The use of

Nadi Field,* an existing airdrome in the Fiji Islands, was granted by New Zealand; the Free French authorized landing rights at Tontouta and Plaine de Gaiacs airfields on New Caledonia; and the Royal Australian Air Force extended the runways at Garbutt airdrome near Townsville, Queensland.

While the fields underwent construction or enlargement, the only other means of ferrying heavy bombers to the Far East relied on a grueling journey that spanned two-thirds of the globe. Starting from MacDill Field in Tampa, Florida, B-17s and LB-30s followed essentially the same route used by Amelia Earhart in 1937: southward to Brazil, across the Atlantic to Africa, then via India, Sumatra, and Java to Australia. Many of the landing sites were inadequate for heavy bombers, and there were no spare parts available for repairs. By the third week of January 1942, twenty-five percent of the bombers that attempted the route were out of commission at various points along the way.[14]

Meanwhile, on December 6, 1941, Short informed Marshall that the construction battalions "were striving very hard" to meet the accelerated deadline for completion of the new ferry route.[15] And despite the surprise attack on Hawaii the next day, which ultimately caused Short's career to implode, the project was completed ahead of schedule. Departing from Hickam Field on January 6, 1942, Ken Hobson led three of his 22nd Squadron B-17s across the string of islands to Australia and thence to Java. According to an official AAF summary, some of the newly developed atolls "had never seen a land [based] plane" prior to Hobson's inaugural flight.[16]

Although the route was considered usable, it had not been properly charted, nor were all of the fields equipped with adequate refueling facilities, accommodations, or defensive garrisons. Despite the limitations, six more B-17s departed from Hickam in mid-January and followed the route as far as Fiji. After mapping the approaches, the crews remained for a few weeks to conduct patrols in support of the aircraft carrier *Enterprise*, which was

---

* The American spelling for the airfield on the main island of Viti Levu was "Nandi," the result of a perpetual misunderstanding or error in pronunciation. Its namesake was the nearby village of Nadi, and the field is still in use: Fijians call it Nadi International Airport, known to countless tourists as the hub of Fiji Airlines.

escorting a convoy to Samoa. Five of the B-17s returned to Hawaii at the end of the month, leaving behind the crew of Lieutenant Ralph Wanderer Jr., whose Fortress had been grounded with a blown cylinder. Weeks passed while the crew camped near their airplane, vaguely hoping that replacement parts to effect the necessary repairs would be delivered.[17]

IN WASHINGTON, DC, the Joint Chiefs of Staff were searching for ways to hit back at the Japanese. Even a small effort, if successful, would provide a boost in American morale. But the military leaders faced multiple obstacles. The most immediate, described by General Marshall as "naval weakness," was not meant as a condescending reference to the shambles that had once been the Pacific Fleet's proud battleship force. Instead he was referring to the serious setbacks that had affected all of the Allied naval forces in the Pacific. The Royal Navy's *Repulse* and *Prince of Wales* had fallen victim to Japanese land-based naval bombers and torpedo planes on December 10; the American cruisers *Houston* and *Marblehead* were damaged by similar "land attackers" of the Imperial Japanese Navy three weeks later; and closer to home, the carrier *Saratoga* had been torpedoed south of Hawaii on January 11. A major overhaul at Bremerton, Washington, would keep her out of action for months.

In mid-January, intelligence reports indicated that the enemy's Mobile Striking Force, the *Kido Butai*, was moving into the Southwest Pacific. The chief of naval operations, Admiral Ernest J. King, recommended a raid on Wake Atoll. Hoping the attack would divert the enemy's attention and exact a measure of revenge for the island's capture, King forwarded his suggestion to Admiral Nimitz, newly appointed as commander-in-chief of the Pacific Fleet, who in turn selected Vice Admiral Wilson Brown to lead the raid. Brown, commander of Task Force 11 aboard the USS *Lexington*, received his orders on January 21, but before he could take action the Japanese intervened. The oiler *Neches*, sent to rendezvous with Brown and refuel his task force, was sunk by a submarine only 135 miles from Pearl Harbor on January 23. Without the oiler's fuel, Brown was unable to conduct the mission.

The Allies were getting nowhere. More than six weeks had now passed since the start of the Pacific war, and every attempt to counter the Japanese had been swatted aside. In the Philippines, General MacArthur had declared Manila an open city barely two weeks after the first Japanese troops landed on Luzon. The battered remnants of his heavy bomber force—only fourteen obsolescent B-17Cs and Ds of the 19th Bomb Group—had initially withdrawn to Del Monte Field on the island of Mindanao, then retreated all the way to Darwin in northern Australia. Tired and dispirited, the crews conducted a few long-range missions, staging back through Del Monte to bomb Japanese positions, but by the end of the year only ten B-17s remained airworthy. On the first day of 1942, they repositioned to Java to help the Dutch defend the Netherlands East Indies. That effort, which sacrificed many more planes and lives, proved to be entirely in vain.

Back on the big island of Luzon, American and Filipino troops and a handful of pursuit aircraft withdrew to the Bataan Peninsula for a last-ditch effort. MacArthur and his staff, determined to hold out for months, hunkered down with the defenders of Corregidor. He pleaded for reinforcements, but the large convoy that had sailed from the States in November—the USS *Republic* carrying the 7th Bomb Group's ground echelon, plus seven other ships filled to capacity with crated A-24 attack aircraft, P-40 fighters, spare parts, ammunition, aviation gasoline, and two regiments of field artillery—was diverted to Australia after the attack on Pearl Harbor. There would be no reinforcements for MacArthur. The eventual capitulation of the entire Philippines archipelago was inevitable.

Things were even worse 2,500 miles to the south. In the predawn hours of January 23 the Australian army suffered its worst-ever military disaster when the same Japanese force that had captured Guam invaded Rabaul, capital of Australia's Mandated Territory of New Guinea. The ill-equipped Australian garrison, known as Lark Force, resisted for only a few hours before the survivors scattered into the jungle in disarray.

The other Allied strongholds in the Far East fared no better. Hong Kong fell on Christmas Day, Singapore was nearly finished, and the Netherlands

East Indies would soon follow. As the overrated bastions toppled one by one, the territory occupied by the Japanese spread like a tidal wave toward Australia.

Protection of the new South Pacific ferry route, the only intact lifeline between the United States and Australia, became paramount. In an effort to distract the Japanese and perhaps induce them to divert resources away from their main thrust, Admiral Nimitz ordered a series of hit-and-run carrier strikes. On February 1, aircraft from the USS *Yorktown*, flagship of Task Force 17, attacked enemy fortifications in the Gilbert Islands. Simultaneously, the USS *Enterprise* air group hammered facilities on Kwajalein and nearby islands in the Marshalls, supported by naval bombardment from warships of Task Force 8. Collectively the raids caused only moderate damage, but throughout the upper echelons of the Imperial Japanese Navy, embarrassment ran deep.

Hailed as victories in the American press, the carrier strikes provided the boost in morale that the Joint Chiefs had been seeking. And additional raids were already in the offing. Five weeks earlier, President Roosevelt had called the Joint Chiefs to the White House to express his intense desire to avenge Pearl Harbor. To their credit, they responded by considering a variety of options, including unorthodox ideas from subordinates. By far the most intriguing concept, the brainchild of a submariner, called for a daring raid on Tokyo using army bombers launched from a navy carrier. Rather than being scoffed at, the idea generated a buzz of excitement and was handed off to Colonel James H. Doolittle to implement. The only downside, from the perspective of the Joint Chiefs, was that the renowned aviator needed three months to prepare for the top-secret mission.

In the meantime, a steady stream of American convoys delivered garrison troops, crated fighters, ground-support personnel, and antiaircraft battalions to fortify the islands along the new ferry route. It was a slow process. New Caledonia, for example, lay approximately 6,500 miles from the West Coast, twice the distance that convoys crossing the North Atlantic had to travel to reach the United Kingdom. And the job of protecting the Pacific convoys placed considerable strain on Admiral Nimitz's limited resources.

In early February, while the *Enterprise* and *Yorktown* hastened back to Pearl Harbor after their successful raids, the *Lexington* and Task Force 11 proceeded into the South Pacific with orders to patrol the ferry route and escort a convoy headed to Canton Island. Orders were changed, however, after Admiral King received credible intelligence that the Japanese were gathering forces at Rabaul prior to launching an attack, presumably against New Caledonia or other positions in the New Hebrides. (The Japanese were indeed planning an operation to invade Fiji and Samoa, but not until later that summer, after the conclusion of major offensives to capture Port Moresby and Midway.)

In response to the perceived threat, King advised Nimitz to place his forces "so as to hit the enemy wherever and whenever he might attack."[18] Aboard the *Lexington*, Vice Admiral Brown received new orders on February 6 to proceed toward the Fiji Islands and rendezvous with the recently created ANZAC Command, a multinational naval force under the leadership of Vice Admiral Herbert F. Leary, the senior American naval officer in Australia.* En route to Fiji, Brown and his staff conceived a plan to launch a carrier strike on the enemy's new stronghold at Rabaul, to be supported by naval bombardment if conditions were favorable. The plan, approved by both King and Leary, was tentatively scheduled to commence at dawn on February 21. To ensure adequate protection for the combined task force, the Joint Chiefs agreed to provide U.S. Navy flying boats and a squadron of AAF heavy bombers to sweep the seas with patrols out of Fiji.

AT HICKAM FIELD, Dick Carmichael anticipated that he would soon take his squadron to Java, following the route pioneered by Ken Hobson in early January. "I had twelve crews and airplanes made up of my 88th Reconnaissance Squadron and the 22nd Bomb Squadron," he would later recall.

---

* An acronym from World War I, ANZAC originally stood for Australian–New Zealand Army Corps. The new command, however, included an American heavy cruiser and two destroyers along with navy patrol planes. Known collectively as the ANZAC Squadron, the warships were commanded by Rear Admiral John G. "Jack" Crace, an Australian with a distinguished career in the Royal Navy.

"Maybe there were a couple of crews from the 38th, I don't remember, but we loaded up those twelve airplanes with as much as we could carry."[19]

Carmichael's recollection, expressed during his official air force oral history interviews almost forty years later, was accurate. Six crews from the 88th, five from the 22nd, and one from the 38th formed the ad hoc squadron, a peculiar combination that likely stemmed from the order in which the twelve B-17s were released to Carmichael by the Hawaiian Air Force. Most ended up back in the hands of the crews who had flown them over from California, although that didn't placate the fliers. Resentful that their planes had been commandeered in the first place, they had spent the past two months patrolling in B-17Cs and Ds, making it impossible to practice with the new turret-mounted guns and other improvements in the E model.[20]

As a consequence of the numerous friendly fire incidents on December 7, all of the Fortresses released to Carmichael had a distinctive new appearance. Their tall rudders wore thirteen red and white stripes to aid with identification, and a red circle still adorned the center of each national insignia. More interestingly, about half of Carmichael's bombers resembled British aircraft. Soon after the Japanese attack, the Hawaiian Air Depot had repainted some of the B-17s with a random, multicolor camouflage pattern similar to that used by the Royal Air Force.[21]

Prior to the squadron's departure from Hickam, Carmichael received amended orders. "We were given a job en route," he remembered with amusement. "Rabaul had been captured by the Japanese, and the Navy was going to attack Rabaul, and they wanted a coordinated attack with land-based B-17s. So they said, 'Well, Carmichael, you do that while you are en route to Java.'"[22]

His lighthearted recollection was oversimplified, but not by much. The impromptu squadron, attached to the navy under Vice Admiral Leary's operational control, adopted a temporary designation as the Southern Bomber Command. The crews were ordered to proceed to Fiji, where they would fly patrols in support of Task Force 11 while awaiting updated plans for the raid on Rabaul. The new orders presented last-minute challenges, especially for Walt Johnson: picked to serve as the squadron's communications officer as well as its adjutant, he was tasked with obtaining and safeguarding "a lot of secret material for communicating with the Navy."[23]

Although regarded as a unified squadron under Carmichael's command, the crews maintained a degree of independence based on their original units. The roster consisted of 112 individuals, of which 52 were officers or aviation cadets. In addition to the nine-man combat crews, the squadron was augmented by Walt Johnson (communications officer), Captain Edward A. Luke (medical officer), Lieutenant Roderick M. Stewart (engineering officer), and Jim Twaddell (weather officer), who also served as the executive officer.

Carmichael subdivided his six crews of the erstwhile 88th Squadron into two flights, which departed from Hickam Field on the morning of February 10. With lieutenants Harry Brandon and Newt Chaffin on his wing, Carmichael flew to Christmas Island, 1,430 miles south of Hickam, while Ted Faulkner led Frank Bostrom and Deacon Rawls to Palmyra Atoll. The next day, accompanied by Dubby DuBose, Fred Eaton, Harry E. Spieth Jr., and John A. Roberts Jr. of the 22nd Bomb Squadron, plus Swede Swenson of the 38th Reconnaissance Squadron, Bill Lewis led the remaining six B-17s aloft from Hickam. They, too, were divided into separate three-ship flights, one going to Palmyra, the other to Christmas Island.

AFTER WEEKS OF patrolling the waters around Hawaii, the crews were universally excited to be heading toward the front lines, though they were still thousands of miles from contested territory. Their two-month stay on Oahu had been interesting, but Hawaii was Americanized, not so very different from home except for the verdant landscape and tropical climate. Now they found themselves landing on tiny, remote atolls unlike anything they had ever seen before. Aviation Cadet Albert J. Hobday, a navigator for the 88th Squadron, described Christmas Island as a tropical jewel "with lots of coconut palms, white sand beaches and the most beautiful ocean surf one can imagine."[24] The crews spent the night in a well-camouflaged encampment in the center of the island, where construction workers, starved for news, bombarded them with questions about life in the United States. "Some of these workmen had been there for a year," noted copilot Wallace Fields, "and were sorta balmy."[25]

Departing in roughly the same staggered order from Christmas Island and Palmyra, the squadron flew to the next far-flung stop, Canton Atoll in the Phoenix Islands. Little more than a thin ribbon of coral and sand surrounding a large central lagoon, the island was difficult to distinguish from the air. "Almost missed it completely," navigator John Steinbinder noted in his diary. "Flew right over it before we noticed the breakwater. This island is so small that it is almost not an island. There is only one tree on it."[26]

The lone palm tree, a landmark in the South Pacific, was put to good use: a crude wooden platform suspended partway up the trunk served as the airfield's control tower. But in contrast with the beauty of Christmas Island, Canton was squat and featureless. A metal Quonset hut held the kitchen and mess hall, with several tents nearby containing dirty cots. In his diary, Cadet Hobday mentioned "lots of rats scurrying around, swarms of flies, and ugly land crabs crawling all around the tent."[27] The fliers were not sorry to be on the way to Fiji, 1,270 miles to the southwest, after an uncomfortable overnight stay.

About half the bombers departed Canton on February 12, which happened to be Al Hobday's birthday. But it lasted only a couple of hours. Upon crossing the International Date Line, the crews advanced their clocks and wristwatches to the morning of Friday the thirteenth. Concerns among the superstitious that the date would bring bad luck were unfounded. Walt Johnson, riding as a passenger in Ted Faulkner's B-17, was moved by the enormity, beauty, and unpredictability of the South Pacific during the nine-hour flight.

> The ocean, a slightly deeper blue than the sky, was at first darkened by shadows of clouds. The play of light and shadows on the surface of the ocean was beautiful. But the clouds thickened, the air became rough, and showers were met at irregular intervals. The ocean was apparently angry and her waves were foam-capped and violent. Faulkner, leading the flight with Bostrom on the right and Rawls on the left, climbed to 8,000 feet

and missed the worst part of the display of nature, and shortly, as the clouds had once before become thicker, they now as surely thinned. A red rainbow circled the nose of the ship, seeming to touch the calming waters below and the sky above.[28]

The remainder of the crews completed the long flight to the airdrome they called "Nandi" on February 14. For most, the trip was uneventful, but Captain Swenson and his crew experienced a few nerve-wracking hours. "We started to lose our two inboard engines about a hundred miles from Fiji," recalled Earl Williams, the assistant flight engineer. "They were back-firing and running erratically."[29]

With two engines sputtering and no assurance that the other two would maintain power, the last hours of the journey must have seemed interminable. To the crew's great relief, the volcanic peaks of Viti Levu, the second of the two main islands, finally appeared on the horizon. Engines popping loudly, the B-17 touched down on the luxuriously long runway on the western side of the island. Soon thereafter, Williams and the crew chief, Leroy Pouncey, discovered that the problem had originated back on Canton Island, where they had refueled from underground storage tanks. The repairs would be time-consuming. "We found out that we had picked up some salt water and sand from one of those pits," Williams remarked. "When we got to Fiji, we had to drain all of the fuel from the tanks and replace the booster pumps."[30]

Intrigued by the dark-skinned Fijians, particularly the muscular, fierce-looking men, the crews of the Southern Bomber Command settled into a tent encampment near their dispersed B-17s. The islanders, far more outgoing than they first appeared, delighted in trading. "They always smiled," wrote Hobday, "and were willing to help us erect tents and bring us fresh pineapples from the fields."[31] Lieutenant Jack L. Carlson, another navigator and prolific diarist, wrote, "The natives are the best-natured people I have ever met."[32]

Carmichael remembered Nadi as "just an old, small British field,"[33] but in this instance his recollection was skewed. The airdrome was neither old nor small, nor even specifically British. Built only two years earlier, it was operated by New Zealanders and had been lengthened to seven thousand feet just prior to the squadron's arrival. The field would serve as their base for the next few days while the crews conducted long-range patrols, scouting ahead of the *Lexington*'s task force for enemy ships or submarines. The planes were fully armed, each lugging four six-hundred-pound bombs, full loads of machine-gun ammunition, and one auxiliary fuel tank.

Carmichael and his crews from the 88th Squadron flew the first series of patrols on February 15, covering ten-degree sectors out to a range of five hundred miles. The remaining crews (except for Swenson, whose B-17 was still grounded) stood by on thirty-minute alert, ready to launch an attack if one was ordered. Their roles flip-flopped the next day, with the five 22nd Squadron crews patrolling the assigned sectors while Task Force 11 rendezvoused with the ANZAC Squadron.

When it began to look as though the B-17s would be called upon to provide extended coverage for the warships, Carmichael decided to find better accommodations for his squadron than a mosquito-infested encampment. But his effort was interrupted by an urgent call to report to Suva, the capital of Fiji, for a conference with members of Admiral Brown's staff. Thus he got to spend a night in the lap of luxury. "I met the admiral's representative over there," Carmichael recalled, "and stayed at the [Grand] Pacific Hotel, with ceiling fans and mosquito nets. The British lived well, so I liked that very much. I was treated like I was really something. The Navy treated me well, too. After all, I had all the land-based support airplanes."[34]

The main purpose of the conference was to discuss Admiral Brown's plan to attack Rabaul. If Carmichael could get his planes to Australia in time, the B-17s were to launch a long-distance mission to bomb Simpson Harbor, the famed anchorage at Rabaul, in coordination with the *Lexington*'s carrier-based aircraft. More than a bold plan, it was a bona fide Hail Mary. Fully two months before Jimmy Doolittle would be ready to mount his raid on Tokyo, Brown and his staff worked out a scheme to strike a heavy blow against the most formidable Japanese stronghold in the South Pacific.

For Carmichael, a twenty-eight-year-old major, the deference shown by the admiral's staff was heady stuff.

Returning to the airdrome on February 17, he prepared to move the Southern Bomber Command (now under official written orders) to Australia. And unexpectedly, he gained several experienced men for his independent squadron. The enlisted crewmen from Ralph Wanderer's B-17, stranded three weeks earlier with a blown cylinder, knew their airplane would be grounded for a long time. Eager to get away from the isolated airdrome, they mentioned to one of Carmichael's pilots that they wanted to join the squadron, and all five were immediately shanghaied.

Within hours, after a chaotic morning of meetings and last-minute instructions, eleven B-17s were ready to get under way. Swenson's crew, still laboring with the tedious job of cleaning their bomber's contaminated fuel system, would follow when they could. The completion of the journey required two long overwater flights, with a refueling stop on the island of New Caledonia, but no one had any confidence in the security of its two airdromes. Strong political and ideological differences had divided New Caledonia's 18,000 French citizens, some of whom were aligned with the Vichy government while others pledged their loyalty to the Free French. Both sides vied for control of the airfields. Carmichael therefore decided to lead half the squadron to New Caledonia that afternoon, leaving Bill Lewis to bring the remaining planes the following day.

Lifting off from Fiji at noon, Carmichael was uneasy. It would be getting dark by the time his flight of six bombers reached New Caledonia, making it more difficult to discern who was in control. The crews who remained at Fiji did not envy their squadron mates. "They left," John Steinbinder wrote in his diary, "not knowing whether they would be taken as prisoners or accepted as friends. . . . So who knows just what our boys will run into. We are not going on until we have definite word."[35]

The uncertainties appeared to be well-founded. Carmichael's formation first headed for Tontouta airfield, twenty-five miles up the coast from the port capital of Noumea, but to their surprise the field was blocked with barricades. Just as curiously, a message had been laid out on the runway in white lettering. While the other B-17s circled the field, Carmichael dropped down to read the message, which directed incoming planes to fly ninety-five miles to the northwest. Faced with no alternative, he led the formation up the coast for the better part of an hour before they found the newly constructed airfield at Plaine des Gaiacs. There was no control tower or radio communication with anyone on the ground, but another message had been placed on the runway in block letters. It simply stated, "OK."

Not knowing what he would find, Carmichael lowered his wheels and landed. The others circled overhead, wondering if the skipper and his crew had become prisoners. Finally, after several long minutes, the position lights of Carmichael's B-17 flashed a signal in Morse code: the field was secure. The new airstrip, carved out of the jungle near the coast, had no servicing facilities, so drums of aviation gasoline had to be trucked from Noumea. There was only enough available to provide seven hundred or eight hundred gallons per airplane, and it had to be transferred into the B-17s by means of a hand-cranked "wobble pump." The slow, laborious method took most of the night. "We couldn't understand the French, and they couldn't understand us," recalled Carmichael. "There happened to be one American there, permanent party, who spoke French. The Frenchmen could understand his French, and we had a hard time understanding his English, but we got along all right, and we safely got gasoline."[36]

Other than fuel, the French had little to offer the American fliers. The local guards shared their food, as there were no messing facilities at the new airstrip for transient flight crews. The only thing in abundance, noted Walt Johnson, was mosquitos. Tired and sweaty, the crews tried their best to get comfortable but resigned themselves to a long, restless night.

SEVEN

STORM CLOUDS

The next stop for the Southern Bomber Command was Townsville, Queensland, seven hundred miles across the Coral Sea. Carmichael and his crews knew almost nothing about their destination, except that Australia appeared to be in deep trouble. Compared with the setbacks suffered by the U.S. military, the war seemed to be going even worse for the ill-equipped Commonwealth. By mid-February 1942, no one had heard from the outposts at Rabaul or Kavieng in more than three weeks, a sure sign that the so-called Northern Barrier had collapsed. Then, on the morning of February 16, Australians awoke to the shocking news that Singapore had surrendered overnight. Along with the humiliation of defeat came the anguish of knowing that the entire 8th Division, a force of more than 15,000 Australians, had been captured along with five times as many British and Indian troops.

Another disturbing story in Australian newspapers that morning described a speech given by Japanese premier Hideki Tojo, who presented the empire's principal war aim to the Diet in Tokyo. In explaining the establishment of a "co-prosperity sphere," he declared that Burma, China, and Malaya were "assured of happiness by Japanese cooperation," then went on to imply that Australia and New Zealand would have the same assurances if they did not resist. It was an ominous threat couched in ideological terminology.[1]

Gravely concerned about their immediate future, Australians faced more bad news over the next few days as Japanese forces swept across Sumatra and bore down on Java with alarming speed. The litany of defeats, coupled with Tojo's menacing speech, rocked the Commonwealth to its core. As one editorial put it, "The succession of recent disasters has shaken the public more than anything else in the war. They see that the war can be lost and everyone is asking apprehensively and impatiently if the conduct of the war is all that it could be."[2]

Australians had plenty of reasons to be concerned. Just north of the continent, the battle for New Guinea had already begun. Lying only a hundred miles across the Torres Strait from Australia, the world's second largest island was firmly in the crosshairs of Japan's regional commander, Vice Admiral Shigeyoshi Inoue. Soon after his South Seas Force captured Rabaul and Kavieng in the Bismarcks, Inoue consolidated his diverse units under a new command, the Rabaul Area Force. He then began to transform the tropical port into a twentieth-century fortress. Construction battalions improved the two main airdromes, and within a week the 24th Naval Air Flotilla, based in the Marshall Islands, shifted its headquarters to Rabaul. Led by Rear Admiral Eiji Goto, the contingent included the Yokohama Air Group with fourteen Kawanishi H6K flying boats for long-range bombing and reconnaissance, and fifteen obsolescent Mitsubishi A5M4 fighters from the Chitose Air Group for local defense.

Mere days after the arrival of the Yokohama Air Group, Goto went on the offensive. In the waning hours of February 2, six of the large flying boats lifted from the dark waters of Simpson Harbor and shaped a course for Port Moresby, five hundred miles to the southwest. Early the next morning, well before dawn, they dropped twenty-one bombs on Seven Mile airdrome, named for its distance by road from Port Moresby. The raid caused little material damage, though one Australian sergeant was killed. Two nights later, nine flying boats bombed the township, demolishing a house and two buildings. The Australian garrison, with no fighters and only a few antiaircraft guns for defense, could only listen helplessly from their slit trenches as the bombs exploded in the darkness. Virtually unopposed, the Japanese had struck the first blows in a battle that would rage back and forth for the next three years.

The Royal Australian Air Force had no land-based planes with the range to strike back at Rabaul, but they did have seaplanes. On January 24, two squadrons equipped with slow, unwieldy Catalina flying boats began a series of night raids against both Rabaul and Kavieng. The results, other than boosting morale for the worried public, were hardly worth the cost. The fifteen-hour missions fatigued the crews as well as the aircraft, several of which were lost in combat. As attrition mounted, it became clear that meaningful counterattacks against Rabaul could not be conducted until carrier-based aircraft or long-range bombers became available. Australia was in desperate need of relief, but it wasn't going to come from Mother England. The only viable lifeline for the shipment of troops, weapons, and airplanes was across the South Pacific to the United States.

As if the Japanese weren't threatening enough, nature also conspired against Australia. It was high summer in the southern hemisphere, hot and humid, with warm waters in the Coral Sea—an ideal gumbo for breeding tropical storms. One cyclone had already brushed the coast of Queensland in early February, and now a powerful new storm developed in the same area. Making landfall midway between Cairns and Townsville on February 16, the cyclone inundated whole cities as it churned south for two days before heading back out to sea. Monsoonal rains caused extreme flooding across a widespread area, resulting in several fatalities and heavy losses in buildings and livestock. At one location northwest of Brisbane, hundreds of miles inland, four thousand sheep drowned.[3]

Across the Coral Sea at Plaine des Gaiacs airfield, Dick Carmichael faced several concerns of his own. The laborious process of refueling his planes on the night of February 17 had filled the tanks to only about three-fourths of their capacity. To add to his worries, a cyclone was raging somewhere out to sea, he didn't entirely trust the Free French, and there was ample reason to believe the Japanese would attack the island soon. As the adjutant observed succinctly in the squadron diary, "New Caledonia was too vulnerable a place for too long a residence."[4]

Carmichael's biggest concern was the storm. Radio messages reported terrible conditions at Townsville, but no amplifying information was available to enable the squadron's weather expert, Jim Twaddell, to forecast the conditions over the Coral Sea with any confidence. The best he could do, despite a degree in meteorology from MIT, was guess. Carmichael therefore decided to proceed south to Brisbane, hoping to dodge the main body of the cyclone. In the meantime, Bill Lewis would lead the remaining B-17s from Fiji later that afternoon, stop overnight at Plaine des Gaiacs, and meet Carmichael's echelon in Townsville on February 19. The fluid plans seemed to change by the hour, requiring everyone to adapt as events unfolded.

Happy to put New Caledonia behind him, Carmichael led his six-plane echelon southwest across the Coral Sea to a point just offshore from Brisbane. There he split off, leaving the other five bombers to circle above Moreton Bay while he searched in the gloomy weather for an airfield. Forty-five minutes later he returned, having located Archerfield airdrome, a shared civilian and RAAF facility a few miles south of Brisbane. He guided the formation down through rain squalls and moderate turbulence to the airdrome, where all six B-17s landed safely on the wet grass. Carmichael had hoped to press on to Townsville immediately after refueling, but the continuing trip was postponed when weather reports from northern Queensland indicated hurricane-force winds. Scrounging for accommodations, the crews found an American encampment at Archerfield and slept fitfully in tents pitched directly on the wet ground.*

The newcomers' frustration with the weather only intensified. That evening, an Australian DC-3 airliner landed on the rain-slicked grass and skidded into two parked aircraft. The first was a Dutch cargo plane, wrecked beyond repair; the civilian plane also hit Lieutenant Chaffin's B-17, damaging the starboard wing, fuselage, and tail. Although repairable, the Fortress would be out of commission for more than a week. The entire echelon was disheartened by the accident. Except for the period that it was under the

---

* The 7th Bomb Group's ground echelon, diverted to Australia from the Philippines, had disembarked at Brisbane on December 23, 1941. About half the troops were detailed to Archerfield, where they assembled A-24 dive bombers and P-40 fighters that had been shipped aboard the convoy in crates (Young, *Death from Above*, 70–71).

control of the Hawaiian Air Force and received its camouflage paint scheme, Chaffin's crew had babied their B-17 since it was brand-new.

The next morning, wary of the soggy airfield, Carmichael decided not to send his remaining bombers aloft in their heavily loaded configuration. All of the baggage, supplies, and most of the personnel were trucked twenty miles west to Amberley airdrome, which had paved runways. The stripped-down bombers then made the short hop from Archerfield and were re-loaded for the flight to Townsville. No difficulty was encountered during the takeoff from Amberley, but the weather north of Brisbane was still so foul that all five aircraft turned back. It now seemed uncertain whether Carmichael's echelon would reach Townsville in time to participate in the mission to Rabaul.

As if things weren't bad enough, more unfortunate news greeted the echelon back at Amberley. Hours earlier, two powerful Japanese air strikes had pounded Darwin, the capital of the Northern Territory. The raids, the first foreign attack on the Australian mainland since its European settle-ment, caused severe damage and casualties: eight ships sunk, thirteen others beached or damaged, two dozen aircraft destroyed (including nine American P-40s shot down), nearly 250 people killed, and hundreds more wounded. As word of the destruction spread across Australia, near-panic gripped the country. Perhaps not by coincidence, a B-17 crewmember was diagnosed with "a nervous illness." Frank Bostrom's flight engineer, whose only taste of combat had occurred more than two months earlier on December 7, was deemed unfit for duty. Staff Sergeant Dan Ehrheart, a member of the 88th Squadron's ground echelon temporarily assigned to Amberley, took the crew chief's place.[5]

Leaving a flight crew behind to await repairs to Chaffin's damaged B-17, Carmichael led the rest of his echelon to Townsville on the morning of Feb-ruary 20. Their initial impressions of Garbutt Field, headquarters of the RAAF Northeastern Area Command Zone, were mixed. Except for a few combat-worthy light bombers, the aircraft parked at Garbutt were trainers or utility types. More disconcerting was the utter lack of defenses, with no modern fighters on hand or any antiaircraft guns.

But the Americans did find a surprise waiting for them. Three of the Fortresses from Bill Lewis's echelon were parked in the dispersal area. Having heard nothing from Carmichael the previous day, Lewis had proceeded to New Caledonia with his five aircraft of the 22nd Bomb Squadron, leaving Captain Swenson to complete the repairs to his contaminated fuel system.[6] The flight arrived at Plaine des Gaiacs airfield without incident, but the wobble pump refueling process was so time-consuming that only three planes got enough gas to reach Australia by the end of the day.[7]

No stranger to bad weather, Lewis decided to fly directly to Townsville despite the tropical cyclone. Taking off from New Caledonia at 2:30 P.M., he led lieutenants Harry Spieth and Jack Roberts across the Coral Sea. By cruising just above the storm-tossed waves, the B-17s avoided the worst of the storm conditions and safely reached Garbutt Field a half hour after sunset. Their arrival caught the RAAF unprepared—no accommodations were available—so the crews spent the night in a vacant garage.

The other two B-17s from Lewis's echelon, piloted by Dubby DuBose and Fred Eaton, arrived at Townsville on the morning of February 20. According to the happy details preserved in the diary of John Steinbinder, the fliers had been entertained in style during their overnight stay on New Caledonia:

> I am writing this after my trip into town with the French schoolmaster. We had a lovely meal (4 course) and I had some of the finest vermouth wine I ever drank. After eating we went around to the various houses and visited some old people who have lived there all their natural lives. Saw some coffee bushes with the beans right on them. Sure enjoyed it all. On the way home, some of the boys who were quite drunk took out pistols and shot up the place a little.[8]

Arriving piecemeal (Swenson finally reached Garbutt Field on the afternoon of February 20), the eleven Flying Fortresses represented the biggest display of aerial strength yet seen at Townsville. The B-17s looked especially large alongside the assortment of mostly obsolete RAAF aircraft, which included several biplanes with open cockpits. "They didn't have much there at all," observed assistant crew chief Earl Williams. "Our arrival was an eye-opener for the Australians."[9]

The city of Townsville, a small but busy tropical port of about 20,000 residents, featured a scenic rock outcropping called Castle Hill that over-looked the harbor, adjacent to the Great Barrier Reef. But there was no time for the Americans to explore. The planned mission to Rabaul was still on and would have to commence before midnight if the bombers were to arrive over the target on schedule. Sweating like stevedores, the crews unloaded supplies, tools, spare parts, and personal baggage they had hauled all the way from Hawaii. By the time that was done, only a few hours remained to effect minor repairs, fill the gas tanks, fuse the bombs, and ready the guns for action.

While the crews worked on the B-17s, Carmichael paid a visit to the senior RAAF officer at Townsville, Group Commander William H. Garing. Known widely as "Bull," the stocky thirty-one-year-old Aussie had earned a Distinguished Flying Cross two years earlier during the Battle of the Atlantic. And he lived up to his nickname. Carmichael considered him "rough and tough," a compliment coming from a Texan. "The Australians were very hospitable . . . fine people," Carmichael observed. "They are a whole lot like Texans as a matter of fact. I felt a real empathy and simpatico for them, so we got along just fine."[10]

After the meeting, Carmichael briefed his crews for the pending mission. Targets were ranked by priority: aircraft carriers, transports, cruisers, and planes on the ground. In coordination with the planned air strike by Task Force 11, the B-17s were to arrive over Simpson Harbor at 6:40 A.M. local time, just after dawn. A high-resolution reconnaissance photograph, taken less than a week earlier by an RAAF Hudson out of Port Moresby, showed merchant ships and big Kawanishi flying boats scattered among the various anchorages. The enlargement also provided details of the township, docks, and the main Japanese fighter strip, Lakunai airdrome, all nestled within the rim of a giant caldera.[11]

With only a few obsolete charts available, the navigators spent hours figuring out the various headings they would use during the outbound leg to the target, then to their refueling stop at Port Moresby, and finally back to Townsville. Much of the first leg, spanning 1,100 miles to Rabaul, would be flown in complete darkness. No alternate landing sites were available in case of emergency. Crews forced down during the mission would face either shark-infested waters or inhospitable jungle.

Tensions increased as the evening wore on. More than a few men began to suffer from stomach ailments, brought on by the stresses of their transpacific journey and the irregular diet of the past week. The result was a common affliction dubbed "Montezuma's Revenge" by the Marine Corps, though the army simply called it the "GIs," a pun on the identical acronyms for "government issue" and "gastrointestinal." Regardless of the nickname, squadron members sweated out their ailments with periodic visits to what the Aussies called "the loo."

Not all of the American fliers experienced symptoms of physical distress, but there wasn't a man among them who failed to grasp the urgency of the pending mission. For more than two months they had received nothing but bad news about Japan's successful offensives and the Allies' grievous losses, capped almost cruelly by the bombing of Darwin the previous day. Tonight, at long last, it was their turn. Shaking off the fatigue of their island-hopping odyssey, Carmichael and his men would finally have a chance to strike back at the hated enemy.

But then a new message arrived, and all the keyed-up emotions deflated like an overbaked soufflé. "After all the labor we had done," wrote Walt Johnson, "the navy gave orders, about 8 P.M, that the venture would not be made. They gave no reason."

THE REASON, IN a nutshell, was Japanese efficiency. Soon after the American carrier raids that had caused embarrassment among the Japanese high command on February 1, Imperial General Headquarters learned that another U.S. Navy task force was heading into the South Pacific. The Japanese went on high alert, broadcasting the known details across the region they referred to as the Southeast Area. Even the lowest ranks were informed. A cook in the 55th Division field hospital at Rabaul entered stunningly accurate details about the task force in his diary on February 7: "Enemy aircraft carrier with 50 aircraft advancing on New Britain."[12] The only carrier force moving in that direction was Vice Admiral Brown's Task Force 11, which had just headed into the South Pacific after Brown received updated orders from Nimitz at Pearl Harbor.

That a low-ranking noncombatant was so well informed can be attributed to Japan's fundamental culture of community. All military units held daily formations, where important messages and motivational speeches were presented to the troops. But the information obtained by the Japanese also raises a critical question: How did the enemy discover Task Force 11's objective so quickly? The answer lies in the high-tech (for its day) intelligence game. A network of listening posts, consisting of radio antenna installations on the mandated islands and powerful receivers aboard ships at sea, effectively intercepted message traffic across the Pacific. The Japanese could hardly miss the bursts of radio dispatches between Washington, Pearl Harbor, Melbourne, and the *Lexington* as the naval commanders discussed the forthcoming raid on Rabaul. Imperial General Headquarters subsequently issued its warnings soon after Task Force 11 crossed the equator, and the high volume of message traffic continued until at least February 16. That afternoon, Brown's ships left the waters near Fiji and headed for the Bismarck Archipelago.[13]

Three days later, a Japanese outpost near Truk notified the edgy commanders at Rabaul that enemy destroyers had been sighted. Although this was later determined to be a false alarm, the warning prompted Rear Admiral Goto, commander of the 24th Air Flotilla, to order a dedicated reconnaissance mission. Early the next day, three H6K flying boats took off from Simpson Harbor to hunt for the American task force.

The crews of the Yokohama Air Group were highly trained. Before midday on February 20, two flying boats made visual contact with Task Force 11. Both of the four-engine aircraft, detected by the *Lexington*'s new CXAM radar, were shot down by F4F Wildcats on combat air patrol, but not before the Japanese reported the position of the task force. The jig was up for Brown, who correctly surmised that he had lost the element of surprise. After reluctantly canceling the planned strike, he continued steaming toward Rabaul. This elicited a strong response from Admiral Goto, who sent all available land-attack aircraft—seventeen Mitsubishi G4M1 medium bombers of the 4th Air Group—to annihilate the task force. But the tables were turned. Only two of the lightly constructed bombers, derogatorily nicknamed "Type 1 lighters" by their own crews, survived the ensuing air-sea battle. The *Lexington*'s Wildcats and the antiaircraft gunners of Task Force 11 accounted for fifteen of the bombers, including five officially credited to Lieutenant Edward H. "Butch" O'Hare of Fighting Squadron 3. His heroism resulted in the first Medal of Honor awarded to a pilot in World War II, and the busy international airport outside Chicago was later renamed in his honor.[14]

On the evening of February 20, Brown turned away from Rabaul, leading his ships to safer waters. But his powerful task force was neither retreating nor intending to exit the Southwest Pacific. In less than three weeks, when the Japanese commenced the first phase of their campaign to dominate New Guinea, Brown's warships and Carmichael's B-17s would find another opportunity to engage the enemy in a joint operation.

THE CANCELLATION OF the strike on Rabaul put the Southern Bomber Command in a quandary. Technically still under the operational control of the navy, the squadron's closest reporting authority was Vice Admiral Leary, headquartered 1,300 miles away in Melbourne. To further complicate matters, Townsville was within range of the enemy's long-range flying boats at Rabaul, and marginally within the combat radius of the land-based 4th Air Group's medium bombers. Furthermore, in light of the recent strikes on Darwin, the Allied commanders were concerned that Japanese aircraft carriers might sail into the Coral Sea and attack Townsville. Given the lack of antiaircraft weapons and fighters at Garbutt airdrome, the B-17s would be sitting ducks. The logical solution was to place the Fortresses under the control of the RAAF, at least temporarily, and disperse them inland to avoid enemy raids.

Well before dawn on the morning of February 21, Dick Carmichael boarded an RAAF Hudson to investigate potential dispersal sites. A new, top-priority airdrome at Charters Towers, about seventy miles southwest of Townsville, was nearly complete but still under construction. Continuing inland, Carmichael landed on a desolate-looking airstrip outside Cloncurry, deep in the outback more than four hundred miles west of Townsville. It was fiercely hot and barren, a place of rust-colored rocks and stunted gum trees. The nearby town, with its wooden buildings, dusty streets, and platform sidewalks, resembled a frontier settlement in the Old West. Although it seemed like a throwback to another century, the town would serve its purpose. By radio, Carmichael sent word to his crews: bring the B-17s to Cloncurry.

The move was not well received. "And now," complained Walt Johnson, "we seem to be on the retreat." Garbutt Field, despite first impressions, had exceeded the expectations of the officers and enlisted men alike. The former, quartered in open-air wooden barracks with a summer camp atmosphere, enjoyed the hospitality of the RAAF Officers Club. Even the enlisted men, housed temporarily in an encampment of pyramidal tents, "did not complain too much" about the overall conditions at the base.[15] Thinking they might not return to Townsville, the crews reluctantly packed their belongings and loaded up the bombers. While taxiing for takeoff, Jack Roberts swung his Fortress too wide, causing the tailwheel to drop off the runway. The wheel immediately sank into thick, clinging mud from the recent cyclone, and the B-17 refused to budge.

Carefully avoiding the mired bomber, the remaining Fortresses completed the two-hour flight across the desert, but the crews found little worth praising in Cloncurry. Walt Johnson characterized it as "a hot, dry place of a million flies per cubic feet of air."[16] John Steinbinder, raised on a dairy farm in Ohio, had never seen such hordes of flies. "Cloncurry sure is a hell hole," he wrote. "Flies fly into your mouth, up your nostrils, into your eyes & ears. Oh! They sure are hell. It's terrifically hot here: 40° Centigrade or 105 Fahrenheit."[17]

Too disgruntled to walk the two miles from the airfield in the stupefying heat, the crews hired trucks to transport them over the winding, unpaved roads to Cloncurry. "Here the 10 crews practically took over the town," wrote navigator Jack Carlson, reasoning that it was "probably more excitement than this little town has had in its history."[18]

The American flyboys had but two options for entertainment: find some elbow room in one of Cloncurry's small pubs, or watch an outdated Hollywood film in what passed for a movie theater. Patrons sat on canvas chairs in a structure with no roof, just "four walls with a ceiling of sky."[19] Whether they quaffed Australian beer (one label, brewed in Cairns, had an alcohol content of 17 percent) or watched old movies under the stars, the newcomers grudgingly exchanged the comforts of Townsville for the relative safety of the outback. "We figured we'd come to stay," Johnson wrote that night, "and we figured Cloncurry didn't offer much the Japs would be interested in."[20]

But the morning of February 22 brought a renewed sense of purpose. The threat of an enemy carrier raid on Townsville had diminished, and aggressive commanders like Dick Carmichael and Bull Garing found it unthinkable to keep the most potent bomber force in Australia on the ground. The time was ripe for another attempt on Rabaul. Verbal orders were issued to fly the bombers back to Townsville, where they would be prepped for a raid on enemy shipping at dawn on February 23. Only nine aircraft flew back to Garbutt Field, however. A mechanical issue, described simply as "engine trouble," compelled Ted Faulkner and his crew to remain behind.

Unfortunately for Carmichael and his fliers, Faulkner's mechanical problem was merely the first in a litany of difficulties that would plague the squadron throughout its first combat mission.

EIGHT

THE FIRST RAID
ON RABAUL

TWO days after Vice Admiral Brown canceled the carrier strike on Rabaul, the Southern Bomber Command was prepared to try again. This time, the B-17s would operate independently.

The postponement had yielded an unexpected bonus. Group Commander Garing, fully aware that the newly arrived Americans had no experience with the unforgiving environment of New Guinea and the surrounding area, had arranged for two RAAF Catalina pilots to assist with navigation and identification of targets. During the pre-mission briefing on the afternoon of February 22, the American crews were introduced to Wing Commander Julius A. "Dick" Cohen, commanding officer of No. 11 Squadron at Port Moresby, and Pilot Officer Norman V. Robertson, who had spent more than a year in New Guinea with No. 20 Squadron.[1]

The allocation of two highly experienced pilots was a strong indication of the RAAF's faith in the B-17. Dick Cohen in particular was an asset the Australians could ill afford to lose. Although just twenty-five years old, he had already seen extensive combat. Posted to the United Kingdom at the beginning of the war, he had earned a Distinguished Flying Cross for a daring rescue mission to Morocco. More recently, after returning to Australia, he had led his Catalina squadron on several harrowing night raids against Rabaul. Although bone-weary from two years of continuous operations, he willingly volunteered to help the Yanks hit Rabaul. He knew the risks better than any of them, yet remained modest about his temporary appointment to the squadron. "I was there for comfort," he later stated. "Carmichael was a very competent pilot and he had a competent navigator. I didn't do anything significant, except that it probably gave them comfort to know they had on board an experienced pilot familiar with the area."[2]

While the pilots, bombardiers, and navigators briefed the mission, the remainder of the crews sweated in the summer heat to ready their Fortresses. It took hours to service nine heavy bombers. Each aircraft, with one auxiliary fuel tank installed, was filled with 2,400 gallons of high-octane gasoline; the lubricant tanks held 147 gallons of engine oil; nineteen oxygen cylinders had to be checked and filled; the machine guns were cleaned and loaded (each plane carried about four thousand rounds of .50 caliber and 610 rounds of .30 caliber ammunition); and the bomb loads were updated. Working under the belly of several B-17s, crewmen manually offloaded two six-hundred-pound bombs and replaced them with four three-hundred-pounders, giving each of the selected aircraft a total of six general-purpose bombs.[3]

With no dedicated ground support available, the crewmembers performed all the work themselves. The veteran crew chiefs, who could practically service a B-17 in their sleep, guided and cajoled their underlings. Experienced and worldly, some had joined the army before the younger crewmembers were even born. Carmichael's crew chief, Master Sergeant Wallace A. Carter, knew the horrors of "evil yellow smoke twisting slowly across the ground" from gas attacks in World War I.[4] Many of the hard-boiled sergeants, like forty-one-year-old Leroy Pouncey, were heavy smokers. Oblivious to the cigarettes constantly dangling from their lips, they orchestrated the myriad chores necessary to prepare a twenty-ton bomber for combat.

At the far end of the field, Jack Roberts and his crew continued to extricate their B-17 from the mud. Gradually, almost predictably, the effort got out of control. Attempts to haul the plane out of the quagmire damaged the tail wheel, making the job of clearing the bomber from the runway far more difficult. "Without equipment that was a huge task," Walt Johnson noted in the squadron diary, "for no weight could safely be placed on the tailwheel.

It was such a big job that it was after dark before he had it completed—and in completing it the fuselage was damaged—the ship made absolutely unfly-able."[5] With a third bomber now out of commission (Faulkner's plane was still at Cloncurry, Chaffin's at Archerfield), enthusiasm among the remaining crews began to wane.

Those who had managed to grab a short nap were awakened at 10:00 P.M. to gear up for the mission. With no standardization in flight clothing or equipment, individual crewmembers wore whatever they possessed. Earl Williams, the tail gunner on Swenson's crew, donned an odd assortment of clothing. "I wore work coveralls over the summer uniform the Australians gave us," he recalled. "When we left the States, we were supplied with wool-lined flying gear and boots, but all that gear burned up when we crash-landed at Hickam Field. So I had to layer my clothing. At 27,000 feet it got quite chilly, and the heat in the airplane didn't do a hell of a lot of good."[6]

After eating a light meal, the crews assembled for final instructions. The formation would consist of three elements, each with three B-17s flying in echelon to the right. Carmichael would have the overall lead, with Bill Lewis and Frank Bostrom leading the second and third elements, respectively. Pilots were reminded to carefully monitor their fuel consumption during the 1,600-mile mission. The profile called for them to fly slightly beyond Rabaul, then make a left turn to set up their bomb run on a southerly heading. After dropping their payloads, the formation would accelerate toward Port Moresby, requiring only a slight heading change. In the event of bad weather over Rabaul, a newly occupied enemy airfield at Gasmata, on the south coast of New Britain, was designated as the alternate target.[7]

When the briefing was complete, the crews and their Australian advisors—Cohen with Carmichael, Robertson with Lewis—headed out to the B-17s. Night had fully settled. With a general blackout in effect and the first-quarter moon not due to rise for several hours, a cloak of blackness swallowed the airfield. Finding their way to the bombers by flashlight, crews climbed aboard and stowed their loose equipment while the pilots initiated the familiar start-up routine, shattering the night with the roar of more than thirty radial engines.

But within moments, the mission hit yet another snag. The first two engines on Dubby DuBose's bomber started normally, but number three refused to run. Repeated attempts proved useless. Although a B-17 could fly comfortably on three engines—and even take off with one dead engine under certain conditions—four good powerplants were absolutely necessary to get a combat-loaded Fortress into the air. For DuBose and his crew, the mission ended before it began. The problem was later traced to water contamination of the fuel system, but the diagnosis did nothing to salve the crew's frustration.

DuBose's mechanical woes were followed by a grim comedy of miscues and setbacks. As the remaining eight bombers began pulling out of the dispersal area in the darkness, Deacon Rawls misjudged his separation from Frank Bostrom's B-17, nicknamed *San Antonio Rose*.* Rawls ran his left wingtip into the spinning propeller of Bostrom's right outboard engine, and everything came to a standstill while the crews assessed the damage. The torn-up wingtip of Rawls's bomber could be replaced, but for the time being the B-17 was grounded. And although the *Rose* appeared unharmed, there was a high probability of internal damage to the engine, the propeller shaft, or both. Two more bombers were therefore scrubbed from the mission, resulting in a clean sweep of Bostrom's entire three-plane element.[8]

Delayed by the collision, the six remaining bombers took off well after midnight. The pilots had been instructed to form up over Magnetic Island, five miles off the coast, but none of them had performed a nighttime rendezvous in months. After fumbling around for several minutes they got themselves sorted out, and Carmichael led the formation toward New Britain.[9] Flying on his wing were Swede Swenson and Harry Brandon, followed by Bill Lewis, Fred Eaton, and Harry Spieth at the rear of the echelon formation.

While the pilots stayed busy maintaining position and the navigators worked their endless calculations, there was little for the other crewmen

---

* One of the few B-17s in the squadron to be named by its crew, *San Antonio Rose* may have been inspired by the song of the same name, first released by Bob Wills and His Texas Playboys in 1938 and made even more popular two years later by Bing Crosby. There is no evidence that the name was ever painted on the aircraft (serial number 41-2416).

to do except wait. The trip to the target would take more than five hours, with nothing but three miles of blackness separating the bombers from the shark-infested ocean.

THUS FAR ALMOST nothing had gone according to plan. Only half the original squadron had lifted off from Townsville, and before they had gone a hundred miles the trend of bad luck continued. Perhaps naively, the American bombers had set off across the warm waters of the Coral Sea at the worst possible time. Seasonal water temperatures, wind patterns, and other meteorological factors combined to form a phenomenon known as an intertropical convergence zone, a semipermanent disturbance that typically drifted over the Solomon Sea east of New Guinea. But on this night, fueled by the cyclone that had swamped Queensland the previous week, the system swirled ominously over the Coral Sea. Too wide to circumvent, with towering thunderheads that rose far above the service ceiling of the B-17s, the storm offered no alternatives. If the bombers were to reach Rabaul, they would have to plow straight through.

Already familiar with the weather system, Wing Commander Cohen had bashed his way through the intertropical front several times in slow, awkward Catalina flying boats. The B-17s were faster, heavier, and more aerodynamic, but puny nonetheless compared to the power of the storm. And this one was unusually severe, a seething malevolence alive with pounding rain, extreme turbulence, and frequent flashes of blue-white lightning. During momentary lapses between the superheated bolts of electricity, the night seemed to Cohen "as black as the inside of a cow."[10]

Carmichael flew as smoothly as he could, trying to feel his way around the densest thunderheads, but at times it was almost impossible to control the bomber. Every few moments the ship would slam into an updraft and soar hundreds of feet, as though riding an invisible express elevator, only to hit a downdraft and plunge thousands of feet in a matter of seconds. With both hands on the controls and his feet on the rudder pedals, Carmichael could literally feel the reactions of the heavy bomber, perhaps even anticipate the turbulence by a fraction of a second. The rest of his crew, wide-eyed in the flickering strobes of lightning, could only hang on for dear life. In the midsection of his B-17, the armed bombs and auxiliary fuel tank jostled against their shackles. Out on the wings, the engines strained mightily, propellers churning through a torrent of rain.

The conditions were even worse for the wingmen. Every updraft and downdraft was magnified as the pilots struggled to maintain formation, constantly jockeying the throttles, using precious fuel. Swede Swenson held onto Carmichael's wing by flying dangerously close. He had the skills to pull it off, but his crowding alarmed the other pilots. In the tail gun position of Swenson's B-17, Earl Williams couldn't hear anything except pounding rain and cracks of thunder due to a broken intercom connection. Seventy-five years later, he vividly remembered the wild carnival ride inside that terrible storm.

> We were all over the sky. Swenson was following too close, which pissed off other members of the formation. The only things we could see were the position lights on the wingtips. It was such a fierce storm. I remember seeing that little red light on another plane, and it was bouncing all over the goddamn sky. I'm sure the other crews were concerned that we'd have a midair collision. And without communications, I really felt like an outcast. I couldn't talk to anybody and had no idea what was happening up front.[11]

For ten or fifteen minutes, an eternity under such conditions, the formation stayed together. Ultimately, however, Bill Lewis realized that he could not maintain his second-element position safely without risking a collision, especially due to Swenson's wild maneuvering. Lewis eased away, and within moments the position lights on Carmichael's three-plane element disappeared into the blackness.

For another three hours, the separate formations experienced severe turbulence. The storm's breadth was enormous, measuring an estimated six hundred miles across. When the weather finally cleared, Lewis's navigator, Jack Carlson, determined they were over the Solomon Sea near the Deboyne

Islands, seven hundred miles north of Townsville. The improvement in the weather brought tremendous relief, but when Bill Lewis glanced around, he discovered that Harry Spieth's bomber was nowhere in sight.

At some point during those dramatic hours, Spieth had been tossed out of the formation. A highly respected pilot, he was not at fault. As the "tail-end Charlie" at the rear of Lewis's echelon, it was virtually impossible for him to hang on indefinitely. "Lost the formation," he simply remarked in his diary, adding dryly that the flight had been "broken up by weather."[12] Having not yet reached the point of no return, and realizing that a solo attack on Rabaul would be senseless, he turned around for the long flight back to Townsville.

DESPITE HAVING ONLY two bombers in his echelon (Fred Eaton had doggedly clung to his wing throughout the storm), Bill Lewis decided to proceed toward the target. Jack Carlson, grateful for clear skies and smooth air, obtained a celestial fix and informed Lewis that they had been blown fifteen miles off course to the west. After making the necessary corrections, Lewis began a gradual climb, unaware that he was miles *ahead* of Carmichael's formation. Somehow, while pushing through the storm, Carmichael had either flown considerably slower or was blown farther off course. Consequently, his three bombers were now more than thirty minutes behind Lewis and Eaton.

Carlson took another fix just as the first glimmer of daylight appeared on the horizon. Lewis's two B-17s were now 180 miles from the target, and ten minutes ahead of schedule. The plan called for them to attack Rabaul between 6:40 and 6:50 A.M. on February 23, so Lewis tweaked the throttles back to reduce speed. Proof that Carlson knew his business came approximately an hour later as the two Fortresses, their bold rudder stripes aglow in the early morning sunlight, arrived over Simpson Harbor at precisely 6:47.

To the crews' dismay, the target area was obscured by cumulus clouds and thick steam, the latter rising from a squat, ugly volcano named Tavurvur on the tip of aptly named Crater Peninsula. One of two volcanoes that had erupted violently in 1937, devastating much of Rabaul and killing several hundred people, Tavurvur had become active again in late 1941, spewing clouds of noxious steam. Tons of ash belched skyward and drifted over the surrounding terrain, including the Japanese fighter strip, Lakunai airdrome, less than half a mile west of the volcano's gaping crater.

Lewis, rationalizing that if he could not see the target, the Japanese could not see him, decided to loiter over Rabaul at 20,000 feet and wait for a break in the cloud cover.

ACCUSTOMED TO PERIODIC night raids by RAAF Catalinas, the Japanese at Rabaul had never been subjected to a daylight attack. Not that they had much reason to worry. During the past four weeks, the army and navy garrisons had established an efficient early warning network and formidable antiaircraft defenses, including a daunting array of gun batteries that encircled the caldera. The first large-caliber antiaircraft guns had been installed by an elite naval infantry unit, the Maizaru 2nd Special Naval Landing Force, which set up four 80mm Type 99 guns to protect the township and wharf areas. Soon thereafter, the army began emplacing numerous 75mm Type 88 "high-angle" guns. Similar in appearance to the legendary German 88mm "Flak" dual-purpose guns, the Japanese weapons were not as lethal, but there were plenty of them. Dozens of Type 88s and Type 99s, which fired explosive shells to an altitude of almost 30,000 feet, were installed at strategic points around the caldera. Allied bombers attempting to attack the military complex would be within range of the guns virtually the entire time they remained over the target area.

In addition to the ring of antiaircraft weapons, Rabaul now boasted a highly trained fighter contingent. Within hours of the invasion, Japanese construction battalions had begun repairing Lakunai airdrome, situated along the northern shoreline of Simpson Harbor. The field, known as "Rabaul East" by the Japanese, had been dynamited by Australian engineers but was quickly repaired. The first fighters, offloaded from an aircraft transporter on January 31, were not the speedy, agile Zeros that had stunned defenders across the Pacific, but outdated Type 96 carrier fighters, known by the Allies as Mitsubishi A5M4s (and later given the recognition name "Claude"). The little fighters, with non-retractable landing gear, open cockpits, and teardrop wheel pants, looked remarkably like the Boeing P-26 Peashooters flown by Dick Carmichael and his fellow pursuit pilots in the mid-1930s.

Aware of the fighters' presence at Rabaul, the RAAF had erroneously advised the American crews that the enemy planes were ineffective above 23,000 feet. "They told us it was no big deal," remembered George Munroe, the navigator on Eaton's crew. "The Japanese didn't have anything that could get up to our altitude."[13]

But the information was neither accurate nor up-to-date. A new composite unit, the 4th Air Group, had been formed at Truk, naval headquarters of the Southeastern Area, on February 10. With an allowance of twenty-seven land-attack bombers and twenty-seven fighters, the unit transferred almost immediately to Rabaul and joined Rear Admiral Goto's 24th Air Flotilla. The fighter component took possession of the obsolescent Type 96 fighters on hand, and six new Zero fighters were delivered on February 17 by the aircraft carrier *Shoho*.

Three days later, the 24th Air Flotilla had suffered a crushing defeat when Goto attempted to destroy the USS *Lexington* task force. Japanese newspapers, strictly controlled by the Johokyoku (Information Bureau), spun the battle as a major Japanese victory, falsely boasting that the "Navy Wild Eagles" had blown up the *Lexington* with suicide dives. Admiral Goto and his men knew the real score, of course, and were eager for a shot at redemption.[14]

AT APPROXIMATELY 7:10 A.M., Lewis found an opening in the cloud layer above Rabaul. With Eaton trailing, he leveled his wings and initiated a bomb run over Simpson Harbor. Electric motors whirred as the Fortresses' heavy bomb-bay doors swung open, sending a blast of cold air into the bombers' midsection. The B-17s had not been fired upon yet by enemy gunners or fighters, perhaps due to the overcast, but it was only a matter of time.

The air-raid alarm had sounded at Lakunai at 7:05. A lookout in the control tower banged rapidly on a metal container—a warning system as ancient as the samurai warlords—sending the standby pilots to their fighters. Two of the older Type 96s were already airborne, having taken off at 6:50

on routine patrol, and over the next several minutes the six newly delivered Zeros scrambled aloft, kicking up volcanic ash as they roared down the unpaved runway.

Lewis's bombardier, Lieutenant Theodore I. Pascoe, selected a large merchant ship tied up alongside the main wharf and toggled his four six-hundred-pound bombs in sequence. The crew thereby earned the distinction of being the first Americans to attack Rabaul, though they did not linger to observe the results. "We made for Port Moresby," Lewis wrote in his official report, "and noticed that Capt. Eaton was staying behind as he had not dropped his bombs yet. As we left the target we noticed five Zero fighters about 6,000 feet below us, but we obtained cloud cover before interception could take place."[15]

Safely in the clouds, Lewis made a beeline for New Guinea. Behind him, the streak of bad luck that had been dogging the squadron continued. "We went over the target in trail," recalled Fred Eaton, "and when we tried to trigger our bombs, they hung up. There was an electrical problem and the bombs did not drop."[16]

Hunched over the bombsight in Eaton's B-17, Corporal Richard E. Oliver, a twenty-one-year-old from Weleetka, Oklahoma, was perplexed. The intervalometer, a black box that was supposed to release the bombs individually at preset intervals, had apparently failed. "I'd been told to drop the 500-pound [sic] bombs to start with, then the 300-pounders," he later stated. "I set the bomb switch to drop them that way, but when we went over the target, it didn't drop *anything*."[17]

Thus far Eaton's flying career had been exciting, even glamorous. He loved flying the big Fortress and was a professional pilot, but until this moment it had all been something of a lark. Now, four miles above a heavily defended enemy base and five hundred miles from the nearest friendly airfield, he faced a critical decision. And he had to make it quickly. Follow Lewis into the clouds, or circle around for another bomb run?

There were no guidelines to consult, no right or wrong answers. Eaton was among the youngest members of the crew, but as the pilot in command,

the decision was his alone.* He made it without hesitation. "We weren't going to come all that way," he acknowledged years later, "and not drop our
bombs."[18]

Eaton keyed the interphone. "We're going back over the target."[19]

Initiating a slow, deliberate turn, he circled around to set up another
bomb run. The elongated orbit, remembered George Munroe, took "at least
fifteen or twenty minutes," an excruciatingly long time to remain over the
enemy stronghold.[20] But Eaton took the risk in order to give Dick Oliver
enough time to pick out a target and dial the necessary settings into the
Norden bombsight. Almost miraculously, the Japanese did not open fire on
Eaton during the lengthy orbit, probably because Carmichael's three-ship
echelon had approached Rabaul a few minutes after Eaton's first bomb run.
Thus it was Carmichael, not Eaton, who attracted the attention of the enemy
fighters.

THE DELAY CAUSED by the intertropical front had been irksome enough
for Carmichael; now he grappled with additional problems as his trio of
B-17s approached Rabaul. Fuel consumption had become a major concern,
he didn't know the whereabouts of Lewis's flight, and the target area was
obscured by clouds. More important, a gaggle of Japanese fighters headed
toward his formation. Pale gray in color, with black engine cowlings and
bold red *hinomaru* roundels (ubiquitously called "meatballs") on their
wings and fuselages, the Zeros and older A5M4s had easily reached the
bombers' altitude. The limitations conveyed by the RAAF had obviously
been wrong.

The interception over Rabaul marked the first combat for the Zero
fighter in the New Guinea theater and the first engagement for the fighter
component of the 4th Air Group. The two A5M4s involved were lightly

---

* At the time, Eaton was twenty-four. Staff Sergeant William E. Schwartz (bottom turret
operator and waist gunner) had just turned thirty, Technical Sergeant John V. Hall (tail
gunner) was twenty-nine, and three other members of the crew were at least twenty-five
years old.

armed, with a pair of 7.7mm machine guns that fired through the propeller arc. Although the guns boasted a high rate of fire and decent range, their rifle-caliber bullets had little real hitting power. The Zero fighters had the same lightweight machine-gun arrangement, supplemented by two wing-mounted 20mm automatic cannons. The latter's explosive shells were capable of causing severe damage, but their low muzzle velocity and rainbow-like trajectory required pilots to get in close before shooting.

The Japanese pilots were well-trained (many had seen combat in China), though none had faced the new B-17Es. Upon seeing the tail guns and power-driven turrets, some were initially hesitant. "We were attacked by fighters," Carmichael recalled, "but . . . it wasn't a real severe attack."[21]

Observing from the copilot's seat next to Carmichael, Dick Cohen was almost giddy. The sturdiness and speed of the B-17, flying at an altitude far higher than his stodgy Catalinas could reach, dazzled him. "I felt very comfortable," he later added. "I had taken the armor plate out of our Catalinas to increase the bomb load, and thought it was great fun being on an armored seat."[22]

Although the initial attacks by the enemy fighters were tentative, the overcast conditions and dwindling fuel convinced Carmichael to forego any attempt to bomb Rabaul. Swinging the formation around, he headed toward the alternate target, Gasmata airdrome, two hundred miles to the southwest. Swenson dumped his bombs over Simpson Harbor, perhaps to ensure that he had enough gas to reach Port Moresby, but Carmichael and Brandon retained their payloads.[23]

As Carmichael's echelon withdrew from Rabaul, the Japanese became more aggressive, slashing at the B-17s from the sides and rear. The Zeros, extremely light by design, weighed about the same as a modern-day SUV, yet they were powered by a 950-horsepower engine. The Fortress gunners had never seen such a combination of power and agility. Their only aerial gunnery training had occurred months or even years earlier, and consisted of shooting at target sleeves towed behind a "tug" airplane flown by a nervous crew. Trailing along on a parallel course at approximately the same speed as the gunnery plane, the target sleeves were relatively easy to hit. Not only was such training unrealistic, some of the crewmembers in Carmichael's echelon had never fired a round from a B-17. Earl Williams's qualification for becoming a tail gunner had consisted of four hours in a classroom at Hickam Field, where he learned to break down and reassemble a .50 caliber weapon—but he'd never actually fired one.[24] Thus, possessing almost no real-world experience, the gunners relied on instinct. But even if they shot wildly, or failed to properly lead the agile fighters that flicked past their gunsights, it felt good to hammer away at the hated Japanese. At long last, the enemy that had caused so much mayhem in recent months was just a few hundred yards away.

Inside the confines of the aluminum fuselages, the deep clatter of the fifties was earsplitting. Vibration from the cyclical rate shook the bombers from nose to tail, especially when the flight engineers, doubling as top turret gunners, opened fire. Streams of brass shell casings rattled to the floor and the acrid smell of spent gunpowder drifted through the bombers' freezing interiors. But the gunners, flushed with adrenaline, were oblivious to the biting cold as they tried to hit the darting fighters. Up forward, bombardiers and navigators poked .30 caliber machine guns through ball sockets in the nose and side windows, though they rarely got a decent shot at the enemy planes streaking past.

In the rear compartment, one of the side gunners typically alternated between the left and right waist guns while the other operated the remote belly turret. They didn't like the awkward system, which required the belly gunner to lie prone, facing aft, on a padded slab of armor plate while aiming the guns through a periscopic system. The sighting mirrors reversed the image, so the gunners had to mentally compensate for left and right as they aimed the guns. Many became airsick.

In the center of Carmichael's formation, Swede Swenson's B-17 received early attention from the Japanese. Lieutenant Roy Reid, the copilot, sarcastically recalled the information given during the briefing. "Here were these poor little airplanes that [supposedly] couldn't get to high altitudes," he later said, "zooming all around us with the greatest of ease. And shooting the hell out of us!"[25]

Numerous bullets punctured the B-17. One slug entered the nose compartment and ricocheted off the navigator's heavy aperiodic compass, then hit the bombardier's right knee, lodging under the skin just below the kneecap. Ignoring the wound, Lieutenant Edwin F. Cihak continued to man his .30 caliber gun.[26]

Flying in the third position of the formation, Harry Brandon suddenly had his hands full when enemy gunfire hit the right inboard engine, which burst into flames. It was the duty of his copilot, Lieutenant Robert L. Ramsay Jr., to close the cowl flaps and set the selector valve for the fire-extinguishing system, while Brandon closed the fuel shut-off valve and determined whether he needed to activate the selected extinguisher. But even as the pilots scrambled to deal with the emergency, the right outboard engine suddenly quit. The likeliest explanation is that Brandon inadvertently closed the wrong fuel shut-off valve—easy enough to do because the small toggle switches were grouped closely together—but he kept his composure. After hastily trimming the plane to fly on two engines, he extinguished the fire in number three and then restarted number four.

With an engine shut down, its prop feathered, Brandon's B-17 had become a "cripple." Flying at reduced speed, trailing a thin stream of smoke as hot oil leaked from the nacelle of the number three engine, the bomber was easy prey. Carmichael and Swenson therefore slowed to keep pace. Tightening up the formation, they forced the Japanese to contend with the combined strength of more than thirty machine guns.

Now that he had a damaged wingman to shepherd, Carmichael decided to head straight for Port Moresby rather than attack the alternate target, Gasmata airdrome. Enemy fighters continued to nip at the B-17s as they flew southwest toward New Guinea, but Dick Cohen remained impressed with the formation's inherent strength. "We were a formidable platform for the Japanese to approach," he said. "The gunners were very good, the aircraft maintained good defensive formation, and I think the Japanese had a pretty rough time."[27]

For all the ammunition expended by the Zero fighters and older Type 96s, only two bullets pierced the fuselage of Carmichael's bomber.

Amazingly, both found a man. The tail gunner, Private First Class Billie B. Sutton, was shot in the left foot. He remained in his confined position, firing approximately two hundred rounds from the twin .50s before they jammed. Even then he remained on his saddle-shaped seat and called out the position of enemy fighters.[28]

In the waist section, Staff Sergeant Ralph E. Mauser tried to fend off Zeros with the remote belly turret. During one enemy attack, a bullet knocked out the sighting mechanism and ricocheted into his left knee. Despite the painful wound, Mauser continued to operate the turret without the gunsight for the duration of the action, which lasted some forty minutes.

Surprisingly, one of the little A5M4s chased the B-17s well beyond the target area. Earl Williams, his communications still kaput, had a ringside view from the tail of Swenson's bomber.

> This one Japanese fighter, an older airplane with fixed landing gear, was persistent. As soon as we dropped our bombs over the harbor we started to climb from 24,000 feet to 27,000 or 28,000 feet—as high as we could get. This little old fighter was still hanging on, still climbing, but he couldn't quite get to us. He'd dip down, then zoom up, and I tried to tell the crew that we still had a fighter on our tail. I picked up empty shell casings and threw them forward, trying to get the side gunners' attention. Stay alert!
>
> But he finally gave up. If he'd gotten closer I would have sprayed the whole area with fifty-caliber, and he might have run into them. He finally gave up though.[29]

After reaching the south coast of New Britain, the formation started across the Solomon Sea. At about 9 A.M., the crews caught their first glimpse of New Guinea, its dark shape both menacing and breathtaking in the morning sun. Just a few miles from the coast, the steep slopes of the Owen Stanley Mountains rose to 12,000 feet, even higher in some places. The densely forested ridges appeared to be covered with dark green carpet, tinted black where clouds cast deep shadows, and the convoluted slopes plunged almost vertically into deep, narrow gorges where rivers and streams resembled twisted strands of silver.

Pointing out landmarks, Dick Cohen guided the formation toward a pass through the mountains near the village of Kokoda.* The B-17s then dropped down the opposite side of the range, arriving at Seven Mile airdrome just twenty minutes later. "We made it to Port Moresby," a relieved Earl Williams recalled, "but with virtually nothing left in the fuel tanks."[30] Harry Brandon, his right inboard engine shut down, had cut the margin too closely. Although he landed safely, all three of his remaining engines quit, out of gas, before he could clear the runway.

Bone-weary, almost debilitated after the combat rush of adrenaline subsided, Carmichael's three crews were met by Bill Lewis, who had arrived ahead of them by ten or fifteen minutes. As it turned out, his was the only other Fortress to reach Port Moresby. Harry Spieth was last seen during the storm, and Fred Eaton had turned back for a second bomb run over Rabaul. The crews reasoned correctly that Spieth had flown directly back to Townsville, but it soon became apparent that Eaton was down somewhere. He had to be, if for no other reason than his fuel was exhausted.

Overall, the raid had been a failure. Of the four B-17s that reached Port Moresby, only Lewis had dropped his bombs on a specific target, with unobserved results. Numerous aspects of the mission had gone awry, but Carmichael and Brandon focused their personal frustrations on Swenson, whose airmanship while flying through the storm drew their wrath. "When we got to Port Moresby, the other pilots in the formation chewed out Captain Swenson for being so damned stupid," remembered Williams. "The possibility for a mid-air collision under those circumstances was great. As I recall, it was a very angry blast at Swenson."[31]

Leaving Harry Brandon behind to await repairs to his shot-up engine, Carmichael, Lewis, and Swenson refueled their B-17s and flew back to Townsville, logging another four hours in the air. Disappointed and

---

* Several months hence, one of the most notorious battles of the war in New Guinea would be fought there, not only at the pass but down both sides of the mountain range on the incredibly rugged Kokoda Trail.

thoroughly exhausted, they reached Garbutt Field at approximately 3 P.M. and turned the wounded men over to Doc Luke, the flight surgeon. By the time they debriefed the mission and arranged repairs for the bombers with combat damage, the crews had invested eighteen stressful hours in the effort. One piece of news cheered them: Harry Spieth had indeed returned to Townsville after becoming separated in the storm.

Eaton's status was still not confirmed. A radio message from the RAAF communications center at Port Moresby indicated that he and his crew were down somewhere in New Guinea, but nothing else about their fate was known. As the afternoon wore on, the men at Townsville waited anxiously for additional word about their missing squadron mates.

NINE

GUNFIGHT OVER
NEW BRITAIN

Three and a half miles above Simpson Harbor, Fred Eaton leveled the wings of his B-17E and commenced his second bomb run. Early morning sunlight glinted from the clear panels of Plexiglas that formed the bomber's bullet-shaped nose, scrubbed clean a few hours earlier by the pelting rain of an intense storm. Corporal Dick Oliver, seated in the nose directly behind the Plexiglas, had a dizzying view of the harbor below—almost as though perched on the edge of a cliff. Bending repeatedly to peer through the eyepiece of his Norden bombsight, he waited for his opportunity to justify the risk the whole crew had taken in making a second attempt. The bombs had hung up in their racks the first time, presumably due to an electrical malfunction, so he had turned off the black box that controlled their release. On this run, he would drop them manually. "Just looking for a ship to bomb, that's all we were looking for," he would later recollect. "I picked one out, couldn't tell whether it was a freighter or a troopship, but dropped 'em all at once—salvoed the whole bunch."[1]

By this time the B-17 had been over Rabaul for some forty-five minutes without drawing the enemy's attention, but the solitude ended abruptly. "All of a sudden all hell broke loose," remembered George Munroe, who shared the nose compartment with Oliver. The phrase has become a cliché, used by innumerable veterans to describe their first experience in combat, but from the perspective of Eaton's crew it was a valid observation. "I mean, the anti-aircraft fire was all around us," Munroe explained. "It was noisy. You *know* when antiaircraft is in your area."[2]

Minutes earlier, the Japanese high-angle gun batteries had fired on Carmichael's three-plane formation. Corporal John Lillback, a twenty-five-year-old radio operator/gunner aboard Harry Brandon's B-17, likened the shell bursts to "blooming fields of dark daffodils spreading out beneath your feet."[3] And now the big guns shifted their aim to Eaton's lone Fortress. Angry black whorls dotted the sky as the artillery shells exploded in rapid succession. Down below, the enemy gunners set time-delay fuses based on the estimated altitude of the B-17, adjusting the delay by rotating a series of rings at the base of each projectile. At the maximum setting of thirty seconds, the shells would reach almost 30,000 feet before exploding, while projectiles fused for less than thirty seconds detonated at correspondingly lower altitudes. Accuracy was a matter of guesswork, but with multiple batteries in action, augmented by the antiaircraft weapons mounted on ships in the harbor, the Japanese were capable of firing well over a hundred large-caliber shells per minute.

Climbing to 23,000 feet, Eaton set the engine and propeller controls for maximum speed, later noting that the Fortress reached an estimated ground-speed of 310 miles per hour. And there, high above Rabaul, the squadron's run of bad luck began to change for the better.

It all came down to timing. A well-trained Japanese gun crew could fire a round every three to four seconds, a rate of fire obtained through rigorous training and synchronized teamwork that relied on agility, physical strength, and efficiency. Each artillery shell, weighing almost twenty pounds, was manhandled into the breech of the gun. A tug on the lanyard fired the weapon, the breech kicked back, ejecting the empty shell casing, and the gun team's loader replaced it with a fresh round. *Boom!* Every three to four seconds. *Boom!* For as long as there were targets overhead. *Boom!* Or the stockpile of ready ammunition held out.

Despite the scores of shells streaking skyward, the probability of a direct hit on a single airplane moving at three hundred miles per hour was infinitesimally small. For that reason, antiaircraft artillery shells were designed to inflict damage with shrapnel that spread outward in every direction when the projectile exploded. A burst within ten yards of an aircraft could be lethal, especially if pieces of shrapnel knocked out an engine or incapacitated the flight crew. But there were no absolutes. Fate and luck shared equal footing with mathematical probabilities. And on this remarkable Monday morning, Fred Eaton and his crew beat the odds—not just once, but twice.

As the B-17 sped from the target area, a large-caliber shell struck the port wing near the trailing edge. The projectile did not explode; it simply punched straight through the wing, slightly damaging the split flap on the underside while leaving a neat round hole in the upper skin. The shell may have been a dud, but in all likelihood it was fused for a higher altitude. If so, the B-17 was out of harm's way by the time the shell exploded.

The truly astonishing aspect of the direct hit was the point of impact. The shell struck directly behind the number one engine, sixteen feet aft of the firewall. Given the bomber's speed, those sixteen feet represented just three-hundredths of a second. In other words, had the shell been fired that tiny fraction of a second earlier, it would have struck the engine. Even if it didn't explode, the kinetic energy of the heavy shell would have caused severe damage to the engine and almost certainly resulted in an uncontrollable fire. Three-hundredths of a second spelled the difference between life and death.

Almost incomprehensibly, another large-caliber shell scored a second direct hit, again on the underside of the port wing. And again, the shell miraculously *did not explode*. Its impact, which occurred between the number two engine and the wing root, blew apart the access panel for the main fuel tank inside the wing. The shell then struck the outer metal skin of the tank itself (the fuel was contained within an inner bladder made of self-sealing rubber), causing a deep upward distortion and breaking all of the mounting straps. The tank, with a capacity of 212 gallons, was mostly empty and did not rupture. More important, the projectile dropped out of the hole rather than lodging inside the wing. Had it exploded there when its timer elapsed, a catastrophic fire and structural damage to the wing root would have caused the entire wing to collapse, sending the B-17 and her crew into a fatal plunge.

The olive-drab Fortress, less than three months old, was suddenly leading a charmed life. Two antiaircraft shells had scored direct hits and failed to explode, whereas dozens of other rounds burst too far away to cause damage. The greatest danger, however, was yet to come.

As the B-17 flew out of range of the antiaircraft guns, fighter pilots of the 4th Air Group swept in to attack. Of the eight fighters that launched from Lakunai airdrome that morning, most of the Zeros and at least one aging A5M4 had scurried to the southwest, hounding Dick Carmichael's formation. Their combat reports were all in agreement regarding one vital detail: an engine on the right wing of the outer B-17 emitted black smoke, an unequivocal reference to Harry Brandon's damaged bomber.[4] The remaining Japanese, meanwhile, focused their attention on Eaton's aircraft. It was a fundamental element of their doctrine to single out an aircraft and overwhelm it, much like wolves chasing down a beast. "We could see the Zero fighters coming up at us," Eaton recalled. "Within five minutes after we left the target, they were shooting at us."[5]

From the limited information contained in the 4th Air Group's *kodochosho* (combat log), the precise number of fighters that intercepted Eaton's B-17 is unknown. Eaton believed there were as many as eleven, though no more than three or four were actually in pursuit. Darting in and out for repeated gunnery runs, the Japanese gave the impression of having several times their actual number.[6]

Most of the attacks came from the rear quarter. At approximately 7:45 the tail gunner, Technical Sergeant John V. Hall, fired several bursts at a Zero from an estimated range of two hundred to three hundred yards and claimed its destruction. Despite what he saw, or thought he saw, no losses occurred among the eight fighters airborne that morning, let alone any significant damage to individual aircraft. Hall, like many gunners, was confident that his shooting was inherently accurate. But complex laws of physics and geometry came into play when firing at fast-moving targets from an equally fast-moving airplane; and even with tracer rounds to help the gunner

The running gun battle covered well over two hundred miles. One Zero after another would slice in, gun muzzles flickering rapidly above the black engine cowling. A heartbeat later, the bullets would rattle against the bomber's thin aluminum skin. Distorted by the impact or smashed into fragments, the 7.7mm rounds zipped and buzzed ominously through the fuselage but had lost some of their energy. The 20mm shells, by comparison, exploded with a ferocious bang as they tore jagged holes in the B-17's skin. One concentrated burst of gunfire struck the upper fuselage near the radio compartment, leaving a large gash from a cannon shell surrounded by at least twenty bullet holes. Two bullets entered the radio compartment and impacted near the release handle for one of the inflatable life rafts, stored in the dorsal bulge behind the upper turret.[12]

The shooting was never constant, but ebbed and flowed with a cacophony of percussion. The rapid chattering of the Zeros' machine guns and the deep jackhammer of the B-17's fifties were occasionally punctuated by the steady *pom-pom-pom* of the 20mm cannons. Crawford, a heavyset twenty-nine-year-old from a small town south of Pittsburgh, somehow survived a burst that raked the left side of the fuselage. A 20mm shell struck just below the gunner's aperture near the trailing edge, another impacted three feet aft of the window, and several bullets pierced the bomber's skin within a five-foot radius. Crawford, evidently manning the gun on the opposite side of the Fortress, received nary a scratch.

Not surprisingly, the billboard-sized vertical stabilizer absorbed multiple hits, most of which passed straight through unless they struck the underlying framework. One 20mm shell penetrated the rudder and exploded above J. V. Hall's head, leaving him unscathed. Another bullet or fragment narrowly missed his left shoulder.

Petty Officer Yoshida personally expended some nine hundred rounds at Eaton's B-17. His combat report did not differentiate between machine-gun rounds and cannon shells, but he must have scored dozens of hits. Incredibly, however, his efforts caused no serious damage. The ruggedly built B-17 flew on as though impervious to gunfire, its crew unharmed. After some forty-five minutes of combat with no visible results, Yoshida disengaged. The other Japanese fighters turned back toward Rabaul, but Yoshida remained behind the bomber at a prudent distance, content to shadow the B-17 as it started across the Solomon Sea toward New Guinea. Technical Sergeant Clarence A. LeMieux, the flight engineer and upper turret gunner, would later describe observing a single Zero that remained "about a half mile up," out of range of his guns. "I would shoot up every now and then," he recalled, "but I couldn't hit him. Anyway it kept him away from us and we got away from there."[13]

Almost. As the Fortress flew over the Solomon Sea, Fred Eaton dropped the empty auxiliary fuel tank, then commenced a shallow descent.[14] Petty Officer Yoshida, perhaps sensing an indication of trouble, decided to continue following the B-17. It was a logical choice, for there was indeed a serious problem aboard the American bomber.

It was about to run out of fuel.

TEN

GREEN HELL

Prior to that 1,600-mile mission against Rabaul, no one had tested the limits of a B-17E's range under actual combat conditions. Crews had conducted shakedown flights in the States with their brand-new bombers, staying aloft for as long as fourteen hours to calculate fuel consumption, and the 2,400-mile flight to Hawaii had further demonstrated the aircraft's range with two auxiliary fuel tanks, but none of those situations compared to the conditions encountered in battle. Bill Lewis, who flew the entire mission to Rabaul without a combat engagement, landed at Port Moresby with only a hundred gallons of gas remaining, nowhere near an adequate reserve. Dick Carmichael's three bombers, which had fought interceptors for approximately forty minutes, landed on fumes, and Harry Brandon actually ran out of gas on the runway. From that comparison alone, it was evident that fuel consumption under combat conditions was considerably higher than anticipated.

And then there was Fred Eaton. Having spent fifteen to twenty extra minutes circling Rabaul for a second bomb run, followed by a dash at "war emergency" throttle settings for forty-five minutes while battling enemy fighters, he had used far more gasoline than the other B-17s. No matter how many times he and navigator George Munroe did the math, they were going to run out of fuel well short of Port Moresby.

The scenario nobody wanted to contemplate was an open-water ditching. Even assuming that a water landing went smoothly and everyone evacuated the plane before it sank, the outlook for survival was dubious. Nine men would be crowded into two inflatable rafts, at the mercy of the winds and currents, with no guarantee of rescue. In fact, they stood a roughly equal chance of being captured by the Japanese.

In an effort to stretch the bomber's range, Eaton throttled back and commenced a shallow descent. But the decision came with at least one negative consequence: the bomber would no longer stand a chance of crossing the Owen Stanley Mountains. The absolute worst scenario would be to run out of fuel partway across the massive range, for there simply was no place to land an airplane among the precipitous, thickly forested slopes. That left the crew with two options: ditch at sea, hopefully just off the New Guinea coast, or bail out over the lowlands near the shoreline. Either way, the towering mountains had become an impassable barrier between the B-17 and Port Moresby.

Steadily losing altitude, the shot-up Fortress finally approached the northern coast of New Guinea. From a distance the mountains dominated the horizon, but as the aircraft drew closer, another option suddenly presented itself. Fred Eaton saw it first. "My gas was running short," he recalled, "when I saw what looked like a perfect natural landing field along the shore—beautiful green grass and very few trees."[1]

"It looked like a wheat field," confirmed the flight engineer, Clarence LeMieux, "just as flat as could be."[2]

Certainly none of the crew expected to find such a large, open space on the notoriously rugged island. And ironically, the eleventh-hour discovery would not have happened if the bomber had been on course. The prescribed route from Rabaul to Port Moresby would have brought the aircraft to the northern coast of New Guinea near the village of Buna, the site of an Australian government station directly in line with the convenient pass through the mountains at Kokoda. Eaton's B-17, however, made landfall sixty miles south of Buna in a largely uninhabited area.

It was just as well. Buna had an emergency landing strip, cleared from the jungle years before the war. Small, neglected, and difficult to spot from seaward, it was never intended for an aircraft the size of a B-17. Eaton might have been tempted to land on the short, overgrown strip if the bomber had been on course, with a high probability of a disastrous crackup. But the Fates were still smiling. By virtue of being miles off course, the aircraft made landfall near the broad, grass-covered clearing spotted by Eaton, which stretched for miles in every direction.

In the vernacular of aviation, an emergency landing on terrain other than a prepared field or runway is considered a "crash landing." Fred Eaton had never attempted one, but the aircraft's flight manual provided the essential guidelines. The main difference from a conventional landing was that the wheels would not be lowered, as there was no way to determine whether the landing site was strewn with rocks, logs, and other hidden obstacles, or if the ground was even firm enough to support the weight of such a heavy aircraft. A certain amount of damage was inevitable in a wheels-up landing, particularly to the propellers and engines, but the B-17's broad, low-mounted wing would spread the impact and provide a smooth surface for the airplane to slide on.

The flight manual recommended a flaps-down approach to reduce the landing speed, but Eaton chose to deviate by leaving the flaps up. His approach would be faster, yet flatter, theoretically resulting in a less abrupt touchdown. While he and copilot Hotfoot Harlow prepared for the landing attempt, the rest of the crew gathered in the radio compartment, which offered the most protection. The doors were braced open to prevent their jamming shut on impact, and the men took assigned crash positions, sitting on the floor with their backs to the forward bulkhead.

Eaton made one pass over the landing area, then banked around 180 degrees to land into the wind. His hands would be full controlling the aircraft, so Harlow stood by to cut all fuel and ignition switches as soon as the plane was fully down, thus minimizing the possibility of a fire. As he lined up his approach, Eaton pressed the alarm button to warn the crew. He gave it four loud rings: brace for impact.

Pointing back toward the sea, propellers barely freewheeling, the Fortress settled lower over the broad expanse of grass. A few seconds before touchdown, Eaton eased back on the control column, raising the nose slightly so that the tail would touch first. Not only would this help him feel the airplane's position, but the tail would act as a brake.

The technique, and the flat approach chosen by Eaton, worked to perfection. When the tail first made contact, he held it there, letting it drag for approximately two hundred feet. The tail lifted momentarily, barely parting the grass for another 150 feet, then the natural laws of physics took over and the bomber settled in. A few hundred feet more and she was fully down, her whirling propellers flinging long stalks of grass high into the air. And that was the puzzling part: neither of the pilots had ever seen such grass, so tall it extended above the wings and engine nacelles. Nothing felt firm beneath the plane as it slid along. Then the right wingtip tilted down and the bomber slewed around hard, decelerating quickly, the propeller blades bending awkwardly as Eaton and Harlow shut down the engines.[3]

After ten hours of roaring motors and the thunder of combat, the sudden silence was bewildering. For a few moments, the only audible sound was the metallic ticking of the engines as they cooled. Congratulating themselves on the smooth landing, Eaton and Harlow rapidly secured the cockpit and unstrapped from their seats. Back in the radio compartment, the rest of the crew took stock of their situation. Only one man, George Munroe, had been injured. Tumbling off balance at the front of the compartment, he smacked into the flimsy wooden door with his head, resulting in a minor but bloody scalp wound. One of the crew opened a parachute, cut out a strip of silk, and made a turban-like bandage for the hard-headed navigator.[4]

With the exception of bent propellers and some dents in her underbelly, the Fortress was remarkably undamaged. But when the crew moved aft and swung open the door at the rear of the gunners' compartment, they made a shocking discovery: water began flowing into the fuselage.

PETTY OFFICER MOTOTSUNA Yoshida's persistence paid off. Exactly how far the Japanese pilot followed the B-17 during its gradual descent is unknown, but the lightly built Zero possessed extraordinary range—enough that Yoshida could follow the bomber all the way to New Guinea and still return to Rabaul. Upon landing at Lakunai airdrome, he claimed one B-17 shot down.

Japanese-born historian Osamu Tagaya, author of several books on the planes and airmen of the Imperial Japanese Navy in World War II, considers Yoshida's claim reasonable, based on the pilot's observations. "Yoshida must have inflicted most of the damage," Tagaya commented in his analysis of the combat. "He must also have pursued long enough to either observe Eaton's crash, or saw the bomber lose altitude significantly and judged it to have gone down, hence his claim."[5]

Yoshida's victory claim was officially accepted, though the Japanese of course had no knowledge that Eaton had crash-landed due to lack of fuel, not combat damage. Regardless, it was the future ace's first aerial victory. Over the next several months, Yoshida would be credited with downing eleven more Allied aircraft and share partial credit for three additional victories with fellow pilots. His record, however, would come to an abrupt end with his death in combat later that year, on the first day of the epic battle for Guadalcanal.[6]

IF THE FATES had been kind in guiding Eaton to one of the few places on New Guinea where he could execute a safe crash landing, the crew's good fortune came at a steep price. The B-17 had literally splashed down in no-man's-land. With her nose pointed southeast, she sat amidst thousands of acres of swampland, seven miles from the coast and approximately a hundred miles from Port Moresby. What had appeared to be a field of wheat was in fact saw-edged kunai grass growing as much as twelve feet high. Beneath the deceptive thickets of grass, the Agaiambo Swamp swirled with water stained the color of tea by decomposed organic matter.

This part of New Guinea was terra incognita, known only to the exotic wildlife that populated the wetlands. The nearest human inhabitants, dark-skinned Melanesian natives, lived along the fringes of the swamp in small, primitive villages. Superstitious, fiercely tribal, scarcely removed from their Stone Age roots, many had never interacted with a white man. In some villages only the *luluai*, or headman, had direct contact with outsiders, limited to occasional visits from government officials or missionaries. Because the lowlands were so sparsely populated and difficult to navigate, territorial representatives and padres rarely showed their faces; instead, the villagers went to them.

Conversely, the American airmen knew almost nothing about the indigenous people. But what they had heard was disturbing. Cannibalism and headhunting had been widely practiced among the hundreds of disparate tribes populating New Guinea, and in some remote locations those practices still existed. The swampland, meanwhile, held many other threats. A few of the worst were summarized by Osmar White, an Australian newspaper correspondent who traveled the island for more than thirty years: "In the New Guinea lowlands men may rot with malaria, typhus, leprosy, hookworm, yaws, and skin diseases of unimaginable variety. There, night and day, the moisture in the air condenses on every surface and trickles back to earth."[7]

Eaton and his crew felt the stifling humidity as soon as they removed the Plexiglas hatch at the top of the radio compartment. The heat pressed down on them like a physical weight while they climbed atop the fuselage to get their bearings. To the west, the dark massif of the Owen Stanley range dominated the horizon, with foothills beginning six or seven miles from the crash site. A small clump of trees appeared to the southwest, but in every other direction the terrain was flat and featureless, nothing but kunai grass as far as the men could see. A gnawing sense of worry set in as they realized the gravity of their situation. Marooned in the wilds, surrounded by an alien and highly unsettling landscape, the fliers were poorly equipped for survival in such an environment. Comprehension left them numb.

Reactions were manifested differently. Dick Oliver felt jinxed, having experienced his second crash in exactly a month. This time no one had been seriously hurt, but on January 23 he had sustained broken ribs when his four-engine LB-30 bomber slammed into the sea during a ditching attempt off Canton Island. Two crewmen had died and several others, including Oliver, were hospitalized.[8]

Twenty-year-old Howard Sorenson, the youngest member of the crew, had the most bizarre reaction of all. Soon after the plane came to a stop he lost his vision. The blindness seemed inexplicable—he had suffered no physical injuries—but he had to be assisted out of the airplane. Although his eyesight returned shortly thereafter, the loss of vision scared him badly.[9]

Any doubts or fears Fred Eaton may have felt remained private. He was still the captain of his ship, and the lives of his crew depended on his leadership and resourcefulness. One of the first requirements was to send out a distress call before the rising swamp water reached the bomber's 24-volt batteries, located inside the leading edge of both wings. Sergeant J. V. Hall, the radio operator, had been busy manning the tail guns for much of the flight, leaving Sorenson in charge of communications, but with the latter suffering from shock, it was up to Hall to relay the crew's status and location to Port Moresby. He managed to tap out the message, then repeated it once more before the batteries shorted out.

Unknown to the crew, the transmission had been encrypted with the wrong daily code. The message was received at Port Moresby and eventually deciphered, but some of the details were either garbled or misunderstood. The crew's location, for example, was reported as 220 miles from Port Moresby, more than double the actual distance. The Australian signals unit sent a reply, instructing the crew to stay with the aircraft and await an emergency supply drop by air, but due to the dead radio, the message was never received.[10]

With no word from Port Moresby, Eaton had to presume the worst. He and the crew, now on their own in that godforsaken land, spent several minutes discussing what to do. One major concern was the possibility of being discovered by the Japanese. If the enemy knew of their location, they might send planes to strafe or even bomb the aircraft. "We decided there was only one thing we could do," recalled Clarence LeMieux. "Get the hell out of there."[11]

The aluminum skin of the bomber was already hot to the touch under the intense glare of the late morning sun, and the sauna-like humidity sapped the crew's energy as they prepared to abandon the B-17. Dick Oliver, remembering his obligation to maintain the secrecy of the Norden bombsight, removed it from the nose compartment. "I had to do something with the bombsight," he recounted. "So I took it out on the end of the wing, pulled out my .45, and shot it a couple of times. It was classified top secret, and we were supposed to ensure that nobody else had access to it." Satisfied that the internal mechanism was destroyed, Oliver performed the coup de grâce by shoving the bombsight into the swamp.[12]

While some men searched the plane for food and water, others opened the storage compartments located on both sides of the upper fuselage. Each held an inflatable life raft. The one on the port side was useless, punctured by bullets or shrapnel, but the raft on the starboard side inflated normally with its CO_2 cartridge. After scavenging for supplies, the crew took inventory. Weapons were limited to a bolt-action rifle (used for guard duty), the crewmembers' .45 caliber pistols, some machetes, and a handful of smaller knives. The inflated raft contained emergency rations along with a few tins of water. Box lunches and snacks the crewmen carried with their personal gear, stowed on the floor of the airplane, had been ruined by swamp water. The emergency rations, too, proved inedible. Packed inside the upper fuselage for months, exposed to terrific heat while the plane was on the ground, then subjected to repeated freezing and thawing in flight, the contents had spoiled. The men had personal canteens, and someone grabbed the bomber's Thermos-type water jug, but the useful supplies amounted to a disturbingly meager assortment.

Before starting out, the crew agreed on a basic plan. "We spotted some trees in one direction, which looked like our most likely destination to reach dry ground," remembered Dick Oliver, "but it was the direction away from the ocean. We were afraid to head towards the ocean for fear of the water getting deeper."[13]

It was not a bad theory. The swamp was essentially a giant basin into which hundreds of inches of annual rainfall drained from the mountains and flowed sluggishly toward the sea. No one was eager to enter the dark water, but after stowing most of their supplies in the life raft, which they intended to tow behind them, the men jumped in. They immediately sank waist deep. The bottom, covered with fine silt, did not adversely affect their footing, but the thick vegetation tugged at their boots and pant legs. And the moment they reached out to push aside stalks of kunai grass, the airmen made a painful discovery: the edges of the stout blades were as sharp as knives.

Hacking with machetes, Eaton and his men slowly cut a trail to the southwest. Exhausted after making less than fifty yards, they concluded that the life raft was too bulky to be dragged through the dense grass. The rubber boat and many of the supplies thought to be essential were abandoned. Men took what they could carry, then pushed on.[14]

The heat and humidity continued to rise. Adding to the general discomfort, the swamp was home to an incredible variety of insects—huge spiders, billions of mosquitos, several types of scorpions—along with enormous populations of frogs, poisonous snakes, and even saltwater crocodiles that ranged up the rivers and estuaries. The tall grass offered one small benefit, providing filtered shade except when the sun was directly overhead, and the water was tepid enough to give periodic relief from the blistering sun. But if the crew had any chance of making progress they would have to continuously hack their way forward. To maintain a steady pace, they took turns wielding the machetes. For a while, beefy Russ Crawford even used the rifle to break the trail.

The crew's progress was excruciatingly slow, measured by the foot. At times, standing in water up to their armpits, the men swung their knives and bolos with little leverage. There was no horizon for guidance, just a wall of grass that towered above them, limiting their line of sight to no more than a few feet. No mention of a navigation device was recorded, but it's almost certain that someone used a hand-held compass to maintain a southwesterly course, otherwise they would have traveled in random circles.

Hour after hour the environment never changed, only the depth of the swamp as it alternated from waist-deep to neck-deep. Sweating, cursing, desperate for something to eat, the men inched forward, hands and forearms sliced and bloody from the abhorrent kunai grass. Temporary relief came late in the afternoon, when the sun finally settled behind the mountains, but dusk was short-lived. At that equatorial latitude, the sun set rapidly.

The men halted to rest, but with the onset of darkness new tortures began. Despite their exhaustion and hunger, they could not sit down because of the depth of the water. And hordes of mosquitos swarmed in after sunset, biting everything above the water, even biting through clothing.

The night also brought loud, unpleasant noises. Most of the insects and other wildlife had been dormant during the heat of the day, but after sunset a constant hum began, gradually building to a steady roar as the night came alive with the sounds of millions of insects, frogs, geckos, skinks, and countless other nocturnal creatures. Above it all, the piercing whine of mosquitos was maddening.

Someone hit on the idea of piling cut kunai grass into mounds high enough to support a man's weight, perhaps allowing everyone a chance to rest. They gave it a hearty try, only to find themselves spiraling further into weary frustration and despair. "The first night," recalled Fred Eaton, "we spent hours cutting and stacking grass, hoping to make a bed, but it all sank in the swamp. I almost cried with disappointment."[15]

But Eaton would not allow himself or his crew to wallow in self-pity. The solution was to keep moving, though everyone was already dead tired, their hands bloody and raw. Men removed their socks and pulled them on like mittens to alleviate some of the discomfort, and one of the crew had brought parachute silk that they wrapped around their heads to discourage the mosquitos. Nothing could be done about their hunger, but rain provided the opportunity to collect fresh water and refill canteens. So they pressed forward in the darkness, taking turns on point, grunting, chopping, swearing, inching forward until they could not lift their arms. Each man worked for as long as he could, then passed his machete off to someone else and moved to the back of the line. By this process, the crew continued slogging throughout the long night, their thoughts dulled by fatigue and the incessant roar of the swamp's busy creatures. Occasional heavy splashes could be heard—crocs, they assumed, which invariably caused a surge of adrenaline.

By dawn on February 24, the castaways were well into their second day without sleep. The roar of the nocturnal swamp ebbed away, replaced with oppressive heat as the sun began to beat down again. As the day progressed and the temperature soared, some men fared better than others. Paradoxically, the strongest and fittest man in the crew was among the first to fade.

Hotfoot Harlow, the twenty-five-year-old copilot, had won a national collegiate boxing title four years earlier. By all appearances he had bulked up even more compared to his 155-pound championship weight, but in the swamp his heavy frame became a liability. It took a greater expenditure of energy to move his muscular limbs than the average person used, and that muscle mass demanded a high calorie intake. Without food, the muscles that normally gave him such great strength began to break down. By the end of the second day, his stamina had declined dramatically. Another thing Harlow didn't have in abundance was hair. Fair skinned and prematurely balding, he all but wilted under the scorching sun.

Stopping only a few times to rest, the crew slashed and hacked at the detestable grass for the entire day. Finally, just before evening, they reached the stand of trees they had seen from the airplane. Having struggled through the swamp for thirty-six hours just to reach this point, they were heartbroken to discover that the trees stood in a foot and a half of water. No one had the strength or motivation to keep moving.

Their drinking water gone, the men could focus on little besides their own misery. Sunburned, blistered, covered with insect bites, their palms sliced to ribbons, legs and feet deeply puckered from constant immersion in the swamp, the entire crew was in bad shape. As darkness settled and the tumultuous sounds of the night began anew, they decided to remain where they were. They had to rest, if the swamp would let them.

That second night was even more excruciating than the first. But the crew's fatigue was also more acute. "We sat down in the eighteen inches of water and leaned up against trees and tried to sleep," recalled Dick Oliver. "The mosquitoes were absolutely terrible; the biggest, loudest things I've ever seen in my life. Swarms and swarms of mosquitoes that nearly drove you crazy. We didn't feel like we slept but I'm sure we must have dozed off during the night, and at least got a little rest sitting down."[16]

Fred Eaton evidently slept very little. Responsibility for the crew was a heavy burden. He believed they would have given up already were it not for the modest shade provided by the kunai grass. "As it was," he would later recall, "half the crew were out of their heads after the first two days. The spiders, scorpions, and mosquitos were terrible, and everywhere, day and night, we could hear crocodiles flopping about in the swamp. It was simply a living hell on earth."[17]

The third day in the swamp differed only slightly from the first two. Survival, the crew came to realize, would depend largely on their willpower. Give up, surrender to despair, and they would perish. The horrid swamp and its scavengers would consume all traces of them in a matter of weeks. Keep moving, continue looking for a way out, and they might get lucky. And so the stranded fliers stirred from their sodden encampment, pushed aside their hunger and thirst, ignored their sliced hands and swollen bites and utter fatigue, and began to explore the stand of trees.

The initial results, remembered Oliver, were encouraging. "In the morning we decided that we had better see what we could find through the trees. Going in different directions we found what looked like a definite river current where the water was clear of kunai grass, and it looked like we would be able to float down to the mouth of the river into the ocean."[18]

The river was surprisingly deep. Thirty-year-old Bill Schwartz, raised on a farm near Champaign, Illinois, confessed that he didn't know how to swim. The straightforward solution, Eaton decided, was to cut down several trees, build a raft, and float down the river. Working with lightweight tools, it took hours to chop through the hard, dense trunks and then lop off the branches. The plan was to tie the logs together with vines or perhaps shoe laces, but no one thought to test the flotation of the trees until several had already been felled. "Somebody rolled one of those trees off into the water and it immediately sank," Oliver lamented. "They were all waterlogged, which was quite a shock to us."[19]

The trees, ironwood or a similar variety too dense to float, defied the widely held myth that all types of wood are naturally buoyant. The fliers were devastated. Physically drained, they reached an emotional nadir as well. But they kept rolling logs into the river, and finally one floated, barely breaking the surface. Determined to give the river a try, the crew decided to use the log to support Schwartz and any others who couldn't swim. Several of the men took off their shoes, tied the laces together, and draped them over the log, reminding Schwartz to look after them. In spite of their fear of lurking crocodiles, the party set off downstream. Schwartz gripped the tree trunk, steered by Crawford, Harlow, and Sorenson. George Munroe clutched the gallon jug, now empty, which doubled as a flotation device. But the plan soon unraveled. Schwartz began to struggle, causing the log to roll. Others came to his aid and the danger soon passed, but the tied-together shoes had slipped off the log. They vanished underwater, condemning three men to go barefoot.

Shortly afterward, Crawford spotted a human skull along the bank of the river. Munroe remembered it somewhat differently, saying they "found a skull in the center of a circle of ashes." Either way, the grisly discovery gave credence to the rumors about headhunters and cannibals. Crawford wondered if it was a sign, a warning of "what they would look like soon."[20]

Bad omen or not, the odds once again were stacked against the wayward fliers. The river carried them only a short distance before disappearing into a tangle of swampland, with no discernible path to follow. "We had to abandon the log and go back and pick our way through with machetes, dragging ourselves along hand by hand where the water was over our heads," explained Oliver. "We continued on this way all of the third day and that night."[21]

No one had eaten or slept since the evening before the mission. Their soggy clothing was in tatters, already beginning to rot. Harlow, frequently delirious, no longer had shoes; neither did Crawford or Sorenson. The crew still had two .45s and the rifle, but the weapons had become too rusted to operate. Desperate for sleep, the men cut and piled stacks of grass again, and in their advanced state of exhaustion a few of them actually dozed off atop the makeshift beds. Within a few minutes, however, they would jerk awake, gasping for air, and find themselves underwater. After a few failed attempts, they resorted to standing in the swamp while leaning on the piles of cut grass for support.

Perhaps the worst part of the night was the discovery of leeches, picked up during their foray in the vanishing river. Dick Oliver never got over his repugnance of the blood-sucking worms: "They were absolutely terrible. We were all covered with leeches that were anywhere from one to two inches long and were black, slimy-looking things that were just driving us crazy. We tried to get them off as best we could by burning them off, slicing them off with machetes, just any way."[22]

For some, the leeches were the final straw. Their nourishment-starved brains literally began to misfire as the trifecta of prolonged hunger, acute fatigue, and physical discomfort triggered hallucinations. Men started to hear and see things that didn't exist. The overriding desire, recalled Oliver, was food.

> J. V. Hall, just ahead of me, turned to me and said, "Dick, let's go down to the mess hall and get some ice cold canned tomatoes."
>
> I said, "That sounds absolutely delicious."
>
> As thirsty and hungry as we were, I said, "Where's the mess hall?"
>
> He said, "Right back behind you there." I turned around and we could both see the lights of the mess hall, and the lights looked just exactly like the lights of any mess hall that we had ever seen. We both turned and probably would have gone down that path and died, but somebody behind us saw what we were doing and stopped us.[23]

Somehow, Eaton got the crew moving again on the morning of February 26, their fourth day in the swamp. The awful routine had not changed. Lightheaded and nauseous, still delirious, the bedraggled aviators hacked through the grass for several hours. Finally they began to notice changes in the landscape. More trees and shallow water indicated that they were at last approaching the fringes of the swamp. The improvements came just in time, for the crew was down to just two machetes. Oliver and Hall, on point, were slowly chopping through clumps of grass when they emerged onto dry ground.

For the first time in more than seventy-two hours, the crew was completely free of the swamp. The effects of their long-term immersion were unpleasant to look at: everyone's skin was chalky white and deeply puckered, open sores had developed where cuts and scratches from the kunai grass had become infected, and all of them limped to some degree. Crawford, Harlow, and Sorenson lagged behind the rest of the crew, their progress both slow and painful as they picked their way gingerly over the ground on bare feet.

The men wielding the machetes suddenly pulled up short. "J. V. Hall and I were cutting in the front of the group," stated Oliver, "when we thought we heard something in the distance that sounded like chopping. We were petrified."[24]

Discovering what appeared to be a footpath, the fliers crept toward the rhythmic sound until they reached a small clearing. On the far side of it, a dark-skinned native was chopping a fallen palm tree. The airmen crouched in place, watching him warily for a few minutes, until the native suddenly spotted them and fled into the jungle. Mindful of the things they had heard, particularly "that all the natives of New Guinea were headhunters and cannibals," the Americans moved cautiously into the clearing. Starving, knowing intuitively that they could not travel much farther without some form of help, they had to risk an encounter with the unknown tribe.[25]

Eventually the native stepped cautiously out of the jungle, accompanied by a second man. The bare-chested Papuans were as frightened of the disheveled white men as the Americans were of them. Each group sized the other up, then Eaton tried a few words in English. He and his men were hungry, he tried to explain, and tired. The natives stared back at the pale, strangely dressed men who had obviously just emerged from the swamp. But Eaton and his men, continuing to experiment with basic gestures of sign language, gradually conveyed the message that they needed help. Deciding that the unkempt strangers represented no threat, the Papuans indicated that the white men should follow them. "They led us to a river and then to their prehistoric village," remembered Eaton, "where there was a population of about thirty."[26]

Weak and defenseless, the fliers had no way of knowing whether the villagers intended to help them or eat them. But no matter what happened, it was a tremendous relief to be out of the swamp. Eaton believed they had traveled eight miles during those seemingly endless days, but in reality they had hacked and chopped less than two miles through the dense grass. Another day or two in that wasteland would have finished them. Ironically, the crew had not taken the shortest distance through the swamp—a heading of due west from the airplane would have accomplished that—but by chance or by grace, their decision to head southwest had brought them to the pair of woodchoppers.

Although the settlement was not as primitive as Eaton implied, that he labeled it "prehistoric" is understandable. Throughout their prewar history, the people of New Guinea had been divided by numerous barriers. Some were natural or geographical, principally the inhospitable mountains; others, such as tribal warfare and perpetual distrust, had further splintered the population. One conspicuous result was the lack of a unified language. In the Papuan territory alone, the population of approximately two million natives was divided into more than a thousand tribes, which were further subdivided by over five hundred "mutually unintelligible" languages. Simply put, a great percentage of the tribes could not verbally communicate with each other. Without a common language to enable the sharing of ideas and developments, their culture scarcely advanced beyond the Stone Age. The variegated tribes had existed in fractured, semi-migratory settings for thousands of years, isolated by their own dialects and the onerous geography of the land. Not until the late nineteenth century, when European commerce and Christian missionaries arrived—and inevitably tried to govern and educate the "savages"—were new developments in medicine, tools, and weapons introduced. Even then, by the time New Guinea became a battleground in 1942, many isolated tribes had rarely experienced outside influences.[27]

The riverside village where Eaton and his men were led, later identified as "Gumbire No. 1," consisted of no more than a dozen huts on stilts. Their construction was extraordinarily simple: a framework of felled trees lashed together with vines, with a thatched roof and walls made of grass. The villagers raised basic crops of taro, sweet potatoes, corn, and melons, but their principal food was sago, a starchy, carbohydrate-loaded staple extracted from the pith of sago palms. The villager first encountered near the swamp, in fact, had been chopping into a newly felled palm to gather raw pith.

Limping into the village that afternoon, the American fliers were met by totally immodest, mostly naked Papuans. Small children wore nothing.

Bare-breasted women wore only sarongs or grass skirts tied around their hips, while the men favored sarongs, simple loin cloths, or even g-strings. Their appearance seemed almost a caricature of the "Fuzzy Wuzzies" depicted in the pages of *National Geographic*, but the vivid sights and smells of the native village came as something of a shock. It was a world of rot and decay, made worse by an almost complete lack of sanitation. As the Americans had already discovered, cuts and scratches easily became infected. Ulcerated sores were common among the villagers, especially on their legs and feet. And like most societies, the Papuans had their vices. They loved to smoke—tobacco was highly coveted—and although the consumption of alcohol was rare, men and women alike got stoned by chewing betel nut. The intoxicating juice stained their teeth, gums, and lips a spectacular shade of red, and the ground where they sat was splattered with red spittle.

The arrival of nine strange men placed a considerable burden on the villagers, who were ill-prepared to care for so many. The crew was therefore guided a short distance downriver to a nearly identical village, "Gumbire No. 2," where the natives had food to share. "They fed us sago, corn, taro, watermelon, and bananas," noted Eaton, who sat together with his crew around a large firepit.[28] The first course, consisting of small ears of roasted corn, was devoured by the famished visitors while the natives stared at them in fascination. But the second dish, sago, challenged the Americans' manners as well as their taste buds. Dick Oliver, who received the first serving, puckered up from the bitter taste and tried to discourage the others from trying it. As he later put it, "everybody was too frightened of the natives" to risk offending them. And so nine half-starved fliers sat by the fire, licking the mash of cooked palm hearts from their fingers while pretending to enjoy it.[29]

In addition to sharing their food, the Papuans provided a hut for their pale, unusual-looking visitors. As was their custom, it was the best and biggest shack in the village, probably the residence of the *luluai*. Accessed by ladder, its elevated floor consisted of tree limbs and saplings woven together. A fire was built under the hut and carefully banked so that its smoke drifted up through the ventilated floor to ward off mosquitos. Although the accommodations were strange and primitive, Eaton and his men collapsed gratefully onto the hard, uneven floor. No one found it uncomfortable. Dick Oliver, thinking the wood "felt like a feather mattress," fell asleep immediately. Later that night, however, he awoke to a scene more surreal than he could have imagined.

I was lying on my back on the floor of this hut, and the firelight was coming up from the bottom and dancing around inside. I opened my eyes and looked up, and I was completely surrounded by natives that were squatting on their haunches all around me in a circle. I thought to myself, "They're getting ready to kill me, and maybe they've killed the others already."

But I laid there, and they didn't move and I didn't move. I finally got up enough nerve to get on my hands and knees and crawl through a small opening where two of them were sitting side-by-side. They made no attempt to bother me, so I kept going and looked around—and here every one of us was surrounded by a group of them just sitting and staring at us. They were just curious as to what a white man looked like.

I woke up some of the others to tell them I didn't know what was going on. They said that at least they could tell they weren't going to kill us and eat us, so we all went back to sleep.[30]

In the morning, convinced that their best hope for rescue depended on reaching a government station or plantation with a two-way radio, Eaton communicated that he wanted to travel downriver to the coast. Even with basic sign language, it was difficult to determine what, if anything, the natives understood. Conversely, the Americans were sure they frequently misunderstood the natives. Eventually, however, both parties forged a mutual understanding. Led to the riverbank, the airmen were helped aboard three dugout canoes, each fashioned from a huge log hollowed out with fire and simple hand tools.

With three crewmen aboard each canoe, villagers steered the party down the swift-flowing river. It soon became obvious that no one had traveled the waterway in a long time—the canoes had to be beached frequently so the natives could chop away fallen trees—and it took all day for the little flotilla to work its way downstream. Although the coast was only eight miles from the village, the many bends and loops in the convoluted river added half again as much to the journey. At last, arriving at the river delta late that afternoon, Eaton and his men were turned over to the inhabitants of another village, called Songada.

Here the crew's fortune took another turn for the better. Not long after they were dropped off, a motor launch pulled up to the village. Out stepped a tall, thirty-six-year-old Australian who introduced himself as Allan Champion, the assistant resident magistrate. Two days earlier, at his Buna headquarters, a radio message from Port Moresby had informed him that an American bomber was missing somewhere in his district. Although he was not aware of any aircraft in distress, Champion decided to search personally for the crew. The predicament was deciding where to look first. There were only two options for traveling, by foot or by boat, and his district was roughly the size of New Jersey.

Borrowing a launch belonging to a nearby Anglican mission, Champion and a Papuan assistant started southward along the coast. They headed first for Oro Bay, stopping at various villages along the way to inquire about the missing crew. Their initial searches came up empty, so they decided to continue for another twenty miles down the coast to the Musa River. After motoring upriver for several miles, as far as their boat could push against the strong current, they turned around. Then, while heading back downstream, Champion spotted another village at the edge of the delta. Determined to investigate, he stumbled upon the wayward Americans purely by luck.[31]

Fred Eaton had never seen "a white man who looked so good as this fine Australian." George Munroe went one better, saying Champion "looked like a savior." As if that weren't impressive enough, Champion also produced dinner: a large kingfish that he and his assistant had caught during their trip. Cooked over a fire, it provided one of the most delicious seafood meals any of them could remember.[32]

Champion informed the Americans that he would take them to Buna in the morning. They would be traveling in the opposite direction of Port Moresby, he told them, but when they reached his headquarters he would radio for assistance—and help them recuperate while they waited to be picked up. Early the next morning, the last day of February, they started out from Songada. It would be a long, slow trip. "The launch was too small to accommodate all the crew," Champion wrote in his memoirs, "so I borrowed a large canoe from the villagers and towed them all to Buna."[33]

What none of them realized was that the Japanese planned to invade the north coast of New Guinea within a matter of days. Champion and his American vagabonds would soon find themselves uncomfortably close to the enemy beachhead. For Eaton and his crew, the journey back to Port Moresby was about to become an odyssey.

ELEVEN

FEVER

The first American raid on Rabaul had been a bust. Of the five B-17s that reached the target area, only two attempted to bomb ships in Simpson Harbor, a third dumped its payload uselessly over the water, and two others did not release their bombs at all. Mishaps and mistakes had contributed to the unsatisfactory results, as did the weather. In his official air force oral history, conducted almost four decades later, Dick Carmichael made no attempt to sugarcoat the outcome: "We attacked Rabaul with whatever number of airplanes we had available or ready to go . . . nine or six or something. As I remember, we had a pretty good formation up there, but we didn't hit anything."[1]

Disappointing though the raid had been, it yielded important benefits. The mistakes, and there had been plenty, became lessons learned. Similarly, the information gleaned from the first encounters with Japanese fighters would benefit the crews on subsequent missions. And regardless of the results, the effort alone provided a boost to Allied morale. Much like the U.S. Navy's carrier raids at the beginning of February, the mission sent a clear message that the United States was capable of hitting back.

The press was quick to put a good spin on the raid, boasting in bold headlines of a "heavy attack" on Rabaul. Reporting from Port Moresby, war correspondent Osmar White described the "extremely bad weather" encountered during the mission, the restricted visibility over the target, even the fact that three crewmembers had been wounded. He referred enthusiastically to a BBC report that claimed "considerable damage had been caused by the raid," and supplemented the account with his own colorful details: "In the dawn raid a swarm of fighters, including Zero types, attacked our bombers high above the clouds."[2]

Some of the details probably came from RAAF participants Dick Cohen and Norm Robertson, who returned to their Catalina squadrons after the B-17s landed at Port Moresby to refuel. Oddly, however, and perhaps deliberately, White's article made no mention of the American bombers or their crews. A single Catalina had bombed Vunakanau airdrome south of Rabaul that same morning, but White credited the entire raid to the RAAF, even stating that the three wounded crewmembers were Australian. Was it a simple mistake, or parochial pride? Most Australians understood that American intervention was essential to stopping the Japanese onslaught, but some probably resented the notion that the United States, not Commonwealth forces, would save the day. The nick of time for the cavalry was not yet at hand.

No matter what Australians thought of the mission, the Southern Bomber Command had shot its bolt. The squadron was in no position to mount another raid against Rabaul, if only because the first effort had demonstrated that it was too far away to hit safely from Townsville. Future raids would have to be staged from advanced bases such as Port Moresby, but the lack of defenses there put the airplanes at risk of being caught on the ground by a Japanese raid.

This was underscored on the morning of February 24, the day after the B-17s bombed Rabaul. Retaliating with his first daylight raid on Port Moresby, Rear Admiral Goto sent the "land-attackers" of the 4th Air Group, escorted by Zeros of the fighter contingent, to destroy Seven Mile airdrome. George H. Johnston, another of Australia's popular war correspondents, grudgingly admired the enemy's skill:

> Moresby's third air raid—the first made in daylight—has just ended, and
> the garrison is a little aghast at the accuracy of the Japanese bombing.
> Nine twin-engine naval bombers came over in as neat a bit of formation
> flying as I have ever seen, and dropped about 70 bombs in a carefully

planned pattern. They scarcely wasted a bomb. One fell smack on one of our Hudson bombers and completely wrecked it. Another blew to pieces the little Gannet monoplane which has rescued so many people from the mining towns. The others pitted the runway and flattened every one of the new buildings of "Yankeeville," the elaborate camp which had just been completed for the American pilots who are coming up here soon.[3]

Harry Brandon and his crew, having completed hasty repairs to the engine that caught fire the previous day, were fortunate to get their B-17 off the ground just before the raid began. Had their departure been delayed by more than a few minutes, the bomber would have presented a fine stationary target. Upon landing at Townsville, Brandon reported his narrow escape, prompting Dick Carmichael to send out a team to investigate potential staging bases elsewhere in Queensland.

Departing before dawn the next morning in an RAAF Hudson, a small party led by Ted Faulkner inspected the Advanced Operational Base (AOB) on Horn Island, a twenty-square-mile chunk of rock in the Torres Strait. Located just off the northern tip of the continent, only ninety miles from New Guinea, the newly built airfield was far enough west of Port Moresby to be relatively safe from Japanese attack, yet close enough to Rabaul to satisfy the fuel requirements.

But even with the discovery of a suitable staging base, no missions were on the drawing board. Ten of the squadron's twelve B-17s were out of commission due to mishap, battle damage, or mechanical issues. One was still in Brisbane undergoing collision repairs, another sat in a swamp, three had been damaged on the ground at Townsville, three others were damaged by enemy fighters during the Rabaul mission, and two were diagnosed with engine or fuel system issues. The only bombers *not* grounded were those of Bill Lewis and Harry Spieth. Thus, in addition to the long hours already devoted to routine maintenance, the crews now had to repair at least six B-17s with varying types of damage at Townsville. Not many months earlier they had been accustomed to the well-equipped machine shops and cadres of skilled technicians at Albuquerque and Salt Lake City. Now, working with basic tools and a small stash of spare parts, the crews had to repair their own engines, replace magnetos, align bomb shackles, fix hydraulic leaks, patch bullet holes in wings and spars, splice cables and wiring, and maintain all of the electrical equipment. Tackling these tasks with a mixture of insolence ("a bitching soldier is a happy soldier") and pride, the overworked crews accomplished the near-miraculous. Many of the officers stripped down to khaki shorts and worked side-by-side with their crewmen.

On the morning of February 23, while the Rabaul raid was under way, Jim Twaddell and a few other pilots inspected the two B-17s that had collided on the ground the previous night. Priority was given to Deacon Rawls's ship, which needed a new wingtip, so the decision was made to replace it with the outer wing section from Bostrom's *San Antonio Rose*. Rawls, who bore primary responsibility for the collision, promised that he would have his airplane repaired in twenty-four hours. Working throughout the day and most of that night, he and his crew successfully removed Bostrom's outer wing and grafted it onto Rawls's B-17 in time for a test hop by the following noon. Unfortunately for Bostrom, the decision to cannibalize his prized bomber, which he had saved during the attack on Pearl Harbor by landing on the Kahuku golf course, relegated the *Rose* to the boneyard. She never flew again, instead becoming a source of spare parts to keep the rest of the B-17s airworthy.

Following an exhaustive maintenance effort, the crews had eight B-17s operational by February 26. However, due to the lack of defenses at Townsville, they were once again sent inland to Cloncurry for dispersal. The crews began to resent their transient existence. They continued to use Southern Bomber Command as the squadron's designation, though as far as anyone knew, the navy had no plans to employ the B-17s in the foreseeable future. And so the "Southern Bombers," as adjutant Walt Johnson called them, remained in limbo, a gypsy unit of U.S. Army aviators attached to the U.S. Navy while operating under the local authority of the Royal Australian Air Force.[4]

Because the squadron was officially on detached duty, the army owed per diem to every member, officers at the rate of six dollars per day, enlisted men at four dollars. Payment was perpetually delayed, however, because there was only one finance officer and he was required to personally witness all payments, no easy task with men constantly moving hither and yon. There were other administrative glitches, too. No mail had arrived, four of the navigators were still receiving cadet pay several months after they were supposed to have been commissioned, and promotions had been held up for most of the junior officers. Isolated from other American units, hosted by Australians on a base halfway around the world from home, the Southern Bombers began to think they'd been forgotten.

For many, the withdrawal to fly-ridden Cloncurry was a step deeper into purgatory. "Just a lot of dust," remembered Corporal John A. Straight, one of the enlisted men shanghaied in Fiji. "It was a desert town, dusty, and the buildings had verandas around them, like the French Quarter of New Orleans. We finally got to drink in their pubs, and they had one that was like a private bar. We ended up there. Seems like we always ended up in a bar somewhere."[5]

With patience already in short supply, the presence of alcohol ignited more than a few tempers, and at least one argument escalated into fisticuffs. On the evening of February 26, Lieutenant DuBose was sent back to Townsville "with two front teeth knocked out from a scuffle," as reported in the squadron diary.[6] No other squadron members were implicated, suggesting that DuBose may have tangled with an Aussie. Wartime or not, it was unbecoming for an officer to brawl, and DuBose spent a few days in Townsville on restricted duty, commonly known as being placed "in hack."

Ironically, all of the crews were recalled to Townsville the following afternoon. Carmichael was eager to hit Rabaul again, if for no better reason than to save face. While his bombers sat idle, the RAAF had been attacking Simpson Harbor every other night with their lumbering Catalinas. The new plan called for the B-17s to fly up to Port Moresby after dark (to minimize their exposure to enemy air attack), gas up, and then launch before daybreak on February 28. Auxiliary fuel tanks would not be required, permitting a full load of bombs.

That evening, Chaffin's repaired B-17 finally rejoined the squadron from

Brisbane. The bomber also brought a VIP passenger, fifty-one-year-old Brigadier General Ralph Royce, the former CO of the 7th Bomb Group at Salt Lake City. Shortly after his arrival in Townsville, the mission to Rabaul was canceled—and the timing was no coincidence. Royce, they soon discovered, had just been appointed chief of staff to Lieutenant General George Brett, the new commander of U.S. Army Forces in Australia (USAFIA). Formerly the deputy commander of the unified American-British-Dutch-Australian command in the Netherlands East Indies (ABDACOM), Brett had evacuated from Java on February 23 and arrived in Melbourne two days later. Royce's visit to Townsville and the subsequent cancellation of the raid on Rabaul were almost certainly connected. The previous day, February 26, Brett had sent a peevish radiogram to Lieutenant General Delos C. Emmons in Hawaii, demanding that the squadron be turned over to him:

> There are at present 12 B-17 airplanes in Australia assigned to Admiral Leary for a special mission. Upon arrival of these airplanes in Australia this headquarters was not informed concerning their status except through information obtained from Admiral Leary's headquarters. They were turned over to the chief of Air Staff RAAF for operational control. These are U.S. Army airplanes operated and manned by U.S. Army personnel. For this reason it is requested that they be turned over immediately for U.S. operational control and that Admiral Leary be informed accordingly. It is urgently requested that these airplanes remain in Australia for operation.[7]

Brett was determined to gain control of the B-17s, but Emmons, who had replaced Lieutenant General Walter Short as commander of the Hawaiian Department, had no jurisdiction over AAF matters in Australia. If he passed Brett's complaint to a higher authority in Washington, he did so without urgency, nor is there any evidence he forwarded the message to Admiral Nimitz's headquarters at Pearl Harbor. For several weeks to come, in fact, Nimitz would continue to receive updates on the B-17s from Vice Admiral Leary.

Thus began a turf war between Brett and Leary, resulting in an extended hiatus for the Southern Bomber Command, and the crews became bored after a few days of leisure in Cloncurry. Aside from the pubs and open-air theaters, there was little in the way of entertainment. With its streets of hard-packed dirt, the city initially reminded navigator Al Hobday of "a small western cowboy town right out of the back lot of Universal Studios." But the hotel where he was billeted was far more refined than the RAAF barracks in Townsville, and excellent meals were served in the dining room. "It was a rather formal dining room, it seemed, for this far into the outback," Hobday recalled. "It had white linen table cloths and napkins, nice china, and crystal, and beautiful and complete silverware."[8] The rate for a room and three meals was ten shillings, equivalent to only $2.25 per day. Depending on their per diem allowance, the American flyboys could pocket between $12 and $26 per week in profits. The Australians soon learned for themselves why the British would often quip that Yank servicemen were "overpaid, oversexed, and over here."

Cloncurry's eligible women had already been cautioned about the Americans. But that didn't stop the town from sponsoring a dance one night in early March. One of the officers who attended was John Steinbinder. Athletically built, dapper in his pressed uniform, he was pleasantly surprised to find "all the women in evening gowns, and many of them very nice." He danced until 3 A.M. with a pretty twenty-two-year-old named Olive. After walking her home, he asked her to go with him to the movies the following night. She agreed but "didn't seem to want the date very much." The next night, after the movies, they had a long talk. "I asked her why she didn't want to give me that date," Steinbinder wrote in his diary. "She replied that she had been warned against American soldiers. The stories she heard concerning them had not been very complimentary. However, she assured me that I had passed her tests of my intentions to her satisfaction."[9]

Aside from the occasional barroom dustup, the army fliers behaved decently in Cloncurry. If not always choir boys, they did nothing egregious enough to add probable cause to the rumors.

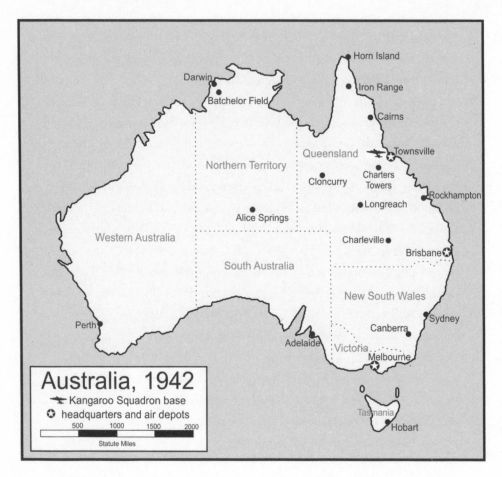

Australia, 1942
🛩 Kangaroo Squadron base
✪ headquarters and air depots

ALTHOUGH THE PEOPLE of Queensland welcomed the airmen, the environment was less kind. On March 4, while waiting to fly the B-17 that had recently been repaired in Brisbane, three members of the assigned crew fell ill. Swede Swenson, Leroy Pouncey, and Bert Lee, all veterans of the fiery crash landing at Pearl Harbor, were diagnosed with dengue fever and sent to Townsville General Hospital. Unfortunately, what might have initially appeared to be a coincidental illness confined to one crew rapidly evolved into a squadron-wide epidemic. Within a matter of days more than thirty officers and men were waylaid with symptoms of the virus. One of those hospitalized in Townsville was Herb Wheatley, the assistant radio operator and tail gunner on Frank Bostrom's crew. A fresh-faced twenty-one-year-old from California, he was afraid he might "go nuts" in the unsanitary hospital, which he described as "a drab, dingy old place overrun with huge cockroaches and other vermin."[10]

Most of the squadron members diagnosed with dengue fever fell ill in Cloncurry, where conditions were ideal for an outbreak. Having no immunity, the fliers had probably become infected within a few days of their arrival in Australia. After a period of incubation, the initial symptoms were typically a mild fever and fatigue, followed by progressively worsening indicators: a distinctive, widespread rash, aching joints and muscles, a raging fever, and fierce headaches. The dust, heat, and flies only added to the sick men's misery.

Wallace Fields, the copilot on Harry Spieth's crew, had spent the leisurely Sunday of March 1 hunting kangaroos. He was feeling feverish by the time he returned to his hotel, and the next day his temperature shot up to 103. By March 3 he was admitted to the little station hospital in Cloncurry, to be joined over the next several days by more than a dozen of his squadron mates, all housed in an open ward.[11]

The shire of Cloncurry, a district covering more than 18,000 square miles, had but one physician. Because the territory was so expansive, he used a small plane to travel from one isolated livestock station to another on a published schedule. He visited patients in the Cloncurry hospital infrequently, leaving their care to a staff of hardworking, underpaid nurses. Fields, from the tiny town of Shamrock in the Texas panhandle, was grateful for their care. "Sorry hospital," he wrote in his diary the first day, "but anything looks pretty good if they can take care of you."[12]

The virus rippled through the squadron, infecting more than a third of the aircrews within a two-week period. With every case, the illness had to run its course before the patient was discharged, though some recovered faster than others. Fields spent an entire week in the hospital, but even after his discharge he remained too weak to fly for a few days.

By March 6, the squadron had more planes in commission than crews to fly them. Newt Chaffin, the operations officer, shuffled the crews and was able to come up with enough healthy individuals to man eight ships, but the squadron needed more personnel. Dick Carmichael and Bill Lewis, fortunate to dodge the virus, flew down to the depot at Brisbane and arranged for replacements. Carmichael then continued south to Melbourne, where he met with General Royce. Batavia had fallen the previous day, all but ending Allied opposition in Java, so the B-17s of the Southern Bomber Command were assured of remaining in Australia. More important, two developments that would have a major impact on the war in the Southwest Pacific were under way, and the squadron would be directly involved in both.

Returning to Townsville that evening, Carmichael shared details of the new developments with his small staff at Garbutt Field. Among them was Walt Johnson, who sensed the winds of war were about to change. Despite the debilitating effects of dengue fever, it was clear that the squadron would soon be back in action. "Today's affairs were routine, ominous in their insignificance," he wrote prosaically, "if one can believe there's an awful quiet before a bomb explodes."[13]

TWELVE

INVASION

Vice Admiral Shigeyoshi Inoue seemed unstoppable. Since the opening round of the Southern Offensive three months earlier, his joint army-navy South Seas Force had met pathetically weak resistance, rolling over defenders with ease. Guam was captured within a few hours on December 10, 1941; ditto for Rabaul and Kavieng in the Bismarcks on January 23; next came Gasmata on the south coast of New Britain, occupied without opposition on February 9. Pleased that the offensive had made "better progress than expected," Imperial General Headquarters was eager to begin the next phase. Inoue and his counterpart in the Imperial Japanese Army, Lieutenant General Tomitaro Horii, were ordered to capture "various important points in British New Guinea and the Solomon Islands . . . as quickly as possible."[1]

The prize was Port Moresby. Once the Japanese gained control of New Guinea, they could launch a prolonged bombing campaign against the entire northern half of Australia. Simultaneous control of the Solomons would extend their aerial and naval superiority over a wide swath of the Southwest Pacific, including the New Hebrides. There was little reason to doubt that Inoue would succeed. When the Rising Sun flag flew over the Netherlands East Indies, New Guinea, and the Solomons, an invasion of the Australian continent would not be necessary. Cut off from both the United States and Great Britain, Australia and New Zealand would be forced to sue for peace.

War correspondent Osmar White had already warned of this in an editorial published on February 18. The fall of Singapore and the pending collapse of the Netherlands East Indies, he argued, made it vitally important to save Port Moresby, Australia's last outpost. He even quoted the commanding general of the garrison, Major General Basil M. Morris, as saying, "If necessary, Port Moresby must become the Tobruk of the Pacific."[2]

The general's reference to the epic eight-month siege in North Africa was an appeal to the War Cabinet for assistance. It was a clever tactic, but the cold reality was that Australia lacked the resources to fortify Port Moresby. The only operational fighters currently in the RAAF inventory were lightly armed CAC Wirraways, a license-built adaptation of the North American T-6 trainer. No match for Zeros, the handful of Wirraways that had bravely tried to intercept the enemy over Rabaul in January had been quickly shot down. For that reason, they were no longer assigned to forward combat areas. Rumors began to spread that a newly formed P-40 squadron was coming to Port Moresby, but weeks passed with no sign of the promised fighters. "For some time now," wrote correspondent George Johnston, "there has been a story in general circulation that a Curtiss Tomahawk squadron is to arrive here. If you ask when they are expected the answer is always: 'Tomorrow!' So now everyone calls them 'Tomorrowhawks.'"[3]

At Rabaul, where the 24th Air Flotilla placed a heavy emphasis on aerial reconnaissance, Vice Admiral Inoue was aware that the Allies were improving the airdrome at Port Moresby. He also knew of the new airfield being developed on Horn Island. Anxious to counter the expansion before it could further threaten Rabaul, the Japanese initiated a campaign to smash Allied air strength in the New Guinea area, sending repeated bombing and strafing raids against the poorly defended positions. The first daylight attack on Port Moresby, as witnessed by George Johnston on February 24, had destroyed a few aircraft and damaged the runway. Four days later the Japanese conducted a two-pronged bombing and strafing raid, which was followed during the first week of March by increasingly bigger strikes. Eighteen Type 1 bombers dropped dozens of small fragmentation bombs, nicknamed "daisy cutters," on Seven Mile airdrome on March 3; the next night, Kawanishi flying boats attacked the airfield and harbor areas; and on March 7, the Type 1 bombers were back in force, dropping some eighty bombs on the airdrome. Despite all the raids, however, surprisingly little damage was done and the garrison's morale actually improved.

Accustomed to easy conquests by this time, the Japanese had become infused with what would later be called *senshobyo*: literally, "victory disease." Rejoicing in one successful campaign after another, they considered themselves invincible. Symptoms of overconfidence could be found throughout the ranks. Planners at the highest level grew contemptuous of the Allies, who thus far had displayed a penchant for surrendering. Victory disease trickled down to subordinate commands as well. The 4th Air Group grossly overestimated the effectiveness of the raids in early March, concluding in a summary of the attacks that "air bases for land and sea planes around Port Moresby were destroyed along with their planes, and the enemy air activities in this area were checked almost completely."[4] Contrary to those claims, the RAAF had lost only five planes to the combined bombing or strafing attacks, hardly the crippling blow invented by the Japanese propaganda machine.

Nevertheless, convinced that Allied air strength had been crushed, the dour-looking Inoue planned to resume his conquest of New Guinea with simultaneous landings at Lae and Salamaua on the northeast coast. The invasion of the adjacent towns, originally scheduled for March 3, had been postponed for several days so that Rear Admiral Goto could replace the many aircraft and flight crews lost during the attack on the USS *Lexington*. Rescheduled for March 8, the effort actually got under way when General Horii's South Seas Force, escorted by eleven warships, sailed from Rabaul on the fifth. By the time an RAAF Hudson crew stumbled upon the Japanese fleet two days later, the convoy was already in the Huon Gulf, mere hours from reaching its objective.

Powerless to stop the landings, the Allies could only spectate as the Japanese began shelling Lae and the smaller town of Salamaua at dawn on March 8. The Australian defenders—local detachments of a militia known as the New Guinea Volunteer Rifles—melted into the jungle without a fight. Thousands of Japanese troops subsequently landed on their respective beachheads and quickly secured both towns, after which construction battalions began repairs to the airstrip at Lae, damaged several weeks earlier by Japanese carrier-based bombers. Within thirty-six hours the field was ready to accept fighters from the 4th Air Group at Rabaul.

The occupation of the two coastal towns not only gave Inoue control over a large region of New Guinea and adjacent waters, it set the stage for a frightening new aspect of the air war. Lae, from which Amelia Earhart and Fred Noonan had set out on their ill-fated flight in 1937, was only 190 miles north of Port Moresby. Warplanes could make the trip in under an hour, though they first had to cross the Owen Stanley range at an oblique angle, which kept them over the treacherous mountains for most of the flight. Salamaua also had an airstrip, built during the previous decade to support gold mining operations, but it saw limited use in the hands of the Japanese. Salamaua's port facilities, on the other hand, were considered superior to the anchorage at Lae. Thus it became a coastal supply center while Lae served primarily as a forward air base to support Admiral Inoue's continuing campaign.

IN SHARP CONTRAST to Inoue's belief that the bombing raids on Port Moresby had crippled Allied air strength, the United States and Australia mounted a strong retaliation to the Japanese invasion. Major Carmichael, informed on March 7 of the pending invasion, called his squadron to action. The B-17s were still dispersed in Cloncurry, with only enough healthy crewmembers to man eight planes due to the outbreak of dengue fever, but by 1:30 A.M. on March 8, all of the able-bodied fliers were preparing for a counterattack.[5] Two hours later, a flight of four B-17s led by Bill Lewis took off for Horn Island, where they would refuel prior to striking the enemy beachheads. The remaining four crews flew to Townsville and took on a full load of bombs, then awaited word on the conditions over the target.

After refueling at Horn Island, the flight led by Lewis took off at dawn to attack shipping off Salamaua. Two of the Fortresses turned back toward the isolated airfield with engine trouble, but Lewis and his remaining wingman, Lieutenant Arnold R. "Skid" Johnson, managed to reach the target area. Finding it socked in by "heavy cumulus clouds and very low overcast," they aborted the mission and returned to Horn Island.[6]

Unknown to the Japanese, the *Lexington* task force was still loitering off the New Hebrides. Vice Admiral Brown had requested, and received, approval from admirals King and Nimitz to attempt another raid on Rabaul, and this time he would wield a much bigger stick. Task Force 17, commanded by Rear Admiral Frank Jack Fletcher aboard the carrier *Yorktown*, had joined Task Force 11 and the ANZAC Squadron on the morning of March 6, giving Brown a combined force of two flattops, eight heavy cruisers, fourteen destroyers, and two oilers.[7] The two-carrier raid, scheduled for dawn on March 10, had the potential to cause heavy damage at Rabaul. Unfortunately for Brown, the Japanese landings at Lae and Salamaua threw a wrench into his plans for the second straight time. Had he proceeded with the strike as scheduled, his planes would have found Simpson Harbor devoid of targets.

Inadvertently, the Japanese handed Brown an even better alternative. The Huon Gulf adjacent to Lae and Salamaua was now full of ships, all of which remained near the coast while the invasion fleet unloaded troops, equipment, and supplies. Brown, recognizing the opportunity to catch a large concentration of vessels in an area where their maneuverability would be restricted, conceived a new plan to strike the Japanese fleet from a position west of Port Moresby. The carrier planes would have to fly over the Owen Stanley Mountains twice, but the Japanese would never suspect an attack from that direction.

At Townsville, crews spent the morning of March 9 pulling the auxiliary fuel tanks from the four B-17s that had flown in from Cloncurry the previous day. Full bomb loads were installed, aided by a newly arrived platoon of ordnance men who helped with some of the workload. At about midmorning, a blue-gray navy dive bomber, adorned with the same colorful rudder stripes as the B-17s, landed at Garbutt Field on a liaison flight from the *Lexington*. Out hopped Commander Walton W. Smith, a member of Vice Admiral Brown's staff, who had arrived for the purpose of coordinating the carrier strike plan with the Southern Bomber Command. Smith also sought advice on mapping a safe route over the Owen Stanleys for the carrier planes. An identical SBD Dauntless flew to Port Moresby for the same purpose, arriving soon after Japanese raiders had concluded yet another attack on Seven Mile drome. Both dive bombers later returned to the *Lexington* with valuable intel on the vagaries of the weather and the best route over the treacherous mountains.[8]

The plan for the B-17s was similar to that of the aborted first raid on Rabaul, wherein the heavy bombers would follow the carrier strikes with a coordinated high-altitude attack on Lae and Salamaua. It appeared that the crews in Carmichael's four-ship flight would be shorthanded due to the viral outbreak, but mere minutes before the bombers were scheduled to take off, five replacement crewmembers arrived from Brisbane. Among them was Master Sergeant David Semple, a bombardier with more than twenty years of army aviation experience. The newcomers got little more than a glimpse of Garbutt Field before they were ushered aboard Carmichael's B-17s, which promptly departed for Horn Island.

By 9:30 the next morning, all eight bombers were airborne from Horn Island and headed toward the Huon Gulf. The event was noteworthy yet ironic, for it marked the first time—and the last—that the squadron would gather so many B-17s in a single formation. As many as ten aircraft might have participated were it not for the impact of dengue fever, which had not yet run its course among squadron personnel. John Steinbinder went on the mission feeling "pretty weak" with a temperature of 103; and back at Townsville, none other than Doc Luke was knocked off his pins by the debilitating virus.[9]

Proceeding across the Gulf of Papua, where the weather was excellent, Carmichael's eight B-17s were spotted by lookouts aboard the American carrier force at 10:15. Conditions deteriorated as the formation flew over New Guinea, however, with buildups of heavy cumulus clouds that reached an estimated 45,000 feet. The similarities to the first raid led by Carmichael were uncanny, but this time he had the advantage of daylight as he guided the formation through a maze of towering thunderheads. He had selected the best navigator for his crew, the affable Lieutenant Kermit E. Meyers, who justified his appointment as "chief navigator for the 88th and the Southern Bombers" by accurately monitoring their position. Despite numerous heading changes, the formation punched through the weather exactly on course. From an altitude of 27,000 feet, the Fortress crews could see an estimated twenty Japanese ships between Salamaua and Lae. Many were near the shoreline, though most of the warships had scattered into the Huon Gulf.*[10]

The strike aircraft from the *Lexington* and the *Yorktown*, collectively totaling more than a hundred planes, had already done their part. Four or five Japanese ships were on fire, two others sunk or sinking. The B-17s, along with eight RAAF Hudsons of 32 Squadron out of Port Moresby, followed as cleanup hitters. "We bombed a cruiser and a transport with success, although the bombsight in the lead ship went out," wrote navigator Jack Carlson in his diary. "Several of our bombs fell long due to this, but on the second run . . . we scored our hits. The enemy's antiaircraft was concentrated on us and the navy's retreat was successful as was planned. The navy had done a good job and we had played our part well."[11]

Lieutenant Theodore I. Pascoe, Carmichael's bombardier since the squadron left the States, was undoubtedly disappointed by the equipment failure. But even if his Norden bombsight had functioned perfectly, the odds of hitting a ship from more than four miles high were poor. Vessels under way reduced the probability even further, as the ship-handlers merely had to observe the falling bombs and maneuver away from their impact point.

Despite the inherent difficulty of hitting a fast-moving ship from high altitude, the light cruiser *Yubari* probably sustained some damage from the B-17s. According to translated records, the warship dodged a total of sixty-seven bombs during the combined attack, of which five were recorded as near misses. Among the U.S. Navy participants, fewer than twenty SBDs dived on the cruiser, which was also strafed by several F4F Wildcats. Thus a good percentage of the bombs can be attributed to Carmichael's B-17s, along with those dropped by the RAAF Hudsons. Which bombs accounted for the near misses is impossible to say, but the cruiser reportedly sustained more than three thousand individual splinter impacts. And those near misses were

---

* The invasion fleet and naval escorts totaled sixteen Japanese ships. A few coastwise vessels probably accounted for the difference.

deadly. The *Yubari*'s crew suffered more than sixty casualties, including thirteen dead, from .50 caliber bullets and scything pieces of bomb shrapnel.[12]

Regardless of how much damage the B-17s caused, the overall results of the joint attack were impressive: three transports sunk or beached, moderate damage to a fourth transport and one seaplane tender, plus light damage to the *Yubari*, two destroyers, and a large minelayer. Japanese casualties totaled 130 dead and 245 wounded, while the only loss to the Allies was the two-man crew of a dive bomber from the *Lexington*, shot down by a shore-based AA battery.[*13]

Although the coordinated attack came too late to thwart the invasion, the Japanese later acknowledged the severity of the damage. By sending his invasion forces to an enemy-held island with only minimal air support, Vice Admiral Inoue had committed a monumental error in judgment. It was a perfect example of *senshobyo*, and he was fortunate the Allies had not been able to muster a more powerful counterattack. As it was, Inoue never repeated his mistake. All of his future operations were conducted with far greater emphasis on aerial support, including aircraft carriers of the *Kido Butai*.

Pleased with the outcome of the raid, Carmichael and his crews returned to Townsville and shared exciting tales of seeing Japanese ships ablaze or sinking. Comparisons to Pearl Harbor were inevitable. The raid was glorious payback, a stinging retribution for the enemy's sneaky (as Americans saw it) attack. After months of doomsday news about the seemingly unstoppable Japanese, the success of the raid provided a much-needed tonic.

So did the arrival of a dozen veterans from the 7th and 19th Bomb Groups, who brought plenty of combat experience. One was a master sergeant with an Ivy League name, Durwood W. Fesmire, long regarded as the best bombardier in the 19th Group. The new arrivals also included four pilots and four navigators who had seen action in the Philippines and Java.

---

* Allied claims were greatly exaggerated: five transports, two heavy cruisers, one light cruiser, one destroyer, and one auxiliary minesweeper sunk, and "heavy damage" to several other vessels.

If they seemed a bit morose or aloof, the stories they told about devastating losses and hairbreadth escapes provided ample justification for their behavior.[14]

Taking some of the shine off the good news, many of the squadron's junior officers were irritated to learn they had been evicted from their RAAF quarters to make room for a newly arrived fighter squadron. The Aussie pilots had unceremoniously piled the Yanks' belongings on the porch of the officers club, and the orderly room had been commandeered by the RAAF without preamble or apology. But the Americans did not stew about it for long. Formed only a week earlier, the Aussie squadron was badly needed. Best of all, making a quantum leap forward in fighter defense capability, 75 Squadron was equipped with twenty-five new Curtiss P-40E Warhawks, which the Aussies called Kittyhawks. They would train vigorously at Townsville for the next ten days before deploying to Port Moresby.

An American light-bomber squadron also moved up to Townsville from Brisbane. Led by First Lieutenant Donald P. Hall, the 89th Bombardment Squadron, part of the 3rd Bombardment Group, would not commence flying until their Douglas A-20s were assembled. Until then, Hall agreed to lend his ground personnel to help the Southern Bomber Command with maintenance and mission preparation. Described as "eager and willing," the newcomers had no experience with B-17s, but their assistance was greatly appreciated by the weary Fortress crews. As noted in the squadron diary on March 11, "The A-20 boys worked all night, and most of the morning and part of the afternoon getting five ships ready to fly."[15]

Lae and Salamaua became the targets du jour for the B-17s. The squadron's next raid, staged from Horn Island on the morning of March 12, was officially led by Jim Twaddell. For the past few weeks his duties as executive officer had kept him out of the cockpit, so instead of flying as the command pilot, he prudently occupied the copilot's seat of Ted Faulkner's B-17. Arriving over the target area at 11:00 A.M., the five-plane formation conducted the squadron's most successful mission to date. John Steinbinder, navigating for Lieutenant Maurice C. Horgan, one of the newly arrived veterans from the 7th Bomb Group, recorded some of the exciting details in his diary.

We arrived over the objective at 27,000 feet indicated. We dropped eight bombs on Salamaua airport, blowing up two hangars, and the other four landed on the mat. We then went to Lae and bombed all the harbor facilities, docks and two ships in dock. Ten minutes from our target we had throttled back & were only making a ground speed of about 255 knots when right out of the sky above us three fighters attacked. At this altitude only four of our eleven guns were working. We were the last ship in a bunch of five. The Zero fighters tried cutting us off from the rest. One of the Zeros just looped completely around us squirting lead like a hose does water. Not a one hit us. As this same fighter came at us from below we throttled forward to a true airspeed of 325 knots which sort of left the Zero exposed to the tail guns of all five ships and it went down, cut in two by the tremendous amount of bullets cutting into it. This was my first sight of a falling ship and it certainly was awe inspiring. The two other Zeros turned back after their encounter.[16]

Some of the particulars in Steinbinder's account dovetail neatly with the combat log of the 4th Air Group, but others, including the destruction of a Zero, do not. The important point is that the Japanese wasted no time developing Lae for offensive operations. In the days to come, approximately half of the 4th Air Group's land-attack bombers and Zero fighters would transfer from Rabaul to defend the new stronghold and conduct daring raids on Allied bases, particularly Port Moresby.

WHILE MAJOR TWADDELL's formation returned from their successful mission over Lae, the squadron's six remaining B-17s, each loaded with fourteen three-hundred-pound bombs, took off from Townsville for another crack at Rabaul. Led by the seemingly indefatigable Bill Lewis, the crews planned to spend the night at Port Moresby prior to launching the raid on the morning of March 13, a Friday. The effort got off to a bad start, however, when Swede Swenson turned back with engine trouble only an hour after leaving Townsville. The remaining five B-17s continued to Seven Mile airdrome, which had just endured its sixth bombing attack in as many days. The crews grabbed a few hours of rest in the new "Yankeeville," built among the hills two miles from the airstrip to avoid the fate of the original encampment, then arose at 1:30 A.M. on the thirteenth for a meager breakfast in the primitive mess tent.

Taking off about an hour later, Lewis climbed to three thousand feet and circled over the airdrome, waiting for the others to join up. But the weather was so foul that he headed west to the alternate rendezvous location, Hood Point, where he circled for another thirty-five minutes. During that time only one Fortress, piloted by Frank Bostrom, successfully joined up; the other three crews, claiming various sorts of mechanical trouble, aborted the mission and returned to Townsville.

Lewis and Bostrom headed for Rabaul, battling what the former described as "very bad weather" over New Guinea and the Solomon Sea. More than halfway to the target area Bostrom was also forced to abort, leaving Lewis and his crew to fend for themselves. Not long after that, one of Lewis's engines began to leak oil. Instead of turning back, an option that no one would have questioned, he descended to 15,000 feet and pressed on. Approximately two hours later his Fortress arrived over Vunakanau airdrome, the primary base for Japanese naval bombers in the region. Climbing to 21,000 feet, Lewis circled for twenty minutes while the crew diagramed shipping in the harbor. He then commenced a bomb run, but just as Fred Eaton's crew had experienced three weeks earlier, the load of three-hundred-pounders failed to release. Despite calls on the interphone that enemy planes had been spotted 10,000 feet below, Lewis circled around for another attempt. In the nose compartment, Master Sergeant Semple, the experienced bombardier from the 19th Group, took over the bomber's guidance using the automatic flight control equipment (AFCE) and picked out a good target: sixteen twin-engine bombers lined up along the south side of the runway. Releasing seven of the three-hundred-pound bombs in train, Semple obtained "two direct hits and one very close, the other bombs falling on the runway."[17]

The enemy fighters never challenged the B-17. Lewis headed initially for Horn Island, but an update of the bomber's fuel state revealed that there was barely enough gas to reach Port Moresby. Once again the combination of prolonged loitering, bad weather, and a second bomb run had used excessive fuel. Lewis told navigator Jack Carlson to forget Horn Island—they needed to go straight in to Port Moresby. When Carlson inquired about using the standard approach, Lewis said, "To hell with that. We've got no gas."[18]

By the time the Fortress reached the Owen Stanleys, the fuel gauges were almost indicating empty. "Put on your 'chutes," Lewis informed the crew. "Wait for the engines to quit, then bail out."

Barely squeaking through the Kokoda Pass, the Fortress glided down toward Port Moresby with the fuel indicators bouncing on zero. The last few miles were going to be a nail-biting, heart-pounding test of the bomber's endurance. Manning the upper turret, Technical Sergeant Karl G. Johansson called on the interphone, "Engineer to crew, couple of fires burning. Moresby must have had a raid this morning. Lucky we're getting there after it's over."[19]

But it wasn't quite over. Led by Lieutenant Shirō Kawai, five Zero fighters had hopped over the mountains from Lae and roared across the airdrome at treetop height. Making multiple strafing runs, they shot up an old Ford trimotor transport and ignited several fires before starting back toward the mountains. Lewis's B-17 happened to approach from the opposite direction at the wrong time. He was descending through five thousand feet, without enough fuel to take evasive action, when the enemy fighters approached from the opposite direction.

Radio operator George R. "Dick" Graf, interviewed later by author Walter D. Edmonds (best known for his novel *Drums along the Mohawk*), described the flight's wild conclusion:

> Our gas tanks were almost dry and we wanted to get on the ground in a hurry. Lewis, instead of circling, turned and dove low, planning to land downwind. We had too much altitude to lose speed—we were going 160 to 170 miles per hour with our wheels down, but the flaps wouldn't go down. We reached the end of the runway and drifted over it about 20 feet in the air.
>
> We had reached the end of the field when more Zeros passed over. An

Aussie Hudson came over just at that moment. The Nips, who still hadn't seen us, started after him.

Lewis wanted to get down in the worst way. He swung off to the right, making a very sharp turn, then made a very tight vertical bank, with the wheels down and the flaps going down. He went into it at about 150 miles an hour and came out of it at about 95 miles an hour, and touched down.

It was the most beautiful landing I have ever seen. You just can't make a tight turn at that speed without losing altitude, but he did it. The wing tip was only 10 feet above the brush when he hit the vertical.[20]

Lewis had pulled off the miraculous landing with not a moment to spare. "One engine cut out due to lack of fuel as we landed," Jack Carlson reported. "Our crew immediately got busy refueling the plane with a hand pump. We loaded just enough gas to get us to Horn Island."[21] Worried about being caught by another raid, Lewis took off immediately, refueled once more at Horn Island, and then started back to Townsville. But there was still one more scare on that Friday the thirteenth.

Lieutenant Don Hall and a few members of his A-20 squadron had joined Lewis's crew for the mission, not only to get a taste of bombing the Japanese but to learn about the hazards of New Guinea. Once the B-17 was pointed toward Townsville, Lewis turned the controls over to Hall, who was flying as copilot. Dog-tired after the strain of the long mission and the hair-raising return to Port Moresby, Lewis moved down to the nose compartment for a nap. The engineer, Johansson, took Lewis's seat to help monitor the instruments, but he soon conked out as well. Hall, flying at only a thousand feet, was getting drowsy himself when the B-17 suddenly approached some scattered rain squalls. Deciding to climb, Hall pulled back on the yoke. "He must have thought he was flying an A-20," recalled Graf, "because he just took the wheel and hauled it back into his belly."

The B-17 soared upward, rapidly bleeding off airspeed, threatening to stall. At such a low altitude, there was no room to recover if the bomber entered a spin. The airspeed had dropped to 110 miles per hour, noted Graf, when Bill Lewis tumbled out of the nose compartment "in a hell of a hurry." Wide awake and more than a little frightened, he quickly got the airplane under control and continued uneventfully to Townsville. That evening, after the Fortress landed safely, a message from Allied Control Headquarters in Melbourne congratulated Lewis and his crew for "completing a difficult mission in the face of the most adverse conditions."[22]

For superstitious members of the squadron, Friday the thirteenth had lived up to its reputation. Thanks to a slew of mechanical issues, only one B-17 from the original flight of six had managed to reach Rabaul. Consequently, Major Carmichael grounded the entire squadron for a few days to allow time for overdue maintenance. But there was also some good news: March 13 marked the last day of the unit's quasi-official attachment to the U.S. Navy. Due to a critical new development, Lieutenant General Brett had finally wrested control of the B-17s from Vice Admiral Leary.

In name, at least, the Southern Bomber Command was no more. The gypsy squadron was officially back in the army.

The final step for brand-new Fortresses: Boeing employees wash and mask off two early-model B-17Es prior to painting them in the camouflage unit. The upper gun turrets, manufactured by a subcontractor, have already been painted OD (olive drab) green. *Boeing, via Glen Spieth*

After arriving at his first operational unit, the 22nd Bomb Squadron/7th Bomb Group, Fred Eaton proudly posed with his two-tone Buick Roadmaster in front of a Douglas B-10. The group's twin-engine B-10s and B-18s were being phased out in favor of the four-engine B-17. *Eaton collection*

Staff Sergeant Lee Embree took the first American aerial photograph of the Pacific war from the side gunner's window of a B-17E on December 7, 1941. Two Japanese dive bombers (Aichi D3As), flying on a parallel course, can be seen above the wing and engine nacelle. *Reid collection*

While a crash crew looks on, the remains of Captain "Swede" Swenson's B-17C continue to smolder at Hickam Field on December 7. Gunfire from Japanese fighters ignited an intense fire amidships while Swenson was on final approach. Three members of his crew were wounded aboard the aircraft, three more hit on the ground during subsequent strafing attacks. *Reid collection*

Crowded around a table draped with an army blanket, seven fliers try their luck at poker. With a dusk-to-dawn curfew in effect across Oahu, options for nighttime entertainment were limited. Slender navigator Hubert Mobley grins at the photographer, navigator Rob Carruthers sits to his left, and balding copilot Henry "Hotfoot" Harlow is at far right. Note at least three packs of cigarettes on the table. *Steinbinder collection*

In early February 1942, Major Dick Carmichael formed an ad hoc squadron consisting of twelve crews from three different units and led them across the Pacific to Australia. A twenty-eight-year-old Texan, West Point graduate, and former pursuit pilot, Carmichael quickly caught the attention of his superiors. Just a captain when the war started, he was a lieutenant colonel in command of the 19th Bombardment Group within eight months. *National Archives*

B-17E number 21-2430 wears the unique camouflage paint scheme applied by the Hawaii Air Depot, along with 13 red and white recognition stripes on the rudder. The photo was likely taken in mid-February 1942 en route to Australia, with Harold "Newt" Chaffin at the controls. *E. P. Stevens via Steve Birdsall*

The crew of *San Antonio Rose* (21-2416) and an extra passenger were photographed upon their arrival in Australia. Led by pilot Frank Bostrom (third from left), the regulars included tall bombardier Earl Sheggrud (far left), navigator Rob Carruthers (second from left), and tail gunner Herb Wheatley (far right). Several are wearing pith helmets obtained in Fiji. *USAF Museum*

A public-relations photo captured the spirit of cooperation between American crews and Australian support personnel as they prepare to "bomb up" a new B-17E with British-made bombs from an RAAF stockpile. Combat crews maintained their own airplanes, but the Aussies provided housing, food, and flight clothing. As one crewman put it, "We had to rely on the Royal Australian Air Force for everything." *Spieth collection*

The curved panels of Plexiglas that formed the bullet-shaped nose of a B-17E gave bombardiers a stunning view of the world. Here, another Fortress flies a few hundred yards ahead on a parallel course, and a reflection of the bombardier's face can be seen in the wedge-shaped center panel. *Boeing via Glen Spieth*

The control tower at Garbutt Field, Townsville, Australia, where the Kangaroo Squadron was based for its entire combat tour. Note the ambulance parked at the base of the tower and the sandbagged gun pit in the foreground. The airdrome also served as the HQ for the Northeast Area. *Eaton collection*

Due to the threat of enemy air attacks following the bombing of Darwin on February 19, 1942, the B-17s were dispersed to Cloncurry, deep in the outback. The wooden buildings, boardwalks, and dusty environment made the Americans feel as though they had stepped back in time to the Old West. *Eaton collection*

A view looking south at the squadron's first target, Simpson Harbor. Heavily defended—and naturally protected by a ring of volcanoes—the anchorage lies adjacent to the town of Rabaul (far right). Dozens of Japanese ships crowd the harbor, and Lakunai airdrome can be seen just below the white cloud in the center of the photo. *Carlson collection*

Almost out of fuel after making two bomb runs over Simpson Harbor on February 23, 1942, Fred Eaton made a belly landing on what appeared to be a grassy field near the east coast of New Guinea. It turned out to be the Agaiambo Swamp, covered with razor-sharp kunai grass. Practically undamaged, B-17 number 21-2446, later nicknamed the "Swamp Ghost," would remain there for more than sixty years. *Spieth collection*

Usually piloted by Harry Spieth at the beginning of the combat tour, this early-version B-17E (21-2435) shows the flat-bottomed remote belly turret and gunner's sighting blister. In the background, the Owen Stanley Mountains are partially obscured by mist. By the end of the war the precipitous mountains were strewn with hundreds of aircraft wrecks. *Spieth collection*

Interior view of the gunners' compartment in an early B-17E, looking forward. The remote belly turret operator would lie prone on the padded cushion, facing aft, while sighting through a complex system of mirrors. Airsickness was common. Note the stowed .50 caliber side guns and racks of small, early-style ammo canisters. *Boeing via Glen Spieth*

Shuttle service: Loading up for a mission, crewmembers toss their wool-lined flying gear into an army truck parked next to the operations shack at Garbutt Field. The heavy clothing would be donned after takeoff, as the temperature plunged from 90-plus degrees Fahrenheit at ground level to -30 degrees at 30,000 feet. *Spieth collection*

During the squadron's first two months in Australia, the combat crews performed all maintenance and repairs on their aircraft in addition to flying 10- to 12-hour missions. Here, the cowling of a B-17's number two engine has been removed for access. *Carlson collection*

Sharing the pasture: Due to the threat of enemy air attack, the Kangaroo Squadron's bombers were dispersed in the woods and meadows surrounding Garbutt Field. It was not uncommon to see cattle taking advantage of the shade beneath the broad wing of a parked B-17. *Carlson collection*

Frank Bostrom's *San Antonio Rose* never flew a combat mission. Damaged in a ground collision on the night of February 22, 1942, it was cannibalized for spare parts. Eventually, only the forward and aft sections of the fuselage shell remained. *Carlson collection*

Nine of the Kangaroo Squadron navigators at Townsville. Standing at left: Hubert Mobley, Albert Hobday, and Harold Snider. Hulet Hornbeck rides on the shoulders of Kermit Meyers, who is seated behind John Steinbinder on the motorcycle. Standing at right: Bob Elliott, Rob Roy Carruthers (partially obscured), and Horace Perry. *Steinbinder collection*

Mabry Simmons, a tall pilot from Texas, tries to round up a young kangaroo somewhere near Townsville. The animal seems to want none of it, but that didn't prevent the squadron from basing its name on one of Australia's most endearing symbols. *Eaton collection*

The first American squadron to operate in New Guinea, the Kangaroo Squadron staged or initiated most of its combat missions from Seven Mile airdrome at Port Moresby. Living conditions in the encampment, situated among the gum trees overlooking the runway, were primitive for the first several months. *Reid collection*

A crewmember on Harry Spieth's B-17 snapped this photo as two bombs hurtled toward what was believed to be a Japanese fleet during the Battle of the Coral Sea, May 7, 1942. But those churning wakes are from the wildly maneuvering warships of an Allied support force centered on the heavy cruiser HMAS *Australia*. Fortunately the bombs missed the friendly ships, splashing near an American destroyer. *Spieth collection*

Major Bill Lewis, the Kangaroo Squadron's oldest pilot, took over as commanding officer in March 1942 after Dick Carmichael was promoted to a staff position. A former airline pilot, Lewis routinely bulled his way through storms or shrugged off mechanical glitches to always reach his target. He was equally effective as a squadron leader, though he led fewer combat missions after assuming command. *Carlson collection*

Due to the tropical heat, nobody was self-conscious about wearing boxers or bathing suits during a spirited game of volleyball. Baseball and sailing trips to Magnetic Island were other popular forms of outdoor recreation at Townsville. *Eaton collection*

Yankee ingenuity: This homemade scooter was built by an enterprising sergeant for pilot John Wallace Fields, who procured two tail wheels from a P-40 fighter, a wrecked maintenance stand, a small engine from a refueling unit, and handlebars from a bicycle. George Munroe rides on the back. *Fields collection*

Army meals typical of forward combat areas were served in this open mess tent at Seven Mile airdrome. Hash, potatoes, hardtack, and coffee were the staples of practically every meal. Poor sanitation meant the hungry aviators fought off swarms of flies for every bite. *Spieth collection*

Living conditions improved marginally after the tents were replaced with native-built structures. Note the thatched roof and walls of the Kangaroo Squadron's operations shack, which contains a worktable, a couple of army cots, and a carefully guarded luxury: an Electrolux refrigerator. *Spieth collection*

Located less than 200 miles from the Japanese airfield at Lae, Port Moresby suffered dozens of attacks by enemy bombers or strafing fighters—sometimes both. Kangaroo Squadron personnel endured many of the raids, including this one on August 17, 1942, which destroyed six Allied aircraft. *Spieth collection*

Most of the squadron's reconnaissance runs were made at high altitude to avoid enemy fighters and antiaircraft weapons, but Japanese seaplane anchorages were an exception. This aerial photo shows two Nakajima E13A floatplanes near a small facility, their "meatball" insignia clearly visible. *Carlson collection*

Flying alone on recon missions, the B-17s sometimes battled upwards of a dozen enemy fighters. Tail gunner Edwin Rhodes, seriously wounded during combat with Zeros of the Tainan Air Group on June 11, missed this crew photo. Note the large cannon hole near the trailing edge of the elevator. *Spieth collection*

During a reconnaissance mission to Guadalcanal and Tulagi on July 9, two Nakajima A62M floatplanes attacked the LB-30 Liberator flown by Wallace Fields. Essentially Zero fighters on floats, the hybrid planes were photographed in action for the first time ever—just before causing considerable damage to the bomber. *Fields collection*

That the solo reconnaissance missions were hazardous was underscored on August 14, 1942, when *Chief Seattle of the Pacific Northwest*, purchased through a highly publicized war bond drive, departed from Port Moresby but never returned. Decades later, Japanese documents revealed that the B-17 had been shot down by the Tainan Air Group. *Spieth collection*

Chief Seattle was the only Kangaroo Squadron bomber lost in action; otherwise the B-17s proved remarkably rugged. This Fortress, flown by Larry Humiston and Roy Reid, crash-landed at Port Moresby on July 30 with two engines shot out and the flight controls partially disabled. Despite 8 cannon holes and 250 bullet holes, the aircraft was repaired and returned to duty. *Reid collection*

In October 1942, a detachment led by Frank Bostrom moved to Milne Bay on the eastern coast of New Guinea, hundreds of miles closer to the reconnaissance lanes. Here, standing near two Kangaroo Squadron B-17Es, ground crews watch Bell P-39 Airacobra fighters take off. Note the pierced steel planking on the ground. *Carlson collection*

Rainfall at Milne Bay was measured in feet, not inches. Conditions in the encampment, surrounded by dense jungle, were constantly soggy and muddy. Nevertheless the necessary chores had to be done, including an attempt to wash uniforms during a downpour. *Spieth collection*

The Kangaroo Squadron's last serious mishap occurred on September 24, 1942, when the B-17E piloted by George Newton (holding propeller blade) made a forced landing on a New Guinea beach north of Milne Bay, apparently due to fuel starvation. A flying boat rescued the stranded crew, but the airplane was written off. *Fields collection*

Raised from the muck of the Agaiambo Swamp on giant airbags, the Fortress crash-landed by Fred Eaton was recovered in the spring of 2006. It took contractor Fred Hagen and his team, aided by local villagers, almost a month to complete the salvage operation. The components, airlifted to a dock at Lae, were seized by the PNG government and held for more than three years. *Hagen collection*

The mystique of the "Swamp Ghost" has not been lost. Currently on display in Hangar 79 on Ford Island, she now resides at the Pacific Aviation Museum in Hawaii. A high-tech interactive attraction is under development to provide a compelling glimpse of the bomber's fateful combat mission. *Peter Dunn*

THIRTEEN

THE EVACUATION OF DUGOUT DOUG

During his meeting with Brigadier General Ralph Royce in Melbourne on March 7, Dick Carmichael had been briefed on two important developments. The first was the discovery of the Japanese invasion fleet, spotted in the Huon Gulf near Lae. The subsequent invasion was indeed a setback from the Allied point of view; for Carmichael personally, the second development seemed potentially more significant.

Two weeks earlier, accepting the reality that the Allied forces in the Philippines could not hold out much longer, President Roosevelt had ordered General MacArthur to evacuate from Corregidor. But it was a complicated issue. Any attempt to spirit the general, his family, and key members of his staff from the enemy-controlled archipelago would not only be risky, it would undoubtedly alienate the tens of thousands of American and Filipino troops left behind. Consigned, at best, to spend the rest of the war as POWs, they would resentfully view MacArthur's departure as a cowardly abandonment. Many troops already despised him. Having ventured only once from his underground fortress on Corregidor to visit the besieged forces on Bataan, MacArthur had earned a disdainful nickname that would haunt him for the rest of his days: "Dugout Doug."

The foregone loss of the Philippines cut deeply in Washington, but the possibility that MacArthur might be captured or killed by the Japanese—a fate likely shared by his wife and young son—would be far more devastating to American morale. The general's capture, in fact, would be the worst scenario imaginable since the Japanese would undoubtedly reap a tremendous propaganda coup by exploiting him as a prisoner. Conversely, the opportunity for MacArthur to start over from a safe haven in Australia, where he could prosecute the war on his own terms, would yield military and geopolitical benefits on both sides of the Pacific. For the worried citizens of Australia, MacArthur represented nothing less than salvation. As historian James Duffy put it, "Of course they wanted American troops, but most of all they wanted an American commander who would ensure that the fight to save Australia from invasion would become an American fight. They wanted MacArthur."[1]

A self-appointed field marshal in the Philippines prior to the war, MacArthur enjoyed an even bigger following in the United States. In terms of overall esteem, especially in the political arena where his name was frequently mentioned as a presidential candidate, he was second only to President Roosevelt as the most popular American of the day. His successful evacuation was therefore highly desirable.

On February 22 Roosevelt sent an encrypted message, drafted with the assistance of General George Marshall and Secretary of War Henry Stimson, directing MacArthur to proceed to the island of Mindanao. The northern portion of that island, the second-largest in the Philippines, was still in American hands. MacArthur was authorized to remain there for up to a week to ascertain the feasibility of Mindanao's defense, after which he was to continue southward to Melbourne and take command of all U.S. forces in Australia.

The order to evacuate dismayed MacArthur, who had declared on several occasions that he was prepared to meet his death on Corregidor, widely known as "the Rock." Although duty bound to follow the president's directive, he considered resigning his commission and then enlisting as a volunteer. Eventually, however, his staff convinced him to leave. Their motives were partly selfish, for it was tacitly understood that key members of the staff would accompany MacArthur and his household (wife Jean, their four-year-old son Arthur, and the child's Chinese nursemaid) when he departed from Corregidor.

MacArthur managed to stall for two weeks but ultimately decided to evacuate his entourage by surface craft. They would rely on Motor Torpedo Boat Squadron 3, led by Lieutenant Commander John D. Bulkeley, whose four remaining PT boats were never designed for long sea voyages. The seventy-seven-foot boats, constructed mostly of wood and powered by triple Packard twelve-cylinder engines, were theoretically much faster than traveling by submarine, but after long weeks of combat operations their engines were badly in need of an overhaul. Naval officers on Corregidor supposedly gave the mission only a twenty-percent chance of success, and additional doubts were raised about subjecting Mrs. MacArthur to the physical and emotional stresses of the journey.[2]

To determine whether his family could tolerate the voyage, MacArthur and Bulkeley arranged a test run on March 1 in the relatively still waters of Manila Bay. Jean MacArthur turned green at the gills aboard PT-41, but gamely assured her husband that she could endure the real thing. MacArthur therefore informed his staff that they would depart at dusk on Wednesday, March 11. Bulkeley would be responsible for getting the party to Mindanao, where army bombers would pick them up for the 1,500-mile flight to Darwin. Twenty-two individuals, selected by MacArthur's chief of staff, Brigadier General Richard K. Sutherland, were authorized to evacuate. The list, based on the estimated weight of passengers and personal luggage that could be safely carried by three B-17s, included MacArthur and his household, Sutherland and fourteen officers from MacArthur's staff, a navy admiral and his chief of staff, and one boyish-looking army clerk.

Down in Melbourne, General Brett had been advised that MacArthur's headquarters would contact him to arrange air transportation from Mindanao. The anticipated radio message, dictated by Sutherland, arrived on March 1:

> You have probably surmised purpose of mission. Request detail best pilots and that best available planes be placed in top condition for trip. B-24s

if available, otherwise B-17s. Ferry mission only. Desire if possible initial landing on return to be south of combat zone. Anticipate call for arrival Mindanao about 15 [March].[3]

Brett had no trouble deducing the nature of the flight, but finding three or four heavy bombers in tip-top shape posed a problem. Only six B-24s, three of which were the vulnerable LB-30 export version, remained in Australia. All were in bad condition. The likelihood of finding three B-17s in comparatively good shape was statistically better—thirty-nine new E models had been ferried to Java in January and February—but nearly two-thirds had been destroyed or abandoned during the ill-fated campaign. Those that had withdrawn to Melbourne required extensive maintenance or even depot-level overhaul before they could return to combat status, although several were being used to fly reconnaissance patrols out of Laverton airdrome.

The B-17 crews down in Melbourne were in equally bad shape. Defeated and demoralized, the survivors of the 7th and 19th Bomb Groups passed the days listlessly, mostly in pubs, with only cursory attempts to maintain military discipline. Brett was therefore in a predicament. "MacArthur would not be pleased with the best we could send," he would later write. "He hated to fly, suffered from airsickness, and would not get into a plane unless he knew it was perfect. He had his wife and child with him, and the trip would be dangerous every minute. He would want bright new ships, fresh off the assembly line."[4]

The twelve B-17Es in Townsville, which had been operating with the U.S. Navy in recent weeks, were as close to brand new as Brett could hope to find anywhere in Australia. Having already sent General Royce to liaison with the squadron, Brett had learned that the B-17s were jealously controlled by Vice Admiral Leary. Knowing the admiral's reputation for turning down requests that did not benefit the navy, Brett paid a personal visit to Leary on March 7. Stating plainly that he "had to get MacArthur out of the Philippines," Brett explained that his own worn-out bombers were not up to the task. Could he borrow three for a special mission? "I'd like to help you, Brett," said Leary, "but it is quite impossible. We need those planes here, and can't spare them for a ferry job, no matter how important it is. You'll have to do the best you can with what you have."[5]

Circumstantially, at least, Leary's refusal to cooperate was defensible. Allied headquarters had just learned of the Japanese invasion fleet off Lae, and plans were already afoot to counterattack. With no alternative but to follow Leary's advice, Brett ordered the dispirited 19th Bomb Group to prepare for a "special mission to the north."[6]

HAVING NOTHING BETTER to do on a Tuesday afternoon, Captain Henry C. "Hank" Godman was sitting in a Melbourne hotel, waiting for the bar to open, when an MP walked in and announced that he was needed back at the airfield. Similar scenes played out at various watering holes and barracks until enough crewmembers to man four B-17s were rounded up. The fliers were told little except that they would be taking off the next morning for an airfield near Darwin, two thousand miles to the northwest on the opposite side of the continent.

Predictably, things began to go wrong almost as soon as the clandestine mission got under way. It took more than two hours simply to get all four of the battle-weary bombers airborne on the morning of March 11. "The planes," Godman acknowledged, "were really in terrible shape."[7] His assessment was confirmed when the bombers landed to refuel at a primitive airfield outside Daly Waters, some 1,600 miles north of Melbourne. The remote outpost was as far as the bomber piloted by Lieutenant Kenneth D. Casper would go. Plagued with mechanical problems, it had to be scrubbed from the mission.

After refueling, the three airworthy B-17s continued to Batchelor Field, forty miles south of Darwin, where the crews were finally informed about their secret trip. They were to fly 1,500 miles across enemy-held territory to the Del Monte pineapple plantation on northern Mindanao, where a base for the Far East Air Force had been constructed just prior to the outbreak of war. After dropping off desperately needed supplies, they would pick up General MacArthur and his party and return immediately to Australia.

Planning to sneak into Del Monte well after dark to avoid enemy detection, the bombers took off from Batchelor Field on the afternoon of March 12. Each had a partial crew of seven men and a full load of cargo including medical supplies, weapons, and other necessities for the garrison on Mindanao, plus spare oxygen masks, parachutes, and inflatable life vests for the passengers on the return flight.[8] Less than an hour after takeoff, however, Lieutenant Jack Adams was forced to turn back due to engine trouble, reducing the evacuation attempt to two B-17s. And their troubles were far from over. The Fortress flown by Lieutenant Harl Pease Jr. developed a hydraulic system failure, affecting the main wheel brakes as well as the waste gates for the four turbosuperchargers. With the latter inoperative, Pease had to fly the route at fairly low altitude, increasing the risk of detection by the Japanese. No further setbacks marred his trip, and Pease landed at Del Monte at approximately 11 P.M. Rolling out in the darkness with no brakes, he stopped the heavily loaded bomber by performing a controlled ground loop at the far end of the runway.

Hank Godman's bomber never made it that far. About halfway through the flight, while transferring fuel from the auxiliary tank in the bomb bay to the wing tanks, a switch was allegedly thrown the wrong way. Godman blamed the flight engineer for the error, which pumped fuel "in Niagara proportions" out of an overflow valve, down the sides of the tank, and out through the bomb bay into the night sky.[9] By the time the blunder was discovered, so much fuel had been lost that the crew faced the likelihood of not reaching their destination. The frightening prospect kept everyone on edge while the pilots continuously monitored the fuel gauges. "I really didn't know if we were ever going to make it," Godman later wrote. "I started to descend lower and lower as we approached Mindanao."[10]

The distraction of the fuel transfer error apparently led to more trouble. Toward midnight, when the bomber finally reached the north coast of Mindanao, Godman commenced a turn over Illigan Bay to get his bearings. While he and his crew searched the darkened shoreline for the familiar shape of Macajalar Bay, which would guide them toward Del Monte plantation, the B-17 suddenly struck the surface of the Sulu Sea in a flat glide.

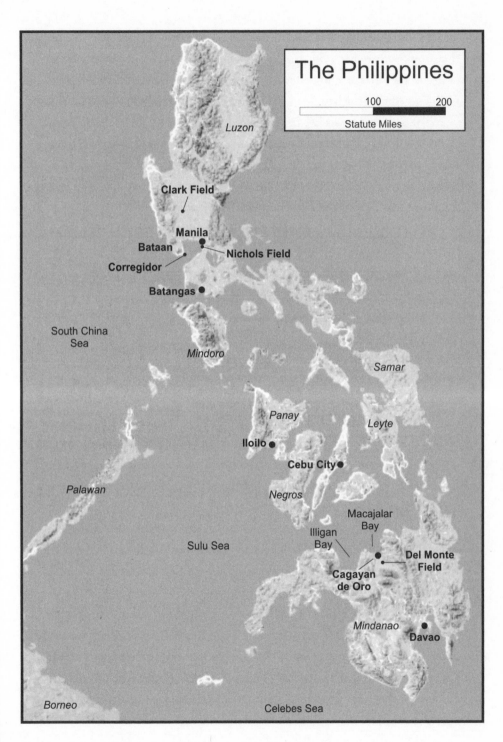

Thankfully Godman had leveled the wings moments earlier, preventing a catastrophic cartwheel, but the Fortress was no longer truly flying. It caromed off the surface, climbed for a few sickening moments, then nosed over and plunged into the bay.

Staff Sergeant Frank W. Lytle and Sergeant Allen G. Whitehead, riding in the rear fuselage where the weapons and ammunition were stowed, never emerged from the sinking wreckage. Godman and four other survivors bobbed to the surface, but all had been injured. Most were bleeding from multiple cuts, raising the terrifying specter of shark attacks. The worst off was Lieutenant Carl E. Epperson, partially paralyzed with a badly strained back and broken ribs. Swimming and paddling throughout the pitch black night, willing themselves to keep moving, the survivors spent almost five hours in the water before they finally crawled onto a beach. Picked up later that morning by Filipinos who had heard the midnight crash, they were eventually transported to Del Monte Field.[11]

The cause of the accident was not due to fuel starvation. Godman would later state that the altimeter had been reading 1,200 feet above sea level at the time of the crash, but aneroid altimeters are only accurate when the correct local barometric pressure is dialed in. Evidently the pilots had never updated the altimeter to the local setting (which would have been provided as part of the weather briefing), perhaps due to cockpit distractions resulting from the dangerously low fuel state. Whatever the cause, as the pilot in command Godman was ultimately responsible.

While Godman and his crew underwent their ordeal, Brigadier General William F. Sharp, the commanding general on Mindanao, had made a cursory assessment of Lieutenant Pease's B-17. He concluded what Brett had already anticipated: MacArthur would never fly in a bomber that had no wheel brakes or functional superchargers. Unwilling to risk the lives of the general and his party, Sharp sent Pease back to Australia with a planeload of 19th Bomb Group personnel. After spending only a few hours on the ground, Pease took off in the early hours of March 13, successfully evacuating seven junior officers and nine enlisted airmen who would otherwise have been left behind.

MacArthur and his entourage reached Mindanao a few hours later, completing a harrowing 650-mile journey aboard Bulkeley's PT boats. The sea voyage was supposed to have taken only nineteen hours, give or take a few, but the exhausted passengers, disheveled and ashen from seasickness, set foot on the island nearly thirty-six hours after leaving Corregidor. The boats had become separated, forcing the party to wait for the late arrivals, after which they still faced a dusty, hour-long ride to the plantation. By the time they arrived at Del Monte, the lone B-17 flown by Harl Pease was half-way to Australia.

After learning that only one malfunctioning B-17 had arrived out of the four sent from Australia, MacArthur fired off a long message to General Marshall in Washington. "Brett had sent four old B-17s of which only one arrived and that was not repeat not fit to carry passengers due to inoperative supercharger," MacArthur complained. "Failure of three planes to arrive not repeat not due to enemy action. The other plane took off before my arrival." Unable to refrain from pointing out his own importance, MacArthur listed his demands: "The best three planes in the United States or Hawaii should be made available with completely adequate and experienced crews. To attempt such a desperate and important trip with inadequate equipment would amount to consigning the whole party to death and I could not accept such a responsibility."[12]

MacArthur also chastised Brett, sending the following reproach to Melbourne:

> Upon arrival discovered that only one of the four planes dispatched here had arrived; and that with an inexperienced pilot, no brakes and super-charger not, repeat not, functioning. This plane was returned to you by Gen. Sharp, since it was not, repeat not, suitable for the purpose intended. It is necessary that only the best planes and most experienced pilots of adequate service be employed for the transportation of such a party. This trip is most important and desperate and must be set up with the greatest of care lest it end in disaster.[13]

Brett, accepting full responsibility "for a situation that was beyond any-one's control," replied to MacArthur that additional planes would be sent as soon as possible. Privately, he objected to the accusation that Pease was inexperienced. Perhaps that was what General Sharp had told MacArthur, as a way to deflect his wrath, but the criticism irritated Brett. "The young man had conducted himself with the greatest courage and skill in combat," he later wrote, "and he had seen plenty of combat."[14]

Knowing it would take far too long to get bombers from Hawaii or the States, and that MacArthur would be twice as demanding about the con-dition of the next planes sent to pick him up, Brett was limited to one op-tion: He had to go back to Vice Admiral Leary. Intending to "get tougher" during his second appeal for help, he found Leary unexpectedly cooperative. Unknown to Brett, Leary no longer had any authority over the B-17s at Townsville. The blistering message MacArthur sent to General Marshall had accomplished in one day what Brett had been trying to do for weeks. Liter-ally overnight, the Southern Bomber Command was removed from Leary's operational control. The bombers now belonged to Brett.

Simultaneously, the entire 19th Bomb Group was reorganized. Crews from the 7th Bomb Group who had escaped from Java were absorbed into the three existing squadrons of the 19th, which would await delivery of new aircraft before training for an eventual return to combat. At Townsville, the former Southern Bomber Command became the 14th Reconnaissance Squadron, attached to the 19th Bomb Group. For all practical purposes, the squadron simply underwent a change in designation. The aircraft assign-ments and personnel remained the same, with Dick Carmichael in com-mand and Jim Twaddell as executive officer.

CARMICHAEL WOULD NEVER forget the telephone call from Brigadier Gen-eral Royce. It came over a secure line on Saturday, March 14, the same day the squadron was redesignated. "Dick," he said, "I want you to pick your best four crews and your best four airplanes and meet me at Batchelor Field. I have a mission for you."[15]

Carmichael hadn't heard about the failed evacuation attempt, but he soon got the full story from Royce. Carmichael and his handpicked crews were to fly a load of supplies up to Del Monte plantation and bring back MacArthur. Fully aware that another failed attempt would be unacceptable, Royce followed his instructions with a pep talk. "Boy, I'm going to make you a real hero this time," he said. "You are going to go up there and get General MacArthur. I have already given him your name, and he is waiting for you with open arms. You will be the hero that Franklin Delano Roosevelt is looking for."[16]

Motivated by Royce's call, Carmichael counted himself in and picked three of his veteran flight leaders—Frank Bostrom, Newt Chaffin, and Bill Lewis—to fly the other three ships. Next, after calling an all-hands meeting, he asked for volunteers to conduct "a dangerous mission."[17] Due to the need for secrecy he didn't reveal the exact purpose of the flight, but virtually every hand went up. The rest of the day was spent preparing four of the squadron's most reliable B-17s, gathering supplies for delivery to the Mindanao garrison, and rounding up flight gear for the passengers on the return leg. The only way to obtain enough survival equipment (fourteen extra oxygen masks, parachutes, and life preservers per airplane) was to strip some of the other Fortresses.[18]

Given the undeniable importance of bringing MacArthur to safety, the attempt had to be thoroughly planned and carefully timed. In late December the Japanese had invaded Davao, a port city at the southern end of Mindanao, and worked their way northward to within thirty miles of Del Monte. For that reason, the B-17s would arrive well after dark on March 16, remaining on the ground only long enough to refuel while the passengers climbed aboard. This raised a new concern for Royce, who knew that none of the pilots in Carmichael's squadron had ever been to Del Monte, let alone at night. (A 19th Bomb Group pilot who had flown numerous sorties from the field described it as "a tricky place to find and safely approach, even in good weather."[19]) Therefore, instead of meeting Carmichael at Batchelor Field as originally planned, Royce gathered four experienced pilots from the 19th Group and accompanied them to Townsville early on March 15. They would serve as copilots, a solution that proved especially helpful for Bostrom and Lewis, already fatigued from the long but ineffective raid on Rabaul two days earlier.

The handpicked crews were awakened early the next morning for a pre-dawn takeoff. A brisk crosswind delayed their departure for over an hour while RAAF personnel manually realigned the smudge pots used to light the runway, but finally the B-17s took off for Batchelor Field. Completing the six-hour flight without incident, Carmichael and his crews arrived at the newly constructed airdrome with hopes of grabbing a few hours of rest before starting the mission. But the Japanese raids on Darwin had led to a lot of jittery nerves in the Northern Territory. Around midday on March 16, while the four crews waited for their scheduled takeoff, an air raid alert forced them to scramble. "So we got in our airplanes and took off in a hell of a hurry," Carmichael recalled, "and flew south to get out of the way."[20]

Forty miles to the north, the RAAF airdrome at Darwin was attacked by fourteen G4M1 bombers of the Takao Air Group. Damages were relatively light, with two Australian fatalities and four wounded, but the early warning network remained twitchy. The air raid alert for Batchelor Field, meanwhile, proved to be a false alarm, and after circling over the desert for more than an hour the B-17s were recalled.

During the return flight, Carmichael's crew chief tapped him on the shoulder. "Oil leak out there on number two," he said, "and it's bad. It must be the tank. I think you ought to shut the engine down, and we'll take a look at it when we get on the ground."[21] Carmichael complied, limping back to Batchelor on three engines. While the B-17s were being refueled for the upcoming mission, the crew chief got up inside the left gear well and traced the oil leak. He was right about the tank, which had cracked. "So that knocked out one airplane," said Carmichael, "but I still wanted to be that hero."[22]

The time had come to begin the mission. Bostrom and Lewis started taxiing out of the dispersal area but the propellers of Newt Chaffin's B-17 were not yet turning, so Carmichael hopped in a jeep and headed toward the parked bomber. He had every intention of pulling rank on Chaffin and taking his airplane, but Carmichael's grand plans were fouled again. "As I got out of the jeep," he explained, "there was a loud bang like a rifle shot. Nature had conspired against me, because that loud bang was the left main tire of Newt Chaffin's airplane. There it sat like a ruptured duck. . . . Somebody up there had denied me the opportunity to be the big hero of the war."[23]

To SAY THAT the past few days had been nerve-wracking for General MacArthur would be an understatement. Everybody at Del Monte was on edge. The Japanese were close, and it was no secret that MacArthur was ensconced at the plantation. Soon after his entourage had arrived, a Filipino woman approached him seeking information about her son, one of the hapless defenders on Luzon. She had walked twenty-five miles just for the opportunity to inquire. Later that evening, while taking a stroll with his wife, MacArthur was almost fired upon by a nervous army captain. Thereafter, keeping a low profile, the general and his family were seldom seen outside their bungalow.[24]

The nearly four-day wait for another attempted airlift probably seemed intolerable to a man like MacArthur. Finally, on the night of March 16, the engines of a heavy bomber could be heard over Del Monte Field. It was Bostrom, "Frank P.," as his crew liked to call him, whose flight to Mindanao on that clear, moonless night had been uneventful. Despite the darkness his experienced substitute copilot, Captain Edward C. Teats, had no trouble finding the valley that led down to Del Monte from the coastal city of Cagayan de Oro. As they neared the plantation the pilots flashed their landing lights. "The third time we blinked," recalled Teats, "they caught our signal and flipped on the field lights right under our right wing."[25]

Bostrom landed at 11:30 P.M., beating Bill Lewis and his crew by almost thirty minutes. The latter had taken off from Australia ahead of Bostrom but encountered more difficulty finding Del Monte in the darkness. "There are three or four bays up there that all look alike," recalled Dick Graf, the radio operator on Lewis's crew. "We milled around them, picked the wrong bay and started to come down, then decided we were mistaken."[26]

With a couple of engines acting up, Lewis finally reached the field at about midnight. "There were very few lights on because the field was subject to attack at almost any time," remembered John Straight, a gunner on Lew-is's crew. "There were just enough lights to get us down, and as soon as we were on the ground those lights went out."[27]

The tired crews, climbing stiffly from their B-17s, could barely see what they were doing. But despite the late hour and the darkness, willing hands promptly began to unload the cargoes of quinine, sulfa, and other sorely needed necessities, none prized more than cigarettes. While the B-17s were being cleaned and refueled, the crews had time to eat. The main attraction, according to Dick Graf, was "some good coffee; we were glad to see it after all the Australian tea we had been drinking."[28] Frank Bostrom, it is widely reported, downed eight cups in an effort to counteract his fatigue.

The arrival of the bombers attracted numerous onlookers. Lieutenant Robert Roy Carruthers, the navigator on Bostrom's crew, recalled spending "a couple of unforgettable hours swapping stories with the many men around the field."[29] Some were undoubtedly hoping to talk their way onto one of the two bombers. Hundreds of USAAF personnel at Del Monte, knowing their days were numbered, were desperate to get away before the Japanese swept in. One who succeeded was Hank Godman. In the days since his deadly offshore crash, he had somehow managed to ingratiate himself with Mac-Arthur. Godman requested permission to meet with the general, whereupon he explained that the crash had cost the lives of two crewmen. Godman felt he deserved to be included in the evacuation and told the general he wanted to join his staff. The plea worked. "Godman," said MacArthur, "anybody as lucky as you who can crash at night into the sea at 170 miles an hour and live to tell about it can work for me."[30]

A few other individuals had also been added to the evacuation list. Dick Graf recalled that while the planes were being refueled, a long line of staff cars arrived and "general after general came piling out."[31]

MacArthur and his family climbed aboard Bostrom's B-17, which had been refueled first. The prevailing mood was one of barely subdued anxiety, the unease intensified by the poor visibility. "In almost total darkness, it was hurry, hurry," acknowledged the tail gunner, Herb Wheatley. "Soon someone placed a G.I. cot mattress in our plane. Then they came. Not only the General and some other rank but a woman and a little boy and his amah. I believed at this time, as young and dumb as I was, that we were into something pretty heavy. I think it was seeing the general's family there under those conditions that really spun my gyro. The rest of the guys felt about the same."[32]

MacArthur, his high-peaked officer's cap making him appear taller than his six-foot frame, wore service dress trousers and a khaki overcoat as he boarded the aircraft. Carrying a wooden cane, an essential part of his public persona, he moved forward to the radio compartment and sat in the operator's seat.[33] "MacArthur said very little," remembered Wheatley. "He had his head down, doing some heavy thinking."[34]

On the floor of the gunner's compartment, the government-issue mattress and a few blankets provided an oasis for Jean MacArthur and four-year-old Arthur (who was half asleep and clutched a stuffed toy), along with Ah Cheu, the Chinese nursemaid. Brigadier General Sutherland, Captain Godman, Brigadier General Harold H. George (air officer), and Brigadier General Richard J. Marshall (deputy chief of staff) also boarded the aircraft. Otherwise, according to Wheatley, the B-17 was lightly loaded.

Lewis's bomber, which had experienced mechanical trouble on the way in, took aboard the balance of the personnel on the list, plus a few extras. "We refueled, and on our plane we loaded 17 of MacArthur's staff and their baggage," John Straight later wrote. "We had some engine problems on the inbound flight and weren't sure we were going to be able to get off the ground. When we saw the amount of baggage and stuff put on the plane, we felt we had had it."[35]

Dick Graf concurred: "Generals, colonels, and admirals started getting aboard our plane loaded down with suitcases, B-4 bags, steamer trunks, foot lockers. We couldn't possibly have taken off with all that luggage, so after some arguing, part of the luggage was finally left behind."[36]

Bags of mail, the last personal correspondence to come out of Corregidor, were also piled aboard. The sight of it was heartrending. Thousands of Americans and Filipinos would hold out for six more weeks on "the Rock," but they were doomed to spend the remainder of the war in captivity. At best. None of them could have fathomed the squalid conditions they would face in POW camps, or the horrors of the "hell ships" that would later transport many of them to Japan as slave labor, or the beatings they would endure. Their last poignant messages to loved ones back home had been scribbled on anything they could get their hands on, from pieces of cardboard to scraps of toilet paper.

One of the last individuals to climb aboard Lewis's B-17 slipped inside as a stowaway. Hank Godman had arranged a reprieve for himself, but the other four survivors of his crash were not included on the evacuation list. Carl Epperson, the navigator, and Staff Sergeant Henry B. Pecher, the radio operator, were recovering from their injuries in a hospital; the other two were left to their own devices. One was an enlisted man with no bargaining power, but the copilot, Lieutenant Richard T. Carlisle, had the advantage of knowing two of the men in Lewis's crew. He explained his plight to John Straight and Private Charles W. Latito, who remembered him from Hickam Field. "Carlisle told us he had to get out of there," recalled Straight. "We told him to stow away in the tail gunner's position. No one would notice because that was supposed to be empty on takeoff. So he got a 'chute, and as the last man loaded, he jumped in the tail."*37

A total of twenty-seven passengers had boarded the two planes, according to eyewitnesses. Not counting Carlisle's surreptitious entry, a few additional men had obviously been added to the list of evacuees from Corregidor. As long as the planes weren't overloaded, the flight crews really didn't care about the headcount. "We had gone without sleep for two nights, and we weren't thinking too much about individuals," acknowledged Bostrom's copilot, Ed Teats. "Our main interest was to get going and get the plane back to Australia with everyone safe on board."38

The tension ratcheted up when Bostrom's right inboard engine refused

---

* Lieutenant Epperson, the navigator, recovered and managed to get aboard a later flight out of Mindanao, but the two enlisted men left behind were captured by the Japanese. The flight engineer, Sergeant Wallace J. Hewston, survived three and a half years of captivity. So did Henry Pecher, who endured the infamous Bilibid prison in Manila, a "hell ship" voyage to Japan, and countless beatings. He weighed only 112 pounds when repatriated.

to start after several attempts using the batteries. Two crewmen jumped out and turned the inertia starter using a long-handled crank, and the engine finally coughed to life on the second try.

Bostrom took off at 2:30 A.M. on March 17, followed by Lewis, whose Fortress had only *one* engine functioning normally. "When we started our takeoff run," recalled John Straight, "we had full power on No. 1 engine, 2 and 4 had about 75% power, and No. 3 was barely idling. The takeoff run was long, but the B-17 being the great airplane it was, finally got airborne."[39]

Soon after takeoff, the passengers were surprised to see an officer crawling out of the tail gunner's position. It was Carlisle, the stowaway. "There wasn't much to do," Straight added wryly, "but add him to the passenger list."[40]

MACARTHUR'S BIOGRAPHERS, IT seems, are not apt to let the truth get in the way of a good story. Nearly all of the popular narratives about him describe the evacuation flight from Del Monte to Australia as fraught with stormy weather and close encounters with enemy fighters. One of the most colorful depictions of the flight was penned by William Manchester in *American Caesar*, a bona fide bestseller. "Neither MacArthur's son nor the amah had ever been on a plane before, and both were excited," he wrote. "They found it wasn't much different from PT-41. Violent turbulence over the Celebes Sea made them airsick, and when they soared over land the pilot repeatedly had to take sharp evasive action. . . . At sunrise Japanese fighters rose to search for the B-17s; but somehow the twisting, diving American flyers eluded them."[41]

Nothing of the sort happened. There were no turbulent storms to contend with, no sightings of enemy aircraft, no stomach-churning, roller-coaster maneuvers in the B-17. Ed Teats described the flight as "completely uneventful." Both pilots struggled with fatigue, but the passengers had no awareness of it. "Bostrom and I took turns at the controls at 30-minute intervals," wrote Teats. "We had to do it to give each other a little chance to rest. . . . The strain of flying by instruments at night is bad enough, and we were fagged. My eyes felt like two red hot coals, and if I closed them, the lids felt as though they were lined with sandpaper. I thought they would pop out of my head."[42]

Rob Carruthers, the navigator, confirmed Teats's recollection. "The weather was excellent," he wrote, "and it is doubtful if General MacArthur ever had as smooth a flight as he had that night. We were thankful for that. Mrs. MacArthur and the General's son both stood up well under the long flight and the General himself was in high spirits as we neared the Australian coast."[43]

Last but not least, tail gunner Herb Wheatley backed up Carruthers's assessment of the conditions. Having manned his guns all night, Wheatley crawled out of the cramped position after sunrise, when the B-17 was safely beyond the enemy-held island of Timor. He was self-conscious about his appearance, knowing that he and the rest of the crew "looked like pirates." Grimy, unshaven, his eyes bloodshot from fatigue, Wheatley was pleasantly surprised when Jean MacArthur greeted him cordially. "Good morning," she said. "How are you?" Her pleasant demeanor left a lasting impression on Wheatley, who remembered her as "a lovely, vivacious lady in spite of all she had been through in that noisy, beat-up B-17."[44]

Manchester and other biographers, including D. Clayton James, further dramatized the evacuation by stating that the B-17s were forced to divert from Darwin to Batchelor Field due to an air raid. This inaccuracy can be traced back to MacArthur himself. "Over Timor," he wrote in his wartime memoirs, "we were spotted and [the Japanese] came up after us. But we changed course from Darwin, where they figured we would land, and came in at Batchelor Field, 40 miles to the south, just as they hit Darwin Field. They discovered their mistake too late, and their dive bombers and fighters roared in at Batchelor ten minutes after I had left in another plane for Alice Springs to the south."[45]

This was pure embellishment. In the first place, Darwin was never the intended destination for the B-17s. The runways at the RAAF facility were not sturdy enough for heavy bombers, as discovered when some of the first B-17Cs and Ds to land there damaged the surface, and they were nine thousand pounds lighter than the E model.[46] Furthermore, the Japanese did not conduct any raids against either Darwin or Batchelor on March 17, although the former had been attacked by land-based bombers the previous day.

In contrast to the dramatized narratives, Bostrom's B-17 touched down quietly at 9:30 that Tuesday morning. "At Batchelor, Frank P. made the smoothest two-wheel landing in his or my career," recalled Wheatley. "While the engines were being cut, I opened the door and a colonel was there to ask who was aboard. I recall telling him, 'We got 'em all.'"[47]

Bill Lewis arrived several minutes later with the rest of MacArthur's entourage. General Royce was there to meet them, and the entire party headed to a "crude little mess that had been set up under the trees" for a breakfast of baked beans and canned peaches.[48]

The evacuation effort had gone almost exactly as planned. MacArthur, whose popularity in Australia and the United States was about to skyrocket, had literally been snatched from under the noses of the Japanese. Even so, because of the threat of enemy air raids in the Northern Territory, his staff was eager to get MacArthur aboard a plane to Melbourne as soon as possible. He and his family, however, raised strong objections.

Most accounts have Jean MacArthur refusing to fly any farther, and who could blame her? The flight to Melbourne would mean another eight to ten hours in the air, an excruciating journey given the lack of comforts in a B-17. But according to Master Sergeant Paul P. Rogers, the only enlisted man to accompany MacArthur's staff from Corregidor, it was the general himself who objected the loudest. "MacArthur had stripped down to his long underwear," he recalled, "when Sutherland came in to report that planes were available for the remainder of the trip to Melbourne. MacArthur lashed out that he would not fly. Sutherland tried to explain that the only alternative would be a truck caravan across the desert to the nearest railhead, but MacArthur was obstinately furious and refused to budge."[49]

Frank Bostrom overheard MacArthur demanding "the best damn rail transportation in Australia"[50] and simply shook his head. The Commonwealth's rail system was terribly inefficient. Instead of using a standardized track width, the various states operated railroads constructed in three different gauges. Passengers as well as shipments had to change trains multiple times on a transcontinental journey. Moreover, there was no rail service this far north. The nearest railhead was more than 750 miles away in Alice Springs, a remote settlement in the central Australian desert.

Informed of this, MacArthur remained stubborn. He contemplated taking a motor caravan, but staff members argued strongly against the idea. The average daytime temperature soared above ninety degrees in the desert, and the journey by vehicle over the winding, unimproved roads would take as much as thirty hours of actual travel time. MacArthur's physician, Major Charles H. Morhouse, finally appealed to MacArthur's better judgment. "Morhouse found the right approach," Rogers wrote. "He told MacArthur that the long trip by truck caravan would be extremely injurious to young Arthur's health. The argument carried the day; MacArthur yielded and allowed himself and his family to be gently hurried to the airplanes."[51]

Unknown to MacArthur or his family, a new air raid warning had just been issued. According to the reliable Rogers, a staff officer quietly informed Sutherland that enemy bombers "had been sighted on a bearing from Bachelor [sic] Field and Darwin." But as previously mentioned, no enemy raids were conducted that day against either Darwin or Batchelor. With the early warning network already on edge, the sighting of a distant reconnaissance aircraft may have been enough to trigger the alert. Another possibility is that the mere threat of a raid was used as a ploy to hasten the departure of MacArthur's party from Batchelor Field. In any case, the tail wagged the dog. Rumors of an inbound raid spread rapidly until the whole base believed it was actually happening.

The situation played right into the hands of Dick Carmichael. The ruptured oil tank that had grounded his B-17 the previous day was now fixed, making his bomber immediately available. The other disabled Fortress was likewise ready. "They had gotten a new wheel for Newt Chaffin's airplane," he explained, "so Newt and I took over with our airplanes from Frank Bostrom and Bill Lewis."[52]

Unfortunately for Carmichael, the flight to Alice Springs started badly. "I almost got court-martialed," he later remarked, "because I spilled all of the people in the back, including MacArthur, with my hasty taxi out and takeoff from Batchelor. They didn't know it at the time, but the red ball had gone up, and word had come through that the field was under attack. The alert came while we were still loading. So I got them in as quickly as I could, and I started the engines and taxied out and took right off. Well, in the process of all this, the back end of a B-17 swings around quite a bit, and it spilled everybody."[53]

MacArthur roared at his chief of staff, Sutherland, to "get that man's name, that pilot's name. I am going to have his head."[54] MacArthur eventually calmed down after the circumstances were explained to him, but the worst was yet to come. Under a cloudless blue sky, the B-17s crossed the desert plateau of central Australia in the middle of the day. Thermals of hot air rising from the desert floor created clear air turbulence, or CATs, which made the ride extremely bumpy. Carmichael was unable to find smooth air anywhere. He tried different altitudes, but without enough oxygen masks for everyone, he dared not fly above 10,000 feet. Even at that height the air was stifling, making the aluminum fuselage feel like an oven. Between the heat and the turbulence, everyone got airsick. "So that," said Carmichael, "ended my big chance to be the hero."[55]

By the end of the miserable four-hour flight, the MacArthurs were physically and emotionally drained. It was probably at Alice Springs, rather than at Batchelor Field as commonly held, that Jean MacArthur said, "Never, never again will anybody ever get me into an airplane! Not for any reason!"[56] Refusing to fly any farther, the MacArthurs and a few staff members, including Morhouse, were billeted in a ramshackle hotel while waiting for a special train to take them the rest of the way to Melbourne. Lieutenant Chaffin and his crew, by comparison, were just getting started. They flew back to Batchelor Field that afternoon, then made the exhausting round trip to Del Monte on March 18–19, returning to Australia with some of MacArthur's baggage, important files, and twenty-one additional evacuees.[57]

From Alice Springs, it would take the MacArthurs three additional days to chug across the outback to Adelaide and thence to Melbourne. The train was pulled by a relic of a steam engine, an iron tortoise, which gave the general plenty of time to dwell on the frustrations of abandoning the

Philippines. The slow journey also provided time to contemplate the statement MacArthur would present when the train finally reached civilization. He drafted a simple pledge to the Filipino people, little realizing that his words would resonate throughout the free world.

When the train stopped at the small town of Terowie, 125 miles north of Adelaide, MacArthur was surprised to discover that a welcoming crowd of citizens and several reporters had gathered at the station. "The President of the United States ordered me to break through the Japanese lines," he told them, "and proceed . . . to Australia for the purpose, as I understand it, of organizing an American offensive against Japan, the primary purpose of which is the relief of the Philippines. I came through and I shall return."[58]

MacArthur eventually made good on his promise, though two and a half years would pass before he waded ashore on Leyte like a returning conqueror. Long before that carefully staged event, he also fulfilled his pledge to Hank Godman by selecting him to pilot his personal aircraft, a B-17 named *Bataan*. It made a great story. But the men MacArthur left behind in the Philippines were having none of it. Those who survived the infamous Bataan death march, followed by three additional years of disease, starvation, and physical abuse at the hands of the Japanese, never forgave the man they called "Dugout Doug."

FOURTEEN

EVACUATION REDUX

The successful evacuation of General MacArthur gave the 14th Reconnaissance Squadron some well-deserved bragging rights. Bostrom's crew in particular, having spent several hours in close company with the famous general, had a lifetime's worth of stories to tell. Spirits also improved as the outbreak of dengue fever began to wind down, though some men were still hospitalized as late as the third week in March. One of the last to get back on his feet, after six days in the Townsville hospital, was navigator John Steinbinder. "Broke out with a terrific rash," he wrote in his diary on March 17. "Had an awful backache. Threw up everything I ate, so for the last five days I ate nothing at all."[1] The day after his release, he went on a mission to Rabaul.

Despite the outbreak of fever and the absence of four handpicked crews during the MacArthur evacuation, the squadron sent raids against Rabaul on three out of four days beginning March 18. In contrast to the huge raids that darkened the skies over Europe and Japan later in the war, however, the missions staged by the 14th Squadron were almost absurdly small. No other heavy bomber units were conducting combat operations in all of Australia. Factories in the United States were still gearing up in early 1942, and the long supply line to Australia provided only a trickle of spare parts. For an independent squadron that conducted ten-hour missions and then had to repair its own planes, every sortie was a major effort. The 14th therefore settled for a modest but sustainable routine, rotating planes and crews in groups of four to Port Moresby for missions against Rabaul. Although the raids caused little material damage, they disrupted the Japanese on a regular basis.

To minimize the effectiveness of enemy fighters, the Fortresses bombed from 30,000 or 31,000 feet, near the limits of their service ceiling. This presented a significant physical ordeal for the crews, as the outside air temperature approached minus fifty degrees Fahrenheit. The unpressurized B-17s were equipped with a heating and ventilating system, which ducted a modicum of warm air to the nose compartment, flight deck, and radio compartment, but the airflow to the rear fuselage had no effect on the large, uninsulated space and there was no ducting whatsoever for the tail gunner. Side gunners bundled up in fleece-lined heavy flying suits to endure the bitter cold, while the tail gunner wore an electrically heated suit that plugged into an outlet. The other essential piece of flight equipment, worn at altitudes above 10,000 feet, was a functioning oxygen mask. Every crewmember wore one and was trained to watch his fellow crewmates for signs of hypoxia. A depleted or obstructed supply of oxygen could be lethal within minutes. ·

As acting CO at Townsville during Carmichael's absence, Jim Twaddell organized and led a raid against Rabaul on March 18. Arriving over the target at 31,000 feet, the crews counted "numerous Jap ships" in Simpson Harbor and bombed a warship believed to be a heavy cruiser. A direct hit was claimed on its stern. That alone was worthy of front-page headlines in newspapers across Australia and even earned praise from Prime Minister John Curtin, who mentioned the damage in a communiqué.[2] According to one reliable account, however, the damage to the cruiser was wishful thinking. Durwood Fesmire, the expert bombardier recently attached from the 19th Bomb Group, had dropped his bombs close to the warship, causing no damage. The others had released their bombs too early, he said, "and all they did was kill a few fish."[3]

The following day, Ted Faulkner led four B-17s from Townsville for an overnight stay at Port Moresby prior to the next raid on Rabaul. Two of the aircraft were flown by First Lieutenant Maurice C. Horgan and Captain Fred M. Key, recent arrivals who had fought in Java with the 7th Bomb Group. Fred was an old-timer, a famed Mississippi barnstormer. He and his brother Al, billed as The Flying Keys, had set an endurance record back in 1935 after helping to pioneer a safe method of aerial refueling. For the Rabaul mission, Fred filled in for Swede Swenson, who had blown a tire while taxiing at Townsville.

Swenson's crew was becoming frustrated with his repeated aborts. On March 12, while staging to Port Moresby for the raid led by Bill Lewis, he had turned back an hour out of Townsville due to engine trouble. Five days later, as part of the effort led by Major Twaddell, Swenson turned back again for the same reason, this time claiming engine trouble only an hour out of Townsville. Although no one could fault him for the flat tire, there were rumblings among the other pilots that Swenson wasn't pulling his weight. His copilot, Roy Reid, considered the captain a likeable person, but felt that Swenson "did his darnedest to find reasons to abort."[4]

The big Swede may have been the nervous type. His hands, according to Reid, were always wet with perspiration while flying. But he wasn't the only one to experience engine trouble. By this time most of the B-17s had accumulated about five hundred hours on their engines, the typical period for an overhaul. Some replacement parts and supplies, including four new engines, had finally reached Townsville; but an engine change required tools and skills beyond the scope of the combat crews.

And so it was not particularly surprising when "Maury" Horgan had engine trouble on March 20, en route to Rabaul with the four-ship formation led by Ted Faulkner. The problem was that *both* engines on Horgan's right wing began to backfire, "missing and acting up" as John Steinbinder put it. Nor were the rough-running engines the crew's only concern. The arctic temperature at 30,000 feet had caused the lubricant in most of the machine guns to freeze. In Horgan's ship, only the tail guns worked. "Well, we figured at that altitude we needn't fear pursuit," wrote Steinbinder, "so we kept on."[5]

Targeting a warship identified as a heavy cruiser, the B-17s released their payloads high above Simpson Harbor. The bombs fell for a long time, taking at least thirty seconds to reach the surface. The winds affected their accuracy, but in the bombardiers' favor, the ship was evidently at anchor. Six days earlier, the light cruiser *Yubari* had arrived at Rabaul for temporary repairs after sustaining damage and casualties in the Huon Gulf on March 10. Thus the B-17s were now attacking her for at least the second time. Although none of the bombs struck home—hitting a slender warship from a height of more than five miles was almost too much to expect—splinters and concussion from near misses opened three large gaps in her plating. Two smoke generators were also damaged, only one of which was repairable. The other generator may have gone up in a flash, prompting the B-17 crews to claim that the cruiser "was seen to explode and burn."[6] More plausibly, the warship fired back with her 5.5-inch main armament, the muzzle blasts from which could easily have been mistaken for a bomb exploding.[7]

High overhead, Horgan and his crew found themselves in real trouble after dropping their bombs. "Just as we closed the bomb bay doors," recalled Steinbinder, "the ship began to shake like a leaf in a cyclone and the #4 engine broke into flames, showering the fuselage with molten aluminum. We shut off the engine and tried to feather the prop but couldn't. Finally we gave up. The three other ships left us. We flew on three engines for five minutes, losing altitude slowly but surely. Suddenly out of the clear blue sky four Zero fighters attacked us, two of them from below and two from the sides."[8]

The combat log of the 4th Air Group confirms that two pairs of Zeros had launched from Rabaul, one section taking off from Lakunai airdrome, the other from Vunakanau. Adhering to the standard doctrine of ganging up on a crippled aircraft, the four fighters caught Horgan's lagging B-17 and attacked independently. One Zero apparently experienced gun failure of its own, perhaps due to the extreme cold. Another, emboldened by the lack of return fire from the B-17, made a frontal attack from below. "They made their initial passes without getting any fire from us," continued Steinbinder, "as we had only two guns working. Suddenly one came under us strafing our belly and came up in full view of the rear gunner. He put in a burst and saw the ship smoking and falling away. The others each made a few more passes but at a respectful distance, all their shells falling short."[9]

No Zeros were lost or damaged over Rabaul that day, once again demonstrating the propensity for combatants on both sides to overestimate the effects of their gunnery. On this occasion, the opponents swatted at each other for half an hour before the Zeros broke off their pursuit.[10]

But the drama was far from over for Horgan and his crew. Still losing altitude, Horgan tried to feather the number four propeller again, but the engine suddenly started up of its own volition, a runaway that shook the Fortress so badly the crew feared the wing might collapse. Everyone donned parachutes, preparing to bail out. Horgan chopped the throttle and the vibration smoothed out, but the engine could not be shut down. Chunks of metal flew off as the nine-cylinder engine literally tore itself apart. "One large piece flew into the upper turret blister," wrote Steinbinder. "Had our crew chief been in the upper turret it would surely have brained him. He, however, was lying down with a raging fever."[11]

Horgan dared not overfly Gasmata, the enemy fighter base on the south coast of New Britain. Instead he headed out to sea, giving the airfield a wide berth to the east, then turned due south. The long deviations added more than a hundred miles to the return flight and put heavy responsibility on Steinbinder, who had to abandon his preflight planning and quickly calculate new heading estimates to get them safely to Port Moresby. The twenty-three-year-old navigator, who held a degree in chemistry from Oberlin College, was up to the challenge. Every ten minutes, while keeping an eye on the dwindling fuel, he gave Horgan a verbal update on their position, groundspeed, and distance remaining. Because of the detour around Gasmata, Steinbinder initially estimated they would run out of gas well short of Port Moresby, but as he continued to update their progress, he realized that a tailwind was gradually helping. If they somehow managed to reach Seven Mile airdrome, they would be shaving it very close.

With fifty miles to go, the propeller on the tortured, red-hot engine suddenly twisted off its shaft and went spinning down into the sea. No longer worried that the prop blades might tear through the fuselage, the crew radioed ahead to warn Port Moresby that they were making an emergency approach on three engines. Moresby radioed back with a warning:

the airdrome was under attack. Lacking the fuel to loiter, Horgan flew straight on in, arriving over Seven Mile just as the raid ended. While he circled in the landing pattern, the right inboard engine quit. Shrugging off the last-second emergency, Horgan quickly retrimmed the plane and applied opposite rudder, then expertly put the big bomber down with both left engines at full power. Shortly after the B-17 cleared the runway, those engines also sputtered and died, out of gas. Close shave indeed. Recounting the day's excitement in his diary, Steinbinder exclaimed, "I never realized just how scared a person could get, and yet act rationally."[12]

THROUGHOUT THE REMAINDER of March, operations continued on a limited scale. A few high-time bombers were flown to Brisbane for depot-level overhaul, while those that could be locally maintained—four or five were typically airworthy at any given time—staged through Port Moresby for missions against Rabaul and Lae.

Down in Melbourne, accepting his appointment as supreme commander of Allied Forces in the Southwest Pacific Area, General MacArthur wasted little time establishing his new headquarters. Distrustful of General Brett's loyalty, he relied almost exclusively on his own staff. Known derogatorily as "the Bataan Gang," they were augmented with personnel who had gained combat experience in Australia. As a consequence, the 14th Reconnaissance Squadron lost its two most senior officers. Dick Carmichael was transferred to the intelligence section of MacArthur's headquarters, and Jim Twaddell became chief of the Allied weather office. With a hasty farewell, they departed Townsville on March 25.

It was an abrupt turn of events for the two West Point classmates, but they left the squadron in the capable hands of Bill Lewis. Still a captain, he had flown more sorties than any other pilot in the outfit, and by coincidence was away at Cloncurry while participating in a joint raid on Timor with the reorganized 30th Bombardment Squadron.

Unexpectedly, in the midst of the turnover, the 14th Squadron received orders to conduct another secret mission to the Philippines. The success of the MacArthur evacuation had everything to do with the new undertaking.

The squadron was not only making headlines in the Australian papers, it was beginning to capture the interest of American war correspondents as well. And despite the fact that it had been operating in the Southwest Pacific for only a month, the 14th had already become one of the few squadrons in Australia that could rightfully boast of its accomplishments. For combat crews and support personnel in any squadron, bragging rights are hugely important. It is far better to be an integral part of a renowned unit on a hot streak than be associated with a downtrodden, ineffective squadron, and the 14th was well on its way to establishing an enviable combat record.

The challenging mission handed down by General Brett's air staff in Melbourne was nearly identical in scope to the MacArthur evacuation. Three B-17s would deliver a load of medical supplies and other necessities to Del Monte, then evacuate Filipino president Manuel Quezon, his family, and his sizable staff to Melbourne.

Quezon and his party had departed from Corregidor by submarine in late February, weeks ahead of MacArthur. Eventually reaching the island of Negros, Quezon remained in regular contact with MacArthur, who sent a letter in mid-March imploring Quezon to evacuate his party to Melbourne. "It is the natural and proper thing for you to do," MacArthur wrote, "to re-join me at my headquarters in Australia in the great drive for victory in the Philippines."[13] Quezon agreed, so MacArthur sent John Bulkeley with his last three PT boats to transport the party from Negros to Mindanao.

Hours before dawn on March 26, a trio of B-17s piloted by Ted Faulkner, Harry Spieth, and Dubby DuBose departed from Garbutt Field. As with the previous mission, they refueled at Batchelor Field, after which they continued another 1,500 miles to Mindanao. Most of the personnel were making their first trip, but five of the enlisted crewmen, including gunners Charlie Latito and John Straight, were veterans of the MacArthur evacuation. All three navigators had also conducted the previous trip, and thus knew their way around Mindanao at night. As a result, the squadron's second flight to Del Monte proved as uneventful as the first. Landing shortly before midnight on the dimly lit field, the crews unloaded their cargo and prepared to take evacuees aboard.

For those who had been there before, the mood at Del Monte was no-
ticeably different. Nobody could predict whether additional evacuation
flights would be sent from Australia, which caused the personnel at Del
Monte considerable uncertainty. Those who were authorized to evacuate
with the Quezon party included some holdovers from MacArthur's staff and
a few others whose qualifications were in high demand, particularly aircraft
mechanics. For the people who would be left behind, the sight of the lucky
ones climbing aboard the B-17s was gut-wrenching. "It was pretty disconso-
late," recalled Spieth's copilot, Wallace Fields. "People were crying, wanting
to be smuggled aboard, and we told them we couldn't take them; that we
didn't have parachutes for them. They would say, 'Well, don't worry about a
parachute; I don't need one; I won't use one.' Anything to get on that plane
and get off that island."[14]

The Quezon entourage included several luminaries from the highest
echelons of the Philippines government and society. Faulkner's passenger
manifest included President Quezon, his wife and children, Dr. Andreas
Trepp (a Swiss lung specialist who treated Quezon's chronic tuberculosis),
and General Basilio Valdes, Quezon's personal physician. An estimated seventeen American passengers, consisting mostly of USAAF mechanics and
members of MacArthur's staff who had missed the previous evacuation,
boarded Spieth's B-17. Last but not least, Vice President Sergio Osména, his
valet and secretary, and several Filipino military officers climbed into Du-
Bose's ship. Quezon had insisted that he and the vice president take separate
planes in case one went down.

The precaution was not an act of melodrama. Taking off from Del
Monte by 1:00 A.M. on March 27, the three Fortresses flew independently
back to Australia. They passed over Mindanao and the Celebes Sea with
no difficulties, but the weather began to deteriorate at the halfway point.
Spieth's navigator, Jack Carlson, reported "very rough" weather conditions
north of Ceram Island. Entering a thunderhead in the darkness, the bomber
hit a downdraft and plunged four thousand feet. With no stars visible for
celestial navigation, Carlson had to rely on dead reckoning to avoid Ceram's
tall mountains. Later, encountering more foul weather about a hundred

miles north of Australia, Spieth descended to three hundred feet but could not get under the storm. Picking his way around it, he finally reached Batchelor Field at 9:20.[15]

After refueling, Spieth continued with his passengers to Alice Springs. This presented a new problem for Carlson, whose only aid for navigation was an old Shell Oil road map. But he reached the destination safely by following a telegraph line that led straight to the little outpost and its dusty airfield. When the engines finally stopped, the crew could barely climb out of their seats. Since their departure from Townsville early the previous morning, the men had flown four back-to-back flights spanning almost five thousand miles. More impressively, they had spent thirty-two of the past thirty-six hours in the air.

Ted Faulkner also made it safely to Australia, though President Quezon required supplemental oxygen during the flight and was frightened by the rough turbulence in the vicinity of storms. General Valdes, unaccustomed to the lack of creature comforts in a military bomber, endured a long, cold night while sitting on the catwalk of the drafty bomb bay.[16]

DuBose's passengers and crew, by comparison, had a series of adventures they would rather forget. Some of the crew managed a catnap or two during the marathon flight, but navigator Rob Carruthers had to remain alert in order to periodically update his estimated position. Shortly before reaching Australia, however, perhaps lulled by the warmth of the morning sun, he fell asleep. He jerked awake when the B-17 made landfall, only to discover that the mainland was obscured by an untimely dust storm. Soon thereafter, grappling with a navigator's worst nightmare, Carruthers had to concede that he was lost. John Straight, one of the gunners on the crew, recalled, "We overflew Batchelor and headed into the interior of Australia. Due to 'Sleepy' Carruthers's little nap, we were off course and missed Alice Springs by about 60 miles."[17]

Extremely low on fuel, and with no airfield in sight, DuBose and his crew searched the immediate area for a safe place to land. Fortune smiled on them in the form of a large, flat field adjacent to an old windmill, where DuBose made a smooth, wheels-down landing at about 10 A.M. Despite being safely on the ground, the occupants were effectively marooned in the middle of Australia's enormous central desert. Embarrassed for the predicament they had placed Vice President Osména and his staff in, the crew pulled out emergency rations and tried to make the VIPs comfortable. The best choice for the passengers was to sit in the shade of the B-17's broad wing, but as the temperature soared, comfort eluded everyone. Perspiring in the arid landscape, the stranded men were tormented by flies—the biggest, stickiest flies John Straight had ever seen. "There were swarms of them," he later wrote. "We had to wear netting over our faces, and where the backs of our shirts were wet with sweat, the flies would gather. Our backs would be black with them."[18]

Technical Sergeant Gaston R. Upchurch, the radio operator, reeled out a trailing wire antenna and tried to establish contact with various airfields and stations on the military net. Assisted by Straight, he also attempted to triangulate their position by charting the lines of bearing from various stations. Reception was negligible, however, so for the remainder of that hot, miserable day they periodically broadcast their position in the blind and tapped out messages in Morse code to relay the fact that they were safely down. That night, Carruthers finally got a fix on their location by shooting the stars, but the information was useless without radio reception.

In the morning, DuBose sent John Straight and another crewman to investigate a distant hill, hoping they would be able to see Alice Springs from its peak. "We got just a couple of hundred yards," recalled Straight, "when we heard an airplane coming. Sure enough it was a plane that was looking for us."[19] The pilot, a Dutch national who had recently evacuated from Java, buzzed the stranded B-17 and reported its position. Shortly thereafter, Ted Faulkner circled the field in his B-17 and landed, bringing two full auxiliary tanks along with a hand pump and an empty fifty-five-gallon drum. Using the wobble pump, the crew transferred gas from Faulkner's tanks into the drum, rolled it over to DuBose's aircraft, then pumped the contents into the stranded B-17. They only needed enough fuel to go sixty miles, and by midafternoon both Fortresses were safely in Alice Springs. The squadron had dodged the proverbial bullet. Although the forced landing could easily have ended in disaster, cool heads and common sense had prevailed, resulting in a satisfactory conclusion.

By that time President Quezon and his immediate circle had already left Alice Springs, which meant that only two B-17s would be needed to transport the rest of the VIPs to Melbourne. The pilots flipped coins to see whose crews would get to enjoy a trip to the big city, and Faulkner lost. This was just as well. Selected as the 14th Squadron's new executive officer, he headed back to Townsville while Spieth and DuBose flew the dignitaries to Melbourne the following day. Thus ended the second evacuation effort from the Philippines, considered a success despite the thirty-hour delay in the outback for DuBose and his crew.

Upon their arrival in Melbourne, the badly worn B-17s (Spieth's aircraft had two blown cylinders) were turned over to the depot at Laverton airdrome for new engines. The facility, run by the RAAF, gave the Americans a new appreciation for their own work ethic. Between the Aussies' daily breaks for tea or a "smoke-o," plus longer stoppages for holidays, the overhaul proceeded slowly. Some of the American fliers enjoyed the hospitality of Australia's second-largest city, a modern metropolis with a population of slightly more than one million, but Wallace Fields became frustrated. "Went out to check on the plane," he wrote in his diary on April 16, more than two weeks after the overhaul began. "This work should have been done in one week at most. [The engines] would have been changed in Salt Lake in one night."[20]

Finally, just as the days turned chilly with the approach of winter, DuBose and his crew picked up their refurbished B-17 and returned to Townsville. But for Spieth's crew, the boondoggle lasted almost a month. By the time they brought their overhauled Fortress to Townsville on April 24, they had missed several important missions, some astonishing stories, and one happy reunion.

FIFTEEN

JUNGLE ODYSSEY

Frank Allan Champion was destined for great deeds. Even his name sounds heroic, as though scripted for a life of mythological proportions. The second son of a Port Moresby government official, he was also blessed with good fortune. Soon after his birth on April 27, 1905, he contracted malaria. A scourge in regions where mosquitos thrive, more insidious than dengue fever, malaria was (and still is) often fatal for infants, the elderly, and those with weakened immune systems. But not for Allan, as he was called. His mother rushed him to the cool climate of a highland plateau, traveling twenty miles into the mountains of New Guinea, and he gradually recovered.[1] Although he would endure numerous bouts of malaria during his lifetime, none was more threatening than that first one. As the saying goes, what doesn't kill you makes you stronger.

After eleven glorious, rambunctious years growing up in Port Moresby, Allan attended a private boarding school in Queensland with his two brothers. A superb athlete, he represented the Southport School in cricket, football, and swimming. Midwinter holidays, the Australian equivalent of summer vacations, were spent on a sheep station in the outback. Keenly interested in engineering, Champion left school a year early to begin an apprenticeship with Burns, Philp, and Company, Australia's biggest shipping conglomerate. That experience led to several years of adventure on the high seas aboard various steamships, from coal-fired tramp steamers to modern tankers. As a junior engineering officer, Champion sailed to the far corners of the globe and visited every civilized continent. He weathered hurricanes in the Gulf of Mexico, was robbed in East Africa, saw his first striptease show in Algiers, and fell in love in England.[2]

Married in 1933 to the niece of his chief engineer, Champion returned with his English bride to New Guinea. His father, now the acting lieutenant governor, resided in Government House in Port Moresby, but that was no guarantee of success for Allan. The worldwide depression was extremely hard on the Australian economy, and even harder on young couples in the Mandated Territory. When an opportunity came for Champion to serve as a patrol officer in Papua, he jumped at it. The pay was meager, the conditions deplorable, and he was forced to travel almost everywhere on foot, but the experience of living among the aboriginal tribes was priceless. Ruggedly handsome, resourceful, fearless, and almost inexhaustible, Champion was a man of quiet modesty and dry humor. Picture a slender Hugh Jackman wearing a patrol officer's khaki shorts and button-down shirt, holstered pistol on his belt, and iconic bush hat cocked to one side of his head, and you have Allan Champion.

By 1938 he had advanced to the position of assistant resident magistrate in the Northern Territory of Papua, headquartered at Buna. His duties included hearing cases of civil law, which he often adjudicated himself unless the circumstances warranted the expertise of a circuit judge. Champion's moral code was firm yet fair, but when asked if he had received any legal training, he would quip, "None. I dispense justice, not the law."[3]

In late December 1941, when the Japanese advance became a direct threat to the New Guinea territory, the government ordered the evacuation of civilian dependents. A few days before Christmas, Champion's wife Emily and their toddler-age son boarded a schooner that took them to Samarai, a bustling island seaport and the capital of the Milne Bay province. From there, joining hundreds of civilians from the trade centers and mission stations throughout the Mandated Territory, his family sailed to Australia for the duration.

But not all of the eligible civilians in Champion's district chose to leave. The bishop of the Anglican church in New Guinea, communicating with his various mission stations by radio, informed his staff that no matter the personal risk, it was their Christian duty to look after their flocks. Thus nearly all of the Anglican missionaries scattered throughout New Guinea—priests, nuns, catechists, nurses, schoolteachers, and more—remained behind. The mission at Gona was no exception. Nine miles from Buna, merely a brisk walk on a jungle path for Champion, the station operated a school and native hospital with a sizable staff that included several teachers and nurses. The Anglicans were good next-door neighbors, and Champion was concerned about their welfare.

After the fall of Rabaul in late January 1942, all able-bodied government administrators in New Guinea under the age of forty-five were inducted into the Australian army. Receiving a lieutenant's commission, Champion continued with his civic duties, but his primary job was to serve as an independent extension of the military. A month later, after receiving a message from Port Moresby about a missing B-17, he started the search that led him to Fred Eaton and his crew.

FIRST IMPRESSIONS LAST a long time. George Munroe thought Champion "looked like a savior" when he first saw him at Sangara village. Decades later, Fred Eaton would state unequivocally that the Australian saved his life. Champion himself was less certain. "Maybe," he wrote to Eaton in his twilight years, "I had something to do with it."[4]

The modest Champion also knew that Papuan villagers deserved credit for their role in the crew's survival. The situation could easily have gone badly for Eaton and his men, since not all tribes cooperated with the Australian government. One thing is certain: the villagers lacked the resources to support nine half-starved men for more than a day or two, and without Champion's timely intervention the Americans would have struggled mightily.

Towing some of them in a borrowed dugout canoe, Champion took his scruffy charges to his station at Buna. The motor launch remained close to the shore, giving the passengers a picturesque view of brilliantly flowering shrubs and tall coconut palms as they traveled north. For the aviators, the

beachfront scenery and ocean breezes were infinitely better than the breath-
less, humid swampland that existed only a few miles inland.

Arriving at Buna shortly before dusk on March 1, Champion radioed
Port Moresby with the good news that he had picked up the missing crew.
He also requested their evacuation by flying boat. He was not provisioned
to care for so many men, and the Americans were in poor shape. Their
hands were cut from handling sharp kunai grass, and at least four men
had developed tropical ulcers. From his own experience, Champion knew
that the festering wounds, the most common type of skin disease in Papua,
could be extremely painful. All it took was a simple abrasion for a bacterial
infection to set in. Such wounds not only refused to heal, they steadily
grew larger, eventually causing necrosis of the surrounding tissue. If left
untreated, an ulcer would gradually eat through skin, muscle, even bone.
Medical treatment was slow and sometimes excruciating, as Champion
could attest.

> One day out on patrol I was crossing a flooded creek when my leg was
> washed against a rock in the water. It took a bit of skin off. It later devel-
> oped into a tropical ulcer which hospitalized me in the Samarai hospital
> for four and a half months. The doctor finally burned it out with bluestone
> and carbolic, a very painful procedure.* He then cut three pieces of skin
> off my thigh, without anesthetic, and did a skin graft. This was about the
> time when sulfa drugs appeared on the medical scene. It all worked, but
> I had to wear a metal guard over the scar for some months, as the doctor
> said if the healed wound was scratched, the whole process would have to
> be done again.[5]

In addition to requiring medical care, the Americans were ravenous.
"We almost ate Mr. Champion out of house and home with the nine of us
descending on him," stated Dick Oliver. "He had limited rations for himself
anyway. In a few days most of that was gone and we were primarily trying to
fill up on ripe bananas that we could find, and coconuts."[6]

---

* Copper sulfate and carbolic acid.

Realizing that it was handy to have some assistance nearby, Champion turned to the missionaries at Gona for help. Soon, the entire crew was under the care of the Anglican staff, notably Sister May Hayman, a British-born nurse in charge of the hospital. By March 4, Fred Eaton felt well enough to pen a letter to his parents. "For the last few days," he wrote, "I have been living with a British missionary among nothing but natives, after quite an unfortunate experience. I am hoping that someone comes and picks me up in a flying boat real soon, but I can't tell much. I am back in good physical shape again after some good sleep and good care by the missionaries we are with. 'Hotfoot,' George, and all the rest of my crew are here with me."[7]

Little did he realize that four months would pass before his letter was postmarked from Australia, or that it would take another two months to reach his parents in Scarsdale.

As for Champion's request for assistance, no word came from Port Moresby regarding an evacuation plan. Headquarters, in fact, seemed more concerned about the abandoned B-17. Champion was instructed to retrieve the bombsight, navigation instruments, and radio equipment, but Eaton assured him the orders were ridiculous. The bombsight had been destroyed, and specialists would be required to salvage the other equipment, presuming they could even get to the aircraft in the first place. Champion therefore ignored the message.

Another transmission arrived from Port Moresby on March 8, but again there was no hint of an evacuation plan. Instead, the decrypted message informed Champion of the Japanese landings 160 miles to the north at Lae and Salamaua. Buna might be next. Duly warned, he decided to move the Americans to a different Anglican mission, high in the mountains along the primitive road to Kokoda.

Before the airmen headed out, Eaton lined them up to say goodbye. Instructing the crew to empty their pockets, he collected about $60 in Australian and American currency to repay their host. Champion feigned insult. "I told him I was not running a boarding house," he later wrote, "that I was also in the army, and the food they ate was supplied by the army." Without batting an eye, aware that Champion had recently jailed six local villagers for gambling, Eaton said, "I'll toss you for it."[8]

Champion accepted, and won the coin flip. In addition to the cash, Eaton handed over the gear his crew had carried out of the swamp, including two rusty .45s and the army rifle. But the item Champion treasured most, and for many years to follow, was "a beautiful one gallon Thermos water carrier with a tap."[9]

Setting off from Buna at 1:30 P.M. on March 8, the airmen followed their Papuan guides along a dirt track that led up into the mountains. Without the natives, famous for their strength, stamina, and agility on New Guinea's steep and treacherously slick footpaths, the nine Americans would have been utterly helpless. It took a day and a half to walk to the village of Higaturu, thirty miles from Buna and a few miles north of Mount Lamington, an ancient volcano.* Arriving on the evening of March 9, the crew stayed at a plantation owned by Jack Mason, a recently commissioned warrant officer. They were also aided by Father Vivian Redlich and his staff from the nearby Anglican mission at Sangara.

Widely scattered across the highlands, the missionaries, plantation owners, and local traders were essentially one extended family. The Anglicans not only shared a common and abiding faith, but Father Redlich was engaged to marry Sister Hayman, the nurse down at Gona. In a broader context all of the residents, Europeans and Papuans alike, were connected by the primitive road that led past their properties to the high mountain pass at Kokoda. They raised their own gardens and some livestock, but relied on the road for everything else. Dry goods, furniture, household items, tools, and even farming equipment were unloaded from coastwise vessels at Buna and manhandled up into the mountains by native carriers. Because of their isolation, the highland residents formed a tightknit community, assisting each other whenever necessary and keeping in close contact by two-way radio or native runners. Their communal spirit was not unlike that shared by Amish families. They thrived on simplicity, education, and Christian goodwill, with a distinctive Papuan flair. It was a happy place, a vibrant place. And then the war came.

---

* In a spectacular 1951 eruption, the slopes of Mount Lamington blew apart with a pyroclastic flow that killed approximately three thousand people.

THE AMERICAN AIRMEN had been delivered inland none too soon. On the morning of March 10, Allan Champion heard an aircraft approaching. A single-engine biplane with a central float and two small outriggers circled over the government station, then headed toward the bay. One of several planes sent out on patrol from the Japanese seaplane tender *Kiyowaka Maru* that morning, the intruder was a Type 95 reconnaissance floatplane, a two-seater known by the Allies as a Nakajima E8N.

Riding at anchor off Buna was the Anglican mission schooner *Maclaren King*, a fifty-footer used by the bishop of New Guinea, the Right Reverend Philip Strong, who was visiting each of his mission stations to discuss wartime expectations. Lining up on the schooner, the Japanese floatplane released two small bombs. One exploded in the water halfway between the vessel and the beach; the other impacted the pathway leading up to Allan

Champion's office. Graced as ever, Champion ducked behind a palm tree an instant before the bomb exploded. "A hunk of jagged metal the size of a dinner plate struck the tree I was sheltering behind," he later recounted. "I then hopped into the radio shack and sent a message in clear language—there was no time to encode it—telling HQ what was happening. The plane then landed in the water and started to machine-gun the radio shack. I got the message away and then took a flying leap through the window and into a slit trench."[10]

At that very moment, motoring back from the Gona mission in a small boat, Philip Strong rounded the northern point of Buna Bay. The Japanese plane took off and machine-gunned the launch, then headed north toward its mother ship. The forty-two-year-old bishop, who had served in France with the Royal Engineers during World War I, was not harmed. Nor was he easily flustered. Within an hour or so, he reached the government station on foot and joined Allan Champion.[11]

THE SITUATION WAS hardly better in the highlands. Most of Eaton's crew, infected with malaria, endured days of misery. At various times they shivered with bone-rattling chills that sapped their energy, then sweated profusely as high fever and delirium took over. The attacks came in waves, leaving patients almost comatose from exhaustion.

Only those who have suffered such attacks could adequately describe the extraordinary discomforts. One fascinating portrayal was written by an Australian artillery officer, Lieutenant David M. Selby, whose infection occurred at precisely the same time as the Americans' and not very far from their location. While making his escape through the jungles of New Britain with members of the defeated garrison from Rabaul, Selby endured a severe attack of malaria in March 1942. Lying helplessly on the veranda of a plantation house near the coast, he experienced bizarre hallucinations.

> From where I lay on the floor I could see, further down the verandah, the legs of a table which, together with an upturned box, comprised the adjutant's office. Those table legs acquired a peculiar significance with the

approach of delirium. As the fever rose, they would grow and grow until, colossal giants, they floated towards me. I struggled in my mind to keep them back, but nothing would hold them. One was kneeling on my chest, crushing my lungs, and, as I panted for breath, it seemed that no breath would come.

Iron fingers were grasping my throat, choking me, and red-hot hands were pressing in my temples, splitting my skull. I felt my struggles against this intangible menace growing weaker, and at last a thick abyss opened up behind me and I slipped headlong down through waves of undulating darkness. Then a gigantic face floated down on me, and I tortured my brain to think where I had seen that face before . . . and a voice a thousand miles away would offer me a drink. I tried to answer but my tongue was sticking to the roof of my mouth and only horrible sounds issued forth.

Then the mists cleared and I felt that by an enormous effort of will I could force the table legs back to their place as they dwindled to their correct size. . . .

Sometimes the whole thing would be repeated; sometimes as I lay, I would feel the fever ebbing away. Every bone and muscle ached and I was soaked in sweat, but I knew that I had fought with death, and won.[12]

During their days with Jack Mason, at least seven members of Eaton's crew endured similar attacks. Eaton would later write that he and Clarence LeMieux were the only two members of the crew to avoid infection, but their turns were coming.

On the crew's fourth day in the mountains, word arrived from Champion that efforts to arrange their evacuation from the coast had been unsuccessful. The only other way to reach Port Moresby, he advised them, would be to cross the Owen Stanley Mountains on foot. Their present location at Sangara mission was only seventy-five linear miles from Port Moresby, but it might as well have been a thousand. The Americans would have to navigate the notorious Kokoda Trail, an extremely demanding hike that took almost two weeks for men in top physical condition. Nobody in Eaton's crew was healthy enough, let alone properly equipped. All the same, the morning of

March 14 found the Americans heading up the road that led up to Kokoda. Most could walk, but a few had to be carried by natives using improvised stretchers.

They had hardly gotten under way, however, when a new message arrived. To the crew's great relief, they were told to meet the government vessel *Elevala* down at Oro Bay. The catch was that they would have to walk part of the way back to Buna, then take a fork in the trail that led south to the village of Eroro. In theory the hike would be much easier than the Kokoda Trail, but the winding trail covered thirty-five miles of rugged, heavily forested mountain terrain. And some of the men were still sick. "When we left the mission I thought I could walk," Dick Oliver recalled, "but I went about 20 yards and collapsed. They had to carry me in a sedan chair with four natives, two on each end of it."[13]

Disoriented, enduring severe aches over his entire body, Oliver was tormented by the jolting of the crude wooden seat. The worst aspect was crossing several deep gorges spanned by primitive suspension bridges. The rickety-looking footbridges, lashed together with lengths of hanging vines, were only wide enough for one person. "To be carried across in one of those chairs," added Oliver, "was an experience that you would rather forget."[14]

At midday on March 16, after two exhausting days of travel, the crew reached Eroro on the shores of Oro Bay. Any hopes of a quick evacuation were dashed, however, for the *Elevala* was nowhere in sight. Nor did she arrive the next day, or the day after that. Plagued with engine trouble for weeks, the vessel finally picked them up on March 19. Over the next two days she limped 250 miles to Samarai Island, her condition so poor that the passengers had to be put ashore while the *Elevala* returned to the New Guinea mainland for repairs.

For the Americans, who had a few blankets and a radio but no food, the delay was akin to being marooned. The once-bustling little port on the lee shore of Samarai, abandoned after the government evacuation in late 1941, was a ghost town. Until the *Elevala* or another vessel came to pick them up, the airmen were on their own. They occupied a vacant house on stilts, where Oliver tried to get creative. "We found some dried apples, a little sugar and some flour that had been left behind," he remembered. "I attempted to bake a pie but because the apples sat overnight it all fermented. Nobody would have any except Harlow, who said it was delicious and ate the whole thing."[15]

A night or two later, the hungry Americans were asleep in their elevated house when shouts of "fresh meat, fresh meat" awakened them. A half-caste native proudly delivered a large portion of recently butchered beef. "We went down and looked," Oliver stated, "and sure enough here he was carrying a quarter of beef over his shoulders. We got everybody up and started cooking as fast as we could. We all ate too much, too fast, and we were all sick."[16]

By their third day in the abandoned port, the Americans were eating beef for every meal. "Thought the *Elevala* might be here today to pick us up, but no such luck," Eaton wrote on March 24, resuming his diary for the first time since the crash landing. "Needless to say, no flying boats took us away, either. Steak for breakfast, lunch, and dinner."[17]

The next morning, a radio transmission included a message specifically for the stranded crew: "LHA to Eaton: send the launch around if you are listening." Presuming the *Elevala* was attempting to make contact, Eaton sent Russ Crawford and J. V. Hall around the island in a small boat. About an hour later, the five-hundred-ton schooner *Matoma* sailed into the harbor. One of her passengers, a major in the Australian army, relayed bad news: The captain of the *Elevala* reported that it might be ten days before he could pick them up. The crew of the *Matoma* took the Americans aboard, departing immediately after Crawford and Hall returned. Before the schooner could clear the harbor, Eaton collapsed to the deck in a dead faint. His luck dodging malaria had finally run out. Put to bed in the main cabin, he later wrote, "This malaria makes you feel so helpless!"[18]

Finally aboard a seaworthy vessel, the wayward Americans were not yet home free. The *Matoma* had several prearranged stops to make on behalf of her other passengers, which included Bishop Strong. Furthermore, her crew would have to carefully navigate some 280 miles of New Guinea's coastline, parts of which had never been properly charted, before reaching Port Moresby. On March 26, while approaching the government station on Abau Island, the *Matoma* ran up hard on a reef and was stuck for eight hours before the shifting tides enabled the crew to work her off the rocks. When she finally docked at the station, the Americans were treated to a full-course dinner and slept in the government house, enjoying real beds for the first time in weeks.

More days of travel lay ahead as the *Matoma* worked slowly along the coast, anchoring just offshore when it got too dark for her captain to see the telltale white water of submerged reefs. On the second day out of Abau, a native came aboard from a dugout canoe to guide them through a particularly treacherous stretch, then paddled ashore. Not five minutes later, the schooner ran aground again. This time she floated off on her own and a short time later was safely in deep water.

Eaton and his crew spent most of March 29 ashore at another government station, Rigo, where one of the Australian officers held court for several natives charged with murder. The station was only thirty miles east of Port Moresby, tantalizingly close. Two days earlier, in fact, a Japanese bomber had crashed in flames near the station, shot down by Port Moresby's newly arrived P-40 Kittyhawks. A search team from Rigo located the aft portion of the wreckage on March 29 and recovered the bomber's 20mm tail cannon along with several rounds of ammunition. Due to the thickly forested jungle, the forward section of the fuselage, with the remains of the crew still inside, was not discovered for another two days.

Following a comfortable night's sleep at Rigo, the Americans witnessed a stirring reminder of their proximity to Port Moresby. "At 0845," Eaton wrote, "we saw 5 B-17s fly almost directly overhead at about 8000 ft., going east. They certainly looked good."[19] Emotionally moved by the sight, the crew returned to the *Matoma*, which promptly got under way. While she paralleled the coastline, the airmen examined the 20mm cannon and ammunition salvaged from the wreck of the Japanese bomber, no doubt gaining some appreciation for the type of weapon that had punched so many holes in their own B-17, now lying in a swamp. A few hours later, bursts of antiaircraft fire appeared in the western sky as Port Moresby underwent its twenty-second air raid. The war was just over the horizon.

Originally intending to land at Seven Mile airdrome on February 23, Fred Eaton and his crew had crash-landed a hundred miles short of their destination. Exactly five weeks later, having walked and sailed approximately

650 miles, they finally reached Port Moresby. Fittingly, a spectacular sunset greeted them as the *Matoma* sailed into Fairfax Harbor. The town, under constant attack for the past two months, was littered with debris, its appearance transformed by slit trenches, stacks of sandbags, and batteries of antiaircraft guns; but the Americans thought it was the best thing they had seen in weeks. As Eaton wrote in his diary; "Civilization, with bomb craters and all, looked mighty good."[20]

The only thing left to do was hitch a ride down to Townsville. Eaton succeeded in securing seats for his crew aboard a four-engine Empire flying boat, which took off early the next morning. Five hours later, the elegant ex-Qantas seaplane taxied into the harbor at Townsville, which looked even better than Port Moresby. Some of the men were still too sick to enjoy their surroundings, but Eaton downed a big lunch at the Queens Hotel. He was joined by Bill Lewis and a couple of other officers who had not yet eaten, so Fred polished off another lunch while sharing the story of his adventures.

That afternoon, the long-lost fliers received a raucous welcome at Garbutt Field. Described as "looking pretty weak and thin, but happy to be back," Eaton and his crew told and retold their tales of "sickness, hunger, thirst, head-hunting natives, crocodiles, jungle rats, and long jungle nights."[21] But for the sake of their own health, the reunion was brief. "Most of us went into the hospital," said Dick Oliver. "Some of us were in there two weeks and then given a week to ten days recuperative leave."[22]

SEVEN HUNDRED MILES from Townsville, an unnamed B-17 sat silently in the waist-deep waters of the Agaiambo Swamp. The nine young Americans who had proudly served as her crew (and owed their lives to her sturdy construction) would never see her again. For decades to come, her only companions would be the insects, reptiles, amphibians, and birds that inhabited the wetlands. But one day, far in the future, human hands would touch her again—and she would have her own fascinating story to tell.

SIXTEEN

THE ROYCE
SPECIAL MISSION

Fred Eaton was impressed with the changes that had taken place during his long absence. Almost everything was different at the squadron level, from its new designation as a reconnaissance outfit to new leadership under Bill Lewis. And, much to the relief of the combat crews, the squadron had finally acquired a dedicated ground-support echelon. Four officers and 106 enlisted men of the 22nd Bombardment Squadron, survivors of the Java campaign, had arrived on March 26. They brought invaluable experience but no tools, having escaped from the ruins of Java with little more than the shirts on their backs. Fifty-six additional ground personnel arrived in Townsville by ship two days later, making it difficult for the RAAF to house and feed everyone.

Eaton also saw that much had changed around Garbutt Field. Observing "many B-26s and P-39s dispersed in the woods,"[1] he realized that the 14th Recon was no longer the sole American squadron at Townsville. A few days earlier, twelve B-26 Marauders of the 22nd Bombardment Group had arrived from Hawaii. Wearing similar red and white rudder stripes, the twin-engine bombers had island-hopped over the same ferry route used by the B-17s, with remarkably similar experiences. As for the P-39 Airacobras, the presence of the uniquely configured American fighters was not only timely but reassuring. Darwin had endured a total of ten bombing raids by the end of March, and Townsville appeared to be in the crosshairs of the Japanese as well. High-flying reconnaissance planes had already triggered air-raid warnings on two occasions, renewing fears of an invasion somewhere on the Queensland coast. As Eaton noted, the combat planes at Garbutt were now dispersed among the gum trees on property owned by local ranchers. It wasn't unusual, in fact, to see livestock lying in the shade beneath an aircraft's wings.

Now that 14th Recon resembled a fully manned combat squadron, Lewis called an organizational meeting on the evening of April 2. The return of Eaton and his men was part of the agenda, and Lewis awarded the crew a week of sick leave. But the primary reason for the meeting was a much-needed pep talk. Acknowledging that he had "inherited a bunch of old planes, a bunch of junk until we get new engines, and a bunch of tired and overworked men," Lewis spoke like a football coach at halftime. His motivational effort paid off. Jack Carlson observed that "the spirit of the squadron is getting better all the time, and it seems as though 90% of us are ready to do anything, go anywhere, until we have the enemy where we want them!"[2]

In the meantime, Fred Eaton was eager to go on leave, and he was drawn to the bright lights. "I'm looking forward to getting south," he wrote, "and seeing some of Australia's big cities. . . . I think a rest down in Melbourne or Sydney will do me a lot of good!"[3] Hopping a ride as far as Brisbane, he ran into Frank Bostrom, who had been there since the MacArthur evacuation while his B-17 was being overhauled. They rode downtown to the posh Lennon's Hotel, where Fred paid for a room and enjoyed a reunion with several acquaintances from Salt Lake City, now stationed at nearby Amberley Field.

At breakfast the next morning, Easter Sunday, Bostrom introduced Eaton to Pat Robinson, an American war correspondent with the International News Service. Enthralled with Eaton's story of survival, Robinson typed up a detailed article and phoned it in to the wire services. His drama-in-real-life account, exactly the sort of inspiring story the American public needed, was published nationally on April 6. The article also spawned a sidebar that featured Eaton's mother, who reflected on Fred's flying career and the anxiety his family had experienced while he was missing.

Unfortunately for Eaton, both his sick leave and his brush with fame were interrupted by another attack of malaria. Sent to a hospital sixty miles from Brisbane, he spent the next week in a funk. Instead of enjoying a vacation in the city, he was kept awake by a noisy generator that ran twenty-four hours a day outside his window. The food was awful, worse than any army chow he had ever eaten. "What a week's leave this has turned into," he complained. "Even the new nurses don't help. I haven't seen a single decent-looking one."[4]

While Eaton fidgeted in the hospital, the 14th Squadron continued bombing Japanese strongholds, but it also commenced its newly designed role. Bob Thacker had flown the squadron's first photoreconnaissance mission on March 28, staging out of Port Moresby for a ten-hour loop that covered Gasmata, Rabaul, Kavieng, and Lae. The solo effort resulted in good intelligence information, yielding a more successful outcome than the typical bombing effort. The problem with the latter was that issues related to the worn-out engines had become endemic, causing one or two Fortresses to abort almost every attempted bombing mission. The blame lay not with the maintenance personnel, who worked miracles using the few spare parts available (and by cannibalizing the *San Antonio Rose*), but with the terribly inefficient, bureaucratic supply system located far from the combat area.

The B-17s, incidentally, looked somewhat different as of April 4. The rudder stripes were removed, and the red circle in the center of each plane's national insignia was painted over to avoid the possibility of being mistaken for a Japanese "meatball." As noted in the squadron diary, "Now the symbol is a white star without the red dot. . . . The Japs have changed our mind about red."[5]

SUBTLE CHANGES TO the bombers' appearance notwithstanding, the Japanese were about to get a surprise. The Townsville-based 19th Squadron of the 22nd Bomb Group was cleared to begin combat operations with its B-26 Marauders. Seventy miles southwest of Townsville, at Charters Towers airdrome, a dozen B-25C Mitchells recently acquired by the 3rd Bomb Group were likewise ready for combat. Originally sold to the Netherlands East

Indies Air Force, the B-25s had been sitting idle at Archerfield airdrome for weeks before members of the 3rd commandeered them from the Dutch. Eager to employ both new types of medium bombers, General Brett and his planners conceived a mission to attack two targets simultaneously using all of the available aircraft. While the B-26s and a few B-17s hit Rabaul, the shorter-range B-25s would bomb Gasmata airdrome on the south coast of New Britain.

At Townsville, the announcement of the joint raid generated considerable excitement. John Steinbinder, who had not flown since March 20 when his B-17 lost a propeller in flight, was motivated, yet apprehensive. He and most of the crew had been compelled to remain in Port Moresby for several days after their dramatic flight, which gave them the unique opportunity to witness jubilant pandemonium when the Kittyhawks of 75 Squadron arrived to defend the outpost. But Steinbinder had also contracted a severe case of dysentery, a consequence of the poor sanitary conditions. Grounded for a week, he had served as the squadron duty officer while regaining his strength. Now, on the eve of the combined mission, he tried to sort out his jumbled emotions. "I must be getting hysterical or something," he wrote in his diary on April 5. "I'm afraid I've been on the ground too long—will finish account of this day's work when I return—if I do return."[6]

Events at Port Moresby on that Easter Sunday provided even more excitement for the weary garrison. The twenty-third Japanese raid had occurred earlier in the day, during which one of the escorting Zeros was shot down. That afternoon, the defenders were thrilled as a steady stream of American bombers entered the landing pattern at Seven Mile airdrome and touched down on the dusty strip. By sundown six B-25s, nine B-26s, and two B-17s were parked in the dispersal area. The crews stretched out on the ground or even slept on the wings of their aircraft for a few hours before the raids got under way early the next morning.

Although often overlooked, the coordinated attacks on April 6 were of no small historic significance. Two of the most famous medium bombers of World War II, the B-25 Mitchell and B-26 Marauder, made their combat debut that day over New Britain. Lieutenant Colonel John H. "Big Jim" Davies, the new CO of the 3rd Bomb Group, participated in a successful raid on Gasmata with five of the ex-Dutch B-25s. A former dive-bomber pilot, he was impressed with the near-flawless performance of the twin-engine Mitchells as they attacked the airdrome from five thousand feet, causing moderate damage.

Meanwhile the two B-17s had taken off from Port Moresby at 2:00 A.M., followed an hour later by eight of the B-26 Marauders. The preflight briefing called for the heavy bombers to hit Vunakanau airdrome ten minutes before the B-26s arrived over Simpson Harbor, but due to stormy weather the plan fell apart. Two of the Marauders turned back after failing to join up in heavy rain squalls, and the remaining six flew a circuitous route that took much longer than expected.

Not that the B-17s fared any better. Lieutenant Jack Roberts got within 120 miles of Rabaul before turning back because of problems with the superchargers and oxygen system. Only the Fortress piloted by Lieutenant Wilbur B. Beezley, a twenty-five-year-old Nebraskan, reached the target area. After making two dry runs over the enemy airdrome, he dropped seven five-hundred-pounders that landed on or near the runway, silencing an antiaircraft gun that had been firing accurately.[7] "We saw three pursuit ships take off but they never reached our altitude," penned Steinbinder. "Antiaircraft, however, was breaking all about us on our last two runs."[8]

On the flight back to Port Moresby, Beezley's left outboard engine suddenly quit. Thus, all of the B-17s assigned to the mission experienced mechanical trouble, underscoring Lewis's remarks a few days earlier about needing new engines and spare parts. Slowed by the loss of the engine, Beezley landed at Seven Mile drome after the rest of the bombers had returned from their respective missions. All were eager to refuel and get off the field before another Japanese raid materialized, but only two aircraft at a time could pull into the designated fuel pits; the others lined up alongside the runway while waiting their turn. At the far end of the field, the bombers that had already gassed up formed another line as they stood by for a green light from the control tower, their signal to take off.

Suddenly, air-raid sirens began to wail and a red ball was hoisted above the control tower. Japanese bombers were inbound. In the nose of Beezley's

B-17, cued up for departure behind several B-26s, Steinbinder stared through the Plexiglas as the attack unfolded. "We had to wait until the B-26s cleared the field," he later wrote. "While we were waiting the Japs bombed Moresby, one bomb hitting 500 feet from us; the other 69 bombs hit the hills."[9]

Worried that a strafing attack would follow the Japanese bombers, Beezley pulled onto the runway as soon as the last Marauder raced aloft. As he swung the tail around to line up for takeoff, one of the wheels of the twenty-ton Fortress sank into a recently patched bomb crater. Sparks and gravel flew as the propeller tips contacted the ground. Thinking the plane had been hit, the crew jumped out and ran for shelter. "The Aussies had a way of repairing bomb craters by merely filling them full of gravel and going off and leaving them," Beezley explained later. "We hit a filled crater and one wheel went into it, down to the hub."[10]

After the all-clear sounded and the crew discovered the two damaged propellers, they spent the rest of the day digging and dragging the big plane out of the crater. Early the next morning, a specialist and two disassembled propellers were delivered from Townsville. Within a matter of hours, using only hand tools, Sergeant Morton Cooper replaced both of the damaged props. A grateful Beezley, who thought it was one of the most remarkable repair jobs he had ever seen, gathered up his crew and took off for Townsville despite the fact that he still had one dead engine.[11] The flight back was no picnic. "Sure was a hectic trip," noted Steinbinder. "Only 3 engines, no lights, lots of clouds, visibility damn near zero. All kinds of rain, glad to get back."[12]

TWO WEEKS AFTER Bill Lewis assumed command of the squadron, he was promoted to the rank of major. Although the bronze oak leaves on his collar were a source of pride, the myriad duties and responsibilities of leadership kept him largely deskbound. Frank Bostrom, already recognized as "the boy who brought out MacArthur," therefore became the squadron's busiest pilot. Promoted to captain on April 8 (along with Fred Eaton, Ted Faulkner, and several other pilots), Bostrom had already made a name for himself when war correspondents Carleton Kent of the *Chicago Times* and Byron Darnton of the *New York Times* paid a visit to the squadron. Their introduction to the pilots and crews, although brief, probably influenced the intense publicity received by Bostrom a matter of weeks later, when his photograph and biographical details were published in newspapers and major magazines nationwide.

The genesis of Bostrom's fame was a plea for assistance from the Allied forces on Corregidor and Bataan. In late March, General Jonathan Wainwright sent a message to MacArthur requesting a bombing operation against the Japanese naval blockade that was preventing supplies from reaching his besieged troops. If a squadron of bombers could attack and scatter the enemy warships, a waiting Allied convoy might be able to slip through. It would be a last-ditch effort. Rations had already been cut so severely that many of Wainwright's holdouts were on the verge of starvation. MacArthur, undoubtedly aware of the bitterness harbored by his former troops, saw an opportunity to save face.

The planning for the mission was left to Lieutenant General Brett. He was an outsider, not a member of the "Bataan Gang," and MacArthur did not deign to approach Brett in person. Instead, he sent Brigadier General Sutherland to inform Brett that he wanted a series of bombing raids in the Philippines. "That doesn't make sense," Brett told Sutherland. "You know what we're up against. . . . We're just holding on by the skin of our teeth, with worn-out planes and exhausted men." Brett voiced several objections to the proposed mission, arguing that the Philippines were already doomed, but of course Sutherland held the trump card. "General MacArthur," he said tightly, "wants the mission accomplished."[13]

Brett subsequently turned the job over to General Royce. At fifty-one and no longer a young man, Royce deliberated for a few days before accepting. By April 3 he produced initial estimates for the mission, which he referred to in code as the "Miami trip." The necessary support was already in place at Del Monte on Mindanao, including hundreds of USAAF personnel, ample stockpiles of bombs, 67,000 gallons of gasoline, and even a handful of P-40s.[14] All that was needed were the bombers and the crews.

On April 8, Royce chaired a four-hour planning conference in Melbourne. Top-heavy with brass, the meeting included brigadier generals

Harold George and Martin F. Scanlon, plus Big Jim Davies and a couple of his pilots from the 3rd Bomb Group. Also there was Frank Bostrom, promoted to captain that very day, as the lone B-17 representative. Already familiar with the demands that would be placed on both men and machines from his previous trip to Mindanao, he undoubtedly emphasized what Royce already knew: Most of the B-17s in Australia were worn out. In fact, Bostrom had just picked up his own Fortress, a replacement named *San Antonio Rose II*, after it completed an extended overhaul in Brisbane. At best, one or two additional B-17s in the 14th Reconnaissance Squadron were mechanically sound enough to withstand such an arduous journey.

That night, placing a rare personal call to Royce to discuss the forthcoming mission, General MacArthur promised him a Distinguished Service Cross upon his return.[15] But MacArthur's own enthusiasm was dashed the next day when he learned that Major General Edward P. King had surrendered the 75,000-plus American and Filipino troops on Bataan. "The light finally failed," MacArthur later wrote. "Bataan starved into collapse. I knew it was coming, but the actual word of the surrender came to me as a shock."[16] The plan to disrupt the enemy blockade was too late to help the men on Bataan, but General Wainwright still held out on Corregidor with 10,000 men. If nothing else, the long-range mission would be good for their morale.

On April 10, with handpicked crews, Frank Bostrom and Deacon Rawls hopped the seventy miles to Charters Towers, where the B-25s of the 3rd Bomb Group were based. Theirs were the only two B-17s from Townsville to attempt the mission, Bostrom flying his freshly overhauled airplane while Rawls piloted a Fortress wearing the camouflage scheme applied in Hawaii. A third B-17, flown by Ed Teats of the 30th Bombardment Squadron, joined them from Cloncurry. Royce arrived that afternoon from Melbourne, and the full crews from the combined squadrons—three B-17s and eleven B-25s—were briefed on the special mission. Many men, aware that Del Monte was surrounded on three sides by the Japanese, considered it a one-way trip. As Lieutenant Robert T. Jones, the navigator in Rawls's crew, put it, "When one considers that these fields were in the middle of Japanese-held territory and apt to be taken at a moment's notice, it portrayed a type of mission closely approximating the suicide type."[17] Despite such concerns, every crewmember eagerly volunteered.

BEGINNING AN HOUR after midnight on April 11, Royce watched the B-25s roar one by one into the night sky, heading for the RAAF facility at Darwin. Shortly thereafter, Rawls and Teats took off in their B-17s, and Royce jumped aboard Frank Bostrom's ship for the long flight to Batchelor Field. Arriving at 7:50 A.M., the Fortress crews spent three hours on the ground to refuel and load supplies for the garrison, then took off again for the 1,500-mile flight to Mindanao.

Past the point of no return, Bostrom's newly overhauled plane developed engine trouble, forcing him to feather the right inboard propeller for the last two hours of the flight. Darkness was falling by the time he approached Mindanao, but the Japanese-held city of Davao was brightly illuminated and countless native fires dotted the surrounding countryside. After a bit of searching in the blacked-out Allied pocket, Bostrom found Del Monte Field and put the B-17 down skillfully at 8:00 P.M. A couple of tense minutes ensued, according to tail gunner Herb Wheatley, while the crew waited to see "whether the first soldier who appeared out of the darkness was an American or a Jap."[18]

The exhausted fliers were met by General Sharp and members of his staff, who promptly ushered Royce and the key mission personnel into the officers club, now serving as an operations room. There they joined Lieutenant Colonel Davies and his B-25 crews, who had safely reached Del Monte that afternoon (minus one ship, which remained at Darwin with a cut tire), for a planning session that lasted several hours. Targets were identified across the Philippines, the idea being that Royce's thirteen-bomber air force would repeatedly attack enemy shipping and strongholds until the stockpile of bombs and gasoline ran out.[19]

Due to events beyond the practical control of anyone at Del Monte, it didn't turn out that way. Field number 1, where the bombers had landed on April 11, was occasionally reconnoitered and even dive-bombed by Japanese floatplanes from Davao. Outlying fields with camouflaged revetments had been prepared, so the staff urged Royce to send his bombers to those locations for their protection. The B-25s were dispersed, but Royce subsequently decided not to move the B-17s.

Many have criticized Royce's decision, almost invariably from the perspective of the B-25 personnel involved, without considering all the facts. The B-25 contingent was led by a group commander, Lieutenant Colonel Davies, but there was no one ranked higher than a captain among the B-17 crews, and Royce was protective of his three heavy bombers. Besides, the crews had already logged fifteen hours in the air since leaving Charters Towers, followed by the planning conference that lasted several more hours. The dispersal field, which lay well to the south near the town of Maramag, was forty-five miles away by road, lending merit to Royce's decision to keep the B-17s nearby. If nothing else, he was reluctant to send the B-17s into an unfamiliar area with exhausted pilots at the controls. It would have been especially hazardous for Bostrom to make the attempt on three engines. Dispersing the bombers late at night made little sense, especially since the crews would be back out on the field before dawn to prepare for the first raid.

In the morning, as the leader of the B-17 contingent, Frank Bostrom pulled rank on Rawls and took his airplane. Though unfortunate for Rawls, it was only natural that the two most experienced crews would fly the two available Fortresses. An oil leak in Rawls's plane delayed Bostrom's departure, so Ed Teats got airborne first. General Royce did not accompany either crew but was on the field to watch their departure.

Teats headed toward Iloilo, a port city on the southern coast of Panay Island, where a heavily protected Japanese troop convoy was believed to be bound from Luzon. If he got lucky and found the enemy ships, he was to radio Bostrom to join him for a coordinated attack; if not, his alternate target was Nichols Field[*] on the outskirts of Manila. Captured by the Japanese, the former FEAF airfield now served primarily as a base for naval fighters. A reconnoiter by one of the few remaining P-40s, operating out of

---

[*] Present-day Ninoy Aquino International Airport.

Panay on April 11, had discovered more than a hundred enemy planes lined up in neat rows. Clearly the Japanese were unconcerned about the possibility of an Allied air attack.[20]

After searching the sea-lanes without luck (the Japanese convoy was actually headed for the island of Cebu, a hundred miles southeast of where he was looking), Teats turned toward Nichols Field. A short time later, just off the southern tip of Mindoro, the B-17's right inboard engine began to run roughly, guzzling fuel at an excessive rate. Realizing that he could not bomb Nichols and still have enough gas to get back to Del Monte, Teats decided to attack the Japanese airfield at Batangas, fifty miles south of Manila. Upon reaching the target area, the crew could clearly see the Bataan Peninsula and the besieged island of Corregidor in the distance. "It was a beautifully clear day," Teats later reminisced, "and from our altitude, almost mockingly, all that we had lost was laid out below us."[21]

The airfield at Batangas was empty. Teats saw no purpose in wasting his bombs, so he made for a nearby harbor instead. Second Lieutenant Maxwell D. Stone, the bombardier, picked out "a nice, big, long boat" that was offloading its cargo next to a box-shaped pier. No antiaircraft fire or enemy planes meddled with the B-17 during its bomb run, and Stone reportedly scored two direct hits, setting the ship ablaze. A few minutes later, while the pilots feathered the number three propeller and turned toward Del Monte, the tail gunner yelled jubilantly, "The whole damn ship blew up!"[22] The crew was thrilled by the spectacular outcome, but their bomber was done for the day. When Teats landed back at Del Monte that afternoon, he gave a thumbs-down to the ground crew: the B-17 needed a cylinder change, if not an entire engine replacement.[23]

Delayed while an oil leak was repaired, Frank Bostrom took off late from Del Monte. Finding no high-value shipping targets, he proceeded northwest toward Luzon, determined to bomb Nichols Field. It was a tense five-hundred-mile flight, the crew expecting strong resistance as they approached the biggest city in the Philippines in a single B-17, but the skies were surprisingly quiet. Powerful emotions surfaced as they glimpsed Bataan, knowing it had fallen just three days earlier. Herb Wheatley felt heartsick as he gazed down on Corregidor, where his kid brother was in a coastal artillery unit. How much longer could the little island fortress hold out?[24]

Wheatley also remembered that the excitable "Frank P." jerked them out of their reverie. "What are you doing down there," he barked to his longtime bombardier, Lieutenant Earl Sheggrud, "reading dime novels? You'd better start looking for that target."[25]

The tall Scandinavian did more than that. Bombing from an altitude of 29,000 feet, Sheggrud walked his string of five-hundred-pounders diagonally across the enemy airfield. Bostrom would later state that the attack "started one big fire, banged up the runway, hit hangars and other buildings." The huge column of smoke that rose above the destruction could be seen from more than forty miles away.[26]

Before turning back toward Del Monte, Bostrom flew west across Manila Bay and descended near Corregidor. Not a single antiaircraft round had been fired over Nichols Field—the Japanese were blithely unaware of the attack until the bombs began to explode—but Bostrom had no intention of tempting the American gunners on Corregidor. Staying safely out of range, he waggled his wings as he passed "the Rock," thrilling the hungry, shell-shocked defenders. By some accounts, Bostrom and his crew were the last outside Americans to see the garrison before it surrendered three weeks later.

Completing the long return trip to Del Monte with no opposition, Bostrom landed that afternoon at 1:00 P.M. Ground crews immediately began to refuel and rearm the B-17 for another mission, which General Royce intended to fly himself. In the meantime, he had been busy coordinating the strikes flown by the B-25 crews, whose sorties against Davao and Cebu City achieved considerable damage.

Before the B-17s could be prepped for another mission, however, the Japanese intervened. Del Monte was simply too close to Davao to keep the bombers' presence a secret. During much of the day, four Japanese Type 0 observation floatplanes (Mitsubishi FM1s) had been shuttling back and forth to the American base from the seaplane tender *Sanuki Maru*, anchored in Davao Harbor. The single-engine biplanes, which carried two sixty-kilogram bombs apiece, could make the trip over the mountains in about an hour. Approaching Del Monte in two-plane sections, they glided almost silently over the field with their engines throttled back. After picking out targets, the pilots suddenly zoomed up, performed a wingover, and then dived from two or three thousand feet before releasing their small bombs. Every few hours, after strapping on more bombs alongside their tender, the two-plane elements repeated the process.

Evidently the Japanese did not find the *San Antonio Rose II* while it was under repair that morning, but shortly after Teats and Bostrom landed in the early afternoon, the biplanes with their big pontoons came back. And this time they spotted the newly arrived B-17s. The bomber crews, relaxing on the field near their planes, heard a series of rifle shots from the surrounding hills (a primitive but effective air-raid warning), and took cover in a drainage gully. Ed Teats later described the raid's outcome: "One bomb fell 25 feet off the tail section of my ship and cut the elevator cables. The tail was riddled. Fabric was torn from the elevators and control surfaces. Rawls's ship—that Bostrom had flown in the morning and which Rawls intended to take out on another mission that afternoon—was badly damaged at the tail. It couldn't possibly fly a mission that afternoon, while mine could not be repaired for a combat mission, if at all, until the following day."[27]

A couple of hours later, some of the pilots were napping in the clubhouse when another flurry of rifle shots brought them stumbling out onto the porch. Wearing only shorts and shoes, they watched as the four Japanese floatplanes orbited overhead. One peeled off and dived toward the B-17s, but before anyone could see what happened, machine-gun rounds from an American antiaircraft emplacement in the nearby hills buzzed over their heads. A .50 caliber slug kicked up dirt and screamed by in a ricochet, chasing the men into a nearby slit trench. They spent the duration of the raid listening to the *whump* of Japanese bombs, then ran down to the field. The aftermath of the enemy attack was almost sickening. "A tall column of smoke was ascending from the parking area," recalled Teats, "and when we reached it, Bostrom's plane was practically consumed."[28]

San Antonio Rose II, struck by a direct hit, went up in flames. Teats's bomber, although appearing relatively intact, had been bracketed by two more bombs. One exploded within fifty feet of the right wing, tearing gashes in the aluminum skin and punching "a hole the size of a man's fist" in the outboard engine's oil tank. The second bomb landed about seventy-five feet from the left wing, damaging the rear spar. Both sides of the fuselage were wrinkled from concussion, the sliding windows in the cockpit had shattered, and the bottom turret was disabled. The only casualty among the crew was the copilot, Lieutenant T. S. "Ted" Greene, who had received painful shrapnel wounds in his lower back.

The enemy bombs also started grass fires that threatened the two remaining B-17s. Dozens of personnel pitched in to smother the flames, and one of Herb Wheatley's lasting memories was the sight of General Royce battling fires in his shirtsleeves. But many others were furious at Royce, particularly those who saw their hopes of evacuation go up in smoke. Three B-17s would have been able to airlift about sixty passengers when they flew back to Australia, including several P-40 pilots who had recently withdrawn from Bataan and other island bases. The loss of *San Antonio Rose II* drastically reduced the number of potential evacuees, since Bostrom's crew would rightfully become passengers on the two remaining B-17s—presuming they could be repaired. The men who were forced off the evacuation list invariably channeled their frustration into anger, which they directed at General Royce for not dispersing the heavy bombers.

The fact that Bostrom and Teats landed back at Del Monte after their first mission, rather than at a remote dispersal field, probably saved both aircraft. By happenstance, Teats had bumped into an officer from the ground echelon of the old 19th Bomb Group earlier that day. In charge of a dozen or so maintenance personnel reassigned to defensive positions north of Del Monte, the lieutenant had asked Teats if he needed any support. Fortuitously, Teats instructed him to bring his men up to the field "in case of emergency." In the meantime, knowing the Japanese floatplanes would return the next morning, the B-17 crews jumped into action to repair the bomb damage. If the two remaining Fortresses were not ready to leave by daybreak, their destruction was virtually guaranteed.[29]

That afternoon, a truckload of 19th Bomb Group maintenance person-nel arrived, excited to have something useful to do after months of manning beach defenses. Over the next fifteen hours, working with basic tools, they spliced severed control cables, patched splinter damage, and cannibalized an oil tank from a wrecked B-17 that had been shoved aside several months ear-lier. Teats was amazed by the scope of the emergency repairs to his Fortress, all the more impressive because the men were hungry, tired, and aware they were not eligible for evacuation. As he later marveled, "they went at the job not only uncomplainingly, but with a dash and a good humor and skill that was beautiful."[30]

Frank Bostrom and Deacon Rawls, meanwhile, worked with their crews throughout the night to repair the other B-17. Issues with the oxygen system and a leak in the hydraulics proved beyond the capability of anyone at Del Monte to fix, which meant that Bostrom would have neither superchargers nor wheel brakes for the long flight back to Australia. Rather than risk it with an overloaded aircraft, he bumped the assigned passengers and even four members of his own crew, giving priority to Rawls's combat crew. After all, it was their plane. First, however, he obtained assurance from General Royce that the B-17 crewmen who stayed behind would be included in the passenger list when the B-25s returned to Australia.

At approximately 5 A.M., giving himself a fifty-fifty chance to reach Australia, Bostrom began his takeoff roll in the morning darkness. Almost reluctantly the patched-up Fortress staggered into the air, barely clearing the boundary fence at the end of the field.[31] For the next nine hours, flying at 10,000 feet or below, Bostrom hedgehopped around Japanese strongholds and occupied islands. Upon reaching Batchelor Field that afternoon, he ground-looped the B-17 to bring it to a stop.

Ed Teats, ready to take off about thirty minutes behind Bostrom, had a full load of passengers plus Bostrom's bombardier and navigator. The pas-sengers were high-priority personnel, among them Lieutenant Commander John Bulkeley, whose PT boats had played such a vital role in recent events. Teats, like Bostrom, was under no illusions about the risks involved in attempting a 1,500-mile flight in a badly damaged airplane. Already exhausted after two nights without sleep, he needed every ounce of concentration simply to stay alert. And then, just as he was about to take off, a Japanese floatplane passed overhead, almost invisible in the gray light of dawn. The crew and passengers held their collective breath until the enemy plane moved on, at which point Teats shoved the throttles forward and got clear of the field. Only a few minutes later, more enemy floatplanes arrived over the field and began their dives. Teats's crew chief, manning the upper turret, saw the flash as the first bomb exploded.[32]

Holding the bomber at low altitude, Teats sneaked across Mindanao just below the ridgetops. Out over the water he climbed slowly, then lost the right inboard engine again. Two other engines, overburdened just to keep the airplane flying, began to show signs of fatigue. Flying just above stall speed, the overloaded B-17 plowed through the air, cold wind howling through the shattered side windows. But she stayed aloft, her tired engines "grinding along," as Teats put it. He gained confidence with each passing hour, mainly because the bomber's weight decreased as fuel was consumed. "Slowly, but stubbornly," he recalled, "the plane was picking up speed and altitude, fighting almost like a living thing for survival."[33]

Ten and a half hours after leaving Del Monte, Teats brought his oil-streaked B-17 to a stop on the parking ramp at Batchelor Field. Bostrom, wearing a huge grin, was there to greet him. "We had about given you up," he shouted. "I didn't think you could get off the ground before daylight!"[34]

While the two B-17s wheezed back to Australia on April 13, Big Jim Davies and his B-25s conducted a second day of raids on Cebu City and Davao. No aircraft were lost and the effort once again proved effective, causing moderate damage to ships, harbor facilities, airfields, planes, buildings, and enemy troops. But ten medium bombers were not going to alter the outcome of the battle for Mindanao. The Allied pocket around Del Monte, some 1,200 miles behind enemy lines, was steadily shrinking. After two days of raiding, General Royce ordered the B-25s back to Australia. A list of passengers authorized for evacuation was circulated, and all four members of Bostrom's crew who had been bumped the previous day were on it. Seeing the crowd of high-ranking officers hoping to be included, Herb Wheatley and the other "dirty, rumpled G.I. fliers" thought they stood little chance of getting aboard the bombers, but General Royce kept his promise.

By the time the B-25s landed in Australia on April 14, word of the special mission to the Philippines had spread. Royce and Davies, who continued to Melbourne to submit their reports to headquarters, were met by a multitude of correspondents. For a few days the "Royce Raid," as it came to be known, received a big play in the press. The *New York Times* exulted, "In the most spectacular thrust of the Pacific war, thirteen United States Army bombers crossed the vast stretches from Australia and heavily assaulted Japanese bases on three Philippines islands to redeem before the world the first installment of General Douglas MacArthur's pledge that the invader would yet be cast out of his lodgments there."[35]

MacArthur did not comment on the raid, instead letting General Brett represent headquarters. In his official statement to the press, Brett said of Royce, "He took the flight into enemy territory, created dismay and destruction at a time most important to our forces, and has returned. . . . I cannot too highly emphasize my pride in the work accomplished by the American air forces participating."[36]

As promised by MacArthur, Royce received the Distinguished Service Cross. So did Davies and Bostrom. Photos of all three men were published nationwide, from the front page of the *New York Times* to prestigious magazines such as *Life* and *Time*. The awards and lavish praise mostly benefited the hero-starved public, particularly in Bostrom's case. His participation was certainly unique—altogether he flew seven thousand miles to drop one load of bombs—but based on the awards criteria applied later in the war, his achievement would not have qualified for a DSC. Furthermore, most of the claims made by the raiders fell short of the actual damage. Four enemy ships were reportedly sunk (three by the B-25s), but the Japanese lost no vessels in the Philippines during that period. This was later confirmed by the Joint Army-Navy Assessment Committee (JANAC), an agency formed by General Marshall and Admiral King in early 1943 to analyze claims for enemy shipping losses.

In any event, the recognition earned by Bostrom and his fellow participants was soon overshadowed. On April 18, just four days after the Royce Raid, a forty-five-year-old lieutenant colonel named James "Jimmy" Doolittle led sixteen B-25s from the aircraft carrier *Hornet* on a one-way mission to avenge Pearl Harbor. Sanctioned by President Roosevelt, the Doolittle Raid on Tokyo resulted in a Medal of Honor for its leader and stole the wind out of Ralph Royce's sails.

For the members of the 14th Reconnaissance Squadron, the Royce special mission would remain a lasting source of pride. They would argue, and rightfully so, that the Doolittle Raid had been a one-and-done affair, whereas the Fortress crews continued to fly lengthy, hazardous missions against a numerically superior enemy for many months to come.

SEVENTEEN

TURNING POINT: THE
BATTLE OF THE CORAL SEA

By the middle of April 1942, the 14th Recon was still adapting to its new role. Bob Thacker had flown the first photoreconnaissance mission on March 27, returning from a 1,200-mile flight with valuable images, but after that first run the "recco" flights were infrequent. Conventional bombing missions continued to dominate the schedule, mainly because the other squadrons of the reorganized 19th Bomb Group had still not reached operational status.

The strain on the B-17s as well as personnel at Townsville remained extreme. Maintenance crews had already used up a small shipment of supplies that arrived in late March, and Frank Bostrom's original *San Antonio Rose*, cannibalized before she flew a single combat mission, had been picked clean of almost every conceivable part. Little more than an aluminum carcass now remained, but even those forlorn leftovers were deemed valuable enough to be shipped to the overhaul depot in Melbourne. Allied headquarters, meanwhile, seemed deaf to the squadron's pleas for new engines and spare parts. "Supply is in terrible shape," Walt Johnson complained on April 9. "The boys behind the lines must have a very good time, indeed. They don't do much work, effective work at least."[1]

Placed in charge of the squadron's supply department when Bill Lewis took command, Johnson hopped a ride down to Brisbane on April 11 to investigate the logjam for himself. He discovered that Lennon's Hotel was "something like a social center where staff men spend their per diem on Australian women,"[2] and his disdain for the rear-area fiefdom grew even deeper when he visited the supply center. Unable to get sensible answers to basic questions about how the system worked, even theoretically, he returned to Townsville and personally inspected railcars for crates allegedly shipped to the squadron. But it was all to no avail. A couple of days later, a parody of the supply quagmire appeared in the squadron diary: "To get a screwdriver, one must first get permission from headquarters, and this, in the case of the quartermaster, requires four signatures, that is: squadron supply, group supply, headquarters, and QM officer. The distance one must travel to do that is approximately eight miles."[3] Shortly thereafter a different diarist noted, "We wired south for the sixth time for parts but received the same answer: 'Will get them to you as soon as possible.'"[4]

Finally, about a week after Johnson's impromptu visit to Brisbane, the situation improved. A dozen new engines arrived in Townsville, of which eight were earmarked for the squadron. The crated engines were "a sight for sore eyes," but the maintenance crew's reaction turned from glee to smirks upon opening another shipment of replacement parts. A consignment of new tail wheel tires proved to be the wrong size. Instead of sending 26-inch tires used by the B-17E, the depot had shipped 23-inch tires that fit the obsolete B-17Cs and Ds.

That same day, April 19, Bill Lewis and Newt Chaffin traveled to Charleville, four hundred miles west of Brisbane, to pick up two brand-new aircraft. The Fortresses were among the first to reach Australia with the new spherical belly turret, a significant improvement over the remote-controlled turret installed in the first 112 B-17Es. The new turret was operated manually by a gunner, ideally someone small in stature because of the cramped space. An abundance of pluck was also a prerequisite. The gunner, noted Johnson, would be isolated "in a little ball beneath the belly of the ship."[5]

The two new aircraft and the shipment of replacement engines did make a dent in the maintenance backlog, but the best gift of all arrived on

Saturday, April 25. It was ANZAC day, a national holiday to commemorate the 78,000 Australians and New Zealanders killed in World War I. The stores, pubs, and theaters in Townsville were closed, but the Americans didn't care as they joyously tore through the first delivery of mail to arrive since the squadron left Hawaii. Fred Eaton, answering a letter from his aunt and uncle mailed four months earlier, replied, "Even though the date was a bit old, I can't tell you how glad I was to get it. Letters mean so much over here that old postmarks don't mean a thing."[6] That same day, John Steinbinder penned in his diary, "I got a few letters written to me prior to my departure from the States and straight away proceeded to answer them. We all got letters today. We got our Christmas presents too that had been following us all about."[7]

But while a holiday atmosphere prevailed briefly in Townsville, no one was celebrating in New Guinea. The punches and counterpunches in the battle for aerial superiority had reached a crescendo, making Port Moresby more dangerous than ever. It was all part of Vice Admiral Inoue's grand strategy as he prepared for an offensive that would put the very survival of Australia to the test.

HAVING SUCCESSFULLY GAINED control of Lae and Salamaua in early March, followed by the bloodless occupation of Finschhafen on the Huon Peninsula a few days later, Vice Admiral Inoue's forces held a powerful grip on the northern coast of New Guinea. As far as Tokyo was concerned, the first stage of the offensive in the Southeastern Area had been successfully concluded. In early April, therefore, Imperial General Headquarters decided to activate the second stage, a series of three operations designed to create a domino effect across the Pacific. The first would be "MO" Operation, the simultaneous invasions of Port Moresby and the island of Tulagi in early May, followed by the seizure of Midway and the Aleutians ("MI" Operation) in June, after which "FS" Operation would capture Fiji and Samoa in July. If all three operations succeeded, the Japanese would effectively blockade Australia and New Zealand from the United States.

The Japanese high command, already troubled by the increasing number of Allied aircraft operating out of Port Moresby, was determined to seize control of New Guinea before the Allies got any stronger. Ordered to proceed with MO Operation, Inoue scheduled the invasion of Tulagi in the southern Solomons for May 3, to be followed by the invasion of Port Moresby on or before May 10. As an offshoot of MO Operation, Inoue also planned to seize Nauru and Ocean islands, north of the Solomons, which held rich deposits of phosphates. But before any of the three elements commenced, he vowed to destroy Allied air strength in the region. Consequently, the air units at Rabaul and Lae were completely upgraded.

The timing of MO Operation benefited from a major restructuring of the Imperial Navy on April 1. As part of the reorganization, the 24th Air Flotilla was transferred from Rabaul to the Central Pacific and replaced by the 25th Air Flotilla. Commanded by the aristocratic-looking, mustachioed Rear Admiral Sadayoshi Yamada, the 25th included Japan's most famous fighter unit, the Tainan Air Group. Organized six months earlier, the group had gained extensive combat experience in the Philippines and the Netherlands East Indies and now boasted many of Japan's top fighter aces. Among them were petty officers Hiroyoshi Nishizawa and Saburo Sakai and their popular *chutai* leader, Lieutenant (junior grade) Junichi Sasai, whose collective exploits elevated the reputation of the Zero fighter during the opening months of the war. Revered in the Japanese press, the pilots fought aggressively and fiercely, always seeking a tactical advantage. Valuing the ancient *bushido* codes, they took the offensive at every opportunity, shunning any equipment that might hinder their performance. Many removed the heavy two-way radios from their fighters, and some even flew without parachutes—anything to reduce the overall weight of their Zeros and gain a slight edge in combat.

During the second half of April, as the Tainan Air Group and bomber units reached full combat strength, Admiral Yamada intensified his aerial campaign against Port Moresby. The Japanese raids came in waves and generally included at least one full division of Type 1 bombers from Rabaul and fifteen or more Zeros from Lae. Only one RAAF fighter outfit, 75

Squadron, was available to defend the outpost. Courageously manning their dwindling supply of airworthy Kittyhawks, the Aussies rose day after day to intercept the Japanese.

IN RESPONSE TO the heavy Japanese raids, General Brett and his staff temporarily shifted their headquarters to Townsville on April 18, hoping to organize a series of counterattacks. Over the next week and a half, the 14th Recon conducted several raids against both Rabaul and Lae. In typical fashion, Bill Lewis led the first effort himself. Collectively the attacks were little more than an aggravating nuisance for the Japanese, but in company with the increasing number of raids conducted by B-25s, B-26s, and A-24 dive bombers, particularly against Lae, the efforts of the Fortress crews contributed to the enemy's overall attrition.

On April 24, the squadron's tenure as the only heavy bomber outfit in New Guinea finally came to an end. That afternoon, four B-17s of the 30th Bombardment Squadron landed at Port Moresby to prepare for their first mission to Rabaul. Early the next morning, however, the newcomers discovered that New Guinea could be even more dangerous than the Japanese. In the process of taxiing in the darkness to begin the mission, the lead aircraft became stuck in a muddy bomb crater. The remaining three Fortresses took off on schedule and began climbing over the mountains, but one slammed into the upper slopes of Mount Obree at an elevation of nine thousand feet, killing the entire crew. A few hours later, fifteen Zeros of the Tainan Air Group swooped down on the airdrome and destroyed the still-mired B-17 along with a parked B-26. The Japanese won the battle of attrition that day, as the American squadrons gained nothing in exchange for the loss of eight men and three bombers.

By April 28, the Aussie fighter squadron was down to its last five Kittyhawks. The commanding officer, Squadron Leader John Jackson, boldly led them aloft that morning to intercept an attack by nine Type 1 bombers and eleven Zeros, but the Japanese simply outgunned the Australians. In the melee that ensued, Jackson and another Kittyhawk pilot were killed in action and a third Aussie was wounded. The next day, when another *chutai* of Type 1 bombers raided Seven Mile airdrome, not a single P-40 rose up to meet them. At Rabaul, Admiral Yamada concluded that Allied air strength at Port Moresby had been crushed.[8]

But the lull in Allied fighter defenses was only temporary. On April 30, hundreds of battle-weary Australians cheered as two squadrons of Bell P-39D Airacobras from the 8th Pursuit Group landed at the airdrome. The Japanese, ever vigilant, resumed their raids with a vengeance. Losses on both sides increased, but the Americans suffered the worst of it. By the end of their first week in action, no fewer than fourteen P-39s had been shot down with the loss of nine pilots.[9]

All across Australia, the public was enthralled by the David-versus-Goliath story of Port Moresby's air war. Detailed accounts appeared in the papers almost every day, written by war correspondents who witnessed the aerial contests from the ground. Osmar White's reports were highly respected as well as influential. "[The] prospect of Japan launching invasion forces against Australia's east coast," he wrote on April 28, "depends now on the outcome of the most thrilling race against time the Pacific has ever seen. The Japanese are racing the organization and disposition of their invasion forces against our ability to build up enough air strength to smash the transports and escorts of those invasion forces."[10]

Two days later, White starkly predicted, "If the Japanese prevail, New Guinea falls, and the sprawling east coast of Australia offers them the choice of a dozen invasion points."[11]

From Darwin to Brisbane, hundreds of thousands of Australians became extremely nervous.

UNKNOWN TO THE Japanese, the Allies held one distinct advantage. For weeks, intelligence centers at Pearl Harbor and Melbourne had been chipping away at the primary cryptographic code used by the Imperial Navy. Known as JN-25, it was never completely broken (at best, analysts could read no more than about fifteen percent of any given message), but by combining the details gleaned from numerous messages with intel gathered from other sources, analysts were able to piece together an outline of MO

Operation. By late April, they knew that two big fleet carriers, a light carrier, and a division of heavy cruisers were moving southward to support the forthcoming operation. In response, Admiral Nimitz ordered the *Lexington* and *Yorktown* task forces to rendezvous in the Southwest Pacific and disrupt the enemy offensive.

General Brett, returning to Townsville on April 28, placed the Northeastern Area on high alert. Soon thereafter an announcement was made that all maintenance troops and support personnel would be issued weapons for the defense of the airfield. This got everyone's attention, trumping the news that the outfit had received a new designation as the 40th Reconnaissance Squadron. Curiously, the designation lasted only a matter of weeks before it was changed yet again. In any event, other than affecting the squadron's mailing address, the new number was practically overlooked. The squadron had more important things to worry about.

Due to the Japanese threat, the last day of April found all personnel restricted to the airfield, where the mood turned as gloomy as the weather. "Well, I saw April go out today," wrote John Steinbinder. "It's been a nasty day, rainy and cold. We are all confined to our barracks as there are persistent rumors that we are in for a raid so we must be on alert 24 hours a day. It seems that the Japs have . . . sent their aircraft carriers into New Guinea and Australian waters. So we are to expect the worst."[12]

As if to amplify the dark rumors, enemy reconnaissance planes appeared over Townsville the following day, triggering two air-raid alarms. The P-39s had already departed for Port Moresby, leaving the defense of the city to the antiaircraft batteries. Their aim was initially poor, noted Steinbinder, but "became more accurate later, driving the planes off."[13]

MO OPERATION GOT under way on April 29, when the transports and warships of the Tulagi Invasion Force sailed from Rabaul. Soon after they cleared Simpson Harbor, even more ships crowded into the anchorage to prepare for the assault on Port Moresby. Hundreds of Australian prisoners, captured when Rabaul fell in late January, labored on the docks to load eleven troop carriers and several large warships. And while the invasion fleet was being loaded, the powerful MO Striking Force, centered on the big carriers *Shokaku* and *Zuikaku*, steamed south from Truk. The total forces available to Vice Admiral Inoue were impressive—three aircraft carriers, six heavy cruisers, three light cruisers, thirteen destroyers, two large minelayers, thirteen transports, and a host of auxiliary ships—but they were divided among several widely scattered groups.

Right in the thick of the reconnaissance effort, lieutenants Jack Roberts and James N. Gibb (a former copilot promoted to 1st Pilot) spent several days in early May flying solo patrols from Port Moresby. Japanese raids had demolished most of the permanent buildings at Seven Mile drome, leaving the crews to seek shelter from the blazing sun in tent encampments or crude native-built structures scattered among the scrub-covered hills. There was little to do between missions except wait for the next unappealing meal served in the open-air mess tent. Steinbinder, now assigned to Gibb's crew, wrote sarcastically, "We have a great variety of food here. For breakfast we have hash, potatoes, hardtack, and coffee; for lunch, hash, potatoes, bread, and tea; for dinner, hash, potatoes, rice, peaches, and coffee, with choice of hardtack or bread."[14]

In addition to the dull food, unsanitary conditions, and oppressive humidity, the crews had to contend with air raids almost every day. On the morning of May 3, while Roberts was out on a 1,700-mile recon, Gibb and his crew watched slack-jawed as an incoming raid was intercepted by the American P-39s. Steinbinder, lost in the pages of *Ben Hur* before the attack interrupted his reading, was fascinated by the air battle. "I've seen movies and read books about this sort of thing," he wrote, "but believe you me, there was never anything written or produced that could compare to the real thing."[15]

The reconnaissance efforts enabled the Allies to effectively track the Japanese fleets. On the afternoon of May 3, the Tulagi Invasion Force was discovered as it approached the southern Solomons. The sighting reports, along with anxious radio messages from the small Australian garrison at Tulagi, were received by Rear Admiral Fletcher's Task Force 17. The next morning, he launched a strike on the Japanese beachhead from the carrier *Yorktown*, sinking two small warships and a couple of wooden minesweepers.

It was a respectable start, but Allied attention shifted immediately to stopping the invasion of Port Moresby. Fletcher, who planned to intervene with his carriers and the multinational ANZAC squadron, spent much of the next two days casting about for the enemy. By the afternoon of May 6, the opposing forces had begun to form a partial picture of each other's whereabouts. At Rabaul, Rear Admiral Yamada ordered his land-attack units, including the veteran 4th Air Group and the newly arrived Genzan Air Group, to conduct dawn searches and prepare for strikes against the American fleet. Fletcher, meanwhile, had correctly deduced that the enemy fleet headed for Port Moresby would attempt to navigate through the Louisiade Archipelago prior to commencing the invasion. Intending to cut them off, he sent the ANZAC squadron, commanded by Rear Admiral "Jack" Crace, Royal Navy, westward across the Solomon Sea to meet the enemy threat.

ON THE AFTERNOON of May 4, Australian POWs had watched in somber silence as the Port Moresby Invasion Force and Support Force sailed from Simpson Harbor. The armada numbered almost thirty ships. English-speaking guards mocked the prisoners, telling them, "Japan take Moresby, then Australia, you go home."[16]

Determined to locate Inoue's scattered forces, particularly the aircraft carriers, the Allies launched dozens of reconnaissance missions. Clear weather gave the aircrews an advantage, and the light carrier *Shoho*, a converted submarine tender displacing just over 11,000 tons, was discovered by a B-25 on May 5. That afternoon, three B-17s loaded with six-hundred-pound bombs flew up to Port Moresby and joined the reconnaissance crews. Harry Spieth, Wilbur Beezley, and Henry Harlow (newly qualified as a 1st Pilot) were probably surprised by the slovenly appearance of their squadron mates. After wearing the same uniforms for several days the unshaven reconnaissance crews looked like vagrants, and the newcomers soon discovered why. Due to overcrowding at the American encampment, no quarters were available for transient crews. Wallace Fields, making his first trip to the embattled outpost, was disgusted with the conditions. "What a hole," he wrote in his diary. "No beds, poor food, hot, dirty."[17]

But the crews were spoiling for a fight. Jim Gibb, scheduled for the next day's reconnaissance mission, worked out a plan with Spieth to locate and attack the enemy carrier sighted earlier that day. The effort almost succeeded. Initially delayed while trying to get an engine started, Gibb took off at 3:45 A.M. on May 6 and found the *Shoho* support force approximately four hours later. Loitering overhead at 14,000 feet, he shadowed the warships while his crew radioed their position to Port Moresby. When two fighters took off from the carrier to intercept the Fortress, Gibb sped off toward the northern Solomons and completed a routine reconnaissance mission.

Standing by on alert, Spieth, Beezley, and Harlow took off immediately and headed straight for the coordinates sent by Gibb's crew. Beezley was forced to turn back when an engine quit, but Spieth and Harlow arrived over the *Shoho* at approximately 10:30 A.M. They commenced a bomb run, but due to a misunderstanding Harlow went after one of the heavy cruisers while Spieth dropped his bombs tantalizingly close to the *Shoho*. "I just missed the aircraft carrier, don't know if I did any damage or not," he admitted in his diary. "We went in under heavy antiaircraft fire and were very lucky not to get hit. Jap planes tried to intercept me, but I pulled away from them."[18]

Spieth also remarked that the cruiser attacked by Harlow appeared to be on fire, but as neither the *Shoho* nor her escorts were damaged that day, he was probably misled by muzzle blasts and lingering smoke from the cruiser's big guns.

Twenty-four hours later, Spieth was still berating himself. "Can't get over missing my great chance yesterday," he wrote. But by that time, the *Shoho* was at the bottom of the sea. An SBD on patrol from the *Yorktown* had rediscovered her on the morning of May 7, and in less than two hours more than ninety aircraft from the *Lexington* and the *Yorktown* were on their way to attack the flattop. Brushing past the few Japanese fighters aloft, swarms of blue-gray dive bombers and torpedo planes blasted the hapless *Shoho* with upwards of twenty direct hits. At 11:35 A.M., only four minutes after the captain issued orders to abandon ship, the carrier disappeared beneath the waves.[19]

SPIETH'S NEXT OPPORTUNITY to attack a capital ship ended with a similar result to his previous attempt. This time, however, he was grateful that his bombs fell wide. On the morning of May 7, Admiral Crace's warships detached from Fletcher's main force and plowed westward at twenty-five knots to intercept the Port Moresby Invasion Force. Soon after, a Japanese reconnaissance floatplane discovered the Allied cruiser force and reported its position to Rabaul. Rear Admiral Yamada, believing this to be the American main carrier force, ordered his land-attack aircraft to destroy it. Twelve Mitsubishi G4Ms armed with torpedoes took off first, followed an hour later by nineteen G3M twin-engine bombers. Both waves were detected by radar aboard the heavy cruiser USS *Chicago*, whereupon Crace's warships gathered into a defensive arrangement known as Formation Victor. Surrounded by a protective screen of American destroyers, the heavy cruiser *Australia*, Crace's flagship, took position in the center of the formation.

The Japanese torpedo bombers attacked first. Due to intense and accurate antiaircraft fire from the warships, only five aircraft succeeded in dropping their "fish," and not a single torpedo scored a hit. The fruitless effort cost the 4th Air Group a total of six aircraft, including four shot down outright, with thirty-one aviators killed in action.

Shortly after the surviving torpedo bombers escaped, the medium bombers of the Genzan Air Group approached the Allied cruiser force from astern. Singling out the *Australia,* which they mistook for a British Warspite-class battleship, the Japanese dropped their bombs in a tight pattern. Whistling down from 18,000 feet, the bombs struck the surface all around the 630-foot *Australia*, sending up huge geysers of spray that totally obscured the flagship. Sailors watching from other ships thought she had blown up, then cheered when the big cruiser emerged from the spray, her upper works doused with seawater. By some miracle no bombs hit the *Australia*, though her stout hull was shaken by near misses.

In all, thirty-one Japanese attackers had failed to score even one direct hit, but Crace's warships were not yet out of danger. A few minutes after the medium bombers passed out of sight, three heavy bombers approached from the north at high altitude. The trio was led by Harry Spieth, who thought the ships were Japanese. The mistake was understandable. For one thing, the B-17 crews had been briefed that no Allied ships would be operating north of a certain parallel, the implication being that any vessels detected above that demarcation were Japanese by default. Not only were the warships north of the line, they were being attacked by B-26s—or so the Fortress crews believed. "We were coming in at about 18,000 feet and could see some planes flying below and diving at low level," recalled Spieth's copilot, Wallace Fields. "We thought those were B-26s, so we lined up on the battleship that they were bombing and dropped our bombs on it."[20]

The case of erroneous identification was also logical. From above, the B-26 Marauder and the Mitsubishi G4M looked almost identical, although either of the Japanese bomber types could easily have been mistaken for B-26s from a distance. According to Rear Admiral Crace, the bombs dropped by Spieth's aircraft landed seven cables (1,400 yards) from the *Australia*, impacting the water near one of the screening destroyers. Lieutenant Commander Thomas E. Fraser, the captain of the destroyer *Walke*, reported that the bombs landed just astern of the destroyer *Farragut*.[21] In this case it was fortuitous that the B-17s were no more accurate than the Japanese had been. If even one six-hundred-pound bomb had hit the *Farragut*, which displaced only 1,365 tons, a tragic friendly fire incident would have resulted.

Other B-17s, flying out of Townsville, fared slightly better. Frank Bostrom led a flight of eight, consisting mostly of "visiting ships" from the 19th Group, on a lengthy mission to find and attack the Port Moresby Invasion Force. Two bombers turned back, but the remaining Fortresses located the convoy near the Louisiade Archipelago, more than seven hundred miles from Townsville. Braving heavy antiaircraft fire from the screening warships, the B-17s attempted to bomb the twisting, turning transports. A few bombs caused minor damage, but as Ed Teats of the 30th Squadron later remarked, the enemy ships proved impossible to hit as they evaded in every direction "like an aggregation of excited water bugs."[22]

THE CLASHES BETWEEN American and Japanese forces on May 7 marked the first time in the history of naval warfare that the opposing ships battled over the horizon, never making visual contact with each other. By the end of the day's actions, the score reflected not only the sinking of the *Shoho* but the loss of thirty-five Japanese aircraft and approximately seventy highly trained aviators. On the American side, the destroyer *Sims* had been sunk, the oiler *Neosho* was a bombed-out hulk, and a handful of planes had been shot down.

The stage was set for an even bigger carrier-versus-carrier showdown the following day, but the Japanese were already losing their resolve. Dismayed by the loss of the *Shoho* and the failure of the MO Striking Force to defeat the American carriers, Admiral Isoroku Yamamoto, commander-in-chief of the Combined Fleet, recommended a brief postponement of the invasion. Vice Admiral Inoue, more immediately concerned about the protection of the Port Moresby Invasion Force, issued a bulletin postponing the invasion for two days. The transports withdrew to the north, sheltering near the New Guinea coast while awaiting the outcome of the pivotal battle to come.

The next day, May 8, the aerial duels between opposing carriers slightly favored the Japanese. The big flattop *Shokaku*, badly damaged by three bombs, withdrew from the battle with 109 fatalities and dozens of wounded. She would be out of action for approximately two months. But in the exchange of roundhouse carrier strikes, the *Lexington* suffered direct hits by two torpedoes and two bombs, and the *Yorktown* sustained damage to her flight deck from a well-placed bomb. The *Lexington* initially appeared to have survived the Japanese attacks, but several hours after the action, persistent fires reached aviation fuel lines deep within her hull, igniting violent explosions. Even then, the beloved "Lady Lex" had to be finished off by torpedoes from an American destroyer. Perhaps the greatest blow on that second day of battle was Japan's loss of more than forty aircraft and several dozen experienced aviators. The attrition was so heavy, in fact, that the *Zuikaku* withdrew as well. Subsequently, neither Japanese flattop was available for the upcoming operation against Midway in early June.

In one of the great ironies of the battle, the Japanese airmen who survived the slugfest submitted outrageous claims. Convinced that two American carriers and several other ships had been sunk, Inoue boasted of a brilliant success to Yamamoto and Imperial General Headquarters. Japanese newspapers reported a smashing victory in the Coral Sea, leading readers to believe the Imperial Navy had "thunder sunk" at least three capital warships and seriously damaged two others. The exaggerations continued to grow, until a total of eight Allied ships had allegedly been sunk or damaged. Not surprisingly, the Information Bureau downplayed the Imperial Navy's losses, admitting only that "a small aircraft carrier" had been sunk and thirty-one Japanese planes "were yet to return."[23]

Despite all the boasting, Inoue lost his nerve. His ships were low on fuel, the *Shokaku* was out of action, and the *Zuikaku* possessed only twenty-one serviceable airplanes. Lacking adequate air support, he decided to postpone the assault on Port Moresby indefinitely. The MO Invasion Force was ordered to return to Rabaul, and literally overnight the entire operation collapsed.

Full realization that the Japanese had called off the invasion took several days to register. The heavy schedule of Allied reconnaissance missions continued unabated, with B-17s reporting fifty-eight enemy vessels in the battle area on May 8 alone. As this was more than the Japanese had assembled for the operation, the total undoubtedly included several redundancies in the overall count, but the aerial coverage was impressively thorough. Even better, while reconnoitering the New Guinea coast that afternoon, Lieutenant "Skid" Johnson spotted what appeared to be a Type 95 reconnaissance floatplane flying at four thousand feet a few miles away. He closed to within four hundred yards of the biplane, and Sergeant George Ryan Jr. claimed its destruction after firing 250 rounds from his waist gun. As it turned out, a Type 0 floatplane (Aichi E13A) failed to return from a reconnaissance flight in the vicinity of the Louisiades. Although Ryan did the actual shooting, Johnson was decorated for his "initiative and determination to defeat the enemy wherever found."[24] As usual, the pilots got all the glory.

Despite the favorable outcome of the naval battle, the heavy reconnaissance effort had an unintended effect on the citizens of northern Australia. Due to the sheer number of enemy ships discovered in the battle area, wild rumors continued to spread that a Japanese invasion fleet was only a few hundred miles from Queensland. Captain John A. Rouse, a pilot in the 30th Squadron who participated in several missions from Townsville, wrote in his diary on May 9, "Other crews [are] here now to relieve us and keep hammering the Japs. Big battle in progress."[25]

The battle was essentially over, yet virtually nobody in Australia realized the enemy had quit the battlefield. The Fortresses and other Allied bombers continued to harass the invasion fleet as it withdrew to Rabaul, but even then the outcome was not apparent. As late as May 10, fears of an imminent attack were still rampant in Townsville. "Alert early this AM in case Japs raid," Rouse penned. "Two carriers reported 300 miles offshore. Scared to death. We would be duck soup for them. Could hardly light a cigarette."[26]

Judging from other accounts, Rouse's anxiety was not exceptional. Radio operator John Lillback, a native of Brooklyn, New York, had found time between missions to date a twenty-year-old nurse from Townsville. By the time of the battle, Lillback was spending considerable time with Sharnée Schmidt at her parents' home. Years later, he reflected on the invasion fears that gripped northern Queensland.

> The nearness of the Japanese caused the Aussie regional commander, [Major General George A.] Vasey, to order strict rules in case of invasion. Wreck water tanks, shoot livestock, burn crops in the field, pack up and start trekking towards Brisbane if you didn't have transport. This was part of the "Brisbane Line" syndrome at the time. It has been hotly denied, but ask any surviving Aussie in the north if it were so. My potential father-in-law asked me to get him a gun to protect himself, his wife, and daughter—which I did. I gave him my Colt .45 pistol, holster, and two clips of ammo. Gordie Schmidt told me that if his area was invaded, he would shoot the Japs as long as he could, saving two bullets for his wife Olga and daughter Sharnée.[27]

The government and the press were slow to suppress the fears of those living north of Brisbane. In a radio broadcast on the evening of May 9, Prime Minister Curtin gave a sobering address intended to prepare Australians for a long, protracted war. "I tell you bluntly," he said, "that the whole world may very well shake within the next few weeks under the blows that full-scale warfare will strike. Australia cannot escape a blow. Happenings of great magnitude are at hand. . . . Australian and American fighting men daily give their lives in defending Australian territory. We face vital, perilous weeks, fraught with exceedingly important happenings for Australia. Invasion is a menace capable hourly of becoming an actuality."[28]

Then, with exaggerations worthy of the Japanese press, Australian newspapers reported on May 9 that the enemy had lost ten ships in the Coral Sea. Two more days would pass before the withdrawal of the Japanese fleet was verified, at which time the press declared a major victory. But soon thereafter, calmer heads reminded the public that it might take weeks for the reports from Allied naval vessels and aviation units to be analyzed.

Over the ensuing decades, most historians have declared the battle a draw, primarily based on the tally of ships sunk during the carrier-versus-carrier battles of May 7 and 8. The seaborne invasion of Port Moresby was stopped cold, but the Imperial Navy lost only one small carrier (the *Shoho*) compared to the Pacific Fleet's loss of the *Lexington*, a destroyer, and an oiler. However, if all three elements of Vice Admiral Inoue's MO Operation are considered, the balance shifts decidedly in favor of the Allies. Before dawn on May 11, an American submarine scored two torpedo hits on the big minelayer *Okinoshima*, the flagship of the invasion force heading for the islands of Ocean and Nauru. She sank the next morning while being towed, and a repair ship dispatched from Rabaul to assist her was sunk that afternoon by a different submarine. The landings on the phosphate-rich islands were subsequently canceled, which meant that Inoue actually accomplished only one out of three stated objectives. The one successful phase of MO Operation had been the occupation of Tulagi on May 4, which cost the Japanese two warships and a few small wooden boats. Altogether, Inoue lost *six* ships, nearly eighty planes, and scores of irreplaceable aviators.

Flying dozens of sorties from Port Moresby and Townsville, the redesignated 40th Reconnaissance Squadron had played a small but vital role in the battle. From the time the enemy began loading ships in Simpson Harbor in late April until the invasion fleet limped back to Rabaul two weeks later, the squadron kept the Japanese under almost constant daytime surveillance. Brigadier General Martin F. Scanlon, who assumed command of Allied aviation units in the Northeast Area just a few days before the battle began, praised the 40th Squadron for its work during "the emergency." But there was also some minor embarrassment. On May 14, an Australian naval officer visiting Townsville complained about the friendly fire incident involving Admiral Crace's cruiser force, saying, "We don't like to get wet."[29]

The mistake was quickly forgotten, in part because the squadron underwent a final change of identity. As of April 22, the War Department had authorized the official constitution of the 435th Bombardment Squadron (Heavy), assigned to the 19th Bombardment Group. Word of the new designation did not reach Australia for nearly a month, by which time the squadron had already adapted to its new role as a reconnaissance outfit, despite the misleading name. The personnel remained the same, the planes remained the same, and in the months to come, the 435th would write a new page in history as the eyes of the Allied forces in the Southwest Pacific.

EIGHTEEN

SILVER STARS

Vice Admiral Inoue's attempt to invade Port Moresby by sea had failed. For the time being, at least, the threat of heavier bombing attacks on the Australian mainland diminished. But the citizens of Australia knew better than to celebrate prematurely. No one doubted that the Japanese would try again to capture Port Moresby, perhaps with a bigger invasion fleet. Deterred only temporarily by the setback, Inoue was already reinforcing his strongholds while simultaneously considering alternative invasion sites on the northern coast of New Guinea. The battle for control of the island was far from decided.

For several weeks after the action in the Coral Sea, the renumbered 435th Reconnaissance Squadron flew an equal balance of bombing missions and photographic flights. Responding to orders generated by Area Combined Headquarters at Townsville, the B-17s covered a vast area of the Southwest Pacific. Lae and Rabaul were the most common targets, but in mid-May, three Fortresses loaded with spare parts and a contingent of maintenance personnel conducted an extended deployment in the Northern Territory. Working out of Batchelor Field alongside eight B-17s from the 30th and 93rd Squadrons, the detachment reconnoitered targets in the Japanese-occupied Netherlands East Indies for more than a week.

Fred Eaton was in charge of the small maintenance echelon at Batchelor. With his old crew broken up after their ordeal in New Guinea, he had been detailed to the squadron's maintenance department until he recovered his strength and received a new crew. It was not a punishment. Eaton continued to suffer malarial chills and his weight dropped to 135 pounds, but he was irritated by the lack of action. "I'm getting mighty tired of sitting here on the ground," he fussed privately. "I wish that I could fly a couple of good combat missions. Even though your bombs don't do as much damage as you would like and your ship gets shot up a bit, you still feel as if you are doing some good in this war."[1]

While Eaton waited to return to combat, the 435th entered a period of transition. Although assigned to the 19th Group, it operated independently from the three original bombardment squadrons (28th, 30th, and 93rd) based at Cloncurry and Longreach. This suited the crews of the 435th just fine. Not only had they developed something of a swagger from their tramp-like days as the "Southern Bombers," their unique status served as an incubator. The squadron's autonomy fostered problem-solving ideas on everything from how to upgrade the B-17s to getting better results from their missions. It began with Bill Lewis, who organized a daily meeting for the combat crews to educate them on useful topics. On any given morning, a Royal Australian Navy officer might lecture on ship identification and maneuvering, or a coast artillery gunner would cover the strengths and weaknesses of antiaircraft weapons. Squadron members often conducted their own workshops, reviewing the lessons they had learned during enemy encounters or while flying in poor weather or navigating on long overwater missions.

One new idea, credited to communications officer Walt Johnson, was to modify the low-frequency coil of the radio transmitters, enabling other planes to home in on the aircraft generating the signal with their radio compasses. Any number of bombers, regardless of type, could join up in the vicinity of a designated target such as an enemy convoy, and make a coordinated attack with a better chance of scoring hits. "Our weakness against maneuvering naval targets has been insufficient area coverage," Johnson acknowledged. "Ships have been maneuvering out from under the bombs during the interval between release and impact."[2]

Another interesting idea came from pilot Harry Spieth, who arranged to have the underwings and belly of his B-17 painted light blue, much as the RAF had experimented with during the Battle of Britain. In theory the unusual color would camouflage the aircraft when viewed from below, and the trial began during the last week of June. "Finally got someone to paint my ship sky blue," he wrote on the twenty-fourth, "hope it comes out ok."[3] Applied to the underside of an older E model with a remote belly turret (service number 41-2421), the blue color was certainly distinctive, but the Fortress was exchanged for a newer plane before the experiment could be properly evaluated.[*]

No idea was considered too unorthodox. On May 29, lieutenants Deacon Rawls and Jack Roberts flew a night raid against Rabaul with a load of incendiary bombs to drop on Lakunai airdrome. The fires ignited by the incendiaries, so the idea went, would "drive the Japs into the woods where the malaria-laden mosquitos can go to work on them."[4] Roberts's bombs failed to release, but Rawls reportedly lit up the field with direct hits. Not that it mattered, because the plan had a fundamental flaw: there were no woods near Lakunai airdrome. Periodic eruptions of Tavurvur volcano had killed off the vegetation around the northern part of the caldera.

Some innovations were derived from combat experience. By the late spring of 1942, the Fortress crews were witnessing a new enemy fighter tactic. "[At first] the Japs attacked the B-17 from the tail," explained Walt Johnson. "After the picnic of the tail gunners in the new E, they had to change strategy. Next the Zeros came in from the bottom, pulling up into a stalled attitude. That does not prove healthy when the bottom turret is working, and the new ball turret does work when properly handled. Now the Japs have a new method of attack, a very frightening one for the pilots, for they pull out in front and come back head-on."[5]

Saburo Sakai, the highest scoring ace from the Tainan Air Group to survive the war, offered a similar but slightly different explanation. "[Our] favorite method of attack against the big planes had been to dive from behind in a sweeping firing pass, raking the bombers from tail to nose as we

---

[*] On July 16, the day after the B-17 was turned over to the 19th Bomb Group, it crashed at Horn Island while loaded with personnel and spare parts. The crew of three and all twelve passengers were killed.

flashed by," he wrote in his bestselling autobiography. "We soon discovered this had little effect on the well-constructed and heavily armored B-17. It was this knowledge—and not primarily the addition of tail armament to the Fortresses—which brought about a sudden change of tactics. We adopted head-on passes, flying directly against the oncoming B-17s, pouring bullets and cannon shells into the forward areas of the enemy bombers."[6]

The frightening new tactic received ample attention on May 13, when Lieutenant Colonel Ken Hobson, now on General Scanlon's staff at Area Combined HQ, led three B-17s on a raid against Rabaul. Flying his first combat mission since the debacle in Java, Hobson had a disturbing experience on the return leg to Port Moresby. Five Zeros intercepted the formation and made several aggressive front-quarter passes. No B-17 crewmen were wounded during the thirty-minute battle, but the sight of enemy planes closing head-on at combined speeds well in excess of five hundred miles per hour was disquieting, especially for the pilots and bombardiers.

The Japanese were taking advantage of the B-17's defensive weak spot. Aside from the upper turret, the only weapon capable of defending against direct frontal attacks was a .30 caliber machine gun, which the bombardier poked through one of the ball-and-socket mounts in the Plexiglas. Awkward to use and too lightweight to be effective, the .30 caliber weapon was considered "a pea shooter."[7]

To remedy this, the 435th Squadron's armament section experimented with homemade single- and twin-fifty mounting points in the nose of a B-17. Rod Stewart, the bookish, slender engineering officer, came up with clever solutions to a number of problems. The .50 caliber weapons, for example, weighed three times more than a .30 caliber gun and produced much heavier vibration from recoil, requiring stout reinforcements to prevent damage to the Plexiglas or the metal framework. As navigator Lieutenant Horace E. Perry explained, necessity is the mother of invention:

> At the time we had a wrecked B-17 that had been stripped for parts. A trial installation was made in this ship to determine if the plastic cell

material would withstand the shock of twin 50-caliber machine guns firing together. The mounting consisted of fitting a steel plate in the center of the nose section. Ball sockets were set in this plate enabling the guns to operate in a 30° cone. Inside the plane the guns were supported by a system of pulleys and shock cord. They worked—and how![8]

Despite a mishap during the first live-fire test on May 22, when tracer rounds ignited a large brushfire on a distant hillside, the installation proved extremely popular. The Boeing company took note of such field modifications, along with feedback from combat crews, and eventually incorporated a powered "chin" turret in the B-17G, the most common production model of the Flying Fortress.*

AT THE SAME time that Stewart began his experiments with the machine guns, the 435th experienced additional turnover among the pilots. Majors Carmichael and Twaddell had already been promoted to staff jobs in Melbourne; Swede Swenson was sent to the transport command at the beginning of May; Dubby DuBose, Newt Chaffin, and Harry Brandon were plucked from the squadron for staff positions elsewhere; Bill Lewis and Ted Faulkner, tied to their respective obligations as commanding officer and executive officer, were rarely available to fly missions; and Frank Bostrom was pulled from combat to serve as the squadron's operations officer. Only a few of the original pilots remained active. Will Beezley, Deacon Rawls, Jack Roberts, and Harry Spieth were among the stalwarts who continued to fly missions day after day, while Fred Eaton got a new crew in early June. To fill the vacancies, Major Lewis expedited the full qualification of the copilots, all of whom had logged hundreds of hours in the right-hand seat. During the next several weeks, a dozen former copilots were checked off, including Wallace Fields, George Munroe (who had completed his obligations as a navigator),

---

* The squadron claimed that Stewart was the first to adapt twin-fifties in the nose of a B-17. This is impossible to verify, inasmuch as similar types of modifications began to appear at various squadrons and depots across Australia in the spring of 1942.

and Roy Reid.* Of course that left several copilot positions open, which the RAAF helped to fill by allocating six enlisted pilots with multi-engine experience. Capable as well as professional, they proved to be excellent copilots and were popular with the crews.

The transition to 1st Pilot was not merely a matter of moving four feet to the left in the cockpit. The pilot in command held the fate of nine or more lives in his hands and routinely faced situations that required quick, firm decisions, the outcome of which might spell the difference between success or failure, life or death. And the transition process was implemented gradually, which meant that some of the newly qualified pilots waited weeks for their first opportunity to run a combat mission. Wallace Fields expected an assignment on May 18, but ten boring days passed while he stood alert duty or loafed in Townsville. Finally, after Harry Spieth was assigned temporary duty in the maintenance department, Fields took over his crew.

On the afternoon of May 28, Fields and Jim Gibb flew two crews to Port Moresby in one B-17, intending to split reconnaissance missions for several days. The more experienced Gibb flew the first mission the next morning, which was just as well. From start to finish, the flight was anything but routine.

Gibb's primary assignment was to photograph the enemy seaplane anchorage at Tulagi, nine hundred miles due east of Port Moresby on the far side of the Solomon Sea. Although scheduled to take off at 10:30 A.M., the crew stood by early in case the Japanese raided the airdrome again. Sure enough, the alarm sounded a few minutes after nine o'clock. Taking off just as the attackers arrived, Gibb hugged the terrain for several minutes to avoid detection, then turned seaward. Almost six hours later he arrived over Tulagi, which reportedly had light antiaircraft defenses consisting of three gun batteries with an effective altitude of five to eight thousand feet. Thinking he was above their limit, Gibb made his photographic run at 11,000 feet.

---

* The others were first lieutenants William H. Campbell, John T. Compton, Wilson L. Cook, Robert M. DeBord, John T. May, Andrew H. Price, Robert L. Ramsay, Mabry Simmons, and Donald O. Tower.

The Japanese gunners were ready. "Just as we made our first turn," noted John Steinbinder, the navigator, "three bursts of antiaircraft broke off to the right of the plane, so we turned again and started taking pictures. We got a complete set of pictures but antiaircraft fire was breaking all around us. I personally spotted six gun positions. The man who said their range was 5,000–8,000 feet sure was a liar. There were shells breaking 10,000 feet above us."[9]

Shaken but unharmed, Gibb's crew completed the long return flight only to find Port Moresby socked in by rain and poor visibility. After six aborted attempts to land, Gibb decided to divert to Horn Island, another 340 miles away. Night fell, enabling Steinbinder to obtain a three-star fix, and he figured they would have barely enough fuel to make it. When they landed that night, the gauges hovered on empty. "I sure was relieved," Steinbinder wrote in his diary. "We found we had about 12 minutes' worth of gas left. Some fun."[10]

The unexpected twists and turns of Gibb's mission provided a clear example of the challenges a 1st Pilot might deal with, especially on long reconnaissance flights. Unlike the pilots in a bomber formation, who primarily flew on the lead aircraft's wing for much of the mission, the "recco" pilots and crews were entirely on their own.

Stranded at Port Moresby for a few days with no airplane, Fields finally flew a mission as 1st Pilot when a replacement B-17 arrived. Target areas for his 1,200-mile reconnaissance loop on June 2 included Lae and Salamaua, the Dampier Strait between New Guinea and New Britain, and the usual run over Simpson Harbor. Chased from Rabaul by six Zeros, Fields was able to elude them thanks to the "rotten weather."[11] It was a good lesson to remember. Although clear skies were ideal for obtaining aerial photographs, the reconnaissance crews much preferred scattered cumulus clouds or even rain squalls, where they could hide if the Japanese intercepted them.

AT THE END of the first week of June, word of the U.S. Navy's stunning victory at Midway reached Townsville. But it was difficult to cheer for an outcome that had occurred four thousand miles away when the enemy in and around New Guinea remained such a dire threat. "The late naval success off Midway is heartening," wrote Walt Johnson on June 7, "despite the growing power of Japan in this region. They are known to have 38 Zeros at Lae now, and several two-motor bombers. The Zero is much better than anything we have, but Jap bombers don't compare with ours."[12]

Johnson's estimate was high, but the Tainan Air Group had accumulated at least two dozen operational Zeros at Lae, and additional fighters were being delivered periodically to Rabaul. That very afternoon, General Scanlon called a meeting at Area Combined HQ to plan an ambitious attack on Lae. General Royce flew in from Melbourne as a high-level liaison for General MacArthur, who had granted permission for several visiting VIPs to participate in the raid as observers. At the top of the list was Congressman Lyndon B. Johnson, a Democratic representative from Texas, who had joined the U.S. Naval Reserve in 1940 and wore the rank of lieutenant commander. Granted a leave of absence from Congress after the attack on Pearl Harbor, the thirty-three-year-old politician had worked his way into President Roosevelt's good graces and was conducting an investigative tour of the Southwest Pacific as FDR's personal representative. Accompanied by Lieutenant Colonel Samuel E. Anderson and Lieutenant Colonel Francis R. Stevens of the War Department staff, Johnson had arrived in Melbourne on May 25, then spent the next two weeks inspecting facilities in Melbourne, Sydney, and Brisbane.

Regardless of Johnson's temporary rank in the navy, his authorization to observe a combat mission, particularly against such a hotly contested stronghold, was unprecedented. Lae was defended by arguably the best fighter group in the Japanese military, which compelled the planners at Townsville to organize the mission so as to minimize the risk to Johnson and the other observers. Their plan, complicated from the start, was to hit Lae with a mixed bomber force. Three B-17s from the 435th Squadron would bomb first from 30,000 feet, hoping to draw any intercepting Zeros northward toward the Markham Valley. Forty minutes later, B-25s of the 3rd Bomb Group would attack the stronghold, engage any late-arriving fighters, and draw them northward into an ambush by waiting P-39s. With the enemy fighters presumably out of the way, B-26s of the 22nd Bomb Group would carry Johnson and the other observers while bombing Lae from medium altitude.[13]

Ted Faulkner was selected to lead the B-17s, with Wallace Fields and Maury Horgan on his wing. The effort started conspicuously on the afternoon of June 8 when Fields, piloting the Fortress with a sky-blue underbelly and lower wing surfaces, blew a tire before takeoff. As soon as repairs were made, the trio departed for an overnight stop at Horn Island. General Royce watched the B-17s take off, followed by twelve B-26s that headed straight to Port Moresby. Later that evening, when the VIPs arrived from Melbourne, Royce joined congressman Johnson and a bevy of army brass at a Townsville hotel for drinks. The highest ranking among them was Major General William F. Marquat, a member of MacArthur's "Bataan Gang" (and a former correspondent for the *Seattle Times*), who was also participating as an observer.[14]

The first stage of the mission got under way at 3:10 the next morning. Bill Lewis took off from Townsville in a Fortress loaded with the VIPs and arrived at Port Moresby at approximately 8 A.M., whereupon the four observers promptly boarded their assigned B-26s. Or at least they started to. The takeoff was delayed while Lyndon Johnson hurried off to find a latrine. Colonel Stevens subsequently swapped places with him, boarding a B-26 named *The Virginian* piloted by Lieutenant Willis G. Bench. After relieving himself, Johnson climbed into Major Walter H. Greer's Marauder, named *Hecklin' Hare*.

At Horn Island, Faulkner's trio of B-17s had departed on schedule, but from that point forward almost nothing went according to plan. Wallace Fields's flight engineer, Staff Sergeant Nicholas V. Stashuk, had fallen ill and was not on board, leaving the assistant engineer, Private Paul Panosian, to take over. His duties included manning the upper turret, but Panosian had little or no experience with the gun system. In the process of testing the weapons after the formation reached altitude, he discovered that they wouldn't fire. Panosian put the turret in the stowed position, facing aft, then reached up and smacked the guns in an apparent act of frustration. And suddenly they began to fire. A solenoid, synchronized to the turret position, was supposed to prevent the guns from firing when pointed at the vertical stabilizer, but inexplicably the guns began blasting away. By the time the runaway weapons were silenced, the tail had been severely damaged. The rudder, shot nearly in two, was useless. Dropping out of formation, Fields dumped his bombs over the Gulf of Papua and diverted to Port Moresby.

Steering with the ailerons, Fields made a smooth landing at Seven Mile airdrome; but instead of feeling relieved, he was dismayed to see Royce and Scanlon speeding toward his aircraft in a jeep. The excited generals wanted to know how many Japanese fighters had attacked the B-17, and where the fight had taken place. It pained Fields to explain that the upper turret guns had run amok, shooting their own tail to pieces. "Well, they were pretty much disgusted," he recalled of the two generals. "They turned around and got in their jeep and drove away."[15]

The rest of the mission was equally discouraging. Faulkner and Horgan, finding the target blanketed by a solid undercast, orbited over the area for fifteen minutes before dropping their bombs. The pilots of the Tainan Air Group did not respond. But when the five participating B-25s arrived over Lae soon afterward, twenty-five Zeros came boiling up to meet them. Unfortunately, the Mitchells raced off to the west rather than northward, thereby dragging the Zeros straight into the approaching B-26s.

Luckily for Lyndon Johnson, *Hecklin' Hare* had developed a faulty generator only thirty minutes after takeoff, forcing Major Greer to turn back well before reaching the target area. When the remaining B-26s came under attack, they dropped their bombs over Salamaua and headed southeast at high speed, battling Zeros all the way to Cape Ward Hunt. The Marauders eventually got help from the P-39 but not before *The Virginian* was fatally damaged and smashed into the sea, killing Lieutenant Colonel Stevens and all on board.[16] Had it not been for Johnson's last-minute latrine call, he would have been aboard the B-26 instead of Stevens. God only knows what sort of ripple effect his death in 1942 would have had on the course of history.

Not only did Johnson survive to become the thirty-sixth president of the United States, his political career received a decided boost from the fore-shortened mission. Although his plane never came in contact with the enemy, he was awarded a Silver Star by General MacArthur. The citation read, in part,

> As our planes neared the target area they were intercepted by eight hostile fighters. When, at this time, the plane in which Lieutenant Commander Johnson was an observer developed mechanical trouble and was forced to turn back alone presenting a favorable target to the enemy fighters, he evidenced marked coolness in spite of the hazards involved. His gallant action enabled him to obtain and return with valuable information.[17]

Much like the Medal of Honor bestowed on MacArthur after his escape from the Philippines, Johnson's award was an obvious political manipulation. Many have decried his Silver Star as a fraud, but no one can argue the fact that he requested the mission and was willing to risk his life. Upon his return to the United States, he met with President Roosevelt, the Navy Department, and members of Congress to report on the weaknesses and generally low morale of MacArthur's forces. Then, parlaying his insider status and "combat award" into a position of power in Congress, Johnson lobbied for across-the-board increases in the shipment of troops and war materiel to the Southwest Pacific. Although his exact influence cannot be assessed, the Silver Star probably had a silver lining.

TWO DAYS AFTER the fouled-up mission to Lae, as if to throw a spotlight on the political nature of Johnson's medal, a reconnaissance mission by the 435th resulted in a more justly deserved Silver Star. Lieutenant Mabry "Tex" Simmons, a twenty-four-year-old from the Lone Star State, was tasked with an extensive list of targets for what was probably his first mission in the left seat. Unusually tall, he was joined in the cockpit by one of the recently assigned RAAF copilots, Sergeant Mervyn C. Bell, flying his first combat mission in a B-17. The 1,300-mile route would test their collective skills for several hours, with no fewer than six separate targets to reconnoiter or photograph.

Starting out from Port Moresby at 7:30 A.M. on June 11, they climbed to 30,000 feet and proceeded to Rabaul, bumping through scattered layers of thick cumulus clouds. A few hours later, during the run over Simpson Harbor, they encountered heavy antiaircraft fire but obtained good photographs of shipping and the two adjacent airdromes. Moments later, as the Fortress turned toward the port of Kavieng on the northern tip of New Ireland, a formation of three Tainan Air Group fighters rose from a layer of clouds and tried to box in the heavily armed B-17. "The Zeros broke formation, one on each wing and one on our tail," recorded Bell in his diary. "Our gunners were awake to their tactics and kept them well out. We eventually lost them in the clouds after our gunners had given them some nasty frights."[18]

Foul weather conditions over Kavieng prevented the crew from obtaining pictures, so Simmons turned southwest to reconnoiter the Dampier Strait, a chokepoint navigated by enemy ships shuttling between Lae and Rabaul. Soon thereafter the ball turret malfunctioned, and as the weather continued to deteriorate, Simmons was forced to descend in order to observe the waterway. The crew then photographed Finschhafen, seventy miles to the south on the tip of the Huon Peninsula, after which they reconnoitered the harbor, port facilities, and airdrome at Salamaua.

To this point the flight had been mostly routine, but soon after Simmons turned northward again for a photo run over Lae, the lone Fortress encountered stiff opposition. "Clouds and rain forced us down to 1,000 feet, which meant we would not be able to pass over Lae," explained Bell, "so we decided to make oblique shots from the clouds' edge. On emerging from the clouds approximately two miles from Lae, we ran into five Zeros who had evidently been waiting for us."[19]

The fighters that Simmons and his crew stumbled upon were led by twenty-four-year-old Lieutenant (junior grade) Junichi Sasai, a graduate of

Japan's esteemed naval academy at Eta Jima. The son of an IJN captain, he habitually wore a meaningful talisman: a tiger's head belt buckle presented by his father. As the leader of the Tainan Air Group's 2nd *chutai*, Sasai had already shot down several P-39s, a B-25, and a B-26. He would soon learn, however, that bringing down a B-17 was far more challenging.

When the Fortress broke out of the clouds, the opposing pilots reacted simultaneously. Simmons rolled into a hard right turn, intent on reaching a fat rain cloud about one mile ahead and slightly above the bomber's altitude. The Zeros, meanwhile, tried to cut the Fortress off before it reached the sanctuary of the dense cloud. One fighter overtook the bomber on the left, another on the right, and three more closed in from behind. Simmons and his crew realized they would reach the cloud before the three trailing Zeros got within range, but the Zero on the left had the angle. To make matters worse, the left waist gun had jammed and the belly turret was already out of commission. Only the upper turret could be brought to bear. The crew watched breathlessly as the first Zero—more than likely flown by Sasai—rolled in from the left.[*] The tense moments were later described in Bell's diary.

> He was now banked and turned from 10 o'clock to make his attack. He was about 200 feet below and 500 yards out. In he raced with four red fangs spitting shells and tracers. The red streams seemed to be coming right into the nose and cockpit, but in the last few feet swerved away to midship and tail. He flashed under our belly, raking the tail with cannon shot, three of which blew great holes in the undersurface. The shrapnel passed through the top surface in hundreds of holes. The tail gunner, Private Rhodes, received shrapnel in his thigh and backside but with great courage he stuck to his guns, and as the Zero flashed out past the tail he gave him the real works and almost certainly bagged him; [but] passing into clouds, beautiful clouds, prevented confirmation. In the meantime,

---

[*] According to the Tainan Air Group's combat log, only Lieutenant Sasai and one other pilot expended ammunition during the interception. As the division leader, Sasai was logically the first to attack Simmons's B-17.

Zero two on our right wing had turned to give us his all as we went into the cloud.[20]

By rights, Private Edwin "Dusty" Rhodes should have been killed by the blast of 20mm shells and machine-gun bullets that sieved the B-17's empennage. However, in preparing to shoot at the Zero as it flashed beneath him, the twenty-one-year-old Californian had risen off his saddle seat in the tail compartment to depress his guns. Instead of slicing through his torso, the shrapnel that struck his body penetrated the muscles in his right hip and upper thigh. Knocked from his seat by the impact, Rhodes crawled back to his guns and fired a burst at one of the attackers. Then, as pain set in, he endured a terrifying ride. The B-17 pitched wildly, as if out of control. No one answered on the interphone. Fearing that the rest of the crew had been killed, Rhodes considered bailing out. He glanced back at the parachute sitting near the escape hatch, then discovered that his legs were paralyzed. *I'll never make it anyway, down on the ocean*, he thought to himself. *That's not for me.*[21]

Unknown to Rhodes, no one else had been hurt. The cord to his headset had been severed during the attack, and the sensation of plunging out of control was the result of the B-17's evasive maneuvering. As soon as the Fortress reached the safety of the clouds, Tex Simmons leveled off and Merv Bell instructed the crew stations to report local damage and injuries. In the rear fuselage the waist gunners were stamping out a small fire, ignited when tracer rounds struck a pile of life jackets, but there was no word from Rhodes. The assistant flight engineer, Sergeant Howard K. Beck, crawled back to the tail to check on him, shouting, "Are you hit?"

Surprised and probably dazed, the wounded private answered, "I'm sure glad to see somebody alive!"

Beck eased him off the seat, dragged him to the floor of the gunners' compartment, and opened his clothing. "Yeah," he said, "you got hit alright."[22]

Rhodes, a former cavalryman who had transferred into the Air Corps two years earlier, was losing a lot of blood. The pilots radioed ahead for an ambulance, which was waiting when they landed back at Port Moresby.

"Naturally we couldn't get out fast enough to inspect the damage," recalled Bell. "The honest old B-17 can take it. After making arrangements to have our ship patched up we set off for a well-earned meal and rest. News from the hospital stated the condition of 'Dusty' as OK."[23]

Carried on a stretcher into the native-built field hospital, Rhodes was anesthetized with chloroform. The Australian doctor had to dig deep to get the shrapnel out, and he later told Rhodes it would have been easier to operate from the front than the back. "We can't sew it up," he added. "It has to heal from the inside out." Facing a long recovery, Rhodes learned to change the bandages frequently. The open wound, which continued to bleed and ooze pus for weeks, "smelled to high heaven," as Rhodes put it. But the wound eventually healed, leaving a permanent indentation near his hipbone.[24]

ON THE MORNING of June 15, three days after Simmons and his crew narrowly escaped disaster over Lae, the men of the 435th gathered in the operations shack to listen to a radio address by President Roosevelt. It was Flag Day back home, the first to be commemorated since the start of the war. Roosevelt did not talk about patriotism, but instead gave a stirring speech about the basic freedoms of humanity and the global fight to end oppression and tyranny. If any of the president's words resonated with the Fortress men listening in Australia, it was probably a passage from his closing prayer: "Most of all grant us brotherhood, not only for this day but for all our years—a brotherhood not of words but of acts and deeds."[25]

By this time, the crews had shared hardships and combat encounters for six months since the attack on Pearl Harbor, forming bonds that would last the rest of their lives. And they knew the true meaning of service. That same afternoon, four crews headed back into harm's way to commence a new round of reconnaissance and bombing missions. Perhaps the president's words provided some encouragement as they boarded their ships. Ted Faulkner, Wallace Fields, and Fred Eaton (who had resumed flying two weeks earlier) headed for Horn Island for an overnight stay before launching a coordinated strike on Lae. The fourth crew was led by Deacon Rawls, who flew to Port Moresby in the squadron's newly acquired photoreconnaissance B-17, equipped with an expensive array of aerial cameras. Over the next few days the special equipment, reportedly worth $50,000, would be used to build a photomosaic of the Solomon Islands, including the soon-to-be-important island of Guadalcanal.[*26]

Appropriately, the day after the president's address, more than two dozen squadron members were officially recognized in an awards presentation. The men put on clean uniforms and stood in formation for the ceremony, attended by generals Brett, Royce, and Scanlon. Dick Carmichael and Jim Twaddell were also on hand, but as recipients rather than observers.

The headline award went to Frank Bostrom, who received a Distinguished Service Cross for his role in the Royce Raid. Then came Silver Star medals for Carmichael, Eaton (in absentia, due to the Lae mission), Bill Lewis, Ralph Mauser, and Billie Sutton, whose citations described their gallantry during the first raid on Rabaul. Next, Harry Brandon, Deacon Rawls (also in absentia), and Bob Thacker received Silver Stars for saving their planes and crewmen at Pearl Harbor. Finally, Jim Twaddell was awarded a Silver Star for his leadership of the successful mission to Rabaul on March 17, praised earlier by Prime Minister Curtin.

After the Silver Stars were pinned on, four squadron members were called forward to receive America's oldest military decoration, the Purple Heart. Ranked as the army's fifth-highest decoration at the time, the medal could be awarded "for any act of singularly meritorious service or act of extraordinary fidelity, and for wounds received in battle." Thus, despite the fact that he had not been wounded, Swede Swenson received a Purple Heart for his part in the first raid on Rabaul. So did navigator Ed Cihak, who was wounded in the knee. Maury Horgan was awarded a Purple Heart on the merits of his

---

* Rawls flew the squadron's first mission with the uniquely equipped B-17 on June 16, 1942. Exactly one year later, that same Fortress (number 41-2666) completed the most highly decorated individual sortie in American combat history. During a mapping mission over Bougainville on June 16, 1943, Captain Jay Zeamer Jr. and his crew battled intercepting Zeros for forty-five minutes. The critical importance of the mission and the crew's individual acts of heroism resulted in two Medals of Honor (one awarded posthumously) and seven Distinguished Service Crosses.

"skill, judgment, and determination" during the March 12 mission against Lae, and Skid Johnson received his for the destruction of a Japanese float-plane on May 8. Of the four Purple Hearts pinned on squadron members that day, only one was awarded on the basis of a combat wound.*

Finally, during the last segment of the ceremonies, the brass awarded the Distinguished Flying Cross to more than two dozen squadron members—officers and enlisted crewmen alike—who had participated in the MacArthur and Quezon evacuations back in March.

As reflected in the various awards, the early months of the Pacific war were an unusually loose time for decorations in the AAF. Between the success of Japan's offensives in the Pacific, the German blitzkrieg in Europe, and the shortages and sacrifices already being felt on the home front, the citizens of America faced the reality of a bitter, bloody, protracted war. Aside from a few brilliant successes during the first six months, much of the war news had been deeply unsettling. Thus, largely in the interest of boosting morale, most of the correspondents who wrote about American boys in combat filled their accounts with hyperbole. Many awards citations were likewise amplified. But even if the newspaper stories and citations were commonly exaggerated, there was a legitimate reason for all the hype: the country needed heroes. And so the military doled out medals, and the press sent home rousing accounts of the action, and the citizens on the home front were duly inspired.

There is also no question that most awardees were pleased and even motivated by the recognition they received. Some generals understood this better than others. Lieutenant General George C. Kenney, who would soon take General Brett's place as the commander of Allied air forces in Australia, pinned decorations on his airmen until his thumbs were bruised. "I knew that little bits of pretty ribbon had helped in World War I," he later wrote, "maybe they would help in this one, too."[27]

Many more medals would be awarded to the men of the 435th in the months to come. A few were already being processed, including a Silver Star

---

* In early September 1942, the War Department announced that the Purple Heart would be limited exclusively to personnel wounded or killed in action.

for Ed Rhodes, grounded while his festering wound healed. Others were yet to be earned, and most would be authentically deserved. As the battle for New Guinea and the Southwest Pacific continued to heat up, the squadron was tasked with longer, lonelier, and riskier missions than ever.

THE AWARDS CEREMONY was a big success. Official recognition for the 435th's many accomplishments, including the first American attack on Rabaul, the MacArthur and Quezon evacuations, the Royce Raid, and other special missions, gave the crews plenty of bragging rights. Morale was high and the squadron enjoyed excellent camaraderie, a product of strong leadership and respect among the personnel. But there was one thing lacking. The 435th needed a brand, a nom de guerre, an identity that would be recognized everywhere. And that summer, thanks to the creativity of an enlisted man from the prairieland of Kansas, it all came together.

Private (First Class) Miley R. "Michael" Crabtree, a veteran of the Java campaign, had been transferred into the squadron back in March when the 19th Group was reorganized. One day, as the story goes, he sketched an emblem for the 435th while sitting in a Townsville pub. It began with a simple circle—the line that has no beginning and no end—enclosing a background of blue sky accented by a billowing cloud. The logo's main feature was a kangaroo, airborne in mid-hop, representing the one animal that almost anyone, anywhere in the world, would associate with Australia. The kangaroo held a spyglass to its stern eye, symbolic of the 435th's adopted role in reconnaissance, and its long tail was wrapped around a bomb, signifying the unit's official designation as a bombardment squadron. Crabtree's design, devoid of any script or motto, was brilliant in its simplicity. Approved by Bill Lewis, the emblem served as a template for local shops that specialized in patches made of leather or embroidered wool. The colorful patches, worn proudly by the combat crews, were displayed prominently on their iconic leather jackets.

Thereafter, the 435th became known by its most famous name: the Kangaroo Squadron.

NINETEEN

THE RECONNAISSANCE GAME

During the summer of 1942, while the three original squadrons of the re-constituted 19th Group conducted most of the heavy bombing raids, the 435th undertook an ever-increasing number of reconnaissance missions. As the schedule became more predictable, Bill Lewis managed to rotate his weary crews to the rear area for short vacations. The announcement of the new policy, recalled Dick Graf, came during one of the morning meetings. "Lewis, who had been my pilot, said, 'Okay, you guys, I know you're all tired. We've all been working hard, and I've been trying to get headquarters to let us relieve one crew at a time for a few days' leave. It might take a couple of months to work through all the crews, but at least you'll have a break.' Then he said, 'Headquarters won't give us permission, but we're going to do it anyway.'"[1]

Graf was delighted to learn that his current crew, led by Will Beezley, would have the first leave. Lewis asked them where they wanted to go, expecting the crew to vote for Brisbane or Sydney. Instead, they all agreed on a place he never expected: the small town of Rockhampton on the Queensland coast. "What the hell," he sputtered. "Rockhampton? That's about the size of Townsville!"[2]

But when the men explained their rationale, Lewis understood perfectly. In mid-May, Beezley's crew had flown a B-17 to Brisbane to pick up spare parts. On the return trip they lost two engines, resulting in an emergency landing at Rockhampton. Aside from a small RAAF refueling detachment the town had no military presence, and the stranded Americans were treated like royalty. The U.S. Army's 41st Infantry Division was due to move into a nearby camp later that summer, but for another month or so, bomber crews that vacationed in the delightful seaside town would have no competition. Simply put, the odds in "Rocky," as Queenslanders called it, were damn good for nine well-paid Yanks. Graf was especially glad for the decision. At one of the crew's parties he was introduced to Phyllis Byrne, whose family owned an auto dealership. Graf was the first American she had ever met, and they hit it off immediately. Several months passed before he could return for another visit, but they eventually married, and Graf later chose to make Australia his permanent home.[3]

As Lewis anticipated, most of the crews opted to fly to Brisbane or Sydney when their turn came. Because his own opportunities to log flight time were limited, he often shuttled the crews back and forth himself. Considerably older than most of the crewmen—he turned thirty-eight that summer—Lewis enjoyed the quiet beaches on the lightly developed Gold Coast. The beach at Southport, about forty miles from downtown Brisbane, was practically vacant during the "winter" months, yet daytime temperatures often rose into the sixties and the warm ocean current kept the water temperature in the seventies.

Naturally most of the younger crewmembers preferred the tourist attractions and nightlife of the cities. During his first overnight visit to Brisbane in April, John Steinbinder found it similar to the biggest city in his home state of Ohio: "Sure reminds me of Cleveland with its structures, buses and cabs," he wrote. "Lots of people here. Plenty of women, wine, etc."[4]

But when he returned in June for a six-day leave with Gibb's crew, the city seemed less appealing. There were swarms of military personnel, making it difficult to find accommodations. After the crew finally got rooms at the landmark National Hotel, Steinbinder ignored his diary for the remainder of the visit. "However," he penned later, "there wasn't much to write about anyway. . . . There wasn't much night life in Brisbane. Went to some movies and one dance."[5]

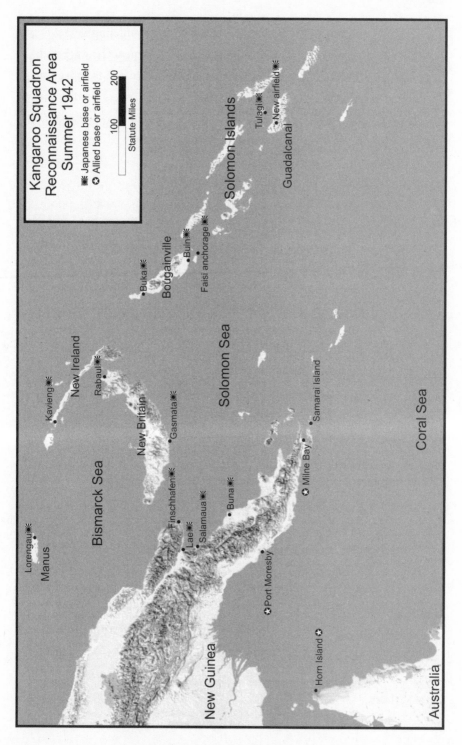

281

Raised only twenty-five miles from Cleveland, then the sixth-largest city in the United States, Steinbinder may have had high expectations. Fellow crewmember John Straight, raised in the oilfields of Wyoming and eastern Colorado, thoroughly enjoyed the trip. "We were able to visit the zoo in Brisbane and other places of interest," he later wrote with humor, "such as all the bars in town."[6]

The mecca for most Americans on R&R was Australia's largest city, with a population of 1.3 million. "Nice in Sydney, which bears up to reports that it is more American than Americans," wrote Walt Johnson. "Has a spare 300,000 women in addition—their men off to war."[7] For self-indulgence, no place could compete with Kings Cross, a dazzling, neon-lit neighborhood of downtown Sydney packed with restaurants, cabarets, cafés, saloons, theaters, and a well-known red light district. Unlike Lewis and a few of the older men who favored quiet beaches, the twenty-somethings played hard after dark. "During that period when we got to places like Sydney and Brisbane," confirmed John Lillback, "our minds weren't quite focused on fun in the sun with kids our own age; it was more like Kings Cross and babes and booze."[8]

The meaning of R&R didn't hold much interest for the young or the young-at-heart. Rather than resting and recuperating, they hardly slept during their week of leave. "As it turned out," admitted John Straight, "we would usually have to go back to New Guinea to get our rest."[9]

THERE WAS NOTHING restful about the combat zone, of course. As the air war over New Guinea intensified, many of the squadron's missions were intercepted by Zeros of the Tainan Air Group at least once and sometimes twice during the same flight, especially if the profile included both Rabaul and Lae. The crews became accustomed to the intercepts. Time after time the speed, firepower, and sturdy construction of their B-17s thwarted all attempts by the enemy to cause serious damage, but as almost every crew learned sooner or later, Japanese fighters and antiaircraft guns weren't the only hazards.

On the afternoon of June 22, Fred Eaton and Maury Horgan took two crews to Port Moresby in one of the early B-17Es (the 435th still had a few Fortresses with the remote belly turret) to hunt for a large Japanese tanker reportedly heading toward Rabaul from Truk. Taking off early the next morning, Eaton searched as far as the northern reaches of the Bismarck Sea but found no sign of the tanker. Turning southeastward to take the usual photographs of Rabaul, he arrived over Simpson Harbor at 28,000 feet in clear weather. As the crew watched, numerous fighters rose up to intercept them.

Once again the Zeros were led by Lieutenant Sasai, whose division had rotated to Rabaul for a break from the primitive living conditions at Lae. Within a matter of minutes, five Zeros had caught up with the B-17. "One made a side attack, another made a direct frontal attack," reported Eaton. "McIntyre* put a good burst directly into the Zero attacking from the front and he never came back for another pass. By this time we were at 31,000 feet, and by using the available clouds, the remaining fighters were evaded."[10]

Or so Eaton thought. About thirty minutes later, three of his crewmembers suddenly collapsed. The side gunner, remote turret gunner, and aerial photographer had fallen unconscious due to hypoxia, and the only way to save their lives was by diving down to an oxygen-rich altitude as quickly as possible. Eaton rolled the B-17 into a rivet-shaking dive, reportedly hitting an indicated airspeed of 455 mph as the Fortress plummeted 13,000 feet in just a few minutes. The radio operator, Sergeant James N. Kokales, fixed the stricken men's oxygen masks—one had a loose connection, the other two were blocked by frozen condensation—enabling all three to regain consciousness at 18,000 feet.

Ironically, much like the situation during Eaton's first mission to Rabaul, a single Zero had followed the Fortress, and it suddenly charged in to attack. Due to the lingering effects of hypoxia affecting three crewmen, the B-17's lower turret and side guns were unmanned. Inexplicably, the Japanese pilot did not capitalize on his advantage. "He made two frontal attacks," recalled Eaton, "but each time I was able to turn into him, and all he did

---

* Lieutenant Jack C. McIntyre, bombardier.

was put a few holes in our elevators. If he had kept attacking from below, he could have gotten us."[11] In his official mission narrative, Eaton subsequently added, "The only thing that saved us was the fact that the Zero, due to range, could not follow us any farther."[12]

Two days after his crew's close call, Eaton was back in the air to resume the search for the Japanese tanker. He flew all the way to the tiny Micronesian atoll of Kapingamarangi, four hundred miles beyond Rabaul, but thick clouds and rain over the shipping lanes prevented an effective search. On the way back to Port Moresby, realizing that he still had enough fuel for a unique opportunity, he descended low over the Agaiambo Swamp and found the Fortress he had belly-landed in the kunai grass four months earlier. After pointing out the airplane and the unforgiving landscape to his crew, Eaton retraced the route his original crew had taken during their journey to Buna, flying up the coast at an altitude of only two hundred feet. As hoped, the sound of the B-17 attracted the attention of the man who had saved Eaton's life. "I heard an aircraft," Allan Champion would later write in his memoirs, "and went out to see a Flying Fortress zooming low. He dipped his wings and flew off to the north."[13]

Knowing instinctively that it was Eaton, Champion would wonder for the next fifty years if his American friend survived the war.

WHILE EATON AND Horgan ranged out daily in search of the elusive Japanese tanker, two crews led by Jim Gibb and Deacon Rawls began a ten-day operation in the Northern Territory of Australia. Their task was to reconnoiter enemy bases in the Netherlands East Indies, particularly Kendari airdrome in the Celebes, 850 miles northwest of Batchelor Field. Stoutly defended by Zeros of the Kanoya Air Group, the stronghold had not been photographed since its occupation by the Japanese in January.[14]

On June 24, lacking any information about the enemy's strength, Gibb and his crew took off from Batchelor for their first attempt to reconnoiter Kendari. Finding a massive thunderhead over the airdrome, they made the photo run at 10,000 feet and were shocked to see dozens of bombers and fighters lined up on the field. Within minutes, three Zeros had chased them down. Gibb attempted to release the empty auxiliary fuel tanks, but only one dropped free; the other remained stuck, and the bomb-bay doors failed to close. Donning parachutes, the crew spent the next forty-five minutes dueling with the persistent Zeros, which knocked out the belly turret and punched numerous holes in the B-17's wings and fuselage as they hounded it down to 2,500 feet.

One of the busiest crewmembers was the navigator, John Steinbinder. A football player and gymnast at Oberlin College, meticulous with his navigational skills and steady in combat, he served with multiple crews and always got them home safely. On this occasion, he periodically jumped up from his chart table to fire at the attacking Zeros with his .30 caliber machine gun. Throughout the long combat engagement, he mentally kept track of his dead-reckoning calculations even while the Fortress twisted and turned to evade the enemy fighters.

Eventually the Japanese gave up and turned back toward Kendari, at which point the bomb-bay doors were cranked up by hand. On the basis of Steinbinder's accurate navigation, Gibb determined that enough fuel remained to proceed to the next objective, so the crew also mapped the Japanese airdrome on Timor before returning to Batchelor Field. Steinbinder was later awarded a Silver Star, in part because the crew had obtained valuable photographs used to plan a successful bombing raid against Kendari on the last day of June.[15]

IN ADDITION TO the almost-daily reconnaissance flights over the Bismarck Archipelago and New Guinea coast, the Kangaroo Squadron's area of responsibility was expanded to include regular missions over the Solomon Islands. The latter were exceptionally strenuous, the flights often exceeding twelve hours due to the distances involved. The Fortresses needed two auxiliary fuel tanks for the trip, which precluded them from carrying bombs to use on targets of opportunity. To compensate for that lack of versatility, the squadron acquired three Consolidated LB-30 Liberators, the first of which arrived on June 19. Piloted by Lieutenant Ken Casper, a 19th Group veteran, the four-engine bomber had been overhauled in Melbourne and was equipped with first-generation ASV (air-to-surface-vessel) radar. An Australian technician accompanied the crew to teach the squadron's radio operators how to use the device, which everyone called "the gadget."[16]

Although the LB-30 had longer legs (an additional eight hundred miles of range) and carried a bigger payload than a B-17, the pilots of the 435th were unimpressed. The Liberator looked dumpy compared to the sleek Fortress and was even ridiculed in the squadron diary as a "flying boxcar."[17] Pilots disliked the fact that the LB-30's Pratt & Whitney engines had no superchargers, which limited the effective ceiling of the bomber to around 12,000 feet. "Good airplane," quipped Fred Eaton, one of the first to be checked off by Casper, "if you can keep it out of combat."[18]

But when Casper conducted the squadron's first mission with the Liberator, the Fortress men took notice. Departing from Port Moresby on June 24, the crew flew a 2,500-mile round trip to photograph the big Japanese base at Truk, completing only the second reconnaissance of the anchorage since the war began.* Four days later Captain Dick Ezzard, a former 88th Squadron pilot who had aborted the flight to Hawaii on the night of December 6, arrived with a second LB-30. Due to their superior range, the Liberators were often employed on the lengthy missions to Tulagi and Guadalcanal in the southern Solomons.[19]

Any reluctance over the acquisition of the refurbished LB-30s (a third was delivered in mid-July) was tempered by the news that the older B-17s would soon be replaced. Over the span of the next few weeks, new Fortresses equipped with radar began to arrive at Townsville, and the last of the squadron's E models with the remote belly turrets were turned over to the 19th Group. As a result of the upgrades, there was always something new to learn. Pilots were checked off one by one in the Liberators, and radio operators attended classes on the ASV equipment. The squadron also conducted experiments with "photo bombs," forty-two-pound flares that produced an estimated 1,000,000 candlepower for night aerial photography. But the flares could be dangerous. During a test drop by the squadron, one became lodged

---

* The first had been flown in early January 1942 from Kavieng, still in Australian hands at the time, by a Hudson of RAAF 6 Squadron.

in the bomb bay and was freed manually by the flight engineer mere seconds before it ignited. A few weeks later the 19th Group lost a Fortress—one of the 435th's former aircraft and a Pearl Harbor survivor—along with its entire crew when the same type of flare exploded in the bomb bay.

With the benefit of replacement planes and new technology, the Kangaroo Squadron's shift to a predominant role in reconnaissance continued. By late June, the increased demand for "recco" missions justified the establishment of a full-time maintenance detachment at Port Moresby. On a rotating basis, two aircraft with four crews began to operate out of Seven Mile airdrome for a week at a time. The daily orders rarely fluctuated throughout the summer, which meant there was always a better-than-average chance of running into enemy opposition. Indeed, the Tainan Air Group maintained shifts of combat air patrols over Rabaul and Lae from dawn until dusk every day, and the Fortress crews knew the enemy would be waiting for them. Many were concerned about the predictability of the flight schedule. "The men are skeptical about this mission since it is run over the same area at about the same time each day," wrote Walt Johnson. "We hope headquarters changes the route order before we lose a ship and crew."[20] His apprehension, voiced in May, was more prophetic than any of them realized.

EVEN AS THE reconnaissance game evolved, bombing missions were still handed to the squadron on a routine basis. On July 2, after spending the past week enjoying the hospitality of Townsville, Fred Eaton was assigned a unique mission. "Bob Thacker, Thad May, and myself are going to Horn Island tomorrow morning at 7 a.m.," he wrote excitedly in his diary. "They are loading our three ships with six 2,000-pound bombs. We are to demolish the runway at Lae and return to Horn. Will probably run another mission the next day. It's about time we got some action. We have been getting soft sitting around going to dances and loafing in general."[21]

Lieutenant John T. "Thad" May, newly qualified as a 1st Pilot, was stymied by engine trouble and did not get off from Townsville the next morning, but Eaton and Thacker reached Horn Island on schedule. After their planes were refueled, they took off again early that afternoon, each carrying two of the huge bombs. Facing heavy but inaccurate antiaircraft fire over Lae, they dropped their one-ton bombs from 25,000 feet with good accuracy. One bomb from each plane was observed to hit the runway at the northwest end of the airfield, while the other two detonated north of the runway. According to Thacker's bombardier, Dave Semple, the release of the first heavy bomb caused the B-17s to jump upward, spoiling the release of each plane's second bomb.[22]

Of equal importance, eight enemy fighters were seen taking off from Lae. Barely a quarter of an hour later, they intercepted the two Fortresses south of the airdrome. During the next forty minutes the Zeros made as many as ten frontal attacks, plus an equal number of side and rear-quarter passes at the B-17s, whose gunners reportedly expended two thousand rounds per plane. They claimed a total of three Zeros shot down, but the Tainan Air Group lost no fighters in the vicinity of Lae that afternoon. To the contrary, the Japanese pilots got the upper hand, hitting both bombers with numerous machine-gun bullets and cannon shells. Aboard Eaton's aircraft, an armor-piercing round struck the heel of navigator Robert W. Elliott's left boot without causing injury. Minutes later another bullet hit the boot of Sergeant Thomas W. Smith, the bombardier, also without wounding him.[23]

Thacker's crew was not so fortunate. The side gunner and remote turret gunner suffered serious wounds, and it was only by scant millimeters that the squadron avoided its first death in combat. Pieces of shrapnel from an exploding 20mm round hit Corporal Clarence E. Hoehn, one of which penetrated his skull; and Private Lonnie D. Wright suffered multiple shrapnel wounds in his legs. Rather than return to Port Moresby, Thacker sped directly to Townsville, where Hoehn underwent a five-hour surgery to remove a piece of metal that was touching his brain. Both he and Wright eventually made a full recovery.[24]

More close calls followed throughout July. Due to a sharp increase in enemy activity, the Kangaroo Squadron stepped up the reconnaissance of both the Bismarcks and the Solomons, where it soon became apparent that the Japanese were gearing up for something new—and something big.

SOON AFTER CAPTURING Tulagi in early May, the Japanese discovered that the nearby island of Guadalcanal offered a suitable location for a new airfield. Engineers and staff from Rabaul visited the big island on May 27 and confirmed the initial estimates. Slightly over a mile inland from Guadalcanal's northern coast, on a grassy plain near the Lunga River, they located an ideal site. A month later, a convoy loaded with two engineering battalions and tons of construction equipment—dozens of trucks, four heavy tractors, six mechanized road rollers, two generators, an ice-making plant, and a pair of narrow-gauge locomotives with a dozen hopper cars—departed from Truk. The ships arrived off Guadalcanal on July 6 and began the slow process of unloading.

Recon missions by the 435th soon revealed the enemy's new activity. Flying the two LB-30s on an armed reconnaissance of Tulagi and Guadalcanal on July 9, Ken Casper and Dick Ezzard observed the Japanese transports off Lunga Point. Both of the Liberators returned the next day, this time with Wallace Fields piloting one of the bombers while Ezzard rode as check pilot. Fields didn't care for the LB-30, which did not maneuver well above 10,000 feet, and he was probably not surprised when the partial load of bombs they dropped fell wide of the Japanese ships.[25] But the worst came soon after, when two single-seat aircraft of a type the crews had never seen before intercepted the two LB-30s at low altitude.

Based at Tulagi with the Yokohama Air Group, they were Type 2 floatplane fighters (Nakajima A6M2-Ns), a hybrid design of the Zero fitted with a large central pontoon and two outriggers. Although heavier and less maneuverable than their land-based cousins, the fighters (later code named "Rufe" by Allied intelligence) had no difficulty overtaking the low-flying Liberators. Corporal Charles R. McBride snapped a picture of both floatplanes—thought to be the first Allied photograph of the A6M2-N in action—as they climbed beneath the bomber flown by Fields. During the mostly one-sided gunfight that ensued, the fighters caused considerable damage. Casper's plane was unharmed, but cannon shells and 7.7mm bullets tore several holes in the lower tail section and starboard wing of Fields's LB-30. A punctured oil line knocked out the number four engine, and when Fields attempted to jettison the auxiliary fuel tank, it jammed halfway out of the bomb bay. The flight engineer courageously tried to kick the tank loose, but gave up when his shoe was sucked away in the turbulent slipstream. Six anxious hours later, after crossing 1,200 miles of ocean on three engines with the bomb-bay doors open, Fields and his crew landed back at Port Moresby.[26]

A week later, on July 17, Lieutenant Bob Ramsay and his crew flew a photo reconnaisance mission over Guadalcanal with a couple of extra passengers in their B-17. "We were carrying two high-ranking Marine Corps officers in the nose as observers," remembered Herb Wheatley. "We were jumped by two bandits while running mosaics."[27] The passengers, Lieutenant Colonel Merrill B. Twining and Major William McKean, were impressed when the B-17's gunners drove off the pair of Rufes that attacked them, but showed even more interest in the airfield being constructed by the Japanese. "I hope they build a good one," said Twining. "We are going to use it."[28]

THE IMPORTANCE OF the Kangaroo Squadron's surveillance of Guadalcanal cannot be overstated. On July 2, eager to capitalize on the naval victory at Midway, the Joint Chiefs of Staff had produced an ambitious master plan for the reconquest of the Bismarck Archipelago and Solomon Islands. The first phase, the invasion of Tulagi and the seizure of the unoccupied Santa Cruz Islands, was scheduled to commence on August 1. Then, just two weeks prior to the amphibious landings, radio messages from Australian coast-watchers and the aerial photographs brought back by the 435th revealed the new enemy airfield under construction. Consequently the American offensive, called Operation Watchtower, was postponed for almost a week while alternative strategies were studied. The operation was substantially altered, making the seizure of Guadalcanal the primary objective. The revised plan called for the 1st Marine Division and supplemental forces to invade Guadalcanal, Tulagi, and nearby Florida Island on August 7.

THE ALLIES WERE also intent on expanding their network of airfields, particularly in New Guinea. One promising site, adjacent to Milne Bay near the southern tip of the peninsula, was a former coconut plantation run by the Lever Brothers company, famous for their soaps. The expanse of low-lands between the wide bay and the nearby mountains was broad enough to support three airstrips, which would provide the Allies with a forward airbase east of the Owen Stanley Mountains. Construction of the new complex, code-named "Fall River," began in late June. Within two months a coalition of Australian infantry battalions, American antiaircraft units, and RAAF squadrons totaling nearly 10,000 personnel were encamped in the coconut groves and jungle surrounding the airfields. Theirs was an uncomfortable existence. Milne Bay was an exceedingly hot, humid, boggy, mosquito-infested hellhole where heavy rains fell almost daily. During a span of five weeks at Airstrip No. 1, which was paved with interlocking sections of pieced steel planks because of the mud, the Australian fighter pilots could count the number of clear days with just one hand.[29]

Committed to further advancing the Allied foothold on the eastern coast of Papua, General MacArthur also planned to establish an airfield at Buna. The village, familiar to many because of the government station run by Allan Champion, featured an old airstrip that might be expanded into a forward base. A scouting party inspected the abandoned strip on July 10 and determined that it did not meet requirements, but a grass-covered plain fifteen miles down the coast near the village of Dobodura looked much more promising.[30]

In Queensland, meanwhile, Dick Carmichael assumed command of the 19th Group on July 10. The following day he moved his headquarters to a new airdrome at Mareeba, a few miles west of Cairns, where he was joined by the 28th, 30th, and 93rd Squadrons from Cloncurry and Longreach. For the first time since the retreat from Java, the original group was consolidated in one location. The exception was the 435th, which remained in Townsville with more independence than ever.

In a similar advance, MacArthur moved closer to the combat area on July 20, relocating his headquarters (known simply as GHQ) from Melbourne to Brisbane. Simultaneously, he lobbied for a new senior airman. Ever since his arrival in Australia, MacArthur's relationship with Lieutenant

General Brett had steadily deteriorated, and after months of complaints to the War Department, he finally got results. Of the two candidates offered for his consideration, MacArthur selected George Kenney, who arrived in Australia on July 28. (The other candidate was Brigadier General Jimmy Doolittle, hero of the raid on Tokyo three months earlier and one of the world's most renowned aviators. But he was simply too famous for MacArthur, who preferred a relative unknown over a subordinate whose star shone as brightly as his own.)

The most explosive new development, both for the Kangaroo Squadron and MacArthur, was an intelligence report indicating that a large Japanese convoy had departed from Truk on July 10. Based on the flurry of enemy activity on Guadalcanal, the convoy was initially presumed to be heading toward the Solomons. Fred Eaton, Hotfoot Harlow, and former copilot Andy Price set off from Townsville the following afternoon to mount a search effort in that direction, while Bob Thacker and Lieutenant Donald O. Tower flew up to Port Moresby to begin several days of reconnaissance over the usual areas of interest in New Guinea and the Bismarcks.[31]

Although recently qualified as a 1st Pilot, Don Tower's extensive experience as a copilot served him well. Jumped by fighters of the Tainan Air Group near Rabaul on July 14, the twenty-five-year-old Oregonian jettisoned both bomb-bay tanks and took evasive maneuvers while his crew fought off three hostile fighters for about forty minutes. Enemy gunfire damaged both wings, knocked out the number four engine, and shattered the windows on both sides of the cockpit. One bullet barely missed the heads of both Tower and his Australian copilot, Sergeant Raymond A. Seabrook, before exiting the right side of the cockpit. After finally losing the Zeros in the clouds, Tower safely brought his shot-up Fortress back to Port Moresby.[32]

Although none of the Fortress crews found the enemy convoy on the first attempt, Tower and his crew eventually discovered the ships in Simpson Harbor on July 19. But the Japanese were not passing through on their way to Guadalcanal, as originally presumed. Instead, three fast transports carrying elements of the South Seas Force, accompanied by several warships of the 4th Fleet, proceeded west across the Bismarck Sea the following evening.

They made good progress under the cover of darkness, then took advantage of foul weather on July 21 as they passed through the Dampier Strait and headed toward Buna. Tower's crew, airborne again with a load of thousand-pound bombs, spotted the convoy twenty miles north of Buna, but their attempt to hit the enemy ships through the rain and scudding clouds was unsuccessful.

That afternoon, upon reaching the debarkation point off the Buna reefs, the enemy warships shelled the landing area while the invasion troops off-loaded. Most of the Japanese were ashore by early evening, although one element mistakenly landed at Gona, farther north than intended.

Once again, despite advance warnings provided by Allied intelligence and aerial reconnaissance, the Japanese had landed on New Guinea without opposition. Adverse weather and the use of fast ships provided a distinct advantage. The best the Allies could do was counterattack with aircraft the next morning, and this time the Kangaroo Squadron enjoyed some success. Lieutenant John M. DeBord, another of the former copilots, scored a direct hit on the transport *Ayatosan Maru* from low level, starting uncontrollable fires. The vessel partially sank, settling by the stern on a submerged reef, but the loss of the ship came too late to alter the outcome of the invasion.

The landings were the first stage of Ri Operation, another attempt by the Japanese to invade Port Moresby. Although the troops succeeded in establishing strong beachheads at Buna and Gona, the entire operation had been planned on the basis of faulty intelligence and careless reconnaissance assessments. The Japanese high command was erroneously informed that a passable roadway led all the way from Buna to the Kokoda Pass and then down the other side of the Owen Stanleys to Port Moresby. Even as additional convoys brought more troops, weapons, and tons of supplies to the Buna-Gona base, advance parties hurried up the same trails that Fred Eaton and his crew had followed into the highlands back in March. And so began the long, bloody, and notorious Kokoda campaign, fought up and down both sides of the precipitous mountains for the next four months.

Allan Champion had managed to avoid the Japanese in the months since Eaton's crew departed, though not without difficulty. "I remained at

Buna until the Japanese invaded," he wrote many years later. "There were only five of us there and we had to let them have the place. I walked to Kokoda and then across the famous Kokoda Trail. It was tough going, took me eleven days from Buna, and the only clothes I wore were the ones I stood up in."[33]

The Anglican missionaries, on the other hand, paid a dear price for remaining in New Guinea at the behest of their bishop. Hiding in the highlands with several other civilians, the missionaries were betrayed by Papuan natives and captured by the Japanese, who beheaded or bayoneted more than a dozen individuals in mid-August. Among them were Father Vivian Redlich and his fiancée, Sister May Hayman (the nurse who had treated Eaton and his crew), Miss Mavis Parkinson (a teacher at Gona), and others from the mission stations at Gona and Sangara. Many months later Champion returned to Buna and was put in charge of an investigation. "The natives responsible were eventually hanged," he wrote in his memoir. "This episode has haunted me all my life. I knew all the unfortunate ones who were executed [by the Japanese]. One was a small boy seven years of age. It sickens me every time I think of it."[34]

FLYING FROM TOWNSVILLE and Port Moresby, the Kangaroo Squadron continued its dangerous game of hide-and-seek with the Japanese. On the afternoon of July 25, one of the veteran crews had a very narrow escape after reconnoitering the sea-lanes between Rabaul and Kavieng. During the return flight, cruising at 14,000 feet as he prepared to cross the Owen Stanleys, Maury Horgan was intercepted by a full division of Tainan Air Group fighters.

Led by Lieutenant Shiro Kawai, the Japanese attacked aggressively, often in pairs. Their frontal attacks were well coordinated, with Zeros approaching simultaneously from both sides of the B-17's nose before zooming up in breakaway turns. Accurate gunfire knocked out the number two engine, damaged number three, and punched holes in the nose, ball turret, both wings, the fuselage, the vertical fin, and the horizontal stabilizers. In short, almost every section of the plane was hit. The ball turret gunner and one side gunner were wounded in the legs, but by some miracle no one was severely injured or killed. After a fifty-minute battle, Horgan finally escaped by diving into scattered clouds.

Upon their return to Port Moresby, Staff Sergeant Dan Ehrheart and Sergeant Harvey D. Joyner were hospitalized, and the crew submitted claims for no less than six Zeros destroyed in combat. Similarly, Kawai and his fellow pilots claimed to have shot down the Fortress, but neither side actually downed any opponents.[35]

Five days later, another veteran crew had an even longer battle with the Tainan Air Group. Lieutenant Leonard S. "Larry" Humiston, formerly of the 38th Reconnaissance Squadron, had been temporarily attached to the squadron in May and was later permanently assigned. During a photoreconnaissance mission over the sea-lanes between Lae and Buna on the morning of July 30, his Fortress was intercepted by Lieutenant Sasai's division of nine Zeros, which included the legendary enlisted ace Saburo Sakai leading the third *shotai*.[36] In an epic battle that spanned more than an hour, the Japanese fired thousands of rounds, shooting out the Fortress's number two engine, the hydraulic system, and the ball turret and later damaging the number three engine. One of the last attacks partially disabled the flight controls. "There was a sharp C-R-A-C-K," recalled Roy Reid, who was on his last mission as a copilot before getting his own crew. "The wheel spun halfway around in my hand, and the plane fell off on the left wing. An aileron cable had been neatly severed by a bullet. By using a lot of rudder and careful pressure on the good aileron, we brought the ship into normal flight. We had lost about 600 feet and were unable to weave and twist. All we could do was climb straight ahead as rapidly as possible."[37]

In spite of the extensive damage no one was seriously wounded, although two crewmen were grazed in the head by bullets. Corporal Earle W. Curtis had climbed out of the damaged ball turret and was manning a side gun when a bullet hit the top of his head, and Staff Sergeant Kenneth A. Gradle, the radio operator, was creased in the forehead. "A fraction of an inch difference," noted the squadron adjutant, "and they would have been killed."[38]

Humiston finally lost the Zeros in a thick layer of clouds, but the next several minutes were no less anxious. Although steadily losing oil pressure, the right inboard engine produced just enough horsepower to help the straining bomber climb slowly inside the clouds. But those same clouds could be a double-edged sword. Literally hundreds of Allied and Japanese aircraft came to grief among the peaks and ridges of the Owen Stanley Mountains during the war, almost always because they lacked sufficient altitude to avoid the mountains at night or in cloudy conditions. In this case, Humiston and his crew were lucky. "By some miracle the engine held together until we broke out at 9,000 feet," recalled Roy Reid, "and there, about three miles in front of us, was a 12,000 foot mountain towering out of the clouds."[39]

Humiston and Reid guided the bomber away from the peak, but still had their hands full. The number two engine was done for, so after shutting it down and feathering the prop, the pilots were forced to maneuver through the mountains on two engines. Making a straight-in approach to Port Moresby with no flaps or wheel brakes, they skillfully put the big plane down. It was still rolling at the far end of the runway, but Humiston used the two good engines to perform a ground loop and the Fortress finally came to rest, its right wheel planted deeply in a bomb crater.

It so happened that General Kenney, who had arrived in Australia only two days earlier and was already touring the forward bases, witnessed the landing. Less than a month later, after settling into his new headquarters in Brisbane, he awarded Silver Stars to the entire crew. His rationale was probably based on the crew's claim that four Zeros had been shot down in flames. Three were credited, though the Tainan Air Group actually lost none.[40]

Despite eight gaping cannon holes and an estimated 250 bullet and shrapnel holes, the indestructible Fortress was dragged out of the bomb crater and eventually returned to combat. The two wounded crewmen were released from the field hospital on August 1, but later that evening, during the seventy-seventh Japanese raid on Port Moresby, Ken Gradle sprained his ankle while jumping into a slit trench.

HAIRY MISSIONS LIKE the ones survived by Horgan and Humiston and their crews became almost routine for the 435th. "Once the Japanese met us with two or three Zeros at a time," wrote the adjutant on August 2. "Now, with a regular patrol in the Buna area, they meet us with 10 to 15 ships. Things are tougher now." It was a gross understatement, but the adjutant's conclusion provided a solid rationale for the squadron's policy of sending crews to the forward area for only a week at a time. They lived in squalid camp conditions, encountered Zeros on almost every mission, and endured systematic bombing and strafing raids. Perhaps the worst aspect was the food, particularly the meals served in the fly-infested mess tent at oh-dark-thirty in the morning. "I had never in my life eaten a baked bean sandwich," attested tail gunner Earl Williams, "but I did in New Guinea—a cold baked bean sandwich."[41]

A week or two of respite in Australia was as close to going home as the crews could rightfully expect, and the Kangaroo Squadron adopted Townsville as their friendly home base. In return, the Americans were warmly welcomed. "They wanted to do the same things we Australians did," recalled Norma Cox, who worked at the registration desk of a local hotel. "But they were well behaved. They didn't make much fuss about anything. They just fit in. My mother said she was so happy to see them."[42] Twenty years old at the time, Miss Cox fell in love with an American P-39 pilot and married him later that year.[*]

Townsville, with all its tropical charm, provided the relief the Fortress men needed. There were daytime picnics on the beach and outings by boat to nearby Magnetic Island. Two buses were obtained for the squadron's exclusive use, and a few men even bought cheap jalopies for getting around. Theaters such as the Roxy, Plaza, Estate, and Wintergarden screened current Hollywood films (referred to as "going to the shows"), and when the men got tired of the bland military food in the mess hall, they went into town and ordered steaks at Atho's Inn, the Bluebird Café, or one of the affordable restaurants on Flinders Street. The Yanks also taught their hosts how to make a proper milk shake, using at least three scoops of ice cream.[43]

True to their independent heritage, the men often dressed casually in defiance of orders to wear proper uniforms in town. At first they ran afoul of the military police, but "Frank P." fixed that. "Captain Bostrom used to

---

* Lieutenant Harvey Eugene "Gene" Rehrer and Norma Cox were married for sixty-five years until his death in 2010.

get the boys out of trouble," recalled Herb Wheatley. "The MPs were thick as flies in Townsville. Bostrom would write us out a pass on hotel stationery, reading: 'This man is a member of the 435th Bomb Squadron, and is authorized to go any place at any time in any uniform.' The boys used to flabbergast the MPs with those passes."[44]

Many Australians invited squadron members to their homes. One of the most generous was Flight Lieutenant Patrick S. J. Primrose, an intelligence officer at Area Combined HQ, whose wife baked delicious desserts. "Primrose got me a chocolate cake and it certainly tasted wonderful," Fred Eaton wrote in his diary in mid-June. "In fact I'm having him get me one every week." The desserts proved so popular that Eaton upped his order to two cakes per week, but even that was not enough. "Chocolate cake day tomorrow," he noted happily on July 9. "We have decided that two are not enough. From now on we will get three a week. What a war!!"[45]

But in late July, the people of Townsville got a taste of the war for themselves. A few minutes before midnight on the twenty-fifth, two massive Kawanishi H8K flying boats (later code-named "Emily") bombed the harbor. No damage was caused directly—the bombs overshot the wharf area and landed in the bay—but two ships had a minor collision as they scurried in the darkness for open water. A couple of nights later, during the early morning hours of July 28, a single H8K targeted Garbutt Field. Its stick of eight bombs, dropped over an uninhabited area that resembled the field from the air, fell harmlessly about a mile from the airdrome. The third and final attack followed less than twenty-four hours later, when another H8K arrived over Townsville in the light of a full moon. Intercepted by American P-39s, the four-engine flying boat dumped its bombs and escaped back to Rabaul. A mass evacuation was considered, but the majority of citizens refused to leave their homes.[46]

In any event, the enemy bombers never returned to Townsville. For the anxious people of Australia and tens of thousands of military personnel scattered across the continent, the war began to take a decided turn for the better.

TWENTY

ALONE AGAINST THE EMPIRE

Compared with the massive formations of bombers attacking targets in the European theater—the Royal Air Force had already flown a thousand-plane raid over Germany in May 1942—the crews of the 435th were under no illusions of grandeur when they pieced together a bombing raid. As adjutant Walt Johnson put it, "Crews are willing to go out, but they are often saying, 'Won't Tojo laugh when he sees our two or three ships coming?' Tojo never sends less than 20, but then Tojo has been preparing."[1]

Whether a bombing raid consisted of three planes or three hundred times that number, the basic profiles were the same: The bombers flew in formation to their target, dropped their bombs, and returned to their home base. Thanks to countless books, magazine articles, and several blockbuster films, that essential profile is relatively familiar, and because of the intense aerial combat and heavy losses that occurred in the skies over Europe during World War II, such accounts are invariably compelling.

By comparison, very few stories of solo reconnaissance missions in the Pacific theater have been published in the mainstream media. For the most part the flights were tedious and lonely. Not much happened during the lengthy transitions between targets. But on virtually every mission there were intermittent periods of anxiety when the aircraft overflew heavily defended strongholds, often receiving antiaircraft fire as well as attacks by enemy interceptors. Furthermore, in contrast to a conventional bombing mission, a B-17 on a reconnaissance flight sometimes climbed and descended multiple times. The circumstances were dictated by the weather. In order to obtain good photographs, a pilot might have to descend below an overcast or storm, as was the case during Lieutenant Gibb's mission to Kendari in late June. Otherwise they typically cruised at high altitude, where the ship was safer from interception. In an unpressurized airplane, the altitude fluctuations affected systems and crewmembers alike. At lower altitudes, condensation formed on guns and in oxygen lines. At high altitudes that condensation turned to ice, jamming the guns and playing havoc with the oxygen system. The plunge in temperature had the harshest effect on the side, ball turret, and tail gunners, whose aft compartments were by far the coldest. Fortunately, unlike the early missions when crewmen pieced together whatever flying gear they could scrounge, the Fortress gunners were better equipped against the frigid temperatures by the summer of 1942. In a humor-laced memoir written years later, radio operator John Lillback provided a unique perspective.

The gear worn by aircrew varied according to the job. Ryan,[*] the ball turret gunner, wore a zippered blue electrical suit, close woven, connected to his shoes and gloves, all wired into a socket inside his turret. It got cold up there! When he was not in his ball, he put on a reverse lamb's wool pants and jacket, like the rest of us. At 30,000 feet it got colder than the testicles of a brass monkey. There was no pressurized cabin. Side gunner windows made sure you got plenty of fresh air. The gun port in the radio cabin was slid back. About the only closed-in spaces were the pilots' and navigator/bombardier's cabin, and those weren't airtight.

My usual gear was Aussie RAAF flight boots, lamb's wool leather jacket, gloves, leather cap. Casual, you might say. It was cool but in spite of the altitude it was still the tropics. We all stripped down rapidly once

---

[*] Sergeant George Ryan Jr.

we descended. I always felt sorry for "Red" Curry,[*] our tail gunner, marooned way back there with his twin fifties, miles away from anyone else. But he was as happy as a hound dog licking a bean pot, because he was able to sneak in an occasional snort of Scotch from a vial he had smuggled aboard in his gear. Everyone knew, of course, but he was a good gunner and did his job.[2]

The crews learned to take whatever the weather gave them. An ideal day would find them cruising in abundant sunshine, with plenty of cumulus clouds to duck into if enemy fighters came along. "Clear skies were desired, yet it was nice to have a handy bank of fluffy clouds nearby, just in case," Lillback explained with his usual jab of humor. "It's not easy to hide a Fortress in a thin line of cirrus: something like a small boy trying to hide in the bedclothes when his mother's calling."[3]

Lillback's quips are a reminder that most of the crewmen were in their early twenties. They shared locker-room banter on the interphone when things were quiet, but during photo runs or while reconnoitering enemy positions, the kidding stopped and their behavior turned strictly professional. "On the crews that I flew with, there was humor," remembered John Straight, "but most of the time we paid attention to what we were doing. That's because most of us had been in the service for a while. We didn't have a bunch of new recruits like they did later on in the war."[4]

No recordings of interphone exchanges are known to exist, but in his postwar writings, radio operator Dick Graf included a re-creation of the dialogue between crew positions during a photographic run.

> *Pilot to crew:* *Rabaul in about 10 minutes—bombardier, use the bombsight to bring us in down the middle of the harbor—at this altitude we should get the airfields on both sides as well.*

---

[*] Corporal Wayman E. Curry.

Two minutes pass.

Pilot to radio: *better get into the camera well.*

One minute passes.

Tail gunner to crew: *I just saw three fighters—they passed between two clouds about 5,000 feet below—I don't think they saw us—they were heading north.*

Three minutes pass.

Bombardier to pilot: *a big cloud has drifted over the harbor—no chance of pictures on this run.*

Pilot to crew: *I'll turn 90 degrees left, hold it for about two minutes, do a 180, and come back across the harbor. Bombardier, pick up Lakunai airstrip in the sight as soon as we head back—that heading should take us across the middle of Simpson Harbor. After that pass I'll turn 90 degrees left which should take us across Vunakanau.*

Thirty seconds pass.

Right side gunner to crew: *several bursts of antiaircraft about 2,000 feet down and well clear.*

Two minutes pass.

Pilot to crew: *starting 180 now.*

Navigator to radio: *at this altitude and speed, picture interval for standard overlap is 43 seconds.*

Radio to navigator: *I'll use 40.*

Two minutes pass.

Bombardier to crew: *harbor clear of clouds now.*

One minute passes.

Bombardier to radio: *start pictures now.*
Pilot to crew: *heavy antiaircraft ahead but well below—if it gets up to our level I'll turn several degrees left.*

One minute passes.

Bombardier to crew: *fighters taking off from Lakunai.*
Pilot to copilot: *give me 35 inches[*] and 2300 RPM—let's get this thing moving. Tail gunner, report on the fighters.*

Thirty seconds pass.

Navigator to radio: *picture interval now 35 seconds.*
Tail gunner to crew: *fighters climbing steeply in our direction.*
Pilot to crew: *there's a big cloud bank up to about 25,000 feet about fifteen miles left. After the last picture, clouds here we come.*

One minute passes.

Navigator to radio: *last picture coming up.*
Pilot to crew: *starting steep 90 degrees left. Bombardier, take us across Vunakanau. That's on the way to the clouds anyway.*

---

[*] Manifold pressure as a barometric reading in the associated gauges, measured in inches of mercury.

One minute passes.

> *Tail gunner to crew:*   *fighters about 15,000 feet and well back. Those things can sure climb.*
>
> *Navigator to radio:*   *start pictures again.*

Two minutes pass.

> *Navigator to radio:*   *last picture.*

One minute passes.

> *Tail gunner to crew:*   *as we entered the clouds, five fighters were 2,000 feet below and 1,000 yards behind.*
>
> *Pilot to copilot:*   *back to normal cruise before something lets go. Navigator, give me a course to Gasmata.*[5]

Graf's re-creation of a typical photo run concluded with a clean getaway into the clouds, but of course that wasn't always the case. In early August, Lieutenant Bob DeBord, with RAAF Sergeant David R. Sinclair as copilot and John Steinbinder navigating, ran into heavy opposition on two consecutive reconnaissance missions. The fiercer of the two occurred on the morning of August 2, when Tainan Air Group fighters jumped DeBord's B-17 at low altitude. The crew reported an interception by a dozen Zeros, although only five, led by Lieutenant (junior grade) Joji Yamashita, were actually involved. One enemy pilot, according to Steinbinder, attempted to ram the Fortress: "As he came in, we could see he wasn't going to pull up in the conventional manner and so DeBord dove down, and just in time. For as he went down, the Zero ran right into our antenna, carrying it away."[6]

The combat lasted approximately thirty minutes before DeBord ducked into rain clouds and eluded the Zeros. Coincidentally, the Yamashita patrol claimed the Fortress as shot down and DeBord's gunners reported the destruction of one enemy fighter, but as so often happened, neither side actually scored a victory.[7]

Nevertheless, attrition from the frequent combat engagements was taking its toll. "This makes the third ship that has been caught at low level in the same area by 10 Zeros or more," noted Steinbinder. "We sure are riding on luck."[8] From a purely statistical standpoint, such luck could not last indefinitely. And less than two weeks later, it finally ran out.

IN LATE JULY, a Fortress with a distinctive history had arrived in Australia via the South Pacific ferry route. Although not especially new (it had been accepted by the army on March 3), the aircraft was arguably the most unique B-17E to roll through the doors of the Boeing factory to that point. Earlier that year, the citizens of Seattle and the surrounding counties had reacted enthusiastically when the *Seattle Post-Intelligencer* launched a campaign to purchase a new B-17 through a special war bond drive. The fund-raising goal of approximately $280,000 was reached quickly. By late February 1942, citizens from across the Northwest had purchased enough bonds to cover the factory cost of one bomber. Picked from the production line for special attention, service number 41-2656 was given the name *Chief Seattle from the Pacific Northwest*, honoring the Native American for whom the city was named while also recognizing the citizens who had contributed to the bond drive. In one of the first officially sanctioned examples of nose art, the name was painted on both sides of the forward fuselage in distinctive, drop-shadow lettering.[9]

The unprecedented attention continued on March 5 with a public ceremony at Boeing Field. Major General Frederick L. Martin, the commanding general of the Second Air Force, officially accepted the bomber from Boeing president Phillip G. Johnson and Seattle mayor William E. "Earl" Millikin. And in the true tradition of a "ship," *Chief Seattle* was christened by the wife of Captain Ed Teats, residing in Seattle while her decorated husband flew combat missions in the Philippines and Java.[10]

Delivered to Colorado after the ceremony, *Chief Seattle* had its ASV radar installed in a modification center at Lowry Field, then flew to Sacramento for the installation of combat equipment at the air depot. By midsummer it had reached Charleville, Queensland, where the 8th Service Squadron performed final inspections and check flights. Initially assigned to the 64th Squadron of the newly arrived 43rd Bombardment Group (Heavy), *Chief Seattle* and three other B-17s were picked up at Charleville in early August and flown across Australia to Fenton Field, a new airdrome eighty miles south of Darwin. But the 64th was weeks away from reaching operational status, whereas *Chief Seattle* and one other new Fortress equipped with radar were sorely needed for reconnaissance over New Guinea and the Solomons. New orders were cut assigning the two B-17s to the 435th, and they arrived in Townsville on August 6.

The acquisition of two additional Fortresses was well timed. The invasion of Guadalcanal began the following day, resulting in a surge of enemy activity as the Japanese scrambled to counterattack the beachhead while simultaneously reinforcing the Buna-Gona garrison on New Guinea. The 435th reconnoitered and photographed both hotspots, eventually sending so many crews up to Port Moresby that the daily combat crew meetings at Townsville were suspended.

Chief Seattle, piloted by Lieutenant Morris N. Friedman, flew from Townsville to Port Moresby on the morning of August 8, then flew the standard Rabaul-Kavieng reconnaissance loop the following day to complete its first combat mission. Friedman and his crew began their second mission on August 11 but were forced to turn back less than two hours after takeoff due to trouble with the left inboard engine. Landing back at Seven Mile airdrome, the boldly lettered Fortress caught the attention of United Press correspondent Frank Hewlett. The fact that *Chief Seattle* was now operating in the combat zone was newsworthy, but Hewlett was even more interested in the story of the crew's veteran bombardier, Sergeant Meyer Levin, who had flown in the Philippines with the late Captain Colin P. Kelly Jr., one of the first aviation heroes of the war.

When repairs to the number two engine of *Chief Seattle* were completed, Friedman and his crew flew back to Townsville. They had conducted only one mission and part of another during five days at Port Moresby, but conditions at the severely overcrowded field justified their return. "We are having a tough fight and the crews are getting irritable, tired, and sick," the adjutant acknowledged on August 12. "High altitude and long hours are getting to them."[11] The reference to long hours was another understatement. During the month of July alone, the hundred-odd individuals on combat status in the Kangaroo Squadron had logged an aggregate of 8,372 flight hours, equivalent to almost a year in the air.[12]

Lieutenant Wilson L. Cook and his crew were next in line for rotation to Port Moresby. Recently checked off as a 1st Pilot, Cook had learned from the best, accumulating hundreds of hours of flight time as Frank Bostrom's copilot. Born in Missouri and raised in Oklahoma, he was only twenty-three years old, four years younger than his RAAF copilot, Sergeant George S. Andrews. The youngest member of the ten-man crew, ASV operator Private David B. Beattie, was not yet twenty. Born in Glasgow, Scotland, he had moved to Michigan with his family as a child.[13]

Taking off from Townsville on the morning of August 13, Cook and his crew flew *Chief Seattle* up to Port Moresby, arriving at approximately the same time that another Kangaroo Squadron B-17 returned from a nerve-jangling mission. For several hours that day, Andy Price and his crew had shadowed a Japanese convoy headed for Buna. Dancing in and out of nearby clouds to avoid antiaircraft fire, they transmitted a constant signal for bombers of the 19th Group to home in on. A gaggle of Zeros subsequently chased Price into some heavy rain clouds, but after twenty minutes he eluded them. He then spotted the approaching B-17s and led them back to the convoy. Due to the foul weather, the formation did not attempt to drop their bombs through the clouds, nor would they descend to get below the weather. John Steinbinder, who flew as Price's navigator that day, described the crew as "very disgusted" during their return to Port Moresby.[14]

The latest intelligence about the enemy convoy was included in a briefing provided that night for the benefit of Cook and his crew, after which they headed to "Yankeeville" to get some sleep.[15] At 6:02 the next morning, one of Cook's closest friends was on hand to watch the crew of *Chief Seattle* begin another reconnaissance mission. Lieutenant John T. Compton, who had shared every squadron assignment with Cook since they were roommates in flight school, noted that the Fortress's exhaust outlets "looked like dim headlights" as it climbed toward the jagged black silhouette of the Owen Stanleys, backlit by the first hint of pink in the predawn sky.[16]

Cook was to reconnoiter the enemy beachhead at Buna and the sea-lanes to Rabaul, then overfly Kavieng before returning to Port Moresby, a route that had been flown dozens of times by crews of the Kangaroo Squadron. But this time something went terribly wrong. Many hours passed, and then evening came and went with no sign of the aircraft, no radio messages from the crew. Word that *Chief Seattle* was missing spread quickly through the camp at Port Moresby. "Sat on our tails all day," wrote Steinbinder. "Heard the Japs successfully landed at Buna and weather was too bad that we could not get in to bomb. My roommate (Mobley) and crew left this morning to attempt shadowing enemy ships as they left Buna.* They haven't returned yet. I'm afraid they were caught or something. I sure hope they return somehow. This is the first time a whole crew of ours has left and not returned or wired in as to what has happened since our first mission when Eaton and crew ran out of gas and crash landed back in February."[17]

John Compton later recorded his own poignant reflection. "I waited that evening until long after there was hope, long after I knew their gas would be gone. Then my hope was that they had landed somewhere on some other island and would be safe. Days, weeks, and now months have gone by. Nothing was ever heard. No radio contact was ever made. Where these brave boys may be, or what their fates might be, whether their lives have been spared, we do not know. But of one thing we are sure: that there are no greater men than those who give their lives in war that we may live ours in peace."[18]

After forty-eight hours of silence, the squadron reluctantly accepted the fact that *Chief Seattle* had met an unfortunate end. "Already Cook and crews' clothing to be crated," wrote Walt Johnson on August 16. "Not a single word from them by radio or otherwise, and where to look for them along their track to Buna, Rabaul, and Kavieng [is] unknown. He would have passed over [a] Jap convoy. They must have got him."[19]

---

* The crew's navigator, twenty-one-year-old Lieutenant Hubert S. Mobley, from Tampa, Florida.

John Compton was probably the last member of the 435th to see *Chief Seattle* as it lifted off from Seven Mile airdrome that morning. As the various musings attest, squadron personnel could do nothing more than speculate about what had become of their friends and comrades-in-arms. For decades, in fact, the disappearance of *Chief Seattle* remained a complete mystery.

Finally, as Japanese and Western researchers began peeling away layers of Pacific War documentation, the combat records of the Tainan Air Group came to light. Details of the *kodochosho* revealed that on the morning of August 14, 1942, a full division of Zeros led by Lieutenant Yamashita took off from Lae to cover the convoy headed for Buna. At 7:35 A.M., Tokyo time, the nine fighters engaged a lone Fortress over the Solomon Sea south of New Britain. Gunners aboard the B-17 seriously damaged one Zero, flown by the leader of the second three-plane element, but the Japanese fighters overwhelmed the Fortress and shot it down. The timing and location of the action, together with the fact that the bomber crashed at sea, explain why no trace of *Chief Seattle* was ever found.[20]

No ONE COULD dwell for long on the missing crew. The action in the Southwest Pacific continued to intensify throughout August as the Japanese reinforced Buna and retaliated against the invasion of Guadalcanal. On the morning of August 17, Bill Lewis flew up to Seven Mile airdrome for a meeting at Area Combined HQ, which had moved to Port Moresby the previous week. Lewis was fortunate that he did not arrive earlier in the morning, or he would have been caught in the seventy-eighth Japanese raid, by far the most devastating attack on Port Moresby to date.

Two dozen Type 1 bombers from Rabaul, escorted by twenty-two Zeros of the Tainan Air Group, approached the airdrome at 20,000 feet and caught the Allies completely by surprise. Ten B-26s were parked alongside the runway, their crews on standby alert as they awaited orders to go after the Japanese convoy. Topped off with fuel, loaded with six five-hundred-pound bombs apiece, the twin-engine bombers were utterly exposed. Numerous transport aircraft were also parked in close proximity on the crowded field, making it almost impossible for the enemy bombers to miss. Opposed by antiaircraft guns but no Allied fighters, the Japanese carpet-bombed the runway and parking ramp, destroying six aircraft including three B-26s. Two of the latter were blown to bits when their bomb loads detonated, and another Marauder, damaged as it attempted a rapid takeoff, crash-landed at a newly built airdrome several miles away. Japanese bombs also damaged seven additional aircraft, destroyed the control tower and operations shack, set fuel dumps ablaze, and smashed several vehicles. Amazingly there were only two fatalities, both Australian. More than a dozen USAAF personnel were injured, some severely, but the relatively low number of casualties attested to the effectiveness of slit trenches.[21]

The runway had been hastily patched by the time Bill Lewis arrived for the conference, where a sense of urgency pervaded the discussions and planning. The Japanese seemed to be everywhere at once and their numerical superiority was undeniable. They controlled the sea-lanes, sending convoys at will to reinforce Buna and Lae; they successfully attacked far-off targets with dozens of bombers escorted by plenty of fighters, something the Allies were incapable of doing; and from all appearances, the Japanese were growing stronger by the day.

Despite this troubling situation, the crews of the Kangaroo Squadron took off day after day from Port Moresby to keep tabs on the Japanese. Unless maintenance issues interfered, one LB-30 and two B-17s reconnoitered different locations every day, each flying hundreds of miles into enemy-controlled territory to look for convoys and photograph installations. Crews maintained radio silence unless they needed to send a sighting report by encrypted Morse code; otherwise they often spent seven or eight hours in limbo, with no one else having any awareness of their whereabouts. The disappearance of *Chief Seattle* starkly emphasized the lonely nature of every reconnaissance flight.

Although the physical and psychological strain of those lengthy missions continued without letup, the living conditions at Port Moresby gradually became more tolerable. The improvements coincided with the replacement of General Brett. During his four-month stint as the commander of Allied air forces in Australia, he had traveled as far north as Townsville on two occasions but never visited Port Moresby. (Neither had MacArthur, for that matter, who was widely scorned as being afraid to fly.) Content to run the air war from Melbourne, two thousand miles from Port Moresby, Brett had only an abstract awareness of the crude living conditions and lack of defenses that prevailed that spring and summer.

Brett's replacement, in sharp contrast, visited Port Moresby within two days of his arrival in Australia. General Kenney toured Seven Mile airdrome and the new airstrips under construction, spoke with troops and airmen, and saw for himself that the living conditions were deplorable. Wasting no time, he sacked subordinates who seemed hidebound or stayed behind a desk. They were replaced with "operators," as he liked to call them: spirited individuals who were willing to take big swings at problems. Kenney was fairly short in stature, but his bulldog personality and sheer force of will resulted in noticeable improvements at virtually every level.

The Kangaroo Squadron, for example, moved into a new encampment at Port Moresby with better quarters, a screened-in mess hall, and even a day-room with an Electrolux refrigerator. The officers' quarters were native-built, as before, with thatched roofs and walls, but the structures were infinitely more habitable than the moldy tents the fliers had previously slept in. In jest, they mimicked the Australian practice of naming the huts after world-famous luxury hotels: the Biltmore, the Hotel Imperial, and the Mark Hopkins among them. Even the enlisted men, who put up with accommodations inferior to the officers' quarters, seemed satisfied. "Our base in New Guinea was newly constructed of tents with wooden floors and open, screened-in sides," recalled John Straight with his inevitable twist of humor. "They were comfortable with the exception of the flies and mosquitoes. Mosquitoes carried away only one or two men each night. . . . The food there was okay, even the vast amounts of blackberry jam we had, blended right in with the flies. We couldn't tell if we were eating blackberries or flies. It was hard to enclose the mess hall to keep the insects out."[22]

FOR A FEW days in late August, Fred Eaton hauled weapons in an LB-30 to the new airfield complex at Milne Bay. With a skeleton crew of six, he and Aussie copilot Merv Bell made the first run on August 18, delivering a Bofors 40mm antiaircraft gun, six gunners, their personal gear, and a ton of ammunition. Two days later they repeated the trip with another antiaircraft gun and crew, but when they arrived over Milne Bay, the Liberator's landing gear failed to extend. The flight engineer diagnosed a total hydraulic failure, and as often happened when things were going badly, the weather began to deteriorate.

For the next hour and a half the crew tried to lower the gear manually but succeeded in getting only the port wheel down and locked. Rain and dark clouds had steadily pushed the ceiling down to less than a thousand feet, so Eaton reluctantly chose to make a crash landing. Concerned about the two thousand pounds of ammunition on board, he ordered the crew to dump it. After opening the bomb-bay doors manually, the men took turns dropping the heavy ammo containers into the sea. By the time they finished, the ceiling had dropped to four hundred feet with visibility of only half a mile.

In preparation for the belly landing, Merv Bell checked on the passengers and the tied-down Bofors gun, then Eaton made two low passes over the strip before initiating a long, flat approach. Attracted by the noise, thousands of Allied personnel stood along the perimeter of the field, holding their breath as Eaton skillfully touched down on the port wheel. He held the wings level as long as possible, but finally the nose dropped and the starboard wingtip crunched into the steel mat with a shower of sparks. Slowing rapidly, the LB-30 slewed around in a perfect ground loop, its nose pointing back down the runway. With minor differences, it was almost a mirror image of his crash landing in the Agaiambo Swamp six months earlier. George Munroe had bumped his head on that occasion; this time the passengers and crew jumped out with nary a scratch.

The big Liberator, which had suffered only minimal damage, was unloaded and dragged clear of the strip. By the following day RAAF maintenance personnel had jacked it up and gotten all three wheels down, but the whole effort turned out to be in vain. After spending five rain-soaked days awaiting evacuation, Eaton and his crew were finally picked up by an ex-Qantas flying boat on the morning of August 25. Their timing was exceptional. Within hours of the seaplane's departure, a Japanese landing force invaded Milne Bay.[23]

Two days later Eaton and Bell returned to the scene of their adventure, this time in a new B-17. After first photographing Buna, they were heading south toward Milne Bay when they overtook a formation of fixed-gear Type 99 dive bombers. One of the escorting Zeros broke away from the formation and raked the Fortress with gunfire, cutting the oxygen line to the flight deck and peppering the radio compartment. Led by Lieutenant Yamashita, the Zeros subsequently strafed the LB-30 that Eaton had crash-landed a week earlier, burning it to the ground.[24]

COMPARED WITH THE first six months of the Kangaroo Squadron's overseas deployment, the final three months blurred together. Much of the impetus behind the accelerated activity stemmed from the arrival of General Kenney, who hit the ground running and did not slow down. Barely a week after reaching Australia, he cabled General Marshall for authority to consolidate all of his American units and personnel into one organization. Approval was received on August 9, and the Fifth Air Force was officially activated on September 3, 1942. In addition to replacing most of General Brett's staff, Kenney successfully campaigned for more air groups, gladly accepting whatever the War Department would send him. The B-17 squadrons of the 43rd Bomb Group would soon become operational, the 38th Bomb Group (Medium) was forming up in Australia with B-25s, and the first P-38 Lightning twin-engine fighters began to arrive in mid-August. A litany of teething problems delayed the combat deployment of the new aircraft, but compared with the mediocrity of General Brett's leadership, Kenney almost single-handedly pulled the Allied air forces out of the doldrums.

In Townsville, a revolving door of new B-17s and crews reported temporarily to the 435th, where they flew several missions to gain experience before moving on to join the 43rd Group. The Kangaroo Squadron's key personnel remained much the same, but the constant rotation of crews— whether headed up to Port Moresby for combat mission, or down to Brisbane or Sydney for R&R—scattered the squadron along a line spanning almost 1,800 miles.

The influx of new personnel was beneficial, especially for the old hands. Bill Lewis was able to relax the squadron's combat policy even further, rotating crews back to Townsville after they conducted two fully completed missions at Port Moresby. Depending on the weather conditions and tasking requirements, it typically took from two to six days to fulfill the requirement. The various routes assigned to the reconnaissance crews also improved. On September 10, the squadron adjutant noted the squadron's new policy of limiting recon missions to "no more than two hot spots on one flight."[25] The length of the flights was likewise reduced, from an average of twelve hours per mission to a more reasonable seven and a half hours.

In early September, much to the delight of the pilots, the two remaining LB-30s were turned over to the transport command. With an ample number of B-17s available, additional emphasis was placed on the detachment at Port Moresby, which now boasted enough ground personnel to support four aircraft and five to six crews at a time. The Kangaroo Squadron became self-sufficient, loading at least one B-17 with sides of beef and other provisions for weekly flights up to Port Moresby.

The improvements were great for morale. The RAAF rations the Americans had become accustomed to were "on the skimpy side," recalled John Lillback. "Sliced beef you could read a newspaper through, coffee/chicory, boiled potatoes, dried eggs and such. Bread if and when available from RAAF stores. Later, when we established our own mess setup, we brought sandwiches, Cokes, etc. along with us from Garbutt. When our mess tents were up, RAAF hats could be seen in the chow lines. Leading aircraftmen, sergeants, even flight sergeants and flying officers weren't too proud to accept invitations to c'mon over and get a good feed."[26]

On their weekly runs to Port Moresby, the B-17s typically delivered as much as a half ton of food, but that wasn't the only thing the 435th was hauling. On one trip, Staff Sergeant Edgar F. "Fred" Formby, a radio operator/gunner from Arkansas, brought along a dog he had acquired in Townsville. The pint-sized mutt, named "Dugout Douglas MacArthur," enjoyed flying even if his namesake did not.

Aptly decorated with little four-star ribbons, Dugout proved to be a legitimate hero. "When flying to New Guinea we usually didn't fly at high altitude," recalled John Straight, "and most of the [heavy] flying clothes were in a pile near the ball turret. On this particular flight the dog was along and all except the pilot and copilot were asleep. Somehow a fire started in the pile of flight suits. Dugout ran to the radio room where Formby was asleep and barked and barked. He woke Formby up and the fire was put out. For this we awarded the dog the Distinguished Service Cross."[27]

Another crew in the Kangaroo Squadron was pressed into temporary service as a troop hauler. In mid-September, upon learning that General MacArthur was sending an American infantry division to New Guinea to support the Australian defense of the Kokoda Trail, General Kenney boasted that he could airlift the troops faster than they could be transported by ship. Skeptics scoffed at the idea, but Kenney corralled every available airplane and began flying the 128th Infantry Regiment to Port Moresby. He even shanghaied Hotfoot Harlow, who had picked up a new Fortress in Brisbane. On the morning of September 21, his B-17 stuffed with American infantrymen, Harlow delivered thirty troops to Port Moresby and then returned to Brisbane. For the next several days he made the same round trip, complying with Kenney's verbal orders to fly the "doughboys" up to New Guinea "at the rate of one load every twenty-four hours."

Kenney thus silenced his detractors. Two days before the 126th Infantry Regiment arrived at Port Moresby by ship, the general's cobbled-together airlift had moved the entire 128th Regiment from Brisbane to Seven Mile airdrome.[28]

WHILE HARLOW (and later a second crew) provided temporary transport service for General Kenney, other crews of the 435th fulfilled numerous demands for reconnaissance over a wide expanse of the Southwest Pacific. Amazingly, during its first seven months of combat operations the squadron had lost only four aircraft (not counting the original *San Antonio Rose*). Two were successfully crash-landed by Fred Eaton, Frank Bostrom's *San Antonio Rose II* was bombed on the ground, and only one plane, *Chief Seattle*, had gone down with its crew. But the loss column grew a little longer in the last week of September, due to what may have been the squadron's first mishap attributed to fuel starvation.

On the twenty-fourth, one of the replacement crews flew a lengthy mission from Port Moresby to reconnoiter the northern Solomons. The pilot was Lieutenant George L. Newton, formerly of the 38th Reconnaissance Squadron, who had flown as Ted Landon's copilot during the unforgettable flight to Hawaii on the "day of infamy." For unspecified reasons—but no hint of combat-related or mechanical issues—Newton landed far short of his destination. The most likely cause was lack of fuel, inasmuch as he made a successful, controlled landing in shallow water just off a beach about eighty miles north of Milne Bay.

Newton and the other eight members of his crew escaped without injury, but they were in no-man's land. Compared with Eaton's crew seven months earlier, they were far more at risk of discovery by the Japanese. Allied forces had retaken Milne Bay after a short, bloody fight a few weeks earlier, but the well-supported enemy beachhead at Buna was merely a hundred miles away. At almost any given moment, an enemy floatplane from one of several IJN seaplane tenders, cruisers, or shore-based detachments might come swooping around a jungle-covered promontory and attack the stranded Fortress with bombs and machine guns. Fortunately for Newton and his crew, it only took a few days to get back to the squadron, not five weeks. They endured only one or two uncertain nights before a flying boat was able to get in undetected and extricate them from the beach. The fliers were soon back in action but the B-17, probably due more to its location than actual damage, was written off as beyond repair.

INDIVIDUALS, SQUADRONS, AND groups didn't have to be polished or perfectly disciplined to suit George Kenney. He wanted achievers. And he didn't care how they looked or behaved as long as they got the job done. Well aware of the defeats and hardships suffered by the 19th Group at the beginning of the war, Kenney knew that the original crews were worn out. "It was principally the veterans of the Philippines and Java fighting who wanted to go home," he would later write. "Most of the crews that had come out from the States in the last three [sic] months were still as cocky as the day they arrived. They were not at all convinced that the Nip was any superman."[29]

Although he didn't identify them by squadron number, Kenney was almost certainly referring to the men of the 435th. The crews, who had actually been in Australia for seven months, not only possessed the confidence and swagger he valued greatly, they displayed a real savoir faire for the reconnaissance role. When writing his memoirs several years after the war, he devoted more than a page to a somewhat embellished rendition of Larry Humiston's two-engine landing at Port Moresby in a shot-up Fortress. And in late September of 1942, no doubt aware of the squadron's success in the MacArthur and Quezon evacuations, Kenney called upon the 435th once again for a special purpose. General Hap Arnold was about to pay a visit. As the commander of the U.S. Army Air Forces and a member of the Joint Chiefs of Staff, Arnold was the highest-ranking American officer to travel to the Commonwealth in 1942. Arriving via the South Pacific ferry route, he paused for a day at Noumea to confer with the Allied leadership involved in the bitter struggle for Guadalcanal, then flew to Brisbane on September 25. After an immediate meeting with General MacArthur, he spent the afternoon discussing George Kenney's needs and recommendations.

One of the latter's priorities was replacing the worn-out 19th Bomb Group. The previous month, in what was supposed to be an "all out" bombing effort against Rabaul, Dick Carmichael's squadrons at Mareeba had managed to prepare a total of twenty Fortresses for the mission. And just like the first raid on Rabaul six months earlier, mishaps and mechanical issues whittled down the participants. By the time Carmichael reached the target on August 7, his formation consisted of only thirteen aircraft. The B-17 flown by Captain Harl Pease, the only pilot to successfully reach Del Monte Field during the first attempt to evacuate MacArthur, was shot down in flames. Aboard the lead bomber, the two side gunners were killed by enemy gunfire, and Carmichael earned a Distinguished Flying Cross for leading the difficult mission. (Pease was awarded a Medal of Honor posthumously. No one realized at the time that he and his tail gunner had survived and were being held in an Imperial Navy prison camp, where the outcome was ultimately the same. Both men, along with several other POWs, were executed two months later.)

Agreeing with Kenney that the time had come to send the tired 19th Group home, Arnold promised to replace it as soon as possible with the 90th Bomb Group (Heavy), currently training in Hawaii with B-24s.[30]

The following day Kenney flew with Arnold up to Townsville, where they toured a new air depot being developed at the much-enlarged Garbutt Field. After the tour, flying with a handpicked crew, Bill Lewis ferried General Arnold and Brigadier General Ennis C. Whitehead, whom Kenney had appointed as commander of the newly established Advanced Echelon (AD-VON), up to Seven Mile airdrome for an inspection of Port Moresby. Radio operator John Straight was proud to ride for a few hours with the legendary Arnold. Having heard the story of MacArthur's aloofness during a recent flight to the same destination, Straight didn't know what to expect from Arnold, but the general put the crew at ease. "Arnold got on the plane, talked with everyone, and sat in the radio room on a parachute like the rest of us," recalled Straight. "He was just one of the guys."[31]

Sergeant Earl Williams, assigned to the Kangaroo Squadron's maintenance detachment at Port Moresby, got a much different impression when the VIPs arrived. "General Arnold came into the mess hall," he explained, "and there were no table cloths on the table. He raised hell with the mess officer, complaining that his table didn't have a table cloth on it. I thought: Jesus Christ, why? Here we were, eating out of mess kits, and he gave a guy crap about a damn table cloth."[32]

It was definitely a step out of character for Arnold, who toured the airdromes and met with the local Australian and American commanders before flying back to Townsville with Whitehead. This time it was John Steinbinder, newly promoted to first lieutenant, who enjoyed a proud moment. "Today flew General Arnold up to Port Moresby and back," he penned in his diary. "He complimented me on my 'splendid navigation.' Said when he returns to USA, he will let mom know he has seen me." Almost as an afterthought, Steinbinder mentioned that one of the B-17's engines had "conked out" during the flight back to Townsville, which took over four hours. Bill Lewis was undoubtedly worried about the situation, if only because of his responsibility for such an important passenger, but there is no indication that Arnold was even aware of it.[33]

The good news, of course, was that they made it safely back to Townsville. On the morning of September 27, after spending barely forty-eight hours in Australia and New Guinea, Arnold returned to New Caledonia to attend another high-level conference. By early October he was back in Washington, where he began to implement the concessions he had promised to General Kenney. Among them was his pledge to bring the 19th Group home.

TWENTY-ONE

THE LONG
ROAD HOME

By the end of September 1942, the buildup of Allied airpower and the tactics introduced by General Kenney led to a shift in momentum in New Guinea. In addition to the B-25s and B-26s that systematically bombed Buna, Lae, and Salamaua, newcomers including twin-engine Douglas A-20 light bombers and RAAF Bristol Beauforts and Beaufighters pounded the enemy strongholds. One of Kenney's personal inventions, the parachute-retarded fragmentation bomb, or "parafrag," proved effective in destroying enemy aircraft on the ground. With the battle for aerial superiority tipping solidly in favor of the Allies, Kenney confidently told General Arnold on September 25 that "the Japs were all through as far as Port Moresby was concerned."[1] He was correct. Just three days later, the half-starved Japanese soldiers who had survived the brutal campaign on the Kokoda Trail began a slow, agonizing withdrawal back to Buna. Although the battle was not yet over, the Japanese would never again threaten Port Moresby.

In the Solomons, the Marines on Guadalcanal were hanging on by the slimmest of margins. Large concentrations of enemy warships at Rabaul and the surrounding waters caused grave concern among the Allied high command, and the steady reinforcement of air units at Rabaul and the northern Solomons foretold a bloody struggle to come. The demand for long-range aerial reconnaissance was greater than ever.

Up at Milne Bay, the Japanese invaders had been soundly defeated in early September after several days of heavy fighting. With the airfield complex now securely in Allied hands, the Kangaroo Squadron was split in half for the purpose of basing a detachment at Airstrip No. 3. Frank Bostrom was assigned as the officer-in-charge, with Newt Chaffin as his exec as well as operations officer, Harry Spieth in charge of logistics, and Earl Sheggrud as adjutant. Approximately half of the squadron's equipment, spare parts, and supplies were crated at Garbutt Field and trucked to the Townsville harbor, then loaded aboard the Dutch merchantman SS *Cremer* for the seven-hundred-mile voyage across the Coral Sea. Led by Sheggrud, seventy-five maintenance and support personnel also boarded the aging coastal trader, which departed from Townsville on October 3.

Despite the fact that rumors had already begun to circulate about the 19th Group's pending return to the States, an air of adventure prevailed among the men going to Milne Bay. They had heard stories of the fighting at Airstrip No. 3, where repeated Japanese infantry charges by units of the elite Special Naval Landing Forces had been cut down by automatic weapons. More than six hundred Japanese lay dead, many of them bulldozed into shallow graves near the end of the airstrip. Although the fighting had ended nearly a month earlier, guns were issued to every member of the detachment in case a few Japanese were still hiding in the jungle.

For the next week, while the *Cremer* made stops along the Australia coast and plodded north to New Guinea, the remaining half of the squadron conducted the usual reconnaissance missions out of Port Moresby. General Kenney, who had been tasked with keeping Rabaul under attack to take pressure off the Marines at Guadalcanal, initiated a series of night skip-bombing raids against shipping in Simpson Harbor on October 2. Three days later, the 19th Group attempted a conventional high-altitude bombing effort with fewer than a dozen B-17s, which were mauled by Japanese fighters. One Fortress, with both inboard engines disabled, was cut out of the formation by Zeros and never seen again. In another B-17, a severely wounded RAAF navigator bled to death before the crew could get back to Port Moresby.

Kenney was exasperated by the negligible results of the costly mission, justifying his intention to send the 19th Group home. But the following day MacArthur called him into his office to discuss an even bigger attack, again in relief of the Marines on Guadalcanal. In response Kenney planned an all-out effort with the combined strength of the 19th and 43rd Groups, though he first gave them a couple of days to perform backlogged maintenance. Subsequently, thirty-six B-17s advanced to Port Moresby on the afternoon of October 8. The event got under way that night with a preliminary raid by four RAAF Catalinas, which attacked Rabaul at approximately 9 P.M. Dropping a total of ninety bombs, more than half of which were incendiaries, the flying boats ignited fires across the township that could be seen from eighty miles away.

At Port Moresby, the B-17s began taking off just prior to midnight. Although six eventually turned back due to malfunctions, the remaining thirty Fortresses began their attacks at 4:00 A.M. on October 9. Unopposed by enemy fighters, they droned over Rabaul for two hours while dropping dozens of general-purpose bombs and incendiary clusters on the township. The rippling explosions damaged a coaling jetty, blew up stockpiles of fuel and munitions, and demolished several buildings.

Following the raiders by approximately four hours, Lieutenant Skid Johnson and his 435th crew reconnoitered Lae before proceeding to Rabaul to photograph the damage caused by the night raid. Aside from confirming or refuting the claims made by various bomber crews, the photos would hopefully provide valuable information about the overall effectiveness of the different types of bombs. The pictures obtained by Johnson's crew confirmed numerous hits throughout the township, but also revealed that Simpson Harbor was still full of warships and merchantmen. Equally disturbing, dozens of fighters were dispersed on Lakunai airdrome.[2]

Seven of those Zeros, flown by enlisted pilots of the Tainan Air Group, scrambled that morning to intercept the lone Fortress.[3] Attrition had been high during the intense air battles over New Guinea and Guadalcanal, whittling the famed group down until most of the elite pilots were either dead or out of action. Petty officer Saburo Sakai, blinded in one eye when a machine-gun bullet struck his head on August 8, was convalescing in Japan. Nearly twenty others had been killed in action over the past two months including the popular Lieutenant Junichi Sasai, whose tiger-head talisman had not protected him from American bullets.[4] But the remaining veterans and replacement pilots were determined and tenacious. Pressing home repeated frontal attacks for approximately an hour, they achieved deadly results. During one of the first head-on attacks, a ricocheting bullet struck the chest of Sergeant Sinclair, the RAAF copilot, knocking him out of his seat. Soon thereafter the young tail gunner, Corporal Ralph C. Fritz, was heard to exclaim that he had bagged a Zero. Moments later, his guns fell silent. By the time someone was able to crawl back to his position and check on him, Fritz was dead, shot squarely in the back.[5]

Despite a collapsed lung, Sinclair began to stir after lying on the floor of the cockpit for several minutes and eventually crawled back into his seat with Johnson's assistance. Flying back to Port Moresby with one propeller feathered (a piston had been shot out of the number four engine), Johnson was confronted with another emergency when the number three engine quit on final approach. Despite two dead engines on the same wing, he put the Fortress down safely, and Sinclair was rushed to the field hospital. John Steinbinder, on standby at Port Moresby that day, noted some of the details of the bloody engagement in his diary: "The fight lasted 60 minutes. One man was killed and the copilot had a bullet enter his chest, piercing the left lung. He may live, however. Here's hoping."[6]

Fritz, a twenty-one-year-old replacement from Detroit, was eulogized in the squadron diary. He had died on just his fourth mission.

> Corporal Fritz, up to fly before dawn, eager to go, smiling—was buried at the Port Moresby cemetery before the sun had set. There's only a cross in the graveyard on the hill by the side of the airport to remind one of an American hero who gave his life for his country.[7]

David Sinclair bounced back quickly, which cheered the Kangaroo Squadron. To a man, they thought highly of their RAAF comrades. "Sgt.

Sinclair, the Aussie copilot who was wounded yesterday, was pronounced on the road to recovery," wrote Steinbinder when he got the good news. "Hurrah!"[8]

Although the 435th had suffered its first confirmed death in combat, the crews reveled in the details of a Japanese radio broadcast that followed the big attack on Rabaul. "The raid was a great success," noted Walt Johnson, "and Radio Tokyo complained the next day. It seems a bomb hit the hotel at Rabaul and 50 Geisha girls were killed. The Japs were angry."[9] The broadcast was intended to elicit guilt, much like the claims fifty years later by Saddam Hussein's regime that American bombs had destroyed a "baby milk factory," but the loss of life was also plausible. During 1942, upwards of three thousand "comfort women," mostly conscripted Koreans, were shipped to Rabaul to provide a sexual outlet for the army and navy garrisons. Many were known to have been killed in bombing raids.

BY THE MIDDLE of October, even as Frank Bostrom's detachment built a new camp at Milne Bay, signs that the squadron would soon be sent home became more apparent. General Kenney, accompanied by the recently appointed head of V Bomber Command, Brigadier General Kenneth N. Walker, arrived at Townsville on October 16 for a formal awards ceremony. The carefully organized event included a color guard and a band from the 197th Coast Artillery Regiment, which honored Kenney with three "Ruffles and Flourishes" followed by the "General's March." While the squadron stood at attention in neatly pressed khaki uniforms and garrison caps, Kenney spent more than an hour pinning fifty-three decorations on awardees. (One, a bronze oak leaf cluster in lieu of a second Silver Star, was presented to tail gunner Ed Rhodes, who had returned to combat despite his still-festering wound. His citation appears in the appendix to this volume.)

Kenney never tired of congratulating and encouraging his young fliers. "By the time I got through," he wrote in his autobiography, "I had worn most of the skin off the thumb and forefinger of my right hand. It was a great show."[10]

His partiality for the Kangaroo Squadron did not end with the awards ceremony. One of the 19th Group's B-17s, damaged in a landing mishap on July 4, was undergoing modifications to serve as Kenney's personal transport, and he wanted a crew from the 435th to fly it. Will Beezley, radio operator Dick Graf, and Sergeant James G. Helton (flight engineer) volunteered to extend their overseas tour for the privilege of chauffeuring the energetic general in his upgraded Fortress, nicknamed *Sally*. The opportunity to remain in Australia especially suited Graf, who was eager to continue his courtship of Phyllis Byrne in Rockhampton.

Squadron morale, already riding high after the awards ceremony, surged even higher a few days later. Around the eighteenth of October, Kenney received notification that the first squadron of the 90th Bomb Group would arrive in Australia within a week. He therefore obtained approval from General MacArthur to send home twelve B-17s and crews of the 19th Group, to be followed by the remainder "as fast as the crews and planes of the 90th Group arrived from Hawaii."[11]

While the veterans at Mareeba prepared to go home, there was little decline in reconnaissance tasking for the Kangaroo Squadron. Missions were flown from Port Moresby almost every day, and on October 21 a pair of Fortresses advanced to Milne Bay to commence operations from the new forward base. The crews had heard all sorts of stories about the jungle camp—Bill Lewis conducted weekly flights to swap out personnel and deliver supplies—but the newcomers were still surprised by their first visit. The scenery appeared idyllic at first glance, like a sleepy tropical getaway, except that a small Aussie freighter lay capsized adjacent to the jetty. The squadron's encampment, located more than a mile from the airstrip, was completely screened from overhead detection by the thickly forested jungle. A few roads connected the airstrips, but they were often impassable due to deep mud that accumulated after the frequent heavy downpours. The rain, so the joke went, measured "136 inches during the short dry season."

The detachment had wisely included seven Farmall-type tractors and a few trailers in the shipment to Milne Bay, which enabled the men to move supplies when conventional trucks bogged down. But nothing could be done about the camp itself. Much like their infantry counterparts in the Pacific, the detachment personnel slept in tents that never dried and stood in the rain with their mess kits for another serving of basic army fare when the chow line was open.[12]

There were some appealing aspects to Milne Bay. Rumors that it was infested with sharks didn't stop the men from swimming in the warm blue waters just off the eastern end of the airstrip, and fresh coconuts were abundant. Their novelty soon wore off, however, and the camp gradually earned a more realistic reputation as "a vacationland of mud and palm trees."[13]

Within a week of the detachment's arrival, half the personnel were sick with malaria or dengue fever, a situation deemed serious enough that Doc Luke and his medical staff were flown up from Townsville on October 14. And for all the logistics and physical effort involved in establishing the detachment—from moving tons of equipment and supplies to building an encampment to enduring constant rain and tropical diseases—the Kangaroo Squadron conducted only a few missions from the forward base.

The primitive camp reminded the veteran crews of the conditions they had found at Seven Mile airdrome when they first arrived back in February. Now, eight months later, the airdrome complex at Port Moresby had been completely transformed. Once considered "a cow pasture" with a crude dirt runway, it encompassed hundreds of acres with graded taxiways, earthen revetments to protect aircraft from bomb fragments, and a parallel runway for emergency landings. Additional improvements were constantly being made, and half a dozen new airstrips had been added (or were under construction) to support Kenney's expanding Fifth Air Force.

WHILE THE OTHER 19th Group squadrons prepared to return home, the Kangaroo Squadron conducted a few more weeks of reconnaissance missions. One noteworthy role was their support of the 8th Photoreconnaissance Squadron, which had been in the combat area for about six months. Because the outfit was experiencing only limited success with its camera-equipped Lockheed F-4 Lightnings (a variant of the twin-boomed P-38 fighter), the

435th was called upon frequently to perform strip-mapping missions or photo mosaics in addition to the regular reconnaissance tasking.

Then, in late October, a new enemy threat ramped up the demand for patrols in the vicinity of the Solomons. Intent on breaking a monthlong stalemate, the Imperial Japanese Army planned a major offensive to recapture Henderson Field* on Guadalcanal. Simultaneously, Admiral Isoroku Yamamoto and his Combined Fleet staff, headquartered at Truk aboard the battleship *Yamato*, conceived a plan to draw the few remaining carriers of the U.S. Pacific Fleet into a decisive battle, thus atoning for the defeat at Midway. By mid-October, three separate forces totaling five aircraft carriers, a battleship, and numerous escorting cruisers and destroyers had sortied from Truk to support the army's attempt to retake Guadalcanal. Every day throughout the rest of the month, the 435th sent at least one Fortress out to reconnoiter the enemy's harbors and far-flung shipping lanes.

The new enemy threat emerged just as the first contingent of Kangaroo Squadron personnel began the long journey back to the United States. With little advance notice, pilots Frank Bostrom, Maury Horgan, and Don Surles took off from Townsville on October 23, hauling fifteen men per plane to Mareeba where they joined Dick Carmichael for the exodus of the 19th Group. Several other pilots accompanied them as passengers, including Skid Johnson, Hotfoot Harlow, Larry Humiston, and Bob DeBord. Enlisted crewmen who had recovered from combat wounds were also among the first to leave.

In an attempt to find a diplomatic solution for determining which members of the 19th Group deserved to go home first, a points system was implemented to assign priority. The number of missions completed was supposed to serve as the deciding factor, but combat wounds and marital status were also taken into consideration. In theory the method was impartial, but as Wallace Fields recalled, the practice wasn't always applied fairly. "We in the 435th felt like the 19th Bomb Group reaped the glory and the 435th did the

---

* After the capture of Guadalcanal in August, the airfield was named in honor of a pilot killed during the Battle of Midway, Major Lofton R. "Joe" Henderson, USMC.

work. . . . In any event, the crews that had been shot up pretty bad and had a little tougher time seemed to be given some preference."[14]

Even within the squadron, the points system was loosely adhered to. Numerous pilots and crewmembers had logged well over fifty combat missions by the end of October, yet some who had completed far fewer missions were among the first to leave. And a few fliers even wrestled with the moral dilemma of going home too soon. In the squadron's daily bulletin, Lieutenant Thad May asked rhetorically, "Do I want to go home? The people at home will say, 'The war isn't over. What are you doing here? You still have two arms and two legs. What's wrong with you?'"[15] Oddly enough, May had flown more missions than almost every other pilot or copilot in the squadron, with almost sixty combat sorties to his credit.

After the departure of the first contingent, the remaining squadron members waited with varying degrees of patience for their turn. Naturally almost everyone was anxious to start the long trip, but there were exceptions. On Saturday, October 24, radio operator John Lillback married Sharnée Schmidt, the nurse he had met at the Roxy Theater. The wedding party was small, consisting of Sergeant Meddie Napoleon Poirer (the assistant flight engineer on Lillback's crew) as best man and one of Sharnée's close friends as maid of honor. There was no time for a honeymoon. After the couple exchanged vows at the Methodist church in Townsville, the entire party went to the movies and watched *Ali Baba and the Forty Thieves*.[16]

With each passing day, members of the Kangaroo Squadron voiced their concerns about the jinx of flying another mission. General Kenney, having already pulled the rest of the 19th Group off combat status, acknowledged the phenomenon. "I never saw a flyer yet who didn't worry about this 'one last mission' business," he wrote in his autobiography. "I don't like it myself."[17] But due to the threat posed by the Japanese forces gathering in the Solomons—which culminated in late October with a three-day carrier clash known as the Battle of the Santa Cruz Islands—the relief of the 435th was not an option. Bill Lewis decided to address the worrisome situation at a meeting of the remaining crews. "The weakest man in the crew may be the one to lose the crew," he told them on October 29. "When you're through, admit that for the sake of the others. Some of you have fought enough that you need no excuse for getting off combat."

One man who had no qualms about flying the hazardous missions was Fred Eaton. If the combat tour had lasted another week or so, he probably would have earned the squadron record. As it was, he had not flown at all for a span of ninety-six days after his forced landing on February 23, but despite such a long hiatus from the cockpit, he logged his fiftieth mission by the end of September and maintained a torrid pace during the final weeks of the tour. Fittingly, he was involved in one of the squadron's last engagements with the Tainan Air Group.

Taking off from Seven Mile airdrome on the morning of October 31, Eaton reconnoitered the shipping lanes between New Guinea, New Ireland, and New Britain in the newest version of the Flying Fortress, a B-17F. Accompanied by his usual crew, which included Aussie copilot Merv Bell and the newly married John Lillback, Eaton made a photo run over Rabaul at 28,000 feet. Due to layers of haze obscuring part of the harbor, he descended a few thousand feet prior to commencing a second run "in order to get better pictures."[18]

Ships in the anchorage put up moderate but accurate antiaircraft fire, and the photo run was terminated when eleven fighters were observed climbing up from below. Racing toward heavy cumulus clouds to the south, Eaton managed to elude or outrun most of the Zeros, but four overtook the B-17 before it reached the clouds. Problems with the ball turret and right waist gun prevented their use, but by aggressively maneuvering the bomber with sweeping banks and turns, Eaton helped to line up shots for Meddie Poirer in the upper turret and Red Curry in the tail gun position. Both gunners claimed to have shot down a Zero, though the combat log of the Tainan Air Group reveals no such losses. Led by Flight Petty Officer Third Class Mitsuo Hori, the four Japanese pilots who intercepted Eaton's B-17 were tenacious, one closing to within fifty yards on at least three occasions. But their collective gunnery was inaccurate. Although they claimed to have shot the B-17 down, the Fortress did not receive a single bullet hole.[19]

The following day, November 1, as part of a complete reorganization of Imperial Navy air units, the Tainan unit lost its unique identity. Officially renumbered Air Group 251, the remnants of the famed group—numbering fewer than twenty original pilots and ground personnel—were retired from combat on November 11 and sailed for Japan to reorganize.[20]

ALTHOUGH THE TAINAN Air Group was no longer a threat, the Kangaroo Squadron had one more close encounter with enemy Zeros. Two combat crews departed Townsville on the morning of November 8, staging to Port Moresby in No. 666 with its special camera array for a priority mission. "We have the enviable task of taking strip map photos of Gazelle Peninsula," John Steinbinder wrote in his diary. "Rabaul is on Gazelle. Seems like whenever there is some dangerous or rather some extra dangerous job to do, they always ask the 435th."[21]

But the mission was changed the next day, in part because someone thought the wrong cameras had been installed. While the photo ship returned to Townsville for the correct equipment, Steinbinder's crew took off in another B-17 to reconnoiter the big island of Bougainville in the northern Solomons. "General Walker needed a special recon of Tonolei and Faisi," noted Steinbinder, referring to a protected harbor at the southern tip of Bougainville and an anchorage off nearby Faisi Island. "As we were the only available recon ship, we were relieved of strip mapping and sent to Faisi."[22]

Piloted by newcomer Lieutenant John I. Murphy, who had joined the squadron in mid-October, the B-17 arrived over the Japanese positions at midday. Based on what the crew observed and photographed from 26,000 feet, it was obvious that Bomber Command's request for reconnaissance had been justified. The waters between Faisi and Bougainville were teeming with enemy ships, including three heavy cruisers, numerous light cruisers and destroyers, several large merchantmen, and a seaplane tender. Bursts of antiaircraft fire blossomed in front of the bomber at the correct altitude— the enemy gunners had the range—so Murphy jinked and dived to a lower altitude. The tail gunner reported four Zeros taking off from Buin, the main enemy airdrome on Bougainville, and within minutes the fighters overtook the Fortress. In his diary, Steinbinder described the tenacity of one Japanese pilot in particular.

> This boy was pretty good. He made nothing but frontal attacks. After two passes on our right front, he made two on our left front. One bullet came in and hit an inch above the bombardier's head and bounced back onto the floor. Two others broke the Plexiglas and thudded through again onto the floor. As he passed by underneath, the lower turret man lined him up and shot him down. Meanwhile, the other three made halfhearted attacks, and after we had dived down to 2,000 feet and entered a small cloud bank, they left us. During the combat, the lower turret door flew off. So after combat, the lower turret man came out, and was he glad.[23]

Unaware that they had participated in the squadron's last combat encounter, Murphy's crew conducted one more mission from Port Moresby the next day. Airborne for more than nine hours, they patrolled the sea-lanes between Buna and the Bismarcks. As they passed over Kavieng at 29,000 feet, five Zeros could be seen taking off from the airdrome, but the enemy fighters never caught up with the high-flying B-17.

At the time, no one realized that the uneventful flight was the last mission flown by the 435th. Murphy and his crew spent an idle Armistice Day at Seven Mile airdrome, then took off for Townsville on November 12. Instead of making the usual direct flight, they detoured to the southwest and landed at Iron Range, where they got a brief glimpse of the brand-new airdrome for heavy bombers on the upper peninsula of Queensland. As Steinbinder later put it, they "stopped in on the boys at Iron Range, looked around, and went on."[24]

It was a symbolic passing of the torch. Iron Range was the new home of the 90th Bomb Group, finally operational after delays caused by a rash of mechanical issues with the B-24s. Led by Colonel Arthur W. Meehan, three squadrons moved in the day after Murphy's crew paused to look around. The group's first mission, in fact, was conducted on November 15 against

Faisi, the anchorage off Bougainville that Murphy's crew had photographed a few days earlier.

As PROMISED BY General Kenney, the rest of the Kangaroo Squadron was ordered home. Numerous personnel had already departed by the time Murphy's crew returned from the last mission, and the rest moved out of Townsville over the next few days. For most, the end of the deployment was anticlimactic. Restricted to fifty pounds of personal baggage, everyone gifted or sold radios, record players, cars, scooters, and other bulky accouterments acquired during nine months in Australia, then waited their turn for travel orders.

The notification came too suddenly for John Lillback. Abruptly collared one day and told to get aboard a plane that was heading for the States, he didn't have time to race into Townsville to see his bride. In desperation, he asked his friend and crewmate, John Straight, to deliver the bad news. "He grabbed a bag full of clothes," recalled Straight, "and then handed me money, I think $300, to give to his wife and tell her he had to go. She was not happy. It would be 1946 before she was able to get on a boat and get to the States to see him again."[25]

Leaving their Fortresses at Townsville, the last crews returned the way they had come. With orders to proceed by air to Hawaii, they first traveled to Brisbane. "Oh Happy Day!" wrote John Steinbinder when he reached the city on the afternoon of November 13. From there, his return home was typical. After waiting for two days, he and several squadron mates caught a transport that flew straight to Fiji, arriving on the morning of November 16. They lounged or slept most of the day, continued overnight to Canton (where it was still the sixteenth after crossing the International Date Line), then made the last hop to Hickam Field on the morning of the seventeenth. "Sure is nice to be back in a civilized world," Steinbinder wrote, though he was unsettled by rumors the 19th Group might remain in Hawaii for several months.

Fortunately the rumors turned out to be false. By late November, all personnel who had reached Hawaii received travel orders to the mainland, but some of the enlisted men endured a much slower journey than the officers.

"We stayed at Hickam a few days and then were put on board a Dutch vessel for the seven-day trip to the States," remembered John Straight. "It was a small ship and pitched and rolled a lot. But, I guess because of the situation, this trip I didn't get seasick. That Golden Gate Bridge looked real good when we passed under it."[26]

Whether they sailed under or flew over the landmark bridge, the sight of the Golden Gate brought a flood of emotions to the returning members of the 435th. Having packed their belongings a year earlier in anticipation of deployment to the Philippines, they returned to a drastically different America. Hundreds of thousands of men and women were now in uniform, the home front was adjusting to the shortages and drudgery of rationing, and in almost every town and city across all forty-eight states, grieving families displayed banners with gold stars, hung in front windows to signify the ultimate sacrifice of a loved one.

There were physical adjustments, too. Most members of the squadron were ordered to a new army airfield at Pocatello, Idaho, under development as a heavy bomber training base. After almost a year in the heat and humidity of the tropics, they were ill prepared for the winter conditions. "We lived in barracks heated by coal stoves," explained Wallace Fields, "and there was about a foot of snow on the ground. The only tracks we made were from our barracks over to the officers club, where we had discovered a record of the Bing Crosby song *White Christmas*. For those of us who had been gone for about a year, this was a most wonderful song."[27]

Released earlier that year, Crosby's smash hit was well timed for the returning veterans, including Fred Eaton. A year earlier, while preparing for deployment overseas, he had sent a heartfelt holiday wish to his family. "I'm certainly going to miss the Christmas tree and the happy gathering," he wrote a few days before the war began. "However, maybe I will be lucky enough to get back by next Christmas."[28]

His wish came true. The returnees were granted furloughs in time for the holidays, and Eaton traveled east for a joyous reunion in Scarsdale. But the innocence of youth was gone. During the past year he had endured physical hardships, the strain of long, arduous combat missions, and the constant stress of wondering if the present day or the next might be his last. Like all of his squadron mates, Eaton had been hardened by his wartime experiences. More important, the war was far from over. For many members of the Kangaroo Squadron, including Eaton, more fighting—and more sacrifices—lay ahead.

Paradoxically, their days in Australia and New Guinea would be remembered, even celebrated, as one of the great highlights of their lives. And a small part of their soul, which no one else could share, remained forever on the far side of the world.

TWENTY-TWO

THE SWAMP GHOST

In the fall of 1941, workers at Boeing Aircraft Company's humongous Plant No. 2 began the methodical, painstaking process of building the fifty-fourth B-17E. A sequential number, 2257, was assigned to track the various subassemblies as they took shape inside the building, a monstrosity that encompassed almost 1.8 million square feet. Starting with aluminum alloy stock and extrusions, employees using massive presses fashioned ribs, spars, and stringers that were fitted together in jigs to form the bomber's structural framework. The forward and aft fuselage sections, constructed separately, were sheathed with panels of sheet aluminum. The two huge wings, built in jigs that stood three stories tall, were wrapped in a corrugated inner skin for strength, followed by a smooth outer skin.

There were no robotics, no automated assemblies in the construction of No. 2257. The entire aircraft was assembled by hand. Every rivet—and there were approximately a million of them in a B-17E—was individually drilled and fastened by a factory worker. The fuselage sections were built up on rolling assemblies and mated together; the wings were then attached with heavy taper pins, and the aircraft gradually assumed its distinctive shape.

Other specialists at Boeing stepped in with their particular skills, such as covering the framework of the flight controls with doped fabric, or installing more than 16,000 feet of electrical wiring, the equivalent of approximately

337

3.15 miles of various gauges of copper. Components manufactured by subcontractors—engines from Wright Aeronautical, propellers from Hamilton Standard, wheel brakes from Bendix, machine-gun turrets from Sperry, and tires from Goodyear—were shipped to the factory for the final stages of assembly. Shortly before completion, the Fortress was assigned a U.S. Army service number, 41-2446, the last five digits of which became its radio call sign. For the final step, the aluminum bomber was rolled into Shop 906, the camouflage unit, where it was washed, masked off, and painted.

In early December, after the completed aircraft was towed out of the factory, the four Wright Cyclones were started for the first time. They had to be carefully broken in, requiring hours of "slow time" operation to ensure that the piston rings and other internal components seated properly. Finally, after passing all inspections and flight tests, 41-2446 was deemed ready for acceptance by the Air Corps. Lieutenant John A. Haig officially took delivery on Saturday, December 6, less than twenty-four hours before the attack on Pearl Harbor.

Assigned to the 7th Bomb Group, and with Fred Eaton at the controls, the new Fortress proceeded with the 22nd Squadron to Hickam Field on the night of December 17–18. Soon thereafter it was requisitioned by the Hawaiian Air Force for six weeks, then released in early February to serve with the Southern Bomber Command. Eaton and his crew flew it across the Pacific to Townsville, arriving on February 21, and took off the following night to conduct the first American raid on Rabaul.

Still new, with only a few hundred hours on her engines and airframe, the olive drab Fortress never completed the mission, winding up instead on her belly in the Agaiambo Swamp.

FOR THE NEXT twenty-three years, 41-2446 sat untouched by human hands. With her bottom half immersed in fresh water and her sides shaded by towering kunai grass, she was remarkably well preserved. The fabric covering the control surfaces eventually rotted away, and most of the paint on her upper surfaces disappeared after years of ultraviolet radiation and the scrubbing effects of wind and rain, but otherwise she was unmolested, a time capsule sitting in the midst of one of the most remote, inaccessible locations on the planet. An aluminum aquarium, she was home to countless fish, amphibians, and reptiles that thrived in the murky waters drifting slowly through her lower fuselage. Above the waterline, her open windows and hatches attracted snakes, lizards, and other swamp creatures seeking shelter or hunting their prey.

One of the first humans known to touch the relic again was Frank Gray, an Australian working out of Popondetta near the New Guinea coast. In 1965 he got a good look at the abandoned B-17 from a circling aircraft, and the pilot marked its precise location on a chart. Gray and a few companions subsequently decided to travel to the site, but on their first two attempts they got only as far as a primitive settlement partway up the nearest river. The village elders, superstitious about the swamp, would not assist them. On their third attempt, the adventurers received help from several villagers who guided them upriver in canoes to a point approximately a quarter of a mile from the wreck site. After hacking their way through the kunai grass for four hours, the party finally reached the aircraft. "It was obvious that no other person had been to this aircraft before us," Gray later stated. "Everything was still in place just as it had been left all those years ago."[1]

All of the machine guns were remarkably preserved, their charging handles still working smoothly. Gray was able to operate the upper turret using the hand cranks. Even some maps and parachutes that had been left by Eaton's crew were intact. Gray and his companions planned to remain overnight, hoping to remove numerous items from the plane, but the villagers were anxious to leave the swamp. Knowing they could not return to civilization without the canoes, Gray and his companions departed reluctantly with a few small items: a navigation light, some gauges and instruments, a compass, and the "Norton [sic] bomb sight." The latter was likely the stabilizer component, based on Dick Oliver's statement that he had removed the optical element, or "sight head," and disposed of it in the swamp after the crash landing.

The story of finding the well-preserved bomber inevitably got out, and visits by curiosity seekers began to occur more frequently. In mid-1972, the crew of an RAAF helicopter "rediscovered" the Fortress during a military exercise. After landing their small whirlybird on the outer section of the starboard wing, they explored the interior. Much as Frank Gray related, the various compartments appeared as though the crew had abandoned the B-17 only a short time ago. Regrettably, on that visit or one soon after, the roof of the radio compartment was hacked open to facilitate the removal of the stowed .50 caliber gun.

The damage to the upper fuselage occurred prior to August 1972. On the first of that month, American helicopter pilot Frank Vanatta, flying a Bell 47 for an Australian charter company, landed on the bomber's starboard wing. His photographs show the kunai grass to be extraordinarily tall, obscuring most of the fuselage and even the main wings, and reveal the gaping rectangular hole that had been chopped in the top of the fuselage. The color slides, together with Vanatta's recollections, also confirm the presence of the twin machine guns in the upper turret and tail position. "Though we could not get to the tail guns themselves," he later stated, "we could see that they were still in place. We could also see that the belts of ammunition running back to those guns were still present. We did get into the cockpit area, and were about to see if we could get to any lower areas of the fuselage. It was at that time that we came across a large snake skin; so, as we did not want to meet its previous owner, we did not try to go lower into the fuselage."[2]

Except for removing a few metal plaques, including the 12446 radio call number, Vanatta left the airplane as he found it. But subsequent visits, presumably by RAAF crews, resulted in significant poaching of the accessible components. Within a year, all of the guns except the two in the inaccessible belly turret had been stripped, along with the seat pans (only the heavy armor plate remained), control yokes, and almost all of the instruments.

On May 22, 1973, during a temporary assignment to Lae, RAAF Pilot Officer Trevor Moxham was the copilot in a Bell UH-1H "Super Huey" tasked with delivering an armorer to the swamp-bound Fortress. Rather than attempting to land the big helicopter, the pilot merely touched the skids to the B-17's wing and held the Huey in a hover while the specialist inspected the bomber for weapons and ordnance. "We dared not shut down for fear of joining the bomber in its demise," recalled Moxham. "We held overhead until the quick internal inspection was carried out, then returned for the pick-up. It was extremely hot and humid, even more so inside the bomber, and the armorer was relieved to be back onboard, gratefully accepting some water."[3]

One visit forever altered the B-17's fate. Charles Darby, a New Zealander with extensive knowledge of aviation relics across the South Pacific, visited the site in October 1974 as part of an extensive trip to identify wrecks in New Guinea and the Solomons. Born the same year that the Fortress landed in the swamp, Darby conducted his trip on behalf of American restaurateur David Tallichet, who had made a fortune as a pioneer of the themed restaurant concept. (A former B-17 pilot himself during World War II, Tallichet was building a collection of vintage warplanes, many of which he flew, called "Yesterday's Air Force.") During his yearlong excursion, Darby explored dozens of abandoned aircraft and took hundreds of compelling photographs, many of which were compiled in a book titled *Pacific Aircraft Wrecks . . . and Where to Find Them*. Published in 1979 and reprinted a few years later, the book kickstarted worldwide interest in aviation relics.

Almost overnight, the obscurity of 41-2446 came to an end. For more than thirty years she had rested undisturbed in the Agaiambo Swamp, but the publication of Darby's book threw a spotlight on the fact that she was not only an extremely rare B-17E, she had sustained only minor damage from the crash landing. The book spawned numerous magazine articles over the years, and the legend of the abandoned Fortress grew exponentially. A thermos found in one of the compartments contained the dregs of what had once been coffee; an ashtray still contained cigarette butts.[4] As if to amplify the mystique, the plane all but disappeared as the kunai grasses grew tall in the wet season but became easier to find during dry spells. The spooky aura of the relic, along with its apparent disappearance and reappearance as the seasons changed, eventually led to a provocative new nickname: the "Swamp Ghost."

THE INTERVENING YEARS had been mostly kind to the former members of the Kangaroo Squadron. After a brief assignment to Pocatello, Idaho, the

19th Bomb Group and the 435th Squadron were ordered to another new airfield—this time in the high desert of West Texas—to form the nucleus of what became known as "Rattlesnake Bomber Base." For the next two years, many of the squadron's veterans taught the lessons they had learned in combat to thousands of heavy bomber crews training in B-17s and B-29s at Pyote Army Airfield.

Three exceptions were Frank Bostrom, Dick Carmichael, and Fred Eaton, who spent several days debriefing Hap Arnold on their role in the air war in the Southwest Pacific. Carmichael was subsequently posted to Arnold's staff for nine months, which he parlayed into a command assignment. In mid-1944 he took the 462nd Bomb Group overseas via the eastern ferry route to China, from which he led the first daylight raid on Tokyo since the Doolittle mission. But the landmark effort on August 20, 1944, was Carmichael's last flight of the war: his B-29 was shot down, and he spent the next twelve months as a prisoner of the Japanese. After repatriation he continued his career in the air force, flying almost forty additional combat missions during the Korean War. Rising to the rank of major general, he retired in 1961.

Fred Eaton also benefited from the special debriefing assignment. Advancing rapidly to lieutenant colonel, he attended the Command and General Staff School before returning overseas with the Fifteenth Air Force. He flew forty-eight combat missions over Europe, mostly from bases in Italy, until he was seriously wounded over Germany in July 1944 while leading the 301st Bomb Group. He received a DSC for that extraordinary mission, the citation of which appears here in the appendix. After the war Eaton joined the corporate world and worked his way up the executive ladder with Sears, Roebuck and Company, eventually becoming the president of Sears in Venezuela.

All of Eaton's original crew survived the war, although three did not live long enough to enjoy the surge of publicity and interest generated by the rediscovery of their abandoned bomber. Tail gunner John Hall, who had earned a commission soon after the war, settled in California and raised a family of nine children but passed away in early 1969 at the age of fifty-six. Lower turret gunner William Schwartz returned to Illinois and raised two daughters. He died in 1970 of complications from a heart attack at the age of fifty-eight. Hotfoot Harlow made a career in the air force and retired at the rank of colonel. But the onetime national boxing champion, known as "the Bull" for his indestructibility, was only sixty when he passed away in 1976.

The other members of the crew were still in decent health when the "Swamp Ghost" became a famous relic. Assistant radio operator Howard Sorenson, who had suffered temporary blindness immediately after the crash landing, was accepted for the aviation cadet program in 1943. He reported to San Antonio, but his goal of becoming a pilot ended on a basketball court. Gouged accidently by another player during physical training, Sorenson lost the use of his right eye. He subsequently served overseas with the Twentieth Air Force as a staff sergeant, then returned to civilian life after the war and eventually retired in California. So did Russ Crawford, the side gunner, who lived in the San Francisco area after retiring from the air force in 1960. The flight engineer, Clarence LeMieux, likewise stayed in the air force, having earned a field commission at Pyote Field in Texas. Stationed at facilities all around the world during his career, he retired as a colonel and returned to his hometown of Spokane, Washington. The career of bombardier Dick Oliver was much the same: he, too, rose to the rank of colonel in the air force, then retired in northern California. George Munroe, who had so patiently accepted his temporary role as a navigator, also remained in the service and enjoyed worldwide postings before he retired. After a second career in the railroad industry, he settled in northern Virginia.

The nine men who formed the crew of 41-2446 for its one and only combat mission had all joined the Army Air Corps prior to the start of World War II. Not only did they survive the war, six of them went on to complete full careers in the U.S. Air Force. Collectively, they devoted more than 130 years of service to their country.

THE RENOWN OF the Swamp Ghost was a double-edged sword. Her fame brought recognition to Fred Eaton's crew as well as the Kangaroo Squadron, and the number of visits to the wreck increased dramatically. Most were made by warbird aficionados, adventurers, and curiosity seekers who had the resources to travel to Port Moresby and charter a helicopter. And eventually, because the airplane was rare and remarkably intact, the Swamp Ghost attracted the attention of well-funded museums, professional restoration organizations, and private warbird collectors.

The inevitable result of all the visits was further damage to the aircraft. Trip by trip, piece by piece, numerous items were carried off by trophy hunters and outright scavengers. An unintended side effect of the visits was the acceleration of decay, particularly to the Plexiglas nose and side windows. For the first thirty years in the swamp, the bomber's flanks and much of her nose and tail were well shaded by kunai grass. But the arrival of frequent visitors altered the immediate environment and affected the man-made Plexiglas. As explained by Chris Henry, an acknowledged B-17 expert and full-time employee of the Experimental Aircraft Association Museum at Oshkosh, Wisconsin, "Every time an excursion would visit, they would cut the vegetation back exposing more of the glass to the extreme sun and heat. The sun's UV radiation would turn the glass to yellow and then brown."[5]

Although kunai grass grows rapidly, once the Plexiglas started to crack and craze, its decay accelerated. After repeated exposure to more intense sunlight over the span of several decades, the nose and side windows turned opaque and brittle. Many broke or simply crumbled.

In fact the swamp itself was changing. By the mid-1970s, when the first visits to the wreck were documented, trees had begun to dot the area where Eaton landed, perhaps even enough that he would not have regarded it as the "perfect natural landing field" he believed it to be in 1942. By the 1980s, there were many more trees in the vicinity of the airplane, though light helicopters could still approach and land on the outer portion of the B-17's starboard wing. This was demonstrated in 1986, when a team that included Richard "Ric" Gillespie, founder of The International Group for Historic Aircraft Recovery (TIGHAR), traveled to the Agaiambo Swamp to evaluate the feasibility of recovering the aircraft on behalf of the Travis AFB Historical Society. That same year, driven by personal curiosity to see where his father had served during the war, attorney Ken Fields (the son of 435th pilot Wallace Fields) hired a helicopter to take him to the wreck. He was accompanied from Port Moresby by Bruce Hoy, the curator of modern history at the National Museum of Papua New Guinea and a frequent visitor to the B-17. "We hovered over the starboard wing and jumped out on the wing," recalled Fields, "as there were no trees there."[6]

But just a decade later, the hover-and-jump method was no longer a safe option. Returning in 1996 as a member of a recovery evaluation team, Ken Fields had an unexpected adventure: "I had to jump out of the helicopter into the swamp, probably 30 yards or more from the plane, because there were too many trees around the plane to hover over it close enough to jump out on it. And I learned that once you are in the swamp in the kunai, you are blind, as you have no point of reference other than the 15-foot wall of kunai in front of you."[7]

Within another ten years, portions of the swamp around the B-17 were thickly wooded, with trees thirty to forty feet tall. In 2005, American researcher Justin Taylan, who has made a career of tracking down missing aircraft among the islands of the South Pacific (and searching for the thousands of airmen still listed as MIA), was able to lead a group of tourists to the "Swamp Ghost" *on foot*. The essential purpose of his visit was to determine whether a business venture was feasible. In a cooperative effort with the local landowners and a renowned fishing camp located downriver from the wreck, Taylan envisioned the "Swamp Ghost" as the focal point of a tourist enterprise that would benefit the Papuan villagers. His experimental visit was conducted in September, during the dry season, using a precut path slightly over a mile in length from a landing point on the navigable river. "Amazingly," Taylan stated, "the trek was easy."[8]

That the swamp had changed so dramatically would have astounded Fred Eaton, as would the knowledge that his B-17 was becoming a boutique tourist attraction. In the mid-1980s, when he described his crew's adventures for a video documentary, he was well aware of the worldwide interest in the wreck. But soon thereafter, he began to exhibit symptoms of Alzheimer's. He lived another six years before succumbing to the disease in 1994.

Two other crewmembers had also died by the time of Justin Taylan's tourism experiment. Side gunner Russ Crawford passed away in 1987, and Howard Sorenson died in early 2004, leaving only three members of the original crew still extant when Taylan led his trek to the abandoned airplane. They, too, would have been astonished to see tourists walking to the plane, covering the same distance in an hour or two that had taken them four terrible days.

THE TRAVIS AFB Historical Society abandoned its efforts to recover the Swamp Ghost, but the bomber had already cast its spell on other restoration organizations and individuals. Pilfered components notwithstanding, the rarity and overall intact condition of the B-17 made it one of the most coveted relics of the Pacific War. Thus, despite the remoteness of the Agaiambo Swamp and its sweltering environment, feasibility studies and speculative visits continued. Ric Gillespie, referring to the prize as "30,000 pounds of bomber sitting in two to four feet of water, thirty miles from the nearest road," remained in favor of the aircraft's recovery. "After consultation with the Royal Australian Air Force, the United States Air Force, [and] the authorities in Papua New Guinea," he stated in 1986, "we're convinced that it can be done, and, in the interest of history, should be done."[9]

The debate over whether the aircraft should be recovered or left in place was polarizing. Many hoped it would remain in the swamp indefinitely. In a position paper submitted to the National Museum of Papua New Guinea in 2002, Justin Taylan highlighted the relic's tourism appeal. Describing the B-17 as "priceless," he voiced the opinion that there were "no signs of exterior deterioration" and went on to state, "The aircraft is not falling apart by staying in the swamp. On the contrary, by leaving the aircraft in the swamp, it will remain intact and unchanged well into the distant future."[10] Although he wrote the study three years before conducting his experimental trip with paying guests, the niche tourism opportunity was already an apparent goal. "It would be very easy to make Swamp Ghost into a world-class destination," he offered, "simply by promoting it as such."[11]

Many others, including Charles Darby, were of the opposite opinion. Half owner of a company that restored vintage P-40 fighters, Darby had no intention of salvaging the B-17 himself but was unequivocal about the necessity of its removal. "If aircraft relics are recovered they have a chance of survival," he stated. "If they are left in situ they will, with no shadow of doubt, corrode into the ground if they are not scrapped, bulldozed, or burnt first."[12]

MUCH SOONER THAN anyone believed possible, the argument became moot. In the spring of 2006, a commercial contractor from Philadelphia named Alfred "Fred" Hagen plucked the airplane out of the swamp. The effort took nearly a month. With military effectiveness, Hagen assembled a team of more than forty individuals, including Ken Fields and Glen Spieth (a former manufacturing engineer at Boeing and the son of 435th pilot Harry Spieth). Working for weeks from a base camp adjacent to the nearest village, the team endured the swamp's unpleasant extremes—relentless heat and humidity, leeches, scorpions, spiders, and mosquitos—while disassembling the bomber. One of Hagen's team members, the owner of a large commercial towing company in Pennsylvania, supplied giant airbags to lift the airplane partially out of the water. Once the engines, wings, and horizontal stabilizers were separated from the fuselage, a Russian-built Mi-8 helicopter hoisted each component and deposited them onto a barge downriver, which was then towed up the coast to Lae. Some salvage experts criticized Hagen's methods, citing the damage caused by cutting the wings off, and much to the team's dismay the waterlogged port wing broke free of its harness during the lift operation and fell back to earth, sustaining minor damage when it was pierced by a tree trunk. But most of the criticism, as often happens when someone succeeds at a difficult challenge, was rooted in professional jealously.

A fully rated pilot himself, Hagen was first drawn to Papua New Guinea on a quest to find the wreckage of a B-25 in which his great-uncle, Major William E. Benn, had been killed in 1943. After finding the wreckage high in the Owen Stanley Mountains, and having already caught the aircraft recovery bug, Hagen fatefully stumbled upon the "Swamp Ghost" in 1996.

Regarding it as "the holy grail of military aviation," he knew immediately that it had to be recovered. It took almost ten years and approximately one million dollars of invested money, much of it in partnership with David Tallichet, before Hagen succeeded in obtaining an export permit from the National Museum of PNG for the agreed sum of $100,000. The funds were deposited by Hagen's restoration company, Aero Archeology, into an escrow account to be divided three ways after the salvage was complete: one half to the National Museum, the other half to be split between the two clans of villagers that claimed ownership of the swampland.[13]

Hagen and his team completed the extrication of the B-17 from the swamp in late May 2006. But as difficult as their effort had been, it would later seem like child's play. As soon as the barge carrying the assorted components of the "Swamp Ghost" arrived at Lae, the project became embroiled in controversy. Opponents to the salvage had launched an effective media campaign, causing the newspaper and TV outlets in Port Moresby to pressure the government into revoking Hagen's export permit. For the next three years, while the dealings between Hagen and the National Museum were investigated by government authorities, the B-17 sat in limbo at the Bismarck Marine wharf in Lae. Hagen, who had hired a Papuan attorney to prepare the original contract, was confident they had an irrefutable case. As he later explained,

> The question floated by [my] opponents to the government and the media was that Travis Historical Society had failed to salvage the plane, other museums had failed, so how is it possible that a contractor from Philadelphia succeeded? The implication was that there was fraud, that there were payoffs. We had set up a legal agreement, we honored it, and we executed it; but the inference was that there was fraud and corruption. That was the basic reason they revoked my export permit: so they could investigate the allegations of fraud. The government didn't find any. They tried. They tried for years. There was nothing. If there had been anything, they would have dug it up.[14]

Hagen's attorney, Camillus Narakobi, countered the government's investigation by filing a lawsuit on behalf of Aero Archeology, reportedly claiming almost $15 million in damages and accrued expenses.[15] After years of negotiations with as many twists and turns as a New Guinea river, Hagen prevailed, mostly through sheer determination. "It basically came down to this," he recalled. "I told them that if the airplane meant that much to them, if it was that valuable, then just give us back what we invested. Give us our money back, and we'll walk away; give us a million dollars back, and it's yours. Nobody agreed to do that, interestingly."[16]

In late January 2010, having languished for three years and eight months on the docks at Lae, the B-17's dismembered components cleared customs and were loaded aboard the container ship *Tasman Pathfinder*. After a circuitous route across the Pacific to California, the forward fuselage of the bomber was unveiled in a public ceremony at Long Beach on June 11. But the homecoming was subdued. In a bitter irony, the long delay caused by the legal bickering had prevented the last three crewmembers from seeing the aircraft back on American soil. Dick Oliver had died in August 2009 at the age of eighty-nine; Clarence LeMieux followed that December, a week shy of his ninety-third birthday; and George Munroe passed away on January 17, 2010, less than two weeks before the "Swamp Ghost" left New Guinea.

David Tallichet did not get to see the B-17 either, having passed away in October 2007. But the unveiling ceremony was held at the first of his themed restaurants, the Reef at Long Beach, and his son became directly involved in determining the ultimate destination of the airplane. As the new CEO of Specialty Restaurants Corporation, John Tallichet assumed part ownership of the B-17 with Fred Hagen. A year after the bomber's arrival in the States, Tallichet contacted Ken DeHoff, executive director of the Pacific Aviation Museum in Hawaii, to see if the museum was interested in obtaining the B-17. Discussions among the museum's board of directors were enthusiastic, especially as the aircraft had direct historic connections with Hickam Field and had flown patrol missions from Hawaii. After a satisfactory inspection of the bomber in July 2011, the museum reached a purchase agreement with Hagen and Tallichet, acquiring the aircraft for $1.1 million.

Shipped in 2014 to the museum, located on historic Ford Island in Pearl Harbor, the "Swamp Ghost" was carefully assessed, with particular attention paid to cataloguing the combat damage sustained during its one and only mission. After a short period of storage outdoors, the bomber was moved into Hangar 79 (which still bears battle damage from the Japanese attack) and partially reassembled to replicate its appearance in the swamp, bent propellers and all.

Although the aircraft had not been named by its crew during its brief period of military service, the nickname "Swamp Ghost" has stuck. To that end, capitalizing on the opportunities for marketing and publicity, the Pacific Aviation Museum was understandably pleased when the Walt Disney Company agreed to create an original nose art design to honor the recovered Fortress. Styled to resemble the studio's iconic logos and insignias of the 1940s—Walt Disney artists produced more than 1,200 such designs during World War II—the tribute features an ethereal Donald Duck, flier's goggles perched on his head, rising up from swamp water in a fighting mood.

Someday, perhaps, B-17E number 41-2446 will be restored. But hopefully not. As a rebuilt, freshly painted bomber, she would resemble all the other B-17s displayed in museums or traveling the vintage air show circuits. As she now sits, perched on cradles in Hangar 79, she exudes an aura that no other Fortress in the world can match. Her eyebrow windscreens make her look almost animate, the missing panels in her Plexiglas nose loom large and eerie, and the clearly evident combat damage and bent propellers tell a compelling story. Wearing her scars and faded paint with quiet pride, she conveys to visitors the many hardships endured by Fred Eaton and the members of his crew; she honors the Kangaroo Squadron's remarkable combat history; and she pays solemn tribute to the millions of men and women who served in World War II.

And that is exactly as it should be.

AWARD CITATIONS

Distinguished Service Cross

Decorations for combat valor during World War II were typically accompanied by citations written for dramatic effect, though the narratives were sometimes misleading or even inaccurate. The highest decoration awarded to a member of the Kangaroo Squadron was the Distinguished Service Cross, second only to the Medal of Honor, presented to Frank Bostrom for his role in the Royce mission to the Philippines. His citation appears below, followed by selections from among the 177 other combat awards earned by members of the squadron during 1942.

> The President of the United States takes pleasure in presenting the Distinguished Service Cross to **Frank P. Bostrom**, Captain, U.S. Army Air Forces, for extraordinary heroism in connection with military operations against an armed enemy while serving as Pilot of a B-17 Heavy Bomber in the 40th Reconnaissance Squadron, 19th Bombardment Group (H), FAR EAST Air Force, while participating in bombing missions during the period 10 through 14 April 1942, in action against enemy Japanese forces in the Philippine islands. On 11 April Captain Bostrom was Pilot of a B-17 bomber under the command of Brigadier General Ralph Royce, who led a daring flight of seven B-25Cs and three B-17s from Australia to a staging field at Del Monte on Mindanao in the Philippine Islands. Over the following two days the B-25s and B-17s attacked the many ships

and the docks at Cebu, the air and harbor facilities at Davao, and Nichols Field on Luzon. The B-25 Mitchells were involved in over twenty sorties. They sank one Jap transport and possibly two others. They also shot down three Japanese aircraft. All but one of the aircraft returned to Australia without the loss of a single flyer, and they brought out a number of important military and diplomatic personnel who had gathered at Del Monte to await evacuation. The personal courage and devotion to duty displayed by Captain Bostrom during this period have upheld the highest traditions of the military service and reflect great credit upon himself, the Far East Air Force, and the United States Army Air Forces.

Silver Star

Approximately two dozen Silver Star medals, ranked fourth in order of precedence in the U.S. Army during World War II (behind the Medal of Honor, Distinguished Service Cross, and the less common Distinguished Service Medal), were awarded to members of the Kangaroo Squadron for combat valor. Here are seven representative citations.

Lieutenant Colonel Richard H. Carmichael: On February 23, 1942, Lieutenant Colonel Carmichael, then a Major, as Commanding Officer of the 40th [sic] Reconnaissance Squadron, led a flight of airplanes in a night attack on enemy installations at Rabaul. Severe weather conditions were encountered but despite the loss of several of his flight Lieutenant Colonel Carmichael finally reached the target area only to find it obscured by low cloud formations over the entire area. Course was then set for Gasmata, the alternative objective, and while on this course the flight was attacked by five enemy fighters, and in the action one engine of one of the airplanes was put out of commission. Lieutenant Colonel Carmichael slowed up the flight so as to protect the crippled airplane and permit it to remain in position. At this point, realizing that the target could not be reached with the fuel remaining, their course was set for Port Moresby, where landing was made with the entire flight almost out of fuel. Lieutenant Carmichael's determination, calm, judgment, excellent leadership, and splendid flying ability were directly responsible for the successful return of this flight through severe weather conditions and enemy resistance.

Captain Frederick C. Eaton: On February 23, 1942, Captain Eaton, on duty as a pilot of a B-17 airplane, was engaged in night attack against enemy installations at Rabaul. Severe weather conditions were encountered which dispersed the formation, but by excellent flying Captain Eaton was able to remain in formation with his flight commander. On reaching the target Captain Eaton was unable to release his bombs due to the target area being obscured. He left his leader, made a second run alone, and successfully dropped his bombs. On the return flight, due to lack of fuel, a forced landing was necessary, and after a calm deliberation a forced landing was made in a swamp on the northeast coast of New Guinea. Six weeks later, by employing almost every means of transportation, Captain Eaton was able to lead his crew back to Port Moresby.

[Editor's note: Eaton was a first lieutenant at the time of the action.]

Captain Harry N. Brandon: On February 23, 1942, Captain Brandon, in command of a B-17 type airplane, was engaged as a member of a formation in a night attack against Rabaul. Despite severe weather conditions, which caused the formation to disperse, Captain Brandon was able to remain with his leader. During the return flight, number four engine was put out of commission by enemy action, but despite this Captain Brandon managed to remain in formation until just before landing, when the other engine on the same side went out of commission. Despite this he was able to successfully land his airplane. During this mission Captain Brandon displayed grim determination, excellent flying ability and calm action under fire, and was directly responsible for the safe return of his airplane and crew.

Lieutenant Colonel James W. Twaddell: On March 17, 1942, an attack was ordered on enemy shipping in Rabaul Harbor. The Commanding Officer, Flight Commanders and Operations Officer were all absent. Lieutenant

Colonel Twaddell, then Weather Officer of the Southern Bomber Command, acting as Commander, received this order, organized and personally led the attack which resulted in the sinking of one heavy cruiser and the damaging of another. The successful results obtained on this mission were due to the initiative and daring of this officer, and demonstrate the highest type of traditions of the Service.

Sergeant Edwin Rhodes: For gallantry in action over Lae, New Guinea, on June 11, 1942. This soldier was a rear gunner of a B-17E type aircraft which was on a reconnaissance mission over Lae. The plane was attacked by a Japanese Zero type fighter and during the engagement Sergeant Rhodes was seriously wounded. In spite of his injuries and severe pain he remained at his guns and by his excellent marksmanship was able to shoot the Zero down in flames. Actions such as these show the fighting qualities of the personnel of the United States Army Air Corps and are in keeping with the highest standards of the Service.

Sergeant Edwin Rhodes (Oak Leaf Cluster): For gallantry in action over Faisi Harbor, Solomon Islands, on September 3, 1942. Sergeant Rhodes was tail gunner on a B-17E type aircraft engaged on a reconnaissance mission over enemy air and naval bases at Buka, Kieta, and Faisi. Weather conditions were so unfavorable and there was such a heavy overcast at Faisi that the run over the harbor had to be made at an altitude of 700 feet. A cargo vessel, two large flying boats and a destroyer, which was one of four warships observed in the harbor, were strafed. Despite heavy antiaircraft fire from the warships and shore batteries, the airplane was able to complete its mission and return to its base without damage. This enlisted man strafed the flying boats and the cargo vessel during the run and manned his gun until danger of interception had passed. Sergeant Rhodes' bravery and skill on this occasion are worthy of the highest commendation.

Corporal Ralph C. Fritz (posthumous): For gallantry in action over Rabaul, New Britain, on October 9, 1942. Corporal Fritz was the rear gunner on the single B-17E type aircraft engaged on a reconnaissance mission to determine the damage which our forces inflicted on enemy air and naval bases at Rabaul during the bomb raid on October 9, 1942. After the observations had been made and the photographs taken, Corporal Fritz's plane was attacked by four enemy Zero fighters. During the running aerial battle, which lasted for one hour, this soldier manned the rear gun and was instrumental in destroying two of the enemy aircraft and in repelling the remaining attacking planes, thereby enabling our plane to return to its home base though badly damaged. Corporal Fritz's ability and courage in the face of enemy fire are in accord with the finest traditions of the Service.

Purple Heart

Prior to mid-September 1942, the Purple Heart could be awarded "for any act of singularly meritorious service or act of extraordinary fidelity, and for wounds received in battle." Based on the existing criteria, several members of the Kangaroo Squadron received a Purple Heart for actions rather than wounds. Three representative citations are presented below.

Captain Raymond T. Swenson: On February 23, 1942, Captain Swenson, on duty as a pilot of a B-17 airplane, was engaged as a member of a formation in a night attack against enemy installations at Rabaul, New Guinea. Despite severe weather conditions, Captain Swenson, with grim determination, succeeded in remaining in contact with his flight leader throughout the trip. While on the return flight the formation was engaged by enemy fighters for about forty-five minutes, during which Captain Swenson demonstrated excellent flying ability by remaining in formation and obtaining the maximum use of his guns during the action. Displaying calm, cool leadership in action, and excellent flying ability, Captain Swenson was successful in returning his airplane and crew intact to Port Moresby.

First Lieutenant Maurice C. Horgan: On the morning of March 19, 1942, First Lieutenant Horgan was the pilot of a B-17 airplane in a flight attacking Rabaul, New Guinea. Shortly before reaching the target, one engine began to lose oil pressure but First Lieutenant Horgan managed to keep his airplane in formation and successfully completed the attack. On the return flight the engine ceased to function but First Lieutenant Horgan completed the trip to Port Moresby with three engines and successfully landed his plane. Realizing that the airfield had been subject to severe raids by enemy ground-strafing airplanes, First Lieutenant Horgan completely unloaded his aircraft of all equipment and prepared to return to Townsville on three engines. With only himself and his copilot in the airplane, and despite the extremely bad condition of the field, he was able by the narrowest margins of safety to get his airplane into the air. After approximately two minutes of flight the remaining engine on one side failed. Faced with a 600-mile flight over water with two engines, or a return to Port Moresby with the possibility of his aircraft being destroyed by enemy action, he elected to and successfully flew his aircraft to the Townsville airdrome. First Lieutenant Horgan's skill, judgement, and determination set an example for his comrades and is another exemplification of devotion to duty placed to the credit of the Army Air Forces.

First Lieutenant Arnold R. Johnson: On May 8, 1942, while engaged in piloting a B-17 airplane on a long range reconnaissance mission over New Guinea, First Lieutenant Johnson sighted a Japanese float plane on a similar reconnaissance mission a few miles away. Realizing the necessity of stopping the enemy reconnaissance, if possible, he immediately engaged the enemy plane in combat, which resulted in the destruction of the enemy aircraft. This officer's initiative and determination to defeat the enemy wherever found truly exemplifies the tradition of the American forces.

Distinguished Service Cross (Eaton)

Finally, although the award was not related to service with the Kangaroo Squadron, the citation that accompanied the Distinguished Service Cross presented to Fred Eaton for a combat mission over Germany in 1944 is well worth including here:

The President of the United States takes pleasure in presenting the Distinguished Service Cross to **Frederick C. Eaton, Lieutenant Colonel**, U.S. Army Air Forces, for extraordinary heroism in action as pilot of a B-17 type aircraft over vital enemy strategic installations in Munich on 19 July 1944. Intense and accurate antiaircraft fire encountered over the target severely damaged his aircraft and seriously wounded Lieutenant Colonel Eaton. Despite the intense pain, shock, and loss of blood, Lieutenant Colonel Eaton courageously led his group through a highly successful bombing run which was instrumental in inflicting grave damage to this vital enemy installation. Lieutenant Colonel Eaton refused to relinquish the controls to the copilot until he had led his group from the target area. Although in a state of semi-consciousness, and in great pain, Lieutenant Colonel Eaton ordered all other damaged aircraft to land before his. His outstanding courage and devotion to duty has characterized his many successful missions against the enemy. Lieutenant Colonel Eaton has upheld the highest traditions of the military service through his gallantry, valor, and intrepid leadership which reflect great credit upon himself and the Armed Forces of the United States of America.

NOTES

Chapter 1: Long Night's Journey into War

1. Pan American pilot R. H. McGlohn, who made numerous transpacific journeys in a Boeing Clipper, wrote in 1939, "The cloud formations over the Pacific are the most beautiful in the world. Great white puffy things, they drift lazily across the blue sky. On [moonlit] nights when we are above them it is like looking down on a field of snow" (*Popular Aviation*, October 1939, 66).

2. Landon, Truman H., oral history.

3. Rawls, David G., quoted in *Squadron Diary*, December 7, 1941.

4. Prange, Gordon W., *At Dawn We Slept*, 490–491.

5. Ibid., 464. Prange characterized Short's understanding and employment of the mobile radar sites as having "no basic faith in their usefulness."

6. SCR-270 "Early Warning Radar at Pearl Harbor," worldwar2headquarters .com/HTML/PearlHarbor/PearlHarborAirFields/radar.html, accessed February 21, 2017.

7. Elliott, George E., Jr., ed. David J. Castello, "There's Nothing Wrong with Our Radar," http://pearl-harbor.com/georgeelliott/, accessed May 2, 2016.

8. Ibid.

9. Quoted in Report of Navy Court of Inquiry, http://www.ibiblio.org/pha /myths/tyler_1.html, accessed May 4, 2016.

10. Prange, Gordon W., *God's Samurai*, 34.

11. Elliott, "There's Nothing Wrong."

12. Regarding order of arrival: "The final radar plot before the attack is of the first arrival of any B-17 . . . a B-17C that ultimately bellied in at Bellows Field," stated Pearl Harbor historian David Aiken. "The [noncommissioned officer in charge] of Opana radar and I went over all the plots and I was able to decipher which plane was which." Correspondence with author, April 21, 2016.

13. Salecker, Gene E., *Fortress against the Sun*, 12, 58.

14. Arakaki, Leatrice R., and John R. Kuborn, *7 December 1941*, 82.

15. "Return to Pearl Harbor," *National Geographic*, December 1991.

16. Quoted in Salaker, *Fortress against the Sun*, 15.

17. Allen, Bruce G., statement to Walter Lord, circa 1956, Reid collection.

18. Williams, Earl T., author interview, November 29, 2015.

19. Ibid.

20. Quoted by Williams, ibid.

21. Reid, Ernest L., "Shot Down at Pearl Harbor," *Air Force*, December 1991, 74.

22. Quoted in the *Argus-Leader* (Sioux Falls, SD), September 5, 1943, 12.

23. Williams, author interview.

24. Ibid.

25. Lansdale, James F., quoting Ensign Harvey N. Hop. "The Lost Pearl Harbor Attack Aircraft," www.jaircraft.com/research/jimlansdale/japanese_losses_ph/Japanese_losses_Pearl_Harbor.htm, accessed September 23, 2010.

26. Reid, Ernest L., "December 7, Pearl Harbor," unpublished article, 1.

27. Swenson, quoted by Williams, author interview.

28. Reid, "Shot Down at Pearl Harbor," 75.

29. Reid, Ernest L., "December 7, Pearl Harbor," unpublished article, 3.

30. Ibid.

31. Williams, author interview.

32. Salecker, *Fortress against the Sun*, 15.

Chapter 2: Boeing's Big, Beautiful Bomber

1. Freeman, Roger A., *B-17 Flying Fortress*, 10–11; also Bowers, Peter M., *Fortress in the Sky*, 6–7.

2. Freeman, *B-17 Flying Fortress*, 13.

3. Ibid.

4. Boyne, Walter J., "The Checklist," *Air Force*, August 2013, 52–53, www.airforcemag.com/MagazineArchive/Pages/2013/August%202013/0813checklist.aspx.

Chapter 3: Off We Go!

1. Borden, Norman E., *Air Mail Emergency*, 25–26.

2. Eaton, Frederick C., Jr., undated letter to *Dartmouth Alumni Magazine*.

3. Craven, Wesley F., and John L. Cate, *Army Air Forces*, volume 6, 569.

4. Coffey, Thomas M., *Hap*, 216.

5. Young, Edward M., *Death from Above*, 64.

6. Dorr, Robert F., *7th Bombardment Group*, 41.

7. *Salt Lake City Tribune*, February 5, 1941, 15.

8. Young, *Death from Above*, 66.

9. Eaton, letter to aunt and uncle, dated "Sept. 1941."

10. Mireles, Anthony J., correspondence with author, February 11, 2017.

11. Eaton, letter to parents, November 1, 1941.

12. Spieth, Glen E., "Missing in Action," unpublished manuscript, c. 1988, mentions the production cost of a B-17E in early 1942 as $280,535.

13. Young, *Death from Above*, 66–67.

14. Eaton, letter to family, November 14, 1941.

15. Nicholas, David. "The Perfect Storm, Part II." *Way We Were*. Park City Museum. http://parkcityhistory.org/wp-content/uploads/2017/04/www20170426-B-18-crash-part-ii-Nicholas.pdf, accessed December 17, 2017.

16. Whittlesey, Lee H., *Death in Yellowstone*, 179; also Carmichael, Richard H., oral history, 41–43.

17. Eaton, letter to aunt and uncle, December 2, 1941.

18. Eaton, letter to mother, December 3, 1941.

Chapter 4: Hap's Farewell

1. Hill, Edwin C., Pottstown *Mercury*, April 29, 1941, 1.

2. Coffey, Thomas M., *Hap*, 223.

3. *Knoxville News Sentinel*, December 4, 1941, 1.

4. Quoted in Dorr, Robert F., *7th Bombardment Group*, 48.

5. *Squadron Diary* (introduction), 5.

6. Ibid.

7. Carmichael, Richard H., oral history, 60–61.

8. Bergdoll, Charles E., statement to Walter Lord, Reid collection.

9. Landon, Truman H., oral history, 147.

10. Prange, Gordon W., *At Dawn We Slept*, 476.

11. Landon, oral history, 148.

12. *Squadron Diary* (introduction), 7.

13. Landon, oral history, 154.

Chapter 5: Surfboards and Submarines

1. Kahlefent, Nicholas H., statement to Walter Lord, Reid collection.

2. Ibid.

3. Ibid.

4. Bergdoll, Charles E., statement to Walter Lord, Reid collection.

5. Embree, Lee R., "Off to the War," unpublished memoir, 44.

6. Ibid., 43.

7. Kahlefent, statement to Walter Lord, 2.

8. Carmichael, Richard H., oral history, 63.

9. Ibid., 66.

10. *Squadron Diary*, December 7, 1941.

11. Rawls, David G., quoted in *Squadron Diary*, December 7, 1941.

12. Bostrom, Frank, quoted in *Squadron Diary*, December 7, 1941.

13. Wheatley, Herbert M., account in Walter D. Edmonds Papers (AFHRA), 2.

14. Joevan, Joaquin, clubhouse superintendent, Kahuku Golf Course, telephone interview with author, June 27, 2017. Born and raised in northern Oahu, Joaquin grew up hearing stories about the B-17 that had landed on the course.

15. Wheatley, account, 2.

16. William R. Schick Clinic dedication article, http://www.erbzine.com /mag7/0718.html, accessed September 20, 2016.

17. *Squadron Diary*, December 7, 1941.

18. *Squadron Diary*, December 9, 1941.

19. Eaton, Frederic C., Jr., letter to parents, December 7, 1941.

20. Eaton, letters to family on December 10 and 11, 1941.

21. Dorr, Robert F., *7th Bombardment Group*, 56.

22. Steinbinder, John J., diary, December 20, 1941.

23. Fields, John W., interview with Kenneth Fields, "Kangaroo Squadron," 30.

24. Eaton, letter to family, December 19, 1941.

25. Eaton, letter to family, December 25, 1941.

26. Reid, Roy, interview with Jack Sigler, April 11, 2002.

27. *Squadron Diary*, December 19, 1941.

28. *Squadron Diary*, December 27, 1941.

29. Ibid.

30. Warlick, Wilbur W., and Allen L. James, "Guardian Angel: A True Story," http://www.pbycat.org/story.html, accessed December 29, 2017.

31. *Squadron Diary*, December 30, 1941.

32. Eaton, letter to family, January 12, 1942.

33. *Squadron Diary*, January 31, 1942.

Chapter 6: To Fiji, and Beyond

1. Trautman, James, *Pan American Clippers*, 47.

2. http://www.clipperflyingboats.com/transpacific-airline-service, accessed May 9, 2017.

3. Ibid.

4. Trautman, *Pan American Clippers*, 83.

5. Ibid., 138–139.

6. Ibid., 140.

7. Ibid., 145–147.

8. https://www.nps.gov/articles/orote-air-field.htm, accessed May 14, 2017.

9. Craven, Wesley F., and John L. Cate, *Army Air Forces*, volume I, 178–179.

10. Ibid., 178.

11. Assistant Chief of Air Staff, *AAF in Australia*, 4.

12. Memo from War Plans Division to General Marshall, February 21, 1941 (quoted in Assistant Chief of Air Staff, *AAF in Australia*, 5).

13. Memo from General Arnold to SecWar, November 26, 1941 (quoted in Assistant Chief of Air Staff, *AAF in Australia*, 6).

14. Assistant Chief of Air Staff, *AAF in Australia*, 6.

15. Craven and Cate, *Army Air Forces*, volume I, 182–183.

16. Assistant Chief of Air Staff, *AAF in Australia*, 8.

17. Straight, John A., interview with author, May 2, 2010.

18. Office of Naval Intelligence, *Early Raids in the Pacific Ocean*, 35.

19. Carmichael, Richard H., oral history, 70.

20. *Squadron Diary*, February 9, 1942.

21. Birdsall, Steve, "Pacific Tramps," *Aviation History*, May 2016, 22.

22. Carmichael, oral history, 70–71.

23. *Squadron Diary*, February 9, 1942.

24. Hobday, Albert J., "Flying into Pearl Harbor and Beyond," published in 19th Bombardment Group CD-ROM compilation,

25. Fields, John W., quoted in Kenneth Fields, "Kangaroo Squadron" compilation, 111.

26. Steinbinder, John J., diary, February 12, 1942.

27. Hobday, "Flying into Pearl Harbor," 4.

28. *Squadron Diary*, February 13, 1942.

29. Williams, Earl, interview with author, November 29, 2015.

30. Ibid.

31. Hobday, "Flying into Pearl Harbor," 4.

32. Carlson, Jack, diary, February 14, 1942.

33. Carmichael, oral history, 71.

34. Ibid.

35. Steinbinder, diary, February 17, 1942.

36. Carmichael, oral history, 72.

Chapter 7: Storm Clouds

1. *Brisbane Courier-Mail*, February 16, 1942, 1.

2. Ibid.

3. "Tropical Cyclone Impacts along the Australian East Coast from November to April 1858 to 2000," https://www.australiasevereweather.com/cyclones/impacts-eastcoast.pdf, accessed June 30, 2017.

4. *Squadron Diary*, 88th Recon/435th Bomb Squadron, February 18, 1942.

5. Ibid., February 19, 1942.

6. Williams, Earl, interview with author, November 29, 2015.

7. Carlson, Jack, diary, February 19, 1942.

8. Steinbinder, John, diary, February 19, 1942.

9. Williams, interview with author, January 15, 2016.

10. Carmichael, Richard H., oral history, 72.

11. Navigator J. J. Steinbinder kept a copy of the reconnaissance photograph, dated "2-14-42." His well-worn pocket notebook contained details of the briefing that included target priorities, a sketch of the Rabaul area, the flight path over Simpson Harbor, and the height of the surrounding mountain peaks.

12. Diary of Private Akiyoshi Hisaeda, February 7, 1942.

13. Lundstrom, John, *The First Team*, 88.

14. Tagaya, Osamu, *Mitsubishi Type 1*, 36–37; "one-shot lighter" nickname: 48.

15. *Squadron Diary*, February 21, 1942.

16. Ibid.

17. Steinbinder, diary, February 21, 1942.

18. Carlson, diary, February 21, 1942.

19. *Squadron Diary*, February 21, 1942.

20. Ibid.

Chapter 8: The First Raid on Rabaul

1. Gillison, Douglas, *Royal Australian Air Force*, 452.

2. Cohen, Julius A., interview with author, November 25, 2005 (originally conducted for the author's book, *Fortress Rabaul*). After the war, to avoid anti-Semitism, Cohen petitioned the courts and changed his legal name to Richard Kingsland. For his many combat awards and contributions to Australia, Kingsland was knighted in 1978.

3. Loads and capacities: B-17 (F model) erection and maintenance manual; bomb load reference: *Squadron Diary*.

4. *435th Overseas*, 34.

5. *Squadron Diary*, February 22, 1942.

6. Williams, Earl, interview with author, January 15, 2016.

7. Steinbinder, John J., pocket notebook containing sketches and notes from the mission briefing.

8. *Squadron Diary*, February 22, 1942.

9. Spieth, Harry E., diary, February 22, 1942: "Left on a bombing attack on Rabaul. Had a difficult time getting the formation together."

10. Minty, A. E., *Black Cats*, 10.

11. Williams, interview with author, January 15, 2016.

12. Spieth, diary, February 23, 1942.

13. Munroe, George B., commentary, *The Swamp Ghost* documentary (DVD), Pacific Ghosts, 2005.

14. Lundstrom, John, *The First Team*, 95; also Hata, Ikuhiko, and Yasuho Izawa, *Japanese Naval Aces*, 146.

15. Quoted in *Narrative History*, combat report, February 23, 1942.

16. Eaton, Frederick C., Jr., commentary, *Swamp Ghost* DVD.

17. Oliver, Richard E., commentary, *Swamp Ghost* DVD.

18. Eaton recollections, *Swamp Ghost* DVD.

19. Quoted in Sheppard Field base newspaper, *Texacts*, July 31, 1943, 1.

20. Munroe recollections, *Swamp Ghost* DVD.

21. Carmichael, Richard H., oral history, 74.

22. Ibid.

23. Earl Williams recalled, "With fighters up and our lack of fuel, we couldn't circle around and come in over Rabaul from the north. The decision was made to simply drop our bombs on the harbor, which we did. (Author interview, October 22, 2016.)

24. Williams, interview with author, August 3, 2017.

25. Reid, Roy, interview conducted by Jack Sigler, April 11, 2002.

26. From a statement by Roy Reid, interview conducted by Jack Sigler, April 11, 2002: "My bombardier got shot in the knee by a ricochet bullet that hit the periodic compass, which is a big, heavy compass, and ricocheted off and then the spent bullet went underneath the kneecap in the little fleshy part."

27. Cohen, interview with author, November 25, 2005.

28. Silver Star citation, awarded June 6, 1942.

29. Williams, interview with author, October 22, 2016.

30. Williams, correspondence with author, July 13, 2017.

31. Ibid.

Chapter 9: Gunfight over New Britain

1. Oliver, Richard E., commentary, *Swamp Ghost* DVD.

2. Munroe, George B., commentary, *Swamp Ghost* DVD.

3. Lillback, John, "One Man's Journey," unpublished manuscript, 2.

4. The *kodochosho* (combat log) of 4th Air Group, translated by Osamu Tagaya, includes references to black smoke.

5. Eaton, Frederick C., Jr., commentary, *Swamp Ghost* DVD.

6. Ibid.; also Eaton, Frederick C., Jr., diary, February 23, 1942.

7. Dunn, Richard L., "Exploding Fuel Tanks," 105: "Zero fighters left a trail of smoke when the engine boost was increased for maximum combat performance. A sudden advance of the throttle might also result in a backfire and momentary flash of flame."

8. Hata, Ikuhiko, and Yasuho Izawa, *Japanese Naval Aces*, 289.

9. Burlingame, Burl, correspondence with author, February 10, 2016. Burlingame is a historian and curator at the Pacific Aviation Museum.

10. Spieth, Glen E., "The Swamp Ghost," unpublished manuscript, 33–34; also battle damage assessment via Burlingame.

11. Quoted in ibid., 34.

12. Ibid.

13. LeMieux, Clarence A., commentary, *Swamp Ghost* DVD.

14. *Narrative History*, Frederick C. Eaton Jr.'s combat report, submitted March 31, 1942, after his return to the squadron.

Chapter 10: Green Hell

1. Eaton, Frederick C., Jr., quoted by Pat Robinson, International News Service correspondent, April 6, 1942.

2. LeMieux, Clarence A., oral history, National Museum of the Pacific War, August 25, 2006.

3. The details and approximate measurements of the B-17's crash landing were extrapolated from aerial photographs taken shortly thereafter, showing obvious disturbances in the kunai grass where the aircraft touched down.

4. Spieth, Glen E., "The Swamp Ghost," 35; also, Oliver, Richard E., oral history, 8.

5. Tagaya, Osamu, correspondence with author, July 28, 2017.

6. Hata, Ikuhiko, and Yasuho Izawa, *Japanese Naval Aces*, 289.

7. White, Osmar, *Green Armor*, 11–12.

8. Oliver, Richard E., oral history, 6–7.

9. Howard Sorenson told of his episode with blindness at a squadron reunion: "Sorenson told me he was temporarily blind after [Eaton] put the Ghost down in the swamp," recalled Ken Fields, the son of pilot Wallace Fields. "He recovered his vision soon and attributed the temporary loss to a psychosomatic reaction to the trauma of the events. He indicated that nothing had happened to him physically to cause it, and mentioned that other crewmembers had to help him out of the airplane. It frightened him greatly but soon went away." (Correspondence with author, August 1, 2017.)

10. Spieth, "The Swamp Ghost," 36–37; also *Squadron Diary*, February 23, 1942.

11. LeMieux, Clarence A., commentary, *Swamp Ghost* DVD.

12. Oliver, Richard E., commentary, *Swamp Ghost* DVD.

13. Oliver, oral history, 8–9.

14. Spieth, "The Swamp Ghost," 40.

15. Robinson, Pat, unpublished dispatch draft, Eaton collection, 4.

16. Oliver, oral history, 9.

17. Robinson, INS dispatch, 3.

18. Oliver, oral history, 9–10.

19. Ibid.

20. Spieth, "The Swamp Ghost," 46; also Munroe commentary, *Swamp Ghost* DVD.

21. Oliver, oral history, 10.

22. Ibid., 11.

23. Ibid.

24. Ibid.

25. Ibid., 12.

26. Robinson, unpublished draft, Eaton collection, 4.

27. White, Osmar, *Parliament of a Thousand Tribes*, 11.

28. Robinson, draft, 4.

29. Oliver, oral history, 13.

30. Ibid.

31. Champion, F. Allan, "Eighty-Three Years," unpublished manuscript, July 1988, 19–20.

32. Eaton, quoted by Robinson, draft, 4; Munroe commentary, *Swamp Ghost* DVD.

33. Champion, "Eighty-Three Years," 20.

Chapter 11: Fever

1. Carmichael, Richard H., oral history, 74.

2. *Brisbane Courier-Mail*, February 24, 1942, 1.

3. Johnston, George H., *New Guinea Diary*, 28.

4. First use of "Southern Bombers" appears in the *Squadron Diary* on March 8, 1942.

5. Straight, John A., interview with author, May 2, 2010.

6. *Squadron Diary*, February 26, 1942.

7. Radiogram, George H. Brett to Delos C. Emmons, February 26, 1942.

8. Hobday, Albert J., "Flying into Pearl Harbor and Beyond," 19th Bomb Group CD-ROM, 4.

9. Steinbinder, John J., diary, March 1, 1942.

10. Wheatley, Herbert M., interview, Walter D. Edmonds papers.

11. Fields, Kenneth W., "Kangaroo Squadron," 44–45.

12. Fields, Kenneth W., diary entries, March 1–11, 1942.

13. *Squadron Diary*, March 7, 1942.

Chapter 12: Invasion

1. Monograph No. 120, *Outline of Southeast Area Operations*, 9.

2. *Brisbane Courier-Mail*, February 18, 1942, 1.

3. Johnston, George H., *New Guinea Diary*, 29.

4. Monograph No. 120, *Outline of Southeast Area Operations*, Part I, 7.

5. Handwritten *Squadron Diary*, March 8, 1942.

6. Ibid.

7. Lundstrom, John B., *The First Team*, 123.

8. Ibid., 125.

9. Steinbinder, John J., diary; also *Squadron Diary*, March 10, 1942.

10. *Squadron Diary*, March 10, 1942.

11. Carlson, Jack L., diary, March 10, 1942.

12. In his seminal work, *The First Team*, John Lundstrom states that two SBDs from VS-2 attacked the *Yubari* first, followed by seventeen SBDs of VB-5, although some of the latter "went after . . . other vessels which had got under way" (129–131); information on the number of bombs evaded, splinter damage, and casualties can be found in the ship's tabular record of movement (TROM) at combinedfleet .com (accessed September 10, 2017).

13. Lundstrom, *The First Team*, 131.

14. *Squadron Diary*, March 10, 1942.

15. Ibid., March 11, 1942.

16. Steinbinder, John J., diary, March 12, 1942.

17. *Narrative History*, combat report, March 13, 1942.

18. Quoted by Graf, George R., undated interview summary, Walter D. Edmonds papers.

19. Ibid.

20. Ibid.

21. Carlson, diary, March 13, 1942.

22. Ibid.; also *Squadron Diary*, March 13, 1942.

Chapter 13: The Evacuation of Dugout Doug

1. Duffy, James P., *War at the End of the World*, 61.

2. Manchester, William, *American Caesar*, 254.

3. Rogers, Paul P., *The Good Years*, 187.

4. Ibid.

5. Ibid., 140.

6. Quoted from extract of 5th Bomber Command journal, 19th Bombardment Group history, 188.

7. Godman, Henry C., *Supreme Commander*, 37.

8. Ibid., 38.

9. Ibid.

10. Ibid., 40–41.

11. Ibid., 42–44.

12. Rogers, *The Good Years*, 192.

13. Ibid., 191–192.

14. Brett, George H., "The MacArthur I Knew," *True*, October 1947, 140.

15. Carmichael, Richard H., oral history, 74.

16. Ibid., 75.

17. Straight, John A., "A History," 13.

18. *Squadron Diary*, March 14, 1942.

19. Teats, Edward C., 19th Bomb Group history, 196.

20. Carmichael, oral history, 76.

21. Ibid.

22. Ibid., 76–77.

23. Ibid.

24. James, D. Clayton, *Years of MacArthur*, volume II, 104; also Manchester, *American Caesar*, 263.

25. Teats, 19th Bomb Group, 196.

26. Graf, George R., interview, Walter D. Edmonds papers.

27. Straight, John, interview with author, May 2, 2010.

28. Ibid.

29. Carruthers, Robert, "The MacArthur and Quezon Evacuations," *435th Overseas*, 32.

30. Godman, *Supreme Commander*, 46.

31. Graf interview, Edmonds papers.

32. Dorr, Robert F., *7th Bombardment Group*, 109.

33. *435th Overseas*, 6.

34. Wheatley, Herbert M., interview, Walter D. Edmonds papers.

35. Straight, John A., "A History," 14.

36. Graf interview, Edmonds papers.

37. Straight, John A., "A History," 14.

38. Teats, 19th Bomb Group, 196. According to Teats, a total of ten passengers boarded Bostrom's plane, while John Straight counted seventeen on Lewis's B-17.

39. Straight, "A History," 14.

40. Ibid.

41. Manchester, *American Caesar*, 266.

42. Teats, 19th Bomb Group, 196.

43. Carruthers, "The MacArthur and Quezon Evacuations," *435th Overseas*, 33.

44. Dorr, *7th Bombardment Group*, 110.

45. MacArthur, Douglas, *Reminiscences*, 145.

46. Alford, Bob, *Darwin's Air War*, 9.

47. Dorr, *7th Bombardment Group*, 110.

48. Royce, Ralph interview, Walter D. Edmonds papers, 2.

49. Rogers, *The Good Years*, 193.

50. McPherson, Irene W., *Four Decades of Courage*, 371.

51. Rogers, 194.

52. Carmichael, oral history, 78.

53. Ibid.

54. Ibid.

55. Ibid., 79.

56. James, *Years of MacArthur*, volume II, 106–107.

57. Harold N. Chaffin and crew, award citation, Eaton collection.

58. James, *Years of MacArthur*, volume II, 109.

Chapter 14: Evacuation Redux

1. Steinbinder, John J., diary, March 17, 1942.
2. *Brisbane Courier-Mail*, March 20, 1942, 1.
3. Mitchell, John H., *On Wings We Conquer*, 102.
4. Correspondence from Joan Reid Ahrens to author, October 17, 2017.
5. Steinbinder diary, March 18–22, 1942.
6. *Squadron Diary*, March 20, 1942.
7. A clear example of this phenomenon appeared in several dramatic photos of cruisers firing their main batteries as antiaircraft weapons, taken by Photographers Mate (First Class) Paul Barnett, whose plane was orbiting over Rabaul during a carrier raid on November 5, 1943.
8. Steinbinder, diary, March 18–22, 1942.
9. Ibid.
10. Claringbould, Michael, assessment of 4th Air Group *kodochosho* (combat log).
11. Steinbinder, diary, March 18–22, 1942.
12. Ibid.
13. Quezon, Manuel Luis, *The Good Fight*, 299.
14. Fields, Kenneth, "Kangaroo Squadron," 59.
15. *Narrative History*, combat report for March 26–27, 1942.
16. Diary of Basilio J. Valdes, March 26, 1942, https://philippinediaryproject .wordpress.com/about/about-the-diary-of-gen-basilio-valdes/, accessed May 29, 2018.
17. Straight, John A., "A History," 17.
18. Ibid., 18.
19. Straight, John, interview with author, May 2, 2010.
20. Fields, "Kangaroo Squadron," 120.

Chapter 15: Jungle Odyssey

1. Champion, F. Allan, "Eighty-Three Years," unpublished manuscript, 1.
2. Ibid., 4–11.
3. Ibid., 14.
4. Champion, F. Allan, correspondence with Frederick Eaton, May 20, 1988.
5. Champion, "Eighty-Three Years," 17–18.
6. Oliver, Richard E., oral history transcript, 14.
7. Eaton, Frederick C., Jr., letter to family, March 4, 1942.
8. Champion, "Eighty-Three Years," 20.
9. Ibid.
10. Ibid., 21.
11. Ibid. According to the diary kept by Bishop Strong, the Japanese floatplane dived on the bishop's motor launch but did not strafe it.
12. Selby, David M., *Hell and High Fever*, 150–151.
13. Oliver, oral history, 15.
14. Ibid.

15. Ibid.

16. Ibid.

17. Eaton, Frederick C., diary, March 24, 1942.

18. Ibid., March 25, 1942.

19. Ibid., March 30, 1942.

20. Ibid.

21. Carlson, Jack L., diary, April 1, 1942.

22. Oliver, oral history, 16.

Chapter 16: The Royce Special Mission

1. Eaton, Frederick C., Jr., diary, April 2, 1942.

2. Carlson, Jack L., diary, April 2, 1942.

3. Eaton, diary, April 2 and 3, 1942.

4. Ibid., April 7, 1942.

5. *Squadron Diary*, April 4, 1942.

6. Steinbinder, John J., diary, April 5, 1942.

7. *Narrative History*, combat report, April 6, 1942.

8. Steinbinder, diary, April 6–8, 1942.

9. Ibid.

10. Beezley, Wilbur B., interview with T/Sgt T. A. McCulloch at Hollandia, Walter D. Edmonds papers, October 13, 1944.

11. Ibid.

12. Steinbinder, diary, April 7, 1942.

13. Brett, George H., "The MacArthur I Knew," *True*, October 1947, 144–145.

14. *435th Overseas*, "The 435th Short History," 8.

15. Royce, Ralph, diary, April 8, 1942: "Gen. MacArthur called me about Miami trip and promised a DSC on my return."

16. MacArthur, Douglas, *Reminiscences*, 146.

17. Jones, Robert T., "Royce's Raid," *435th Overseas*, 40.

18. Wheatley, Herbert M., interview, Walter D. Edmonds papers.

19. Martin, Adrian R., and Larry W. Stephenson, *Operation PLUM*, 181.

20. Bartsch, William H., *Doomed at the Start*, 393.

21. Teats, Edward, 19th Bomb Group, Edmond papers, 224.

22. Ibid.

23. Ibid.

24. Wheatley interview, Edmonds papers.

25. Ibid.

26. Martin and Stephenson, *Operation PLUM*, 184.

27. Teats, 19th Bomb Group, 225.

28. Ibid., 225–227.

29. Ibid., 226.

30. Ibid.

31. Jones, "Royce's Raid," *435th Overseas*, 41.

32. Teats, 19th Bomb Group, 227.

33. Ibid., 228.

34. Ibid.

35. *New York Times*, April 16, 1942.

36. *Brisbane Courier-Mail*, April 16, 1942.

Chapter 17: Turning Point: The Battle of the Coral Sea

1. *Squadron Diary*, April 9, 1942.

2. Ibid., April 11, 1942.

3. Ibid., April 13, 1942.

4. Carlson, Jack L., diary, April 14, 1942.

5. *Squadron Diary*, April 19, 1942.

6. Eaton, Frederick C., Jr., diary, April 25, 1942.

7. Steinbinder, John J., diary, April 25, 1942.

8. Bullard, Steven (translator), *Japanese Army Operations in the South Pacific Area*, 64.

9. Stanaway, John C., and Lawrence J. Hickey, *Attack and Conquer*, 48.

10. *Brisbane Courier-Mail*, April 28, 1942, 1.

11. Ibid., April 30, 1941, 1.

12. Steinbinder, diary, April 30, 1942.

13. Ibid., May 1, 1942.

14. Ibid., May 5, 1942.

15. Ibid., May 3, 1942.

16. Quoted in Bowman, Alice, *Not Now Tomorrow*, 83.

17. Fields, Kenneth, "Kangaroo Squadron," 121.

18. Spieth, Harry E., Jr., diary, May 6, 1941.

19. CombinedFleet.com, Shoho tabular record of movement.

20. Fields, "Kangaroo Squadron," 65.

21. Office of Naval Intelligence, *Early Raids in the Pacific Ocean*, 55.

22. Teats, Edward C., 19th Bomb Group, 237.

23. Quoted in *Osaka Mainichi* (English language newspaper), May 10, 1942, 1.

24. Citation quoted in General Order No. 18, HQ AAF SWPA, June 6, 1942.

25. Rouse, John A., diary, Walter D. Edmonds papers, May 9, 1942.

26. Ibid., May 10, 1942.

27. Lillback, John, "One Man's Journey," unpublished memoir, 43.

28. Quoted in *Brisbane Courier-Mail*, May 9, 1.

29. *Squadron Diary*, May 14, 1942.

Chapter 18: Silver Stars

1. Eaton, Frederick C., Jr., diary, April 30, 1942.

2. *Squadron Diary*, May 28, 1942.

3. Spieth, Harry E., Jr., diary, June 24, 1942.

4. *Squadron Diary*, May 29, 1942.

5. Ibid., May 13, 1942.

6. Sakai, Saburo, *Samurai!*, 75.

7. Quoted in Salaker, Gene E., *Fortress against the Sun*, 109.

8. Perry, Horace E., "Nose Guns," *435th Overseas*, xxiv.

9. Steinbinder, John J., diary, May 29, 1942.

10. Ibid.

11. Fields, Kenneth, "Kangaroo Squadron," 124.

12. *Squadron Diary*, June 7, 1942.

13. Evans, Don L., et al., *Revenge of the Red Raiders*, 105–106.

14. Royce, Ralph, diary, June 8, 1942.

15. Fields, "Kangaroo Squadron," 71–72, 124.

16. Evans, *Revenge of the Red Raiders*, 107.

17. Quoted in an article by Foster Hailey, *New York Times*, September 21, 1964, 22.

18. Bell, Mervyn C., diary, June 11, 1942.

19. Ibid.

20. Ibid.

21. Rhodes, Edwin, video transcript via Laurie Rhodes Kroger.

22. Ibid.

23. Bell, diary, June 11, 1942.

24. Rhodes, video transcript.

25. Roosevelt, Franklin D., United Flag Day speech, June 14, 1942, American Presidency Project, http://www.presidency.ucsb.edu/ws/?pid=16276, accessed January 8, 2018.

26. *Squadron Diary*, May 15, 1942.

27. Kenney, George C., *General Kenney Reports*, 43.

Chapter 19: The Reconnaissance Game

1. Graf, George R. ("Dick"), interview, August 10, 2002, via Peter Dunn.

2. Ibid.

3. Ibid.

4. Steinbinder, John J., diary, April 15, 1942.

5. Ibid., June 5–10, 1942.

6. Straight, John, "A History," 21.

7. *Squadron Diary*, September 8, 1942.

8. Lillback, John, "One Man's Journey," unpublished manuscript, 56.

9. Straight, "A History," 20.

10. *Narrative History*, combat report, June 23, 1942.

11. Eaton, Frederick C., Jr., diary, June 23, 1942.

12. *Narrative History*, combat report, June 23, 1942.

13. Champion, F. Allan, "Eighty-Three Years," unpublished manuscript, 20.

14. Gibb, James N., "A Most Interesting Mission," *435th Overseas*, 73.

15. Ibid.; also Steinbinder, diary, June 24, 1942.

16. *Squadron Diary*, June 19, 1942.

17. Ibid., June 20, 1942.

18. Eaton, diary, June 21, 1942.

19. Livingston, Bob, *Under the Southern Cross*, 26.

20. *Squadron Diary*, May 28, 1942.

21. Eaton, diary, July 2, 1941.

22. *Squadron Diary*, July 3, 1942.

23. Eaton, mission narrative, July 3, 1942.

24. Eaton, diary, July 3 and 6, 1942; also Eaton, mission narrative, July 3, 1942.

25. Fields, Kenneth, "Kangaroo Squadron," 127.

26. Ibid.; also Livingston, *Under the Southern Cross*, 27.

27. Wheatley, Herbert M., correspondence to Kenneth Fields, April 8, 1985.

28. Johnson, Walter H., "The 435th Short History," *435th Overseas*, 2.

29. Duffy, James P., *War at the End of the World*, 154–155; also Livingston, *Under the Southern Cross*, 30.

30. Duffy, 123.

31. *Squadron Diary*, July 11–12, 1942.

32. Ibid., July 14, 1942; also Ruffato, Luca, and Michael Claringbould, *Eagles of the Southern Sky*, 204.

33. Champion, F. Allan, correspondence with Frederick Eaton, May 20, 1988.

34. Ibid.

35. Ruffato and Claringbould, *Eagles of the Southern Sky*, 212–213.

36. Ibid., 218.

37. Reid, Ernest L., "Mission to Lae," unpublished manuscript, 5.

38. *Squadron Diary*, July 31, 1942.

39. Reid, "Mission to Lae," 6.

40. Kenney, George C., *General Kenney Reports*, 68; also Ruffato and Claringbould, *Eagles of the Southern Sky*, 218.

41. Williams, Earl, interview with author, October 22, 2016.

42. Rehrer, Norma (Cox), interview with author, February 11, 2017.

43. Lillback, "One Man's Journey," 32.

44. Wheatley, Herbert M., interview, Walter D. Edmonds papers.

45. Eaton, diary, June 19 and July 9, 1942.

46. Piper, Robert K., *The Hidden Chapters*, 45, 47–49.

Chapter 20: Alone against the Empire

1. *Squadron Diary*, June 25, 1942.

2. Lillback, John E., "One Man's Journey," unpublished manuscript, 48–49.

3. Ibid., 35.

4. Straight, John A., interview with author, May 2, 2010.

5. Graf, George R., essay titled "Photo Mission" in correspondence to Peter Dunn, May 30, 2002.

6. Steinbinder, John J., diary, August 2, 1942.

7. Ruffato, Luca, and Michael Claringbould, *Eagles of the Southern Sky*, 220.

8. Steinbinder, diary, August 2, 1942.

9. Spieth, Glen E., "Missing in Action," unpublished manuscript, 3.

10. Ibid.; also *Life*, March 30, 1942, 90.

11. *Squadron Diary*, August 12, 1942.

12. Ibid. This figure is a conservative extrapolation. The squadron had flown 8,372 hours as of July 31.

13. Spieth, "Missing in Action," 5–6; also findagrave.com/memorial/56772156 /david-beattie.

14. Steinbinder, diary, August 13, 1942.

15. Ruffato and Claringbould, *Eagles of the Southern Sky*, 247; also *435th Overseas*, 65–68.

16. Compton, John T., "The Chief of Seattle [*sic*] and Crew," *435th Overseas*, 67.

17. Steinbinder, diary, August 14, 1942.

18. Compton, "The Chief of Seattle [*sic*] and Crew," 69.

19. *Squadron Diary*, August 16, 1942.

20. Ruffato and Claringbould, *Eagles of the Southern Sky*, 248.

21. Evans, Don L., et al., *Revenge of the Red Raiders*, 129–132; also pacificwrecks .com, accessed January 24, 2018.

22. Straight, John A., "A History," unpublished memoir, 18.

23. Livingstone, Bob, *Under the Southern Cross*, 29–30.

24. Bell, Mervyn C., diary, August 20, 1942; also Ruffato and Claringbould, *Eagles of the Southern Sky*, 254–255.

25. *Squadron Diary*, September 10, 1942.

26. Lillback, "One Man's Journey," 31–32.

27. Straight, "A History," 25.

28. Kenney, George C., *General Kenney Reports*, 108, 110–111. Kenney's memoirs and the squadron diary are in exact agreement regarding Harlow's verbal orders.

29. Ibid., 68.

30. Arnold, Henry, *Global Mission*, 343–345; also Kenney, *General Kenney Reports*, 112.

31. Straight, "A History," 25.

32. Williams, Earl, interview with author, October 22, 2016.

33. Steinbinder, diary, September 26, 1942.

Chapter 21: The Long Road Home

1. Kenney, George C., *General Kenney Reports*, 113.

2. Gamble, Bruce, *Fortress Rabaul*, 248.

3. Ruffato, Luca, and Michael Claringbould, *Eagles of the Southern Sky*, 271.

4. Hata, Ikuhiko, and Yasuho Izawa, *Japanese Naval Aces*, 387–379.

5. *Squadron Diary*, October 9, 1942.

6. Steinbinder, John J., diary, October 9, 1942.

7. Johnson, Walter H., "The 435th Short History," *435th Overseas*, 10.

8. Steinbinder, diary, October 10, 1942.

9. Johnson, "The 435th Short History," 10.

10. Kenney, *General Kenney Reports*, 122.

11. Ibid., 125.

12. *Squadron Diary*, November 4, 1942.

13. Ibid.

14. Fields, Kenneth, "Kangaroo Squadron," 87.

15. May, John T. ("Thad"), quoted in the *435th Daily Bulletin*, October 31, 1942.

16. Lillback, John E., "One Man's Journey," unpublished manuscript, 56.

17. Kenney, *General Kenney Reports*, 122.

18. *Narrative History*, combat report, October 31, 1942.

19. Ibid.; also Ruffato and Claringbould, *Eagles of the Southern Sky*, 273.

20. Hata and Izawa, *Japanese Naval Aces*, 138; also Ruffato and Claringbould, *Eagles of the Southern Sky*, 276.

21. Steinbinder, diary, November 8, 1942.

22. Ibid., November 9, 1942.

23. Ibid.

24. Ibid., November 12, 1942.

25. Straight, "A History," 26.

26. Ibid., 27.

27. Fields, Wallace, interview with Kenneth Fields, October 9, 1982.

28. Eaton, Frederick C., Jr., letter to aunt and uncle, December 3, 1941.

Chapter 22: The Swamp Ghost

1. http://www.theswampghost.com/photos/1965/index.html, accessed January 10, 2018.

2. Vanatta, Frank, correspondence with author, January 7, 2018.

3. Moxham, Trevor, correspondence with author, March 24, 2016.

4. Darnton, John, "Swamp Ghosts," *Smithsonian Magazine*, October 2007, 80.

5. Henry, Chris, correspondence with author, February 7, 2018.

6. Fields, Kenneth, correspondence with author, August 11, 2017.

7. Ibid.

8. Taylan, Justin, public forum post, June 6, 2006, www.pacificwrecks/forum, accessed January 15, 2018.

9. Gillespie, Richard, appearance in *Lady in Waiting* video documentary produced by TIGHAR, 1986.

10. Taylan, Justin, "Papua New Guinea's Aviation Icon: WWII Bomber B-17 'Swamp Ghost,'" report for the PNG National Museum's director, curators and board of trustees, 2003, 11, www.theswampghost.com/news/sources/sg-report.pdf.

11. Ibid., 24.

12. Darby, Charles, interview, www.pacificwrecks.com/people/authors/darby/index.html, accessed February 11, 2018.

13. Hagen, Alfred, correspondence with author, February 5, 2018.

14. Hagen, interview with author, November 29, 2017.

15. Darnton, "Swamp Ghosts," 87.

16. Hagen, interview with author, November 29, 2017.

SELECT BIBLIOGRAPHY

Official Histories and Military Documents

Arakaki, Leatrice R., and John R. Kuborn. *7 December 1941: The Air Force Story.* Honolulu, HI: Pacific Air Forces Office of History, 1991.

Assistant Chief of Air Staff, Intelligence, Historical Division. *The AAF in Australia to the Summer of 1942.* Washington, DC: Army Air Forces Historical Studies, 1944.

———. *The AAF in the South Pacific to October 1942.* Washington, DC: Army Air Forces Historical Studies, 1944.

Bullard, Steven (translator). *Japanese Army Operations in the South Pacific Area: New Britain and Papua Campaigns, 1942–43.* Canberra, ACT: Australian War Memorial, 2007.

Craven, Wesley F., and John L. Cate. *The Army Air Forces in World War II,* volume I, *Plans and Early Operations, January 1939 to August 1942.* Chicago, IL: University of Chicago Press, 1948.

———. *The Army Air Forces in World War II,* volume IV, *The Pacific: Guadalcanal to Saipan, August 1942 to July 1944.* Chicago, IL: University of Chicago Press, 1950.

———. *The Army Air Forces in World War II,* volume VI, *Men and Planes.* Chicago, IL: University of Chicago Press, 1955.

Gillison, Douglas. *Royal Australian Air Force, 1939–1942*, Series 3, volume I, *Australia in the War of 1939–1945.* Canberra: Australian War Memorial, 1962.

Monograph No. 120 (Navy). *Outline of Southeast Area Naval Air Operations, Part I, December 1941–August 1942.* Second Demobilization Bureau, circa 1946.

Monograph No. 143 (Army). *Southeast Area Operations Record, Part I, January–May 1942.* Second Demobilization Bureau, circa 1946.

Office of Naval Intelligence. *Early Raids in the Pacific Ocean, Combat Narrative, February 1 to March 1942.* Washington, DC: U.S. Government Printing Office, 1943.

Published Works

Alford, Bob. *Darwin's Air War: 1942–1945: An Illustrated History.* Darwin, Australia: Aviation Historical Society of the Northern Territory, 1991.

Arnold, Henry H. *Global Mission.* Blue Ridge Summit, PA: Tab Books, 1989.

Bartsch, William H. *December 8, 1941: MacArthur's Pearl Harbor*. College Station: Texas A&M University Press, 2003.

———. *Doomed at the Start: American Pursuit Pilots in the Philippines, 1941–1942*. College Station: Texas A&M University Press, 1992.

Borden, Norman E., Jr. *Air Mail Emergency: 1934*. Freeport, ME: Bond Wheelwright, 1968.

Bowers, Peter M. *Fortress in the Sky: The Story of Boeing's B-17*. Granada Hills, CA: Sentry Books, 1976.

Bowman, Alice. *Not Now Tomorrow: Ima nai ashita*. Bangalow, NSW, Australia: Daisy Press, 1996.

Chihaya, Masataka (translator). *Fading Victory: The Diary of Admiral Matome Ugaki, 1941–1945*. Pittsburgh, PA: University of Pittsburgh Press, 1991.

Coffey, Thomas M. *Hap: The Story of the U.S. Air Force and the Man Who Built It: General Henry H. "Hap" Arnold*. New York: Viking Press, 1982.

Dorr, Robert F. *7th Bombardment Group/Wing: 1918–1995*. Paducah, KY: Turner Publishing, 1996.

Duffy, James P. *War at the End of the World: Douglas MacArthur and the Forgotten Fight for New Guinea, 1942–1945*. New York: New American Library, 2016.

Dunn, Richard L. *Exploding Fuel Tanks: Saga of Technology That Changed the Course of the Pacific Air War*. Annapolis, MD: Self-published, 2011.

Edmonds, Walter D. *They Fought with What They Had: The Story of the Army Air Forces in the Southwest Pacific, 1941–1942*. Washington, DC: Center for Air Force History, 1992.

Evans, Don L., et al. *Revenge of the Red Raiders: The Illustrated History of the 22nd Bombardment Group during World War II*. Boulder, CO: International Research and Publishing, 2006.

Freeman, Roger A. *The B-17 Flying Fortress Story: Design-Production-History*. London: Arms and Armour, 1998.

Gamble, Bruce. *Fortress Rabaul: The Battle for the Southwest Pacific, January 1942– April 1943*. Minneapolis, MN: Zenith Press, 2010.

Godman, Henry C. *Supreme Commander*. Harrison, AR: New Leaf Press, 1980.

Hata, Ikuhiko, and Yasuho Izawa. *Japanese Naval Aces and Fighter Units in World War II*. Annapolis, MD: Naval Institute Press, 1989.

Haulman, Daniel L. *One Hundred Years of Flight: USAF Chronology of Significant Air and Space Events, 1903–2002*. Montgomery, AL: Air University Press, 2003.

Huston, John W. *American Airpower Comes of Age: General Henry H. "Hap" Arnold's World War II Diaries*. Montgomery, AL: Air University Press, 2002.

James, D. Clayton. *The Years of MacArthur*, volume II, *1941–1945*. Boston, MA: Houghton Mifflin, 1975.

Johnson, R. W., and N. A. Threlfall. *Volcano Town: The 1937–43 Rabaul Eruptions*. Bathurst, Australia: Robert Brown and Associates, 1985.

Johnston, George H. *New Guinea Diary*. Sydney, Australia: Angus and Roberson, 1943.

Kenney, George C. *General Kenney Reports: A Personal History of the Pacific War.* Washington, DC: Office of Air Force History, USAF, 1997.

Livingston, Bob. *Under the Southern Cross: The B-24 Liberator in the South Pacific.* Paducah, KY: Turner Publishing, 1998.

Lundstrom, John B. *The First Team: Pacific Naval Air Combat from Pearl Harbor to Midway.* Annapolis, MD: Naval Institute Press, 1984.

MacArthur, Douglas. *Reminiscences.* New York: McGraw-Hill, 1964.

Manchester, William. *American Caesar: Douglas MacArthur, 1880–1964.* Boston, MA: Little, Brown, 1978.

Martin, Adrian R., and Larry W. Stephenson. *Operation PLUM: The Ill-Fated 27th Bombardment Group and the Fight for the Western Pacific.* College Station: Texas A&M University Press, 2008.

McPherson, Irene W. *Four Decades of Courage: Development of United States Air Power and the 7th Bombardment Group.* Bloomington, IN: Author House, 2006.

Minty, A. E. *Black Cats: The Real Story of Australia's Long Range Catalina Strike Force in the Pacific War: Solomons to Singapore, Cairns to the Coast of China.* Victoria, Australia: RAAF Museum, 2001.

Mitchell, John H. *On Wings We Conquer: In Alis Vicimus.* Springfield, MO: G.E.M., 1990.

Piper, Robert K. *The Hidden Chapters: Untold Stories of Australians at War in the Pacific.* Carlton, VIC: Pagemasters, 1995.

Prange, Gordon W. *At Dawn We Slept: The Untold Story of Pearl Harbor.* New York: Penguin, 1982.

———. *God's Samurai: Lead Pilot at Pearl Harbor.* Washington, DC: Brassey's, 1990.

Quezon, Manuel Luis. *The Good Fight.* New York: D. Appleton-Century, 1946.

Rogers, Paul P. *The Good Years: MacArthur and Sutherland.* Westport, CT: Greenwood Books, 1990.

Ruffato, Luca, and Michael Claringbould. *Eagles of the Southern Sky: The Tainan Air Group in World War II,* volume I, *New Guinea.* Boulder, CO: Tainan Research and Publishing, 2012.

Sakai, Saburo, with Martin Caidin and Fred Saito. *Samurai!* Garden City, NY: Nelson Doubleday, 1957.

Salecker, Gene E. *Fortress against the Sun: The B-17 Flying Fortress in the Pacific.* Conshohocken, PA: Combined Publishing, 2001.

Selby, David M. *Hell and High Fever.* Sydney, Australia: Currawong Publishing, 1956.

Stanaway, John C., and Lawrence J. Hickey. *Attack and Conquer: The 8th Fighter Group in World War II.* Atglen, PA: Schiffer, 1995.

Tagaya, Osamu. *Mitsubishi Type 1 Rikko "Betty" Units of World War 2.* Botley, England: Osprey, 2001.

Trautman, James. *Pan American Clippers: The Golden Age of Flying Boats.* Erin, ON: Boston Mills Press, 2007.

Wallenfeldt, E. C. *The Six-Minute Fraternity: The Rise and Fall of NCAA Tournament Boxing, 1932–1960*. Westport, CT: Praeger, 1994.

White, Osmar. *Green Armor*. New York: W. W. Norton, 1945.

————. *Parliament of a Thousand Tribes: A Study of New Guinea*. Indianapolis, IN: Bobbs-Merrill, 1965.

Whittlesey, Lee H. *Death in Yellowstone: Accidents and Foolhardiness in the First National Park*. Lanham, MD: Roberts Rinehard, 2014.

Young, Edward M. *Death from Above: The 7th Bombardment Group in World War II*. Atglen, PA: Schiffer, 2014.

Unpublished Memoirs and Private Collections

Champion, F. Allan. *"Eighty-Three Years of Memories, 1905–1988."* Typewritten manuscript, July 1988.

Eaton, Frederick C., Jr. Untitled collection containing the subject's diary, personal correspondence, and service-related records.

Embree, Lee R. *"Off to the War."* Typewritten manuscript, undated.

Fields, Kenneth W. *"Kangaroo Squadron: Memories of a Pacific Bomber Pilot."* Compilation of interviews, diary entries, and articles related to the overseas tour of John Wallace Fields, circa 1983.

Lillback, John E. *"One Man's Journey: Pearl Harbor to the Coral Sea."* Typewritten manuscript, undated.

Reid, Ernest L. Untitled collection containing articles, interview transcripts, service-related records, and unpublished material.

Spieth, Glen E. *"Missing in Action."* Illustrated manuscript, circa 1988.

————. "The Swamp Ghost: B-17E 41-2446." Illustrated manuscript, circa 1986.

Straight, John A., Jr. *"A History: The First 70 Years in the Life of John Straight, Jr. 1920–1990."* Typewritten manuscript, 1998.

Magazine Articles, World Wide Web, and Multimedia

Listed individually in chapter notes.

Personal Diaries and Interviews

Listed individually in chapter notes.

Dissertation

Pierce, Marlyn R. "Earning Their Wings: Accidents and Fatalities in the United States Army Air Forces during Flight Training in World War Two." PhD dissertation, Department of History, Kansas State University, Manhattan, KS, 2013. https://krex.k-state.edu/dspace/bitstream/handle/2097/16879/Marlyn Pierce2013.pdf?sequence=1.

Oral Histories

Carmichael, Richard H. U.S. Air Force History Office, Bolling AFB, 1980.

Landon, Truman H. U.S. Air Force History Office, Bolling AFB, 1977.

LeMieux, Clarence A. National Museum of the Pacific War, Fredericksburg, TX, 2006.

Oliver, Richard E. National Museum of the Pacific War, Fredericksburg, TX, 2006.

Official Squadron Documents

(Air Force Historical Research Agency, Maxwell AFB, Montgomery, AL)

435th Daily Bulletin. Notices and miscellaneous commentary from September 3, 1942 to November 10, 1942.

435th Overseas. Mission experiences and human-interest stories written by squadron members.

Narrative History: The 435th Bombardment Squadron (H), 6 December 1941 to 20 December 1942. Includes pilots' combat reports, aerial victory statements, and mission records.

Squadron Diary. Day-to-day entries and commentary, December 6, 1941, to November 8, 1942.

Walter D. Edmonds Papers

(Air Force Historical Research Agency, Maxwell AFB, Montgomery, AL)

Extensive collection of interviews and personal observations of pilots and crewmembers from the 19th Bomb Group and 435th Bomb Squadron, compiled by historian Edmonds during 1942.

ACKNOWLEDGMENTS

THIS WORK WOULD not have been possible without the enthusiastic support of numerous friends, family members, and colleagues over the past ten years. Special recognition goes to my agent, Wendy Strothman, who provided superb recommendations, and to veteran editor Bob Pigeon: thank you for your rock-steady guidance and patience.

Family connections were very important. My cousin, Karen Steinbinder Holyer, not only made available my uncle's footlocker containing his military papers and personal diary, she provided additional documentation along with copies of his personal letters. Karen's youngest daughter, Margaret Holyer Compton, also caught the history bug: in addition to transcribing her grandfather's diary, she spent years tracking down his missing Silver Star award, lost when his service record was destroyed in the 1973 fire at the National Personnel Records Center.

Similarly, the sons and daughters of several other Kangaroo Squadron members provided invaluable help by contributing diaries, memoirs, newspaper clippings, military records, and photographs. They are (in alphabetical order) Joan Reid Ahrens, daughter of pilot Ernest "Roy" Reid; Scott Carmichael, son of pilot and squadron commander Dick Carmichael; Ken Fields, son of pilot John Wallace Fields; Christie Eaton Leininger, daughter of pilot Fred Eaton; Laurie Rhodes Kroger, daughter of tail gunner Ed Rhodes; Glen Spieth, son of pilot Harry Spieth; and Torjie Carlson Sweeten, daughter of navigator Jack Carlson.

The recollections of Pearl Harbor photographer Lee Embree were made available by his friend Alan Barnard; Barb Coghlin assisted with information on Pearl Harbor survivor GC Beale; and Gus Breymann provided selections from the personal diary of General Ralph Royce.

Individuals who helped with details of daily life in Australia include Rod Cardell (resident of Townsville), Norma Cox Rehrer (former resident of Townsville), Peter Dunn (creator of the incomparable Oz@War website), Debra Close (City Libraries, Townsville), and Will Wood (State Library of Queensland).

Assistance with numerous military and technical aspects of the book, including but not limited to Japanese aircraft and units, was graciously provided by fellow members of the Pacific Air War History Associates: David Aiken, Bob Alford, Bill Bartsch, Steve Birdsall, Michael Claringbould, Jim Lansdale, Edward Rogers, Jim Sawruk, and Osamu "Sam" Tagaya. Thank you, gentlemen, for your time and expertise.

For matters pertaining to the B-17 Flying Fortress and piston-engine aircraft in general, I turned to Chris Fahey, Chris Henry, Anthony Mireles, Keith Perry, and Brian Thrailkill. And for the specific story of the B-17E known today as the "Swamp Ghost," I owe a special thanks to several people who are closely associated with that extraordinary airplane, each in their own unique way: Burl Burlingame, Ken DeHoff, Fred Hagen, Trevor Moxham, Justin Taylan, and Frank Vanatta.

Others who helped with general research matters were Joanna Bouldin, John Bruning, Bob Brunson, Jim Davenport, David Nicholas, John Snyder, and Bill Syrett. I'm also indebted to Nathan Howland and Craig Kelsay for their assistance with photo restoration, and Greg Wilsbacher for digitizing seventy-five-year-old photographs.

Saving the best for last, it was my personal privilege to spend time with two original members of the Kangaroo Squadron to conduct detailed interviews: radio operator John Straight in Abilene, Texas, and assistant flight engineer/tail gunner Earl Williams in Riverside, California. As of this writing (2018), Earl is the last known surviving member of the squadron at the age of ninety-nine.

INDEX

Page numbers followed by the letter f *refer to footnotes.*